Rob Percival is a writer, campaigner and food policy expert. His commentary on food and farming has featured in the national press and on prime-time television, and his writing has been shortlisted for the *Guardian*'s International Development Journalism Prize and the Thomson Reuters Foundation's Food Sustainability Media Award. He works as Head of Food Policy for the Soil Association. *The Meat Paradox* is his first book.

'A fascinating book, part cultural history of meat, part manifesto, part pilgrimage ... Percival is a gifted writer, marshalling evidence, weaving together interviews and offering descriptions that at times verge on the poetic' *Sunday Times*

'This provocative book presents a challenge that most haven't even begun to confront – and few are ready to meet' *Guardian*

'Brilliantly provocative, original, electrifying' **Bee Wilson, *Financial Times***

'Impressively nuanced' *The Week*

'A funny, reverent reminder that meat has always been central to our story as a society' **Dan Barber, author of *The Third Plate***

'Utterly brilliant, in the range of its erudition, the power of its argument, its revelatory profundity and its compelling storytelling' **Jay Griffiths, author of *Why Rebel***

'Passionate, sophisticated, urgently important and compulsively readable ... an exhilarating and salutary record of our stuttering conversation with the non-human world, and a robust interrogation of our whole way of being' **Charles Foster, author of *Being a Beast***

D1585509

'Combines great storytelling with the latest findings ... this book is a page-turner that will spin your head around' **Hal Herzog, author of *Some We Love, Some We Hate, Some We Eat***

'A fearless exploration of the question that has shaped human evolution ... Percival takes a detailed look at the history and the arguments and ultimately answers the question of how to be an ethical carnivore' **Louise Gray, author of *The Ethical Carnivore***

'A fascinating must-read ... Percival grippingly guides the reader through the psychological complexity of our challenges, finding a middle ground in the debate and helping people decide where they may sit in the midst of it all' *Bristol Magazine*

'An erudite and entertaining excavation, but it also brings us to the present, prompting us to ask what relationship animals, both wild and domesticated, we should choose now, in a warming world where very few of us need meat to survive ... It's one of the big questions of our age, and Percival compellingly insists we mustn't shrink from it' **Hugh Fearnley-Whittingstall**

'Fascinating and unsettling, this is a book about how we became what we are – and where we go from here' **Dougald Hine, co-founder of the Dark Mountain Project**

'Beautifully written ... written by someone who clearly cares deeply about animals and our planet, this book provides much needed nuance in an often polarized debate' **Tobias Leenaert, author of *How to Create a Vegan World***

'An even-handed and nuanced exploration of our deeply complex moral relationships with other animals ... a compelling journey into the evolutionary past, potential future, and conflicted psyche of the planet's most dangerous and empathetic predator: us' **Tovar Cerulli, author of *The Mindful Carnivore***

THE MEAT PARADOX

Eating, Empathy and the Future of Meat

Rob Percival

abacus
books

ABACUS

First published in Great Britain in 2022 by Little, Brown
This paperback edition published in Great Britain in 2023 by Abacus

1 3 5 7 9 10 8 6 4 2

Copyright © Rob Percival 2022
Illustrations: Bethan McFadden

A CIP catalogue record for this book
is available from the British Library.

Paperback ISBN 978-0-349-14457-3

Typeset in Sabon by M Rules
Printed and bound in Great Britain by Clays Ltd, Elcograf S.p.A.

Papers used by Abacus are from well-managed forests
and other responsible sources.

Abacus
An imprint of
Little, Brown Book Group
Carmelite House
50 Victoria Embankment
London EC4Y 0DZ

An Hachette UK Company
www.hachette.co.uk

www.littlebrown.co.uk

CONTENTS

INTRODUCTION

The artefact was unearthed in the Swabian Jura, at the rear of a cavern carved into a limestone rib. Geologist Otto Völzing made the discovery. He was leading an excavation financed by the German military, and time was pressing. Europe was poised for the Second World War, and it was the final day of the dig. In the hindquarters of the cave, folded through archaic sediment, Völzing came upon a fragment of engraved ivory. There were hundreds of them. By dim torchlight, the geologist made his excavation.

It would take many years for the fragments to be reassembled. Archaeologists returned to the cave in the 1980s, and further pieces of the puzzle were exhumed. Völzing had unearthed a statuette, a hybrid figure, upward standing and humanoid in form, but with the head of an animal. It was only in 2013, following the discovery of more than a thousand additional fragments, and after years of painstaking reassembly, that the restoration was declared complete. The figure was named *der Löwenmensch*, the Lion Man. The statuette had been carved from a mammoth's tusk 40,000 years ago.

As scholars pored over the figure, archaeologist and craftsman Wulf Hein set out to create a replica using the tools and materials available in the Upper Palaeolithic. Hein sat among hammerstones and rabbit trails and chipped away at his laborious task. The Lion Man, he says, would have taken more than four hundred hours to sculpt – the equivalent of working for six weeks, seven days a week, eight hours a day. This was a phenomenal length of time for our ancestors to have spent on a task that had no obvious pragmatic value. Europe was a windswept steppe. Our forebears were nomadic hunters who tracked reindeer across its expanse, armed with wooden spears. They dressed in animal skins. They burned bones for warmth. Those four hundred hours could have been spent in more practical pursuits: hunting, foraging, planning, parenting, cooking, sewing, tending to the camp. The Lion Man did not aid their survival directly, but he was of evident importance to the community.

'You scratch and scratch, and days and days of working and working, and blisters on my hands, my finger was aching,' Hein recalls. 'A real artist made this. He was set free by his community to do this piece of artwork. If you do this, you can't go hunting, you can't go fishing, you work all day on it.'

Who – or what – was the Lion Man? The statuette stands thirty-one centimetres tall, the head of a cave lion perched atop human shoulders. The eyes gaze and the ears are alert. The arms, which rest close to the body, have been enhanced with the paws of a feline, while the lower body belongs to a human. The figure appears to be standing on his toes, or perhaps he is floating. Was this a mythical monster, a hunter in disguise, a shaman draped in an animal hide? What did the Lion Man mean to the sculptor's community? Why did the artist choose to depict this, of all possible images?

The cave provides some clues. The mouth faces north, rendering the site cold and unsuitable for habitation. No one lived here, but they might have visited on ceremonial occasions. The Lion Man had been stashed forty metres from the cave entrance, along with a handful of perforated fox teeth and a cache of reindeer antlers. Some scholars have suggested that these might have formed part of a decorative garment. Perhaps a group came here to perform a ritual. Someone entered the cave, their dressing room, to retrieve the Lion Man and don their ceremonial attire. Analysis of the carving shows that the surface has been rubbed and smoothed, as though the statuette was passed from person to person, from hand to hand, to be held and beheld. We imagine a fire at the mouth of the cave, a group before the flames. A story is told, a tale in which the Lion Man features. The statuette is passed as the story is spoken.

The Lion Man is the oldest figurative sculpture in the archaeological record, among the very first works of art. He is also the oldest known representation of a supernatural being – we do not know who or what the Lion Man was, but we know that this human-feline anatomy is not found in the natural world, only in the meeting of that world with the human imagination. The statuette provides the earliest evidence that our ancestors had entered a psychologically 'modern' relationship with the animals around them. They were entangled in a web of ecological relationships with these animals, but they were also entangled in a web of cultural narrative; they told stories that helped them understand their place in the world in relation to other species.

I sought out the Lion Man – tracking him down in the Natural History Museum in London – because I was searching for evidence of this archaic storytelling. I wanted to know when we first began to tell tales about the animals around us. I wanted to know how our cultural narratives today derive from those earliest accounts. I found the statuette in the corner of the Human Evolution gallery. He was surrounded by hominid skulls and flaked stone tools, primate teeth and fractured jaw bones.[1]

That wasn't the only reason I sought him out. There was another reason I went to the Natural History Museum and found my way through the Human Evolution gallery to the Lion Man.

I had come to pick a fight.

*

The Egyptian vulture (*Neophron percnopterus*) was perched high on the wall, its talons wrapped around a short branch. Wings bowed. Shoulders hunched. Most vultures are bald – an adaptation that prevents their feathers from being matted with blood when they stick their head into a carcass to feed – but the Egyptian vulture wears a crown. A white crest atop an egg-yolk face. A haggard old monarch. Beneath the bird there was a sign. 'Endangered.'

There were other birds arranged across the cabinet. Ou, Steller's sea eagle, St Vincent parrot, rufus-necked hornbill, Gurney's pitta. Only a fraction of the Natural History Museum's avian collection is on display; its research repository holds close to a million specimens drawn from more than 95 per cent of the world's bird species. Many are decades or even centuries old, but new birds are donated from time to time and are passed to the museum's taxidermist for preparation. Those heading to the research repository will be laid out flat, in preordained posture, their wings tucked to the side, while those destined for the public galleries receive more elaborate treatment, bodies contorted to mimic their living kin. The Egyptian vulture had been suitably contorted. It stood erect but stooped, its hooked beak primed for the kill.

As necrophagous scavengers, vultures have inhabited an ambivalent position in the human imagination. In the Old Testament, vultures (*rachamah*) are named by Yahweh as 'unclean' and among the animals not to be eaten. The dead were protected from vultures, in the belief that passage into the afterlife required a proper burial. But vultures were also perceived to be far-sighted and portentous. In the book of Job, the narrator says the path to divine wisdom lies even beyond the judicious vision of the vulture. 'There is a path which no fowl knoweth, which the vulture's eye hath not seen.' In other societies, the vulture has been venerated *because* it consumes carrion. In ancient Egypt, the deity Nekhbet, associated with the cycle of death and rebirth, was portrayed as a vulture-headed woman. In various Neolithic cultures the dead

were fed to vultures, believing this to be a noble end. The poet
Robinson Jeffers says he would welcome such a death:

> To be eaten by that beak and
> become part of him, to share those wings and
> those eyes –
> What a sublime end of one's body, what an enskyment;
> what a life after death.[2]

There are cultures which practise enskyment today, committing their dead to 'sky burials', including Tibetan Buddhists and
Zoroastrians in India. In the Zoroastrian tradition, the dead are
laid out upon 'towers of silence', circular structures that elevate
the corpse to be consumed by carrion birds. This practice is
cosmologically nuanced and ecologically intelligent; the vulture
aids the migration of the soul as it departs the body, and the
body is consumed before it begins to decompose, lessening the
risk of pathogenic disease.

In recent years the practice has become more difficult in India,
particularly in Mumbai, a centre of modern-day Zoroastrianism.
Three of Mumbai's towers of silence are located on Malabar Hill
among fifty acres of scattered trees and woodland. Hundreds of
vultures used to sit among the branches, hooded, unkempt and
hungry. Bodies left upon the towers would be consumed within
hours – picked at by an unruly throng – but in recent years
vulture populations have fallen into steep and abrupt decline
across India, including in Mumbai. This decline has left the
dead piled up, posing cultural and public health challenges to
the Zoroastrian community.

The cause of the vultures' demise was a mystery, and its
rate was alarming. Between 1992 and 2007, populations of
key vulture species declined by between 97.5 and 99.9 per cent
throughout India. Populations of the Egyptian vulture declined
by more than 80 per cent.

The ramifications were felt far beyond the towers. Vultures

also helped to dispose of cattle, which were reared for milk but not typically eaten. These cattle would often be reared in towns and villages, in urban environments, and their meat would sustain a large vulture population. In these birds' absence, the cows were left to the dogs. Carcasses rotted in the street, and the stray dog population ballooned, leading to the spread of diseases such as rabies. Food poisoning and dysentery also became more common, as flies fed on the corpses and then landed in kitchens.

The Zoroastrian tradition dates back roughly 3,000 years, but the origins of sky burial are far older. The earliest evidence is found in southern Turkey, at the temple of Göbekli Tepe, built between 10,000 and 12,000 years ago. Göbekli Tepe is formed of finely carved pillars decorated with images of animals, including vultures. On one pillar, known as the Vulture Stone, the bird is depicted holding what appears to be a disembodied human head. At nearby Çatalhöyük, a habitation site, there are painted frescos showing vultures hovering over headless bodies and scavenging human remains. Excavations at the site have found vulture skulls embedded in the plaster walls of houses, along with human bodies in various states of disarticulation, including headless corpses buried under the floors.

Mythology has always been informed by ecology. Animals have embodied intuitions and emotions, giving form to the inchoate, helping us understand our place in the world and the forces that shape our lives. Other frescos at Çatalhöyük depict the life cycle of a bee, and a butterfly emerging from a chrysalis, suggesting a cultural preoccupation with processes of regeneration, transformation and rebirth. The disembodied head at Göbekli Tepe has been interpreted by some scholars as the soul released from the body, ready to be guided to the afterlife by the bird. The vulture is a dishevelled carrion eater, a corpse-hungry scavenger, but it has also been seen as a mediator between worlds, possessed of the ability to transform death into winged flight, granting rebirth upon the deceased.

The cause of the vultures' decline was eventually identified as diclofenac, a drug approved for veterinary use that was routinely given to cows. Diclofenac is an anti-inflammatory which helps to ease pain resulting from injury or sickness, but it is poisonous to vultures, causing fatal renal failure within a few days. India's vultures were eating cattle carcasses laced with the drug and were dying soon after, collapsing from the branches of trees.

Veterinary diclofenac was finally banned in 2006, after years of campaigning. There is evidence that the birds' decline has been slowed, and perhaps put into reverse. India's vultures might yet achieve their own rebirth. But the drug remains in use in other parts of the world, including in Europe, where it was controversially licensed for use in Italy and Spain in 2013.

Conservation NGOs Bird Life International and the Royal Society for the Protection of Birds (RSPB) sounded the alarm. 'What we have here is an immensely risky situation: key European vulture populations (mostly in Spain, but also in Italy) feeding on domestic carcasses that now have the potential to contain veterinary diclofenac. The consequences could be catastrophic, similar to what has happened in India.'

Four vulture species live in Europe: the Egyptian vulture, the cinereous vulture (*Aegypius monachus*), the griffon vulture (*Gyps fulvus*) and the bearded vulture (*Gypaetus barbatus*). Spain is home to 3,000 Egyptian vultures, 85 per cent of the European population.[3]

In Spain, as in India, vultures have traditionally fed on the carcasses of domestic livestock, including free-ranging cattle in fields and pigs deposited in 'carcass dumps' called *muladares*. A 2016 study estimated that diclofenac might be killing more than 6,000 vultures each year, with pig carcasses of primary concern. 'Whether feeding on cattle or pigs,' the authors of the study wrote, 'more than half of the vultures feeding on a carcass were expected to die if the animal died immediately after diclofenac treatment, but this proportion declined rapidly with increasing time.' With no adequate restrictions on use, veterinary use of diclofenac in Spanish pig farming has opened a new frontier in the vultures' struggle for survival, implicating Spanish pork in the Egyptian vulture's demise – pork that the Natural History Museum was buying and serving in its restaurant.

I love the Natural History Museum. I love the character of the place, its Romanesque architecture, its panelled ceilings and vaulting arches, its ornate staircases and hewn pillars. I love its gargoyles, the detail of its exterior carvings: pterosaurs and sabretooth cats; dragonfish and geckos. I love wandering aimlessly through its galleries, getting lost in its corridors, happening upon obscure scientific treasures: the skull of the first Neanderthal to be discovered; the skeleton of the first bird, *Archaeopteryx*; moon rocks from the lunar landings. I love the ethos of the museum. I love that entry is free. I love that the place is always packed with children and families. I remember visiting as a child, soon after the film *Jurassic Park* was released, and standing in awe before the animatronic dinosaurs. I love all that the museum aspires to be, as a repository that celebrates the abundance of the natural world, and a research centre committed to tackling wildlife loss and climate change.

I did not love the museum's restaurant.

'We face a planetary emergency,' the museum's strategy document says. 'Humanity's future depends on the natural world, but we are not taking effective action to combat our destructive impact on the planet's survival systems. Climate change, biodiversity loss and extinctions, habitat destruction, environmental pollution, soil erosion and loss, deforestation, desertification, ocean acidification and many other crises all flow from unsustainable human activity.'

I was auditing the food served at attractions and institutions around the UK, and the Natural History Museum emerged as an oddity. I had studied dozens of menus and interviewed scores of caterers. I had seen restaurants go to impressive lengths to ensure their menu was healthy and sustainable, promoting a dietary pattern that would help to resolve these ecological crises. But not here.

There is a Ted Hughes poem that moves through a zoo. 'The apes yawn and adore their fleas in the sun.' The parrots are 'cheap tarts' and the tiger is 'fatigued with indolence'. The animals have been deadened by captivity. 'Cage after cage seems empty.' Hughes might have been walking through the taxidermy collection at the Natural History Museum, gazing at the empty eyes of the elephant, the solitude of the dodo, the vacant grimace of the badger. But there was one animal that stood apart, 'where the crowd stands, stares, mesmerized ... / He spins from the bars, but there's no cage to him'.[4]

There is something about the jaguar. If any of the animals on display in the museum could have been reanimated, roused from taxidermic slumber to step free from their enclosure, pacing the corridors, prowling to the restaurant door to protest at the menu – I imagine that it would have been the jaguar, Panthera onca.

The jaguar is the largest feline in the Americas, the apex predator, occupying a unique position in the native ecology and the mythology and imagination of the indigenous population. The rainforests of the Amazon are the cat's preferred habitat, but it will also be found in savannah grasslands and in the cloud forests that skirt the mountains. The jaguar hunts by ambush, close to rivers, swamps and water sources, and is adept at swimming and climbing. This ability to move between worlds – the water, the land and the trees – has conjured associations with shamanism both in the Amazon and the high Andes. In many Amazonian cultures, the shaman identifies with the jaguar and converses with jaguar spirits; some shamans drink a hallucinogenic brew in the hope of being transformed into a jaguar. The jaguar is understood to be the guardian of the rainforest, the Master of Animals, arbitrating between human and animal communities. Yet, for all the cat's cultural and ecological significance, the jaguar faces grave threats and is now an endangered species. Its habitat has been eroded by soy plantations and cattle farming, both in the forests and in the Cerrado.

The Cerrado is a savannah biome located to the south of the Amazon. It is less well known than its rainforest neighbour, but as the world's richest and most ancient savannah, it is one of the planet's most important ecosystems. More than 11,000 plant species grow in the Cerrado, and nearly half are found nowhere else; hundreds are on the verge of extinction. Its animal inhabitants include giant anteaters, maned wolves, anacondas, howler monkeys and armadillos, and at least sixty species are endangered. The jaguar is listed as 'Near Threatened' on the International Union for Conservation of Nature (IUCN) Red List of Threatened Species, which means that it is likely that it will be classified as threatened with extinction in the future, and as 'Vulnerable' on the Brazilian Red List, which means it is facing a high risk of extinction, partly because of the clearing of the Cerrado.

Our appetite for meat is to blame. More than half the native vegetation of the Cerrado has been lost since the 1960s to cattle grazing and soy production; more than a million hectares have been swallowed by soy in the past two decades alone, with destruction progressing at a faster rate than in the Amazon. The UK diet is contributing to this destruction. Around 3 million tonnes of soy are imported into the UK each year to be fed to our farm animals, primarily our chickens and pigs. Most of these imports come from ecologically vulnerable areas of the Americas, and only 20 to 30 per cent are certified as sustainable. Our diets are known to be contributing to the destruction of the Cerrado and the demise of the jaguar.[5]

The UK is not unique in this regard. In most affluent countries, including those of Europe and North America, our diets are rich in meat provided by industrial farming systems. These are systems where animals are removed from the land, housed at high densities, and fed on intensively grown 'feed crops' such as soy and maize, produced using fossil fuel fertilisers and chemical inputs. The sheer number of animals that we consume means that huge swathes of land must be given over to the production of feed crops, putting increasing pressure on the planet's remaining habitats and resources. The science is clear. If we are to stem the tide of ecological degradation, preserve our planet's riches and resolve the climate crisis, we will need to change the way we eat – and that will include eating less meat.

Given its concern for the living world and its designation as a 'Cathedral of Nature', the Natural History Museum should have been in the vanguard of this dietary change. The museum restaurant, of all restaurants, should have been sourcing environmentally sustainable ingredients and promoting a dietary pattern oriented towards human and planetary health. But the restaurant was a grill, offering a meat-laden menu. The meat had not been sourced from nature-friendly or organic farms. The animals had not been reared on farms that prohibited the use of ecologically damaging feed crops. There were no plant-based options. No information about the provenance of the meat was available in the restaurant, and the staff were reluctant to discuss the issue. The museum had made no public commitment to serving sustainable fish. It was not monitoring the provenance or volume of soy in its supply chain, and it was not assessing the menu's impact on vulnerable animal populations, for example in relation to the restaurant's purchase of Spanish pork, which posed a threat to European vultures. The menu was also unhealthy, particularly for children.

It was extraordinary. As a visitor to the museum, you could explore its galleries, stand face to face with hundreds of rare and endangered animals – creatures captured by taxidermic craft in frozen expression – and then you could sit down in the museum restaurant and contribute to those animals' demise.

One day, after visiting the restaurant to speak with the chef, I decided to seek out the jaguar. I found the creature, and a crowd gathered before the cabinet. Children in anoraks and tourists with cameras. Their eyes were fixated upon the feline, entranced by its angular brow, its bristling jaw. I was holding a map of the museum, and my gaze followed theirs. The taxidermist had achieved a rare feat – they had captured the jaguar's essence, the spirit of the beast. Or perhaps, by some old shamanic impulse, the jaguar had refused to relinquish its spirit when it was captured and killed. The Master of Animals, poised to prowl free. I waited for the crowds to disperse. I waited for them all to leave. I waited until we were all alone, and I took a single, low bow. *Panthera onca ... Panthera onca ...*

In a 1956 essay, Aldous Huxley wrote:

> In the history of science the collector of specimens preceded the zoologist and followed the exponents of natural theology and magic. He had ceased to study animals in the spirit of the authors of the Bestiaries, for whom the ant was incarnate industry, the panther an emblem, surprisingly enough, of Christ, the polecat a shocking example of uninhibited lasciviousness. But, except in a rudimentary way, he was not yet a physiologist, ecologist, or student of animal behaviour. His primary concern was to make a census, to catch, kill, stuff, and describe as many kinds of beasts as he could lay his hands on.[6]

Sir Hans Sloane was one such collector of specimens. The foremost of a generation of explorers and naturalists who sought out rare and unusual treasures, Sloane provided the nucleus of the collection which would become the Natural History Museum. He was active in a period of intensive scientific discovery in the seventeenth and eighteenth centuries, an era characterised by a ferocious appetite to collect, study and classify the natural world. The scientific method has advanced since those days – it is ecologists and zoologists and not collectors who further our understanding today – but the task of documenting the diversity of life is far from complete. On one recent estimate, some 86 per cent of all plant and animal species are yet to be described. Many could be lost before we have the chance.

In the past half-century, the global population of farm animals has tripled, while populations of wild animals have declined by two-thirds. These statistics are squarely related. Our appetite for meat has become the leading driver of habitat loss and species extinction globally. The sheer scale of transformation in the balance of populations is mindboggling. Measured by biomass, humans and our farm animals now comprise 96 per cent of all the mammals on the planet, with only 4 per cent being wild. Poultry destined for human consumption make up 70 per cent of all living birds, and we are still hungry. Global demand for meat is anticipated to rise 73 per cent by 2050, relative to 2010. Our attempts to satisfy this demand will place an impossible burden on the already fragile fabric of life.[7]

Easing this burden is my profession. I work for the Soil Association, an organisation campaigning for healthy and regenerative food and farming, including organic food and farming. In recent years, as veganism has entered the mainstream and the climate crisis has escalated, a heated societal debate has erupted, focused on our consumption of meat and animal foods. As the organisation's head of food policy, I have been intimately involved in the debate. I've spent my days studying the science, surveying the evidence, campaigning for dietary change. The investigation at the Natural History Museum was undertaken in this context, and the campaign that followed was a success. The museum restaurant was forced to overhaul its menu.

This was a symbolic success, yet far from transformational. The Natural History Museum should have been leading by example, but a museum cannot fix the global food system or resolve the climate crisis single-handedly. A resolution will require something much more challenging.

There are parts of the meat industry that are highly consolidated, with power and production concentrated in the hands of a small number of corporate actors. The ten largest meat and dairy companies per sector are responsible for the lives and deaths of over 10 billion animals, but most of us are unaware of who these companies are. Most people in America will probably be unaware that the four largest companies (JBS, Tyson, WH Group and Cargill) process 85 per cent of all beef, 71 per cent of all pork and over 50 per cent of all chicken. These businesses offer over sixty meat-focused brands between them, creating the illusion of choice and diversity, a façade that hides these companies from view. In the UK, most people will similarly be unaware that 70 per cent of all chicken is processed by just four companies (Moy Park, 2 Sisters, and Cargill and Faccenda, who are joint owners of Avara). These businesses also hide in plain sight, secluded behind retailers' rustic-sounding brand names. Cargill and Moy Park are partly responsible for 'Willow Farms', Tesco's chicken brand, and Faccenda for 'Farm Stores', Asda's seemingly wholesome meat brand. This consolidation also extends to the supply of feed crops. If you have eaten chicken from high street brands such as Tesco, Lidl, Asda, McDonald's or Nando's, you have eaten birds fed soy supplied by Cargill, a company accused of involvement in deforestation and the destruction of the Cerrado, human rights violations, and the dispossession of indigenous people of their lands.

These corporations are disproportionately responsible for the damaging social and ecological impacts commonly attributed to animal farming. JBS, Tyson, Cargill, Dairy Farmers of America and Fonterra between them emit more greenhouse gases than fossil fuel barons ExxonMobil, Shell or BP. The twenty largest meat and dairy companies together emit more greenhouse gases than the entire German economy. Industrial animal farming is on course to exhaust most of our remaining emissions budget within a couple of decades, and these companies are simultaneously complicit in the overuse of antibiotics, the emergence of zoonotic disease, the destruction of wild habitats, the disempowerment of individual farmers, and the suffering and exploitation of billions of animals. It is not the smallholder in Colombia or the hill farmer in Wales that is fuelling the 'planetary emergency', it is the corporate players behind industrial animal farming.[8]

Curbing the power of these businesses will require action on multiple fronts, including action to cut the industry's financial fodder. These companies are bankrolled by investment firms, banks and pension funds, including those that might handle your finances. Between 2015 and 2020, meat and dairy companies received over £350 billion ($478 billion) from these funders, with high street banks such as Barclays and HSBC in the UK providing billions in loans to the companies behind the production of 'chlorinated chicken' in the US. If we are to create a more humane and equitable food system, it will require divestment, stronger government regulation, and rapid investment in a viable alternative for farmers. But it will also require action from each of us. It will require that we eat differently, withdrawing our custom.[9]

This dietary change is proving difficult to achieve, even though most of us are sympathetic to the cause. Most of us agree that the 'factory farming' of animals is undesirable. Almost nine in ten Americans (89 per cent) are opposed to industrial animal farming, citing animal welfare, worker safety and public health risks as their top concerns. In a recent poll, 85 per cent of the UK public said they would support an immediate ban on factory farming, and three-quarters said they want to do more to support British farmers producing to high standards. But these good intentions are inconsistently translated into purchasing choices and eating behaviours. We say one thing, but the food on our plates tells a different story. In recent years, as the urgency of the change has grown more acute, scholars have pored over the barriers, trying to understand the forces which inhibit our adoption of a more sustainable diet, the personal, political, social, cultural and psychological dimensions of dietary change. This book is concerned with the last of these, the psychological.[10]

The 'psychology of meat' might strike you as a peculiar arrangement of words. What can psychology tell us about sausages? What does the science of the human mind have to tell us about our appetite for chicken nuggets and lamb chops? Quite a lot, it turns out. In the past decade, a rich vein of research has probed the cognitive and emotional tensions inherent in our relationship with meat. In a 2010 paper published in the journal *Appetite*, Steve Loughnan, Brock Bastian and Nick Haslam coined the term 'meat paradox' to describe these tensions. This research is revealing the power of our empathy and the unexpected consequences of our consumption, and it is now set to transform our understanding of the way we eat today.

I began studying the meat paradox because I thought this psychological science might illuminate the dynamics of dietary change. The climate and ecological crises demand that we eat differently, and I thought the paradox might offer insight into how to elicit that change. I wanted to know what was happening in Britain, where our consumption of meat has been the focus of so much heated debate, but I suspected the investigation would be of wider significance. I was amazed at what I discovered. The meat paradox is shaping the way that we eat throughout the world, from Europe to North America, in meat-hungry nations such as Australia and Argentina, and far beyond. Regardless of who you are and where you come from, and regardless of your dietary orientation, whether you are an enthusiastic carnivore, a committed vegan or something in between, this book will introduce you to facets of your psychology of which you are probably unaware, landscapes of your mind which might feel unfamiliar.

I was soon drawn into the meat paradox on a personal level, lured beyond a detached appraisal of the science into more visceral and intimate territory. I could not have known how deep I would be drawn or the destination I would reach. This book tells of my passage into the paradox, my immersion in the emotional complexity of meat. In the pages that follow, I speak to farmers and philosophers, archaeologists and scientists, activists and poets. I pursue the paradox through farms and slaughterhouses, across cultures and continents, and through millions of years of human evolution. We meet hunters on the Arctic tundra and trappers in the forests of Siberia. We search for the origins of the paradox in our prehistory, asking when our relationship with meat became emotionally complicated. When did we begin to empathise with the animals we consume? The journey concludes in the most unlikely of places, beyond the painted caves of the Palaeolithic, on the far side of the climate crisis, a place where jaguars prowl and vultures rasp.

Like those collectors of centuries past, we are going in search of an unlikely creature in an alien land. That creature will seem no less implausible than the giraffe or the duck-billed platypus would have seemed to early explorers. Unlike those explorers, we have no desire for conquest, and we do not hope to catch or kill our quarry. On the contrary, we are interested in the behaviour of the beast. The Lion Man is the true protagonist of this tale. Völzing's hybrid *is* the meat paradox. This fusion of human and animal forms tells us what it meant to eat animals so many years ago, and what it might mean to eat them today. Come, the creature is close at hand. Lower your voice. Gather your senses.

1

MEAT

Have you ever had the feeling, when on the verge of sleep, that you are suddenly falling? Your limbs jerk and your muscles jolt. It's called a 'hypnagogic jerk', and it is understood by some scholars to be 'an archaic reflex' – the brain 'misinterpreting the muscle relaxation accompanying the onset of sleep as a signal that the sleeping primate is falling out of a tree'. It is our body's memory of another life, of the precarity of the high canopy, an existence edged with the fear of falling.

'We need these cows,' the farmer was saying, his voice loud and decisive, his eyes bright. 'We need ruminant animals in our farming system. We need to farm them, and we should be eating them.'

The farmer was talking, and I should have been listening. I should have been listening, and I should have been responding, but my attention was with the tree and with the branches.

We were living in the branches when this all began. We were in the canopy when we started to eat meat, and memories of that dietary transition are still inscribed within us.

It was between two and three million years ago, and we were fringe-dwellers, gracile and curious. We lived at the tree line, moving between the shaded woodland and the savannah scrub. Our bodies were different then. We were bipedal, adapted for two-legged locomotion, and by day we roamed the grasslands foraging for food, but we had not yet relinquished our arboreal aptitudes – we had strong arms and long curved hands, and feet that helped us to climb into the foliage above.

From our elevated vantage point, we watched the sabretooth hunt. These great predatory cats stalked the tree-covered areas that dotted the savannah. They specialised in hunting large herbivores, such as elephants, which they attacked by ambush, pouncing with razor claws and sabre teeth, enlarged upper canines that stabbed and slashed, inflicting mortal flesh wounds upon their prey. We watched, cooing and fretting as they passed beneath, and we waited, listening for the howling.

We were plant-eaters, herbivorous by nature. We did not consume animals, at least not habitually. Our bodies were adapted to a diet of fruit and seeds, shoots and roots, and the occasional egg or insect. But we were opportunistic, and we were hungry, and the sabretooth was a generous killer.

It was those terrible teeth, those jutting canines. The sabretooth was a deadly predator but unskilled at disarticulating carcasses. They made the kill, ate their share and then departed, leaving the scraps for the scavengers. We were those scavengers. Canny, we possessed stone tools, bone breakers and flesh slicers, hammerstones and sharpened flakes, which we used to pick at the remains, extracting nutrition that the sabretooth could not reach. We watched, hushed and humming, as the cat fed upon the elephant. We waited until they were satiated, and then we rushed down from the canopy.

We do not know that this was how it began – our transition from an herbivorous to a meat-inclusive diet – but it is one scenario that archaeologists have proposed. It probably began in many ways, in many places, and at many times. It certainly began when we were still adapted to life in the trees.[1]

The earliest evidence dates from 3.4 million years ago – animal bones unearthed in Dikika in Ethiopia show signs of butchery at the hands of a hungry hominid. Our forebear *Australopithecus africanus*, who lived around 3 million years ago, appears to have eaten a varied diet that included a moderate amount of meat, while *Homo habilis*, who evolved soon after, ate a greater volume still. There is evidence from Afar in Ethiopia that by 2.5 million years ago we were regularly eviscerating carcasses and filleting the limb bones of ungulates, while multiple sites at Olduvai Gorge in Tanzania suggest we were consuming mammals ranging in size from hedgehogs to elephants. By the time the first early humans evolved, members of the species *Homo erectus*, around 1.8 million years ago, we were squarely omnivorous – meat formed an important part of our diets. We were also fully bipedal, no longer adapted to life in the branches.[2]

The word 'meat' should be understood here to mean 'animal matter of various kinds'. We did not only eat the muscle tissues that we typically consume as meat today. The fat and viscera were often more important, for they were nutrient rich and energy dense. In the beginning, we hungered for the liver, the heart and the kidneys of the animals we consumed. Wielding our hammerstones, we cracked femurs, and we sucked the marrow from their core. We split skulls and we lapped brains warm from the cup.

Omnivory changed us. Those capable of procuring and digesting nutritionally rich animal matter were at an advantage, and this advantage propelled our evolution. Our digestive system changed, and as our guts grew shorter, our brains grew larger. The iron, zinc, vitamin B12 and fatty acids found in animal foods allowed us to build and maintain more complex neural networks. (While many of these nutrients are found in plants, they typically occur in lower quantities and in less bioavailable forms.) In time – we can't say exactly when – a feedback loop emerged. Our consumption of animal foods fuelled the growth of our brains, and this brain growth enabled us to procure a diet richer in meat. Increased cognitive function enabled greater behavioural complexity, and we became skilled scavengers and hunters. By 500,000 years ago, we were embedded in an 'eclectic-feeding dietary niche that probably included significant meat-eating'. We became a top-level predator, alongside the carnivore guild.[3]

But we were not carnivores. Throughout our evolution, our diets have been characterised by variety, flexibility and diversity. We have always eaten plants. The contribution of meat to our diets was often qualitative, rather than quantitative. We relied on animal foods for the essential fatty acids and micronutrients that fuelled infant and adolescent growth and the maintenance of health, but our diets changed with the season, the landscape and the climate. 'A message for public health nutrition that emerges from studying the evolution of human diets is that there is not, nor has there ever been, a "set" human diet,' says nutritional anthropologist Stanley Ulijaszek.[4]

We were not carnivores, but neither were we herbivorous. A society subsisting solely on plants has never existed among our species. We have always needed to extract high-quality nutrition from our environment, balancing the needs of our biology with the possibilities of our ecology, and this has always meant eating animals, one way or another.

'We certainly should be eating less meat,' the farmer was saying. 'We need to end all forms of industrial animal farming. This should be a priority. But we need to understand that animals can be part of a sustainable farming system.'

The farmer had his arms spread wide.

Above his head, the branches were bowing.

Beneath his feet, billions of microbes were thrumming through the surface of the earth.

There are hundreds of millions of microorganisms in a single gram of healthy soil. They are bacteria, fungi, actinomycetes, algae and protozoa, and they perform a host of ecological functions essential to life on this planet. We are only just beginning to understand these functions, the biology of the soil. Scientists mapping the 'soil microbiome' compare the complexity of the task to that of mapping the stars of the cosmos, the galaxies of the distant universe.

'Look around you,' the farmer said. 'What do you see?'

I hauled my attention down from the branches. We were in the English countryside, on a farm in Gloucestershire, a group of us standing at the upper margin of a meadow edged with oak. There were cows, and the cows were browsing the grasses, their heads bowed.

'These cows are doing what wild herbivores do,' he continued. 'They're grazing. You're looking at a farming system that functions in harmony with nature, without fossil fuel or chemical inputs. Ruminant animals are an important part of the system.'

Farmer Patrick Holden wears a forceful gaze and when he speaks it is with the simmering intensity of the evangelist. He is warm and personable, but his voice is conviction distilled to its purest form.

'I like this word "harmony" because it implies that there are pre-existing patterns and processes that a farmer must understand when farming the land. In organic and regenerative farming, you aim to work *with* those processes to produce healthy food and healthy soil.'

Patrick has been studying the mechanics of health and harmony for a long time. He began farming in 1973, following a stint in the San Francisco Bay Area in the United States, where his father had taken up a visiting professorship. 'When I was about twenty, I went out there, drank the Kool-Aid, came back and decided I wanted to get back to the land and live self-sufficiently,' he recalls. Upon his return, he moved from London to west Wales with a small group to establish a commune. They were known as 'the hippies on the hill', and Patrick is still on the hill almost half a century later. He farms eighty-odd Ayrshire cows across three hundred acres at Bwlchwernen Fawr, producing a cheddar-style cheese called Hafod.[5]

When Patrick arrived on the land, the organic movement was still in its adolescence. The principles of organic farming had been outlined in the 1930s and 1940s by a group of farmers, scientists and doctors concerned by the industrialisation of agriculture and the use of synthetic fertilisers and chemical pesticides, but organic standards (today defined in law) were still being formalised. Patrick drafted the world's first organic dairy standards, and he went on to become a leader in the organic movement, acting for fifteen years as CEO of the Soil Association, and going on to establish the Sustainable Food Trust, an organisation that works 'to accelerate the transition to more sustainable food and farming systems that nourish the health of both people and planet'.

'The intensive, chemical-based farming systems of the past half-century have been a disaster, at least for the environment,' Patrick continued, as we descended the meadow, striking a path towards the stile at the far corner. 'The application of nitrogen fertilisers has contaminated rivers and polluted our atmosphere. The excessive use of antibiotics in intensive livestock has fuelled resistance. We've thrown pests and predators out of balance, creating the need for chemical pesticides. We've done terrible things to the soil. But we know better now. The most exciting innovations are taking place in the regenerative farming space.'

The word 'regenerative' describes an approach to farming which enriches the soil and the natural world, instead of depleting it. This typically means curtailing or eliminating fossil fuel and chemical inputs and building soil carbon and soil fertility through a mixed rotation of crops and animals. Organic farming is regenerative – in that it has been shown to benefit humans, animals, nature and the climate – but it is distinct from the broader bucket of 'regenerative' approaches in that it has defined standards backed by certification and inspection. (If you eat organic, you know what you're eating and how your food was produced.)

The cows had begun to follow us across the meadow.

'In a regenerative system, you need to include a fertility-building phase in your crop rotation; in most cases this means a mixture of legumes and grasses that fix nitrogen from the atmosphere,' Patrick explained. 'Ruminant animals like these cows enable a farmer to produce food during this fertility-building phase. They turn something we can't eat – grass – into something we can – meat and dairy. They help to recycle fertility, and they make sensible use of land that cannot be cropped.'

We were trailed by trampling hooves and nudging snouts. Puffing exhalations. The slap of dung on wet grass. As they followed, the herd had their heads bowed, as though before the pulpit. In that moment, they were Patrick's gospel and his congregation.

'Organic farmers have always understood the value of ruminant animals, but we are still learning. Farmers are now experimenting with novel grazing patterns. Mob grazing. Holistic grazing. I've been introducing the principles of this approach into my herd management over the last few years. I've divided the farm into small paddocks, and we graze the herd intensively for a short period in each paddock before moving them on. This short duration, high intensity grazing allows for a longer grass recovery period, and it seems to be good for the soil. In the wild, herbivores will always be on the move, driven by predators, so you're mimicking the predator–prey relationship.'

This notion of mimicry is important. The most sustainable farming systems are often those which emulate in some respects the dynamics of a wild ecosystem. In the UK and across Europe, this often means farming with herbivores, ruminant animals such as cows. In the semi-wild, semi-managed landscapes that preceded industrial civilisation, these animals would move across the land, chomping, nibbling and trampling, and the pattern of their movement and consumption created a mosaic of habitats and vegetation types. The pasture, woodland and wood pasture ecosystems indigenous to these shores were formed under the influence of bison, red and roe deer, wild horses, aurochs and wild boars.

'Large herbivores are crucial for the functioning of a bio-diverse ecosystem,' the organisation Rewilding Europe explains. 'The plants and animals we know today from our managed fields, meadows, forests and moors, have evolved from natural plains, herbaceous fields, thickets and ancient forests. These natural areas were rich in both species diversity and numbers. This natural wealth was largely the result of the presence of large grazing animals.'[6]

The aims of rewilding and farming sometimes seem to be at odds – one demanding the removal of farmers from the land so that nature can regenerate, the other rooted to the land and intent on producing food – but there is a healthy middle ground. There are wilder forms of farming, ways of producing food which allow the natural world to flourish. This mode of farm-ing doesn't always require grazing animals, and not all grazing is good – in the UK and globally, over-grazing by ruminants has caused enormous ecological damage – but animals can be beneficial. Cows, sheep and pigs, in the appropriate niche, will trample and chomp, rewilding the soil, helping to restore and maintain the complexity of the landscape.[7]

'There are additional benefits when the grazers are native breeds,' the second farmer said, as we approached the lower boundary. 'We have a number of such breeds here at Home Farm: cattle, sheep and pig. We have Irish Moiled and Gloucester, Shetland and Welsh Black, Aubrac and Sussex, Tamworth and Large Black, Cotswold and Shropshire, Hebridean.' He recited the names as a monk recites his holy verse. 'The Prince is very enthusiastic about native breeds.'

David Wilson was our host for the day. We were at Duchy Home Farm, the property of Prince Charles, and David was the farm manager. Wiry and energetic, he resembled a farmer that Quentin Blake might have drawn for a Roald Dahl book.

'We work a seven-year rotation here,' David continued, as

we clambered over the stile. 'We do three years of grass and clover, which we graze. At the end of the third year, the cover is ploughed for winter wheat, and then spring oats or barley and rye. The grazing is important; it helps to build fertility and it benefits the wildlife we have here on the farm.'

David led us around the perimeter and the hedgerows were bustling, insects busy in the margins. It was evident that Home Farm was heaving with life, and this fecundity and profusion was both a product and a function of the organic system. Scientists have established that organic farms have on average 50 per cent more abundant wildlife compared to non-organic farms, with a third more species, including 50 per cent more pollinator species and 75 per cent more plant species.[8]

'Native breeds of grazer are more hardy, resilient,' David explained. 'It's a different mentality, seeing animals this way, as part of a farm system, an ecological system, instead of simply reared for meat. It's the very opposite of "factory" farming. Here at Home Farm we try to farm *with* nature, and that means farming less intensively, with good grazing. That's what organic is all about.'

All farming involves the imposition of simplicity upon complexity. To produce food, we must impose human rhythms upon an unruly chorus. But there are differing degrees of imposition. The chorus can be choked with chemicals and contorted into compliance, or our voices can join the biotic refrain. We can apply a crude extractive logic to the land, forcing industrial repetition upon the soil, or we can align food production with the babble of the encompassing biome. This is true of both animal and crop farming. The manipulation of animal biorhythms in industrial farming, as repetition and simplicity are forced onto instinct and lifespan, differs from the management of animals in organic and regenerative systems. Sometimes less is more. If we were to farm far fewer animals, giving them a much better life, we could craft a more resilient food system. If we returned native breeds to the land, hardy animals that are less far removed from their wild ancestors, then we could bring colour and complexity back to the countryside. But this will require us to eat differently.

'Of course, you don't have to be organic,' Patrick interjected. 'Not all farmers can go organic, and not all farmers should. Organic isn't the answer to everything. What we need is for all farmers to be regenerative, to adopt more regenerative approaches.'

'Do we really need to farm animals though?' I asked, testing the waters. 'Can't we achieve all this without them?'

'I think we would be unwise to try,' Patrick said, disapproval seeping into his voice. 'I think we should be very worried about attitudes towards meat and dairy, the crude misrepresentation of farming that you see in the newspapers. Ruminants get blamed for everything, from cancer to climate change, but a farming system without them leaves us reliant on fossil fuel fertilisers and chemical pesticides. That's the problem.'

David seemed to share Patrick's frustration.

'We need to help people understand,' David said. 'We need people to choose to eat the produce of a sustainable farming system, or else farmers won't be able to farm like this. That doesn't mean that everyone needs to eat meat, but we need to get over the idea that all animals are bad.'

It felt like an appropriate moment to ask the question.

'Patrick ... '

'Yes?'

' ... what do you think of vegans?'

What does the High Priest think of the Apostate?

Patrick took a deep breath.

We need to consume a combination of macronutrients and micronutrients to be healthy: proteins, fats and carbohydrates, plus dietary fibre and water, and an assortment of vitamins and minerals. Nutritional science tells us to eat an abundance of some foods, those that contain more of the good stuff, and to limit consumption of others, where the food in question contains compounds that might be harmful to our health. Red meat, for example, contains lots of saturated fat. A body of evidence suggests that diets rich in red meat are associated with a heightened risk of heart disease, and this is understood to be related to the saturated fat. 'Too much fat in your diet, especially saturated fats, can raise your cholesterol, which increases the risk of heart disease,' authorities in the UK warn.[9]

The status of red meat as an 'unhealthy food' has become a dietary dogma in some quarters, but research is beginning to reveal a more complex picture. In a 2020 paper titled 'The unmapped chemical complexity of our diets', biochemist Joseph Loscalzo notes that our 'understanding of how diet affects health is limited to 150 key nutritional components' – the macronutrients and micronutrients that form the basis of our dietary guidelines – but 'these nutritional components represent only a small fraction of the more than 26,000 distinct, definable biochemicals present in our food'. Some of these components are believed to affect our health, yet most have not been thoroughly studied. Loscalzo describes these biochemicals as the 'dark matter' of our diets.[10]

Consider garlic. A close relative of onions and shallots, and commonly eaten by billions of people, garlic is understood by scientists to contain sixty-seven key nutritional components, including manganese, vitamin B6 and selenium. Yet a clove of raw garlic contains more than 2,306 distinct biochemicals, and within this 'dark matter' are compounds of importance to both our health and garlic's role in our culinary traditions. Luteolin, for example, is believed to protect against heart disease. Diallyl disulphide is a biochemical known to contribute to garlic's smell and taste, now understood to support good health. Allicin is a sulphur-containing compound, responsible for garlic's distinct aroma, which might also help to protect against heart disease.

The biochemical complexity of our food is accentuated by the interaction between this 'dark matter' and the trillions of microbes that inhabit our intestinal tract, our 'gut microbiome'. Emerging evidence suggests this interaction might play an important role in shaping the health risks associated with red meat.

The association between red meat and heart disease has been linked in some studies to the production of an organic compound called trimethylamine N-oxide (TMAO). Research has found that patients diagnosed with heart disease have a significantly greater risk of dying over the next five years if they have high levels of TMAO in their blood. Red meat has been identified as a potential contributor. Red meat doesn't provide TMAO directly, but it contains L-carnitine and choline, two compounds metabolised by microbes in our gut microbiome and then transformed into TMAO in the liver.[11]

This transformation is inconsistent, however. The Mediterranean diet, which regularly pairs red meat with fresh garlic (as well as extra virgin olive oil and red wine), is believed to derive some of its health benefits from two biochemical components secluded in the 'dark matter' of the diet which inhibit the process by which L-carnitine and choline are metabolised into TMAO. This suggests that the association between red meat and heart disease might be shaped by the context in which the meat is eaten, the other foods on the plate. In keeping with this complexity, the association between red meat and negative health outcomes has been more commonly observed in studies where people are eating a highly processed 'Western' diet. Studies of healthy omnivores eating a diet rich in plants have failed to find consistent evidence that red meat is unhealthy. Context matters.[12]

The contribution of meat to our diet is further complicated by the fact that not all meat is produced equally. Different farming systems, which provide animals with very different lives, produce meat of varying nutritional quality.

There is evidence to suggest that chickens reared in industrial farming systems – which is most chickens on the planet – contain fewer essential micronutrients than chickens farmed in traditional systems. They might also contain much lower levels of essential long-chain omega-3 fatty acids. Chickens and eggs have long been one of the few land-based sources of these omega-3s, but the grain-based feed and the lack of access to external forage in industrial systems means that chicken now contains five times less than in 1970. This is unhelpful from a nutritional perspective, for these fatty acids are an important component of a healthy diet, and most of us don't eat enough of them. Fish are another primary source, but the nutritional quality of fish is also being depleted. A 2016 study of over 3,000 salmon farmed in Scotland found a significant decrease in omega-3 levels, meaning a double portion size was required in 2015 relative to 2006 to obtain the same intake. A study published in the same year, however, found that meat from organic farms, including red meat and dairy, can provide a valuable source, with organic meat and dairy containing around 50 per cent more omega-3s than non-organic.[13]

In the prevailing nutritional paradigm, beef is beef, chicken is chicken, red meat contains saturated fat, and too much saturated fat can heighten the risk of heart disease. But the emerging picture is considerably more complicated. We now understand that organic meat and dairy are nutritionally different to non-organic, that the health risks associated with red meat might be mediated by the microbes in our gut and the context in which the meat is eaten, including the diet as a whole, and the 'dark matter' present in the other foods on the plate. This same suite of complexity arises when we consider the healthfulness of vegan diets.

Veganism is an ethical stance which typically entails the exclusion of animal foods from the diet. Health authorities in both the UK and the US have endorsed vegan eating, with the British Dietetics Association (BDA) and the American Academy of Nutrition and Dietetics (AAND) saying that well-planned vegan diets can be healthy for everyone. The BDA says that vegan diets can 'support healthy living in people of all ages', and the AAND says they can be 'appropriate for all stages of the life cycle, including pregnancy, lactation, infancy, childhood, adolescence, older adulthood, and for athletes'. The two largest observational studies of vegan eating to date, the EPIC-Oxford study and the Adventist Health Study 2, found evidence of distinct health benefits, with vegans expected to live between three and seven years longer than the general population.[14]

But the collusion of genes and gut microbiome might complicate this picture. Tim Spector, Professor of Genetic Epidemiology at King's College London, and the UK's foremost authority on the gut microbiome, says that he struggled to maintain adequate vitamin B12 levels when he removed animal foods from his diet. B12 is a common challenge for vegans, as it isn't found in plant foods. During a medical check-up, Spector was told that his blood levels of B12 and folate were low and his homocysteine level – a mark of heart disease risk – was high. He was eating plenty of folate in his vegetables, but his low B12 levels were blocking its absorption.

'I started taking increasingly large amounts of B12 supplements each morning,' Spector says, 'but they had little effect on my blood levels. I tried eating a few eggs a week as they have some B12, but that didn't work either. Finally in desperation I tried B12 injections in my bottom. They worked, and my B12 and my homocysteine level too finally returned towards normal.' Faced with a lifetime of injections, 'I decided I should eat just one steak a month and see what happened. So that's what I did – either a rare steak or a raw French-style steak tartare, once or twice a month, did the trick, and gave me the vitamins I needed without any artificial supplements.'

I asked Spector why his B12 supplements had been ineffective. 'The body's ability to absorb and metabolise nutrients is shaped by our genes and the microbiome, mostly the microbiome,' he told me. 'Responses to a vegan diet will vary from person to person. I've tended to have low B12 and folate levels ever since, as an eighteen-year-old, I suffered a bout of dysentery which altered the composition of my gut. Culture also plays a role. If you're from a vegetarian or low meat culture such as in India, your body's relationship with B12 might be different, again because of your microbiome. Some people will need to eat meat to be healthy. There is no one diet that works for everyone.'

Anecdotes like this should not be read as an argument against veganism, but Spector's experience illustrates that there are gaps in our understanding. The way the microbiome and other confounding influences might shape individual responses to vegan eating has not been thoroughly researched.[15]

Accounts from individuals who say that they struggled to be healthy on a vegan diet are not hard to find. Among the more high-profile testimonies in recent years are those of lapsed plant-based influencers, a cascade of whom have renounced their diet on YouTube. Yenova Mendoza (with 478,000 subscribers) was among the first; having been caught eating a fish in a livestream video, she was forced to admit that doctors had persuaded her to eat animal foods for health reasons. Rebecca (353,000 subscribers) was another, posting a monologue titled 'Why I'm No Longer Vegan' in which she explained that 'bacterial overgrowth' in the gut had forced her, after repeated encouragements from doctors, to consume fish and eggs. High-profile figures beyond the world of YouTube have also shared their stories. Actress Anne Hathaway said she'd broken her diet with Icelandic salmon and felt healthier as a result, saying her 'brain felt like a computer rebooting'.

According to a 2015 study by Faunalytics, 'there are more than five times the number of former vegetarians/vegans compared to current vegetarians/vegans' in America. The study found that health concerns were the second most common reason cited by those who had returned to meat or animal foods (following dissatisfaction with vegan foods). Respondents said they returned to omnivory because of perceived or actual nutrient deficiencies; because they were feeling fatigued, light-headed and weak; because they gained or lost too much weight; because they were pregnant; or because their doctor had recommended it. These responses should be treated with caution, for these individuals might have thrived on a more nutritious diet. Several of the lapsed YouTubers had overlaid their diet with a raw food regime and regular fasts and 'cleanses', and it is likely that these contributed decisively to their ill health. But ex-vegans remain under-studied. We don't know why some individuals might struggle to be healthy on a vegan diet.

There have been no long-term randomised control trials (considered to be the 'gold standard' for nutrition research) of vegan diets, and it's possible that people who become vegan and thrive may differ in important ways from those who don't. 'Those advocating vegan diets should be open-minded and curious about any reports of failure to thrive from vegans or ex-vegans,' says Stephen Patrick Kieran Walsh, research fellow at Vrije Universiteit Brussel and chair of the Vegan Society. Walsh recalls that within ten years of the Vegan Society's foundation in 1944, British vegans experienced multiple health issues, including amenorrhea (the absence of menstruation), sore tongue (inflammation of the tongue), paresthesia (abnormal sensations such as pricking and tingling) and 'poker back' (a rigid spine). Vitamin B12 was isolated by scientists in 1948, and the symptoms were identified as those of B12 deficiency. Once supplementation became viable, the worst consequences were alleviated. Walsh says that a vegan diet can be healthy for everyone, but he warns that another 'Factor X' might still be found; 'there may be other, as yet unknown, lessons to be learnt.'[16]

We know much more about vegan nutrition these days, but deficiencies still occur. A 2010 study of UK vegans found that 73 per cent were deficient in vitamin B12, compared with 24 per cent of vegetarians and 2 per cent of omnivores. Calcium intakes can be low, with one meta-analysis finding vegans to have a 6 per cent lower bone mineral density than omnivores, equivalent to about a 10 per cent increase in fracture risk. Dietary intakes of vitamins B2, niacin (B3) and D, and iodine, zinc, potassium and selenium are typically lower for vegans. Blood levels of long-chain omega-3s are often lower.[17]

There are, of course, plenty of malnourished omnivores in the population – any diet must be well planned – but the gaps in the evidence and the recurrence of deficiencies mean that some health authorities do not recommend vegan eating for everyone. Several nutrients critical for foetal and infant development can be more challenging to obtain on a diet that excludes animal foods. Iron, for example, is needed for the growth and branching of neurons in the womb; zinc is found in high concentrations in the hippocampus, a crucial region for learning and memory; vitamin B12 maintains the sheaths that envelop and protect nerves. Iodine is another important mineral, mediating the effects of thyroid hormone on brain development, and even a mild deficiency may have adverse effects on the infant during pregnancy and lactation. Iodine deficiencies are common among vegans and can be chronic. A 2020 study found that one in three vegans in Germany exhibited levels lower than the World Health Organization threshold value for 'severe iodine deficiency', while levels in UK and US vegans are also low. Contrary to the BDA and AAND endorsement, some authorities consequently caution against vegan diets for high risk groups. The German Nutrition Society 'does not recommend a vegan diet for pregnant women, lactating women, infants, children or adolescents', saying that those who follow such a diet should 'receive advice from a nutrition counsellor and their supply of crucial nutrients should be regularly checked by a physician'. A group of doctors from the Royal Society of Medicine in Belgium put forward a proposal in 2019 to make feeding infants and children a vegan diet *illegal*, while other European health authorities are cautious, the Spanish Association of Paediatrics and the Danish National Health Authorities being among those who advise against vegan diets for infants.[18]

Should we eat animals? The picture that emerges from the evidence is complicated and sometimes contradictory. A robust body of science says that those of us living in more affluent countries would benefit from eating lots more plants, and we should cut out heavily processed foods. It's likely that most of us can be entirely healthy on a diet that includes little or no meat, if the diet is balanced and wholesome. It's also likely that lots of us can be very healthy on a vegan diet, though it's not certain that we all can, and for some groups the risks are much higher than for others.

An equally robust body of science says that we have been eating animals alongside plants for well over a million years, and we are biologically adapted to benefit from both. If Patrick is right, and animals have a role to play in our farming system, then it seems certain we would benefit nutritionally from eating them.

'What do I think of vegans?'

Patrick's eyes widened. 'I think that we need to convert them back!' he thundered.

But then he softened his tone and struck a more conciliatory note.

'Look, I understand it, the vegan thing. I really do. I understand the rationale and I respect anyone's decision. But we need ruminant animals if we are to farm sustainably.'

'What would you say to them?'

'To vegans? I would say we farmers need your support, even if you don't consume our produce. We need to work together to end industrial livestock. I am with you on that; many of us are with you on that. But as a society we must be discerning and understand that there are animals that are part of the problem and animals that are part of the solution.' With a sweep of his arm, he indicated that David's cows fell into the second category.

I think Patrick is right. I believe his analysis is largely accurate.

Consider, for example, the nutrient cycles on which food production depends, including the nitrogen and phosphorus cycles. These elements are needed for crop growth and for the formation of bones and teeth in animals, along with other metabolic functions. Plants obtain nitrogen and phosphorus from the soil, but the pool is limited. When a crop grows, it extracts these nutrients from the land, and when the crop is harvested and taken elsewhere, the soil is left in deficit. All farmers must find a way of replenishing the store, and most farmers rely on synthetic nitrogen fertilisers, which are manufactured using fossil fuels, and mined rock phosphate, a dwindling non-renewable resource.[19]

The organic alternative typically means farming with animals. Nitrogen in organic systems is provided by soil microorganisms, but manures can help to transfer and recycle that nitrogen. A cow can produce 70 kilograms of manure per day, providing enough recycled fertiliser in a year to produce one hectare of wheat, equivalent to 128 kilograms of synthetic nitrogen that would have otherwise been manufactured using fossil fuels. Phosphorus is also recycled and returned to the soil as plant and animal residues, including manures and rendered animal remains, mimicking the return of animal bodies that occurs in the wild. Cattle populations must be reduced if we are to resolve the climate crisis, as ruminant animals burp methane, a potent greenhouse gas, but if we are to end our food system's reliance on fossil fuels and unsustainable inputs – as we surely must – then animals will have an important role to play.[20]

We concluded the tour, and David led us across the estate to Highgrove House, the nearby royal residence where Prince Charles has planted lavish gardens. 'The gardens need to be seen to be believed,' a besuited staff member whispered as we approached. The gardens are truly extraordinary, and in their grandeur, the detail of their design and the extravagance of their intent, they seem an obvious indulgence, a decadence of monarchical proportions, but they also express an underlying intelligence, a set of principles which the Prince holds dear.

I explored the gardens: the meandering paths lined by opium poppies and salvia; the promenades edged with topiaries of golden yew; stumpery and sanctuary; pond and drooping vine. I came to the Carpet Garden, an arrangement of fig, pomegranate and olive trees sculpted to resemble a Persian rug, the 'magic carpets' of tradition and lore. There were purple pelargoniums, trimmed hedges, and a fountain spilling water over brightly coloured ceramic tiles. The Carpet Garden was designed, the Prince explains, to exhibit the proportion and balance character-istic of Islamic art, the pattern of the rug's design mirroring the architecture of the heavens, the geometry of the cosmos. 'They were called "magic carpets" because they have the capacity to transport us to another place,' he says. When people journeyed through the desert, they would unroll these carpets beneath their tented pavilions at night, a portable garden. Smoking hashish or hemp, they would feel themselves begin to levitate, the carpet flying, the pattern of the garden rising to meet the constellations above. A short walk from the Carpet Garden, beside the Prince's house, there is a gate adorned with Egyptian hieroglyphics. *The flowers in the garden are a reflection of the stars in the sky.* As above, so below.[21]

The Prince's commitment to these 'principles of harmony', as he calls them, might sound whimsical, but their intelligence becomes more patent as the gardens spill into the surrounding farmland. Rare and heritage varieties of vegetable grow in the kitchen garden, an act of quiet defiance against the loss of local variety intrinsic to intensive production. At the garden's edge, a wildflower meadow extends across four-and-a-half acres. The meadow is managed in the traditional manner, scythed by human hands and grazed by sheep, and erupts seasonally into a riot of colour and scurrying life, as scabious ox-eyed daisies, knapweed, poppies and various types of orchid provide habitat and sustenance for insects and pollinators. The gardens, like the farmland, are managed organically, meaning that pests and predators must be kept in balance without resort to chemical sprays. As the sheep sculpt the meadow, providing a haven for the pollinators who have elsewhere been poisoned by pesticides, hundreds of chickens cluck and roam among the surrounding fruit trees. Their peck and forage helps keep would-be orchard pests under control, while their manures fertilise the soil (and the trees, in turn, provide the chickens with shelter from the elements). Think of an ecosystem as a constellation of relationships. In organic farming, the constellations that emerge in the wild are emulated, in part, and deliberately cultivated in service of food production. The living world dictates the design of the system, biology taking precedence over chemistry, diversity over uniformity. In a quiet corner of the gardens, the Prince has erected a bust of Vandana Shiva, the scholar and food activist who has campaigned for indigenous and peasant land rights in India, taking on the 'poison cartel' of the pesticide and GM industries. 'We have made the celebration of diversity our mode of resistance,' Shiva says. This celebration is the creed of the organic farmer.

In 2017, Patrick convened the pioneering 'Harmony in Food and Farming Conference', exploring how the principles of harmony shape sustainable food production, binding prince and peasant in a shared ecological ethic. This is an ethic of entanglement. Ever since we clambered down from the branches, hungry for a slither of elephant steak, we have been snared in a pattern of predation, our feet in the soil and the geometry of life painted red. We evolved as omnivores, reliant on meat and enmeshed in a web of ecological exchange, the needs of our biology pitted against the possibilities of our environment. Though we over-consume animals today and often treat them abysmally, though many of us can choose to consume a plant-based diet, free from meat or animal foods (hugely more of us than currently make that choice), there has always been a nub of necessity that we have been forced to grapple with.

You might think of this as a *residual* necessity, if you like, a vestige that speaks more of our past than of our future. Perhaps our reliance on animal foods is akin to the hypnagogic jerk, a remnant of our evolutionary history which we are already in the process of growing beyond. Perhaps a different world is already on the horizon. After all, there are technologies in development, lab-grown meats and synthetic proteins, precision fermentation and novel biotechnologies. Some say the rapid emergence of these will render animal farming obsolete in the not-too-distant future, and perhaps they are right. Perhaps we can remove all animals from our diet without undermining our health or the resilience of our food system. Perhaps. But that is not the world we are living in today.[22]

I believe that we sometimes need to farm animals, and it can be necessary that we eat them. I am conscious that in the context of a polarised debate, this assertion places me squarely at one end of the spectrum, camped among the omnivores and flesh-eaters. Let me lay my cards on the table and tell you that I eat both plants and animals.

Yet I am caught in a paradox, for I also find myself camped in the blizzard of the opposing pole, gazing up through furling winds towards the vegan flag. You see, I believe they are correct, these vegans. I think they speak the truth. Notwithstanding our omnivorous entanglement, there is a word for what we do to these animals, those that we consume. Murder.

2

MURDER

'Aim carefully or you'll be splattered with blood.'
Siobhan handed me the gun.

'Here's how it works. The cartridge is already in the chamber. To arm the mechanism you move this lever, like this. When you pull the trigger, the charge will explode, shooting the bolt. If you aim correctly then the bolt will penetrate the cranial cavity and enter the brain, just like that.'

The slaughterman carried over the head and positioned it upon the hook hanging at waist height before me. Here she was. Fuck.

'Now, pay attention everyone. Look at how Rob is holding the gun. That's very good, Rob.'

I felt nauseous. I wondered if I should feel ashamed, but there was no time for that. I needed to focus on this dripping head and on what I needed to do to it. I could see where the first bolt had entered, moments before. Now all eyes were upon me.

'This is an essential part of your training, vets,' Siobhan continued. 'You must shoot the bolt and you must watch others shoot the bolt. Bovine slaughter. Once you're qualified and in practice, you might have to euthanise a farm animal, so watch closely – you must know how to do it properly.'

I felt sorry for them, these veterinary students. How had their childhood love of animals come to this? I understood why they were there, though, the necessity of it. Why was I there?

'We call this gun the "cowpuncher" and the other one the "bulldozer". Given the age, breed and gender of the bovine, this is the correct mechanism.'

No one said anything.

'To identify the optimal position for stunning, draw two imaginary lines from the top of the eyes to the base of the opposite horn bud.'

Siobhan drew two intersecting lines, eye to horn bud. X marks the spot.

'Now, grip the gun, release the safety, aim and fire.'

I looked at the head dangling before me. I wanted to drop the gun and run, but I didn't.

I released the safety. I aimed. BANG.

The evening before all this happened, I sat down to read the tale of Peter Singer's peculiar tea party.

Philosopher Peter Singer is among the founding figures of the animal rights movement. *Animal Liberation*, his 1975 masterwork, remains a keystone text in animal advocacy, its adherents including many of those who promote a vegan diet. *Animal Liberation* popularised the term 'speciesist', describing 'a prejudice or bias in favour of the interests of members of one's own species and against those of members of other species'. Just as, in recent decades, we have recognised racism and sexism as forms of arbitrary and reprehensible discrimination, we will someday look back on speciesism with shame and moral regret, Singer says.[1]

Singer's case is partially based on an argument from marginal cases. Why do we think that it's wrong to kill humans, but morally acceptable to kill animals? The omnivore's response typically names a faculty or capability which humans possess but animals do not, this faculty or capability marking a morally relevant boundary between species. Rationality. Consciousness. Language. Singer notes, however, that examples can be found where a human lacks this essential faculty, or where animals appear to possess it in a higher order. Newborn babies, for example, do not possess language or much in the way of intelligence. Cognitively impaired adults in a psychiatric ward might be less conscious or rational than an octopus. Yet we care for these people, recognising their moral value.

Singer's philosophy falls under the banner of 'utilitarianism', meaning that he broadly proposes that we should act to achieve the greatest wellbeing for the greatest number. He follows renowned utilitarian philosopher Jeremy Bentham in suggesting that animals should be included in this moral calculation. Writing in 1789, Bentham said:

> The day may come, when the rest of the animal creation may acquire those rights which never could have been withholden from them but by the hand of tyranny. The French have already discovered that the blackness of skin is no reason why a human being should be abandoned without redress to the caprice of a tormentor. It may come one day to be recognized, that the number of legs, the villosity of the skin, or the termination of the *os sacrum*, are reasons equally insufficient for abandoning a sensitive being to the same fate ... the question is not, Can they reason? nor, Can they talk? but, *Can they suffer?*[2]

Singer also sees the capacity for suffering as the essential moral criterion. 'If a being suffers,' he says, 'there can be no moral justification for refusing to take that suffering into consideration.'[3]

An extensive body of science affirms that other animals can experience a range of sentient states, including pain and suffering. 'The science simply supports what so many people have known for centuries,' animal scholar Marc Bekoff tells me, 'namely, that other animals are indeed sentient and feeling beings who care about what happens to themselves, their families, their friends, and other individuals.'

Bekoff is a giant in the animal movement. The author or editor of more than a thousand essays and dozens of books, including the *Encyclopaedia of Human-Animal Relationships*, he exudes enthusiasm when talking about animals, his hair gathered in a ponytail, a silver band wrapped around his ear. 'The good news is it's very difficult to find anyone who will try to convincingly argue that we really don't know if other animals are sentient and conscious beings, or who will argue that they're not,' he continues. 'This view would not only be anti-scientific given all we know, but downright inane.'

Bekoff points to the Cambridge Declaration on Consciousness, published in 2012 by a group of neuroscientists, as evidence of scientific agreement on the issue. 'Convergent evidence indicates that humans are not unique in possessing the neurological substrates that generate consciousness,' the declaration asserts. 'Non-human animals, including all mammals and birds, and many other creatures, including octopuses, also possess these neurological substrates.'

In Singer's eyes, the shared capacity for conscious and sentient experiences – pain and suffering, pleasure and joy – generated by these neurological substrates, means we should take the interests of other animals into account. This remains true when we are deciding what to eat. We should weigh the life of the animal against our desire to consume their flesh; we should ask whether the enjoyment or benefit that we glean is of more moral value than the animal's life.[4]

Singer has exercised enormous influence over the animal rights movement, but his philosophy has also been contentious, even among animal advocates, and this contention begins with the events narrated in the opening pages of *Animal Liberation*.

In the preface to the work, Singer tells a story. He recounts that he was invited to tea – he was living in England at the time – by a lady who had heard that he was writing a book about animals. 'She herself was very interested in animals, she said, and had a friend who had already written a book about animals and would be *so* keen to meet us.' It quickly becomes apparent that Singer was unimpressed by the situation. In disparaging tones, he says that the hostess's friend was already there when he arrived, 'and she certainly was keen to talk about animals.'

'I do love animals,' the woman said, telling him about her dog and two cats, and about Mrs Scott, 'who runs a little hospital for sick pets.' Midway through her speech, she began eating a ham sandwich. 'But you *are* interested in animals, aren't you, Mr Singer?' she asked.

Mr Singer – the great animal rights philosopher – insisted that he was *not* particularly interested in animals. He had never been inordinately fond of dogs, cats or horses. He didn't *love* animals. But he was interested in preventing unnecessary suffering. '[I] simply wanted them treated as the independent sentient beings that they are, and not as a means to human ends – as the pig whose flesh was now in our hostess's sandwiches had been treated.'

Singer's antipathy towards the woman starts to make sense at this point. It was her ham sandwich that affronted him.

But there was more to it than that. Singer didn't include this tale in the preface of *Animal Liberation* to illustrate the hypocrisy of professing to love animals while eating pigs in sandwiches; it was the *sentimentalism* insinuated by the woman's line of questioning that he objected to. It was the idea that his commitment to animal ethics was rooted in a 'love' of animals. He was concerned that such sentiment might devalue the rational case for animal rights: 'The portrayal of those who protest against cruelty to animals as sentimental, emotional "animal lovers" [has meant] excluding the entire issue ... from serious political and moral discussion.'

Accordingly, we should not allow emotion to guide our ethical thought. It is right to treat animals with moral concern, in ways which include refraining from eating them, not because our emotions have dissuaded us from doing so, but because the careful application of reason requires it.

This anti-sentimentalist view was echoed by Tom Regan, a second founding figure in the animal rights movement. In his 1983 book, *The Case for Animal Rights*, Regan similarly stressed that our ethical concern for animals should not be governed by our emotions. 'We can give lie to these accusations [of sentimentalism] only by making a concerted effort not to indulge our emotions or parade our sentiments,' he said, adding in a later essay that 'reason – not sentiment, not emotion – reason compels us to recognize the equal inherent value of ... animals and ... their equal right to be treated with respect.'[5]

Singer's tea party was still on my mind as I stood, several steps inside the slaughterhouse, gasping before a viscid pink thing that was swinging from a chain.

I had barely made it through the door when the pink thing appeared. A flush of exposed flesh, and I was left reeling. There was a man pulling at it, peeling something away. There came a ripping sound, and I realised (belatedly) that this was a man flaying a sheep. The sheep had been hoisted by one ankle, and the man had his knees bent. He was leaning back, committing his body to the task. I watched as he heaved and exhaled, as fleece was torn from ovine flank.

As I observed the flaying, I realised that it is not easy separating one's feelings from one's ethical perception. This separation might be the forte of the philosopher, and perhaps there is value in it, at least in some circumstances, but in that moment, it felt like an entirely unfeasible prospect. Can we really look at such a scene with rational detachment? *Should we?* Scholars working in the feminist tradition of animal ethics have criticised Singer and

Regan for being, in Josephine Donovan's words, 'hyperrational' in their exclusion of emotion. Singer paints a false picture of moral reasoning, they say. It isn't possible to divide our thoughts from our feelings. We bring our whole being to bear in arriving at a moral judgement; it is neither desirable nor possible to discard our emotions.[6]

Singer's concern was partly with the *pliability* of our emotions, the risk that they might be exploited, undermining the rational case for animal rights. And it is true that emotions can be exploited. You should be aware that in writing this chapter, I have your emotions in mind. What are my intentions? What if I told you that I backed away from the man and the flaying, towards the corner of the space, where three sheep heads were lined up upon a table, their teeth exposed in rictus grins. What if I told you that their pluck – heart, lungs, liver, spleen – had been skewered upon hooks arranged around a pyramidal metal frame, like baubles upon some sort of hellish Christmas tree. Why choose these words and these images? What emotive or ethical stance am I trying to draw you into?

There is really no way of describing the slaughterhouse that is void of affective impact. I need only tell you the job titles of those employed on a traditional slaughter line – the *knocker*; the *shackler*; the *sticker*; the *bleeder*; the *legger*; the *flanker*; the *rumper*; the *side-puller*; the *head-dropper*; the *gutter*; the *horn-sawer*; the *back-splitter*; the *tail-ripper*; the *tongue-plucker* – to begin to stir your feelings. Perhaps the least moving thing I can tell you about the slaughterhouse is that the clichés are all true. It is exactly as you might imagine it. The chains clanking. The knives slashing. The walls white and splattered, blood frothing hot in the drain. If clichés weaken dramatic effect then perhaps I should tell you about the cows in as many trite truisms as I can muster – for the men soon moved from sheep on to cows – and then perhaps you will trust me as a narrator.

Or perhaps, with effort, it can be done. Perhaps I can strip all emotion from the scene, distil the events down to the purest mathematics:

$$KE = \tfrac{1}{2}mv^2$$

Killing a cow is a two-stage process. First, she must be stunned. This involves shooting a bolt into her skull, rendering her unconscious and insensible to pain. Second, having been hoisted by the ankle, her throat must be cut, severing the major blood vessels in her thorax. This causes a loss of blood and death from a lack of oxygen to the brain. Here's where the mathematics comes in. To render her unconscious, the bolt of the gun must strike the skull with the appropriate kinetic energy. The kinetic energy (KE) of the bolt when shot from the gun is proportional to the mass of the bolt (m) and its velocity (v), which is created by the charge. The propulsion of the stun can be determined according to the formula, $KE = \tfrac{1}{2}mv^2$. (Got it?)

The cow is led into the stun cage. The slaughterman is standing above her. He holds the gun to her brow, and he pulls the trigger. The bolt shoots from the gun and strikes, applying a sharp, heavy blow that causes the brain to impact against the inside of the skull. This impact causes a sudden, massive increase in intra-cranial pressure, which is followed by an equally sudden drop in pressure, disrupting the normal electrical activity of the brain. The damage to the nerves and blood vessels causes brain dysfunction and impaired blood circulation, rendering the recipient of the blow immediately unconscious. 'Non-penetrating' stunning is typically used for calves. For adult cows, the bolt will penetrate the skull and enter the brain, eliciting a similar result.

The gun fires, and the few seconds that follow are intense. The stunned cow collapses. She stops breathing and begins to exhibit 'tonic' activity. Her body becomes rigid, with her head extended and her hind legs flexed towards the abdomen. This period of rigidity lasts for ten to twenty seconds and is followed by a period of involuntary kicking movements which gradually subside. Her eyes roll and her tongue lolls from her mouth. She is hoisted by the ankle.

There is a moment, somewhere in the middle of all this, when a minded animal becomes a torso of meat. The gun fires with a blast, and the sound recedes. The men get to work, but there are ripples that continue to fill the space. It is as though a stone has been thrown into a pool, and the splash has ebbed, but the surface is moving still. I could feel those ripples, lapping against the nape of my neck, as though the cow's soul-stuff, thrown from her body in the decisive moment, was swelling upon my skin, searching for a shore upon which to land.

See, I can't do it.

I can't peel away the affective dimension of the experience and present these events to you in rational prose. I can't pretend that mechanistic clarity exists when I am a bundle of raw and tender tissues assaulted by extraordinary scenes. The philosopher's fantasy of reason removed from emotion is just that, a fantasy.

But that's OK. I was not hoping to follow in Singer's footsteps. I did not go to the slaughterhouse to hone a line of reasoned argument. I didn't set out to write a book that led you, step-by-rational-step, towards a clear and unambiguous moral conclusion. I went for the very opposite reason. I went because I wanted to be confronted by the complexity of it. I went because I was seeking immersion, a visceral encounter with the meat paradox.

In hindsight, it was a naive and somewhat reckless ambition, for some things, once seen, cannot be unseen. I crossed the slaughterhouse. I climbed up onto the stun cage.

Slaughter is a dangerous business. Workers must handle sharp cutting tools at rapid production speeds. Their movements are monotonous and often repetitive – the same gash, the same slice, snip-and-snap, over and over. A slip of the hand can lead to serious injury, and injury rates are high. A 2018 investigation found two injuries occurring each day in slaughterhouses in the UK, and two a week that were classified as serious. Across a single year, eighteen workers lost fingers or limbs, and over one hundred suffered serious injuries including damage to eyesight, and crush injuries to the head or torso. The picture is similar in the US. American slaughterhouse workers are three times more likely to suffer serious injury than the average worker, and workers on pork and beef slaughter lines are nearly seven times more likely to suffer repetitive strain injuries. Beyond these physical perils, workers are also exposed to the possibility of emotional injury – psychological damage resulting from the slaughter process.[7]

'The initial experience of starting on the slaughterfloor seems to be inevitably traumatic, eliciting feelings of shock and abhorrence,' wrote the authors of a 2016 study. 'Thereafter, participants report many disturbing and conflicting emotions but emphasise how these emotions change and they start to feel emotionally hardened by the work. Dreams and nightmares seem to occur frequently during the first couple of months.'

Anecdotal accounts attest to the disturbing experience of arriving on the job. 'The first time I killed it was not easy for me,' one worker recalls. 'I felt pity. I felt I just wanted to close my eyes, turn around, and run away.' 'When I shot my first animal, I started shaking,' another says. 'I was so scared, even when holding the gun, I was shaking.'[8]

The psychological consequences of slaughterhouse work have not been extensively studied, but the research that has been conducted suggests that workers are susceptible to perpetration-induced traumatic stress (PITS), described by Rachel M. MacNair as a form of post-traumatic stress disorder (PTSD) that results 'from situations that would be traumatic if someone were a victim, but situations for which the person in question was a causal participant'. PITS arises when someone perpetrates of an act of violence and is traumatised by the act. MacNair's study was concerned with the PITS experienced by soldiers, policemen, executioners and Nazis, but she highlights that slaughterhouse workers are also likely to be susceptible.[9]

PITS sufferers sometimes re-experience the traumatic event in recollection, dreams, hallucinations and flashbacks. Some of the most well documented cases are from soldiers. In the First World War, for example, there were accounts 'from hospital nurses who said that delirious soldiers are again and again possessed by the same hallucination – that they are in the act of pulling the bayonets out of the bodies of the men they have killed'. The risk of trauma associated with killing is accentuated by proximity and presentation, being face-to-face with one's victim. In the Second World War, bomber crews reported that killing was less disturbing from a distance; it was only when they were returned to the ground and faced with their victims that they found the experience traumatic. 'They can't stop the eyes of the man I killed from starin' into mine,' one war veteran recalled.

Nazi soldiers appear to have succumbed to PITS in relatively high numbers. There are accounts of soldiers having nervous breakdowns, turning to alcohol or committing suicide, having been forced to murder Jewish people and other minorities. In response, execution squads tried killing from a different angle, so as not to be face-to-face with their victim, 'but it was discovered that necks, like faces, also individualize people ... these necks came to haunt their dreams.'

Emmanuel Levinas wrote at length about the ethical significance of the face. We might organise our society around moral norms and seemingly rational ethical principles, he observed, but there is a deeper stratum to our ethical experience, rooted in the face-to-face encounter. Levinas viewed the 'face' as an assemblage of features – mouth, nose, eyes, chin, brow – and as something more intangible. In the face of the other, he says, we encounter an *ethical demand* that reaches out and takes hold. This demand is primal and compelling. It demands that we do no harm. 'The face is a living presence,' Levinas says. 'The first word of the face is, *Tu ne tueras point*, "Thou shalt not kill". It is an order.'

It is certainly not the case that every slaughterhouse worker is traumatised or beset by nightmares, or that all experiences of slaughterhouse work are the same. The conditions and welfare standards in meat processing plants vary greatly from country to country and from facility to facility; we don't know how prevalent emotional issues are. But the evidence, though not extensive, implies that slaughterhouse work *can* be psychologically damaging. Killing animals for food can be traumatic or disturbing. Crucially, the *potential* for trauma or psychological injury remains, even in the 'best' circumstances, even in a well-managed facility where the worker has every reason to believe that what they are doing is right and morally justifiable.

There are well-documented accounts of PITS arising in situations where the killing could be deemed right and morally justifiable. Nazi executions certainly don't fall into this category, but the policeman forced to kill in self-defence when arresting a violent criminal, or the soldier defending their country from an invading army, might. Similarly, the slaughterhouse worker might have every reason to believe that their work is respectable and just. They might belong to a society that endorses the consumption of meat. They might be able to provide a rational explanation of their actions. They might even take pride in their work. Yet the reach of reason is limited when confronted with the ethical demand. The face of the other, Levinas warns, is indifferent to our rationalisations and arguments. 'The eye does not shine; it speaks.'

'There was one night I'll never forget as long as I live,' a slaughterhouse worker from the US recalls. 'A little female hog was coming through the chutes. She got away ... [but] I grabbed her and flipped her over. She looked up at me. It was like she was saying, "Yeah, I know it's your job, do it." That was the first time I ever looked into a live hog's eyes.'

That moment of shared gaze made a lasting impression on the worker, and this is a recurring theme in the literature. Slaughterhouse workers attest to the significance of being held in the animal's look. 'You see eyes,' one slaughterhouse worker says, describing his nightmares. 'I saw [the] eyes of the animal. It's like it's watching me. That thing, that dream, I didn't feel well even when I came back to work.' Another worker says that he dreamt of his death, saying he arrived at heaven's gate and was confronted by the eyes of all the animals he had killed. 'Sometimes I think how many animals I have killed since I've been here; I think maybe thousands or millions. Someday I am going to stand before these animals.'

One worker recalls his experience in a poultry processing plant. 'The chickens are panicking. Many of them are squawking loudly, some are just sitting there trembling. Sometimes you catch one looking up at you, eye to eye, and you know it's terrified ... No one can convince me that that chicken did not know what was about to happen.' The worker was beset by nightmares of chickens and recalls a fellow worker being 'hauled off to the mental hospital' suffering severe recurring dreams.

'At the end of the slaughter line there was a huge skip, and it was filled with hundreds of cows' heads,' another worker in the UK recalls. 'Each one of them had been flayed, with all of the saleable flesh removed. But one thing was still attached – their eyeballs. Whenever I walked past that skip, I couldn't help but feel like I had hundreds of pairs of eyes watching me. Some of them were accusing, knowing that I'd participated in their deaths. Others seemed to be pleading, as if there were some way I could go back in time and save them.'[10]

Levinas describes the ethical demand as a 'summons' that reaches out from the face of the other, speaking through their gaze. This summons confronts us in the face of 'the orphan, the widow, the stranger', arising in a dynamic of vulnerability, demanding that we act for the sake of the life before us, whatever the consequence.

While the Nazis were killing Jewish people across Europe, a few brave individuals tried to help, risking their lives to save both friends and strangers from the murderous pogroms. These individuals had little in common with one another. They held a wide range of moral and religious viewpoints; they were Catholic, Protestant, Jewish, Muslim, atheist, Marxist, Kantian and utilitarian (they even included the odd principled anti-Semite who thought it right to exclude Jewish people from universities but not to murder them). Some were notably virtuous in other areas of their life; others were not. A significant number of these individuals were later interviewed, and when they were asked why they acted as they did – why they risked their lives to help those who were threatened by the Nazis – most of them voiced a similar response. They did not invoke wider moral or religious beliefs; they did not appeal to moral rules or ethical theories; they did not appeal to reason or logic. They typically answered briefly, saying that 'it was the only thing to do'. It was demanded of them.[11]

We often fail to heed the demand. We walk past the man who is fraying and begging in the street. We put our head down and pretend he isn't there. As we walk away, something inside us is prised open, a fissure in the margins of the mind. We might call this 'conscience', but Levinas would have us know that it is the demand still grasping at us. In more extreme cases, where the failure is severe, we can be split on a more fundamental level, traumatised by our failure. The soldier plagued by visions of his victim. The policeman haunted by the face of the deceased criminal. The slaughterhouse worker who dreams of so many staring eyes. Beware the failure of the demand, Levinas warns, for we are held 'hostage' by the consequences.[12]

I climbed up onto the stun cage. The door at the far end slid open.

I met a man named Kumar, who was short in stature and broad in heart. He was born in Kandy in Sri Lanka, his full name Sivalingam Vasanthakumar, and he arrived in the UK in 1983, in flight from the Sri Lankan civil war. Having been raised on the family dairy farm, and coming from several generations of farmers, Kumar sought work on dairy farms upon his arrival, moving to the south-west. He studied agriculture at university, and he acquired land in Devon, where he began farming sheep and goats.

Kumar was a farmer, through and through. He had farmed animals his entire life. But one day he turned the wheel left when he was meant to turn right. Kumar was driving his lambs to slaughter, but he never arrived at the slaughterhouse. He turned and drove two hundred miles in the opposite direction to a sanctuary where his twenty lambs were released.

'It took me forty-five years,' he says, 'to see that I couldn't do it any more.'

The decision cost Kumar almost £10,000, and he arrived home to a quandary. There were seventy sheep still grazing his land. As Kumar tells me of these animals and the dilemma they pose, as he says he will not kill them and cannot afford to keep them, as he speaks of the financial difficulties the decision could pose, his eyes glow and his face beams. 'It's such a relief.'

Kumar never enjoyed saying goodbye. His eyebrows arch as he describes loading the lambs onto the truck, driving them to the slaughterhouse. Often, they refused to be unloaded. 'They understood where they were,' he says; 'they could smell it.' They huddled at the back of the truck and he would have to climb in to herd them out.

Kumar was not soft. He had worked with livestock for decades. He had slaughtered pigs by his own hand. He'd farmed animals since he was a child. But enough was enough. Kumar is now a vegetarian.

'You arrive, and they are on the truck, and they don't want to get off. You look at them, and they look at you, and it was very difficult,' he tells me.

There is something that happens when we stand face-to-face with an animal, when we look into their eyes in the last. Or, more precisely, there is something that might happen, something that sometimes happens, something dangerous, for it eludes our control. *You look at them. They look at you.*

She looked at me.

I was on the far side of the stun cage.

She had almond eyes. A thick white chest. Cautious hooves. A slight squint in her gait.

Siobhan had told me about cortisol, the stress hormone released when an animal is anxious or afraid. One can 'read' an animal through changes in their blood chemistry, she explained. When stressed, cortisol levels are higher, heart rates increase, and the animal exhibits telling behaviours. The slaughter process had been designed to minimise stress. This was mainly for the sake of the animals, she said, but also because stress reactions interfere with the quality of the meat. The cows that passed through her slaughterhouse weren't anxious or afraid. She was confident of that.

And she didn't seem stressed, she who was standing before me. Yet she was evidently anxious. She seemed to intuit that something was amiss. It was clear that she did not want to step into the stun cage. She looked around the space and stood stubbornly where she was. Nope. Not going to happen.

But then she saw me, a goofy primate dangling beyond the bars at the far end. Cows are curious by nature. She looked me in the eye.

That was when it happened.

I witnessed a murder.

I use these words deliberately, for that is what I saw. I did not witness an illegal act, but her death was murder.

She stepped forward, and she was still looking into my eyes when the door slid shut, when the slaughterman bent down and reached out and ...

... I not only witnessed a murder; I was complicit in it.

I felt the demand gripping me long after the bolt had fired and her body had collapsed, long after I had climbed down from the stun cage and rejoined the group. Siobhan walked over, the gun in her hand. The slaughterman carried over the animal's head and arranged it on the hook hanging waist high before me. *Aim carefully or you'll be splatted with blood.*

We tend to think of empathy as something that *we do*. Edmund Husserl has described empathy as 'imaginative projection into the place of the other'. 'I try to picture myself, standing *here*, how I would look, how I would feel, and how the world would appear if I were *there* – in the place of the body which resembles mine and acts as I might.' But this 'active' mode of empathy is only part of the story. Empathy is not always something we do, sometimes it is *done to us*. The resonance of another body within ours, an alien rhythm beating upon our bones. Not a projection into the place of the other, but the experience of being grasped by an external power. I witnessed a murder.

I have asked myself many times: Was I mistaken? Was I simply being sentimental? Was I guilty of squeamishness? Was I straightforwardly naive, disconnected from the realities of food production? But then I think of the slaughterhouse workers plagued by disturbing dreams. Are they being sentimental? Are they being squeamish? I think of Kumar. Was he disconnected from the realities of food production? Kumar is not the only farmer to turn his back on animal farming, perceiving that meat involves murder.[13]

I have no idea whether 'meat is murder' is true as a blanket statement; I suspect it's probably not. I could not tell you whether the other animals who passed through the slaughterhouse that day were murdered; I wasn't close enough to see.

An important distinction can be made between the philosophical aspirations of Peter Singer and those of Emmanuel Levinas. While the former was primarily concerned with *ethical justification*, the latter was interested in our *ethical experience*. Singer wanted to define a moral framework within which we might determine whether an action is right or wrong. Levinas was more concerned with the shape and colour of his everyday experiences, those that might be described as 'ethical' in nature. He wanted to know what characteristics these experiences had in common, what lent them their ethical slant. In Singer's world, everything needs to make sense. Ethics is a rational pursuit, in which we must act as good moral accountants, ensuring the books are properly balanced. This might be very worthy (especially for a philosopher), but Levinas would retort that our ethical experience is *not* wholly rational. We stand before the face of the other and we are grasped by a primordial demand that precedes our flailing attempts at reason, indifferent to what is rational or sensible.

The book *Sacred Cow* was published in 2020, with a film of the same name following months later. Written and produced by Diana Rodgers and Robb Wolf, *Sacred Cow* makes the case for ethical meat consumption and sustainable animal farming, looking at the nutritional, environmental and moral dimensions of the argument. 'Meat and animal fat are essential for our bodies,' the authors state, unequivocally. 'A sustainable food system cannot exist without animals.' Rodgers and Wolf proceed from the position that meat is nutritionally and ecologically necessary, to argue that meat consumption is also morally justifiable, given certain caveats about animal welfare. This all appears to be very reasonable. The ethical conclusion seems to flow logically from the strictures of necessity. If it is truly *necessary* that we eat meat, if we have no choice but to farm and consume animals, then it makes little sense to say that consumption is *unethical*. We are in the domain of ethical justification here, acting as good moral accountants, ensuring the books are balanced.

On the other hand, if animal farming and meat consumption are *not* necessary, then the case for veganism becomes more compelling. 'Other animals kill out of necessity whereas humans do not,' says Ed Winters, popularly known as Earthling Ed, co-founder of animal rights outfit Surge. 'In contemporary society we don't need to eat animals or their secretions and in doing so we are shortening our lifespan, destroying our planet and causing an unimaginable amount of unnecessary harm to innocent, living beings.' Following this logic, when we look beyond our society to very different societies, such as indigenous hunting cultures, where survival genuinely depends on animal foods, necessity would appear to provide moral justification. 'Eskimos, for example,' Ed says in one of his podcasts. 'I'm not going to point the finger at them. This idea of necessity is what I think is most pertinent.'[14]

These are simple illustrations, but they point towards the intuitive importance of the question, the fault line running through the debate. *Is it necessary that we consume animals?* In the rational realm of ethical justification, the question becomes all-important, for it would appear to tip the moral scales one way or the other. The question is undoubtedly important, but in the realm of our ethical experience, it proves to be less than decisive. Our empathy responds to the face before us, even when necessity binds us. The ethical demand takes hold, indifferent to the requirements of our biology. This world was not made by a moral philosopher, and the books do not always balance. *Meat is necessary. Meat is murder.* Sometimes both these statements are simultaneously true. Just ask the Eskimos.

3

HUNTING

In the far north, where flesh is precious and plants are scarce, the Inuit (or Eskimos) subsist by hunting. There are few edible plants upon the snow-blown tundra. Trees cannot survive at these latitudes; the soil is gripped with permafrost and vegetation struggles to take root. Yet the land is not without life. A mat of shrubs and lichens supports small mammals and migratory birds; there are caribou and moose; fish in the rivers; and seals, whales and walruses at the land's edge.[1]

In the dead of winter, the hunter stands over a seal's breathing hole. The ocean has frozen, and the hunter is on the ice, wind whipping his sleeves, snow blurring his vision. The hole beneath has been capped by a fragile cupola, a semi-transparent dome that sits atop a tunnel carved through the floe. The dome, formed by the sloshing of the seal as they breach the surface to breathe, is cracked, and the hunter peers down and through, into folds of black and green, and there are bodies turning below, silver sheening on the flank of a fish, finned forms pursued (perhaps) by a hungry seal.

The Inuit call these breathing holes *allus*, and in the shamanic tradition they are understood to be a portal that opens between worlds. The shaman is the community's representative in these other worlds, the sky above and the sea below. They earn their right to represent their community by being killed and consumed. The apprentice is initiated in isolation, seeking a secluded spot upon the tundra where, according to tradition, they will be consumed by a bear or attacked by bees. Having been eaten – having been preyed upon and lived to tell the tale – they are endowed with unusual abilities, including the ability to step beyond the human world. The *allu* marks the boundary.

The hunter tends to the boundary over winter, searching for *allus* on the pack ice that forms when the ocean freezes. This is perilous hunting, for while land ice is stable and predictable, the pack is protean and capricious; it might crack as the wind changes or the currents shift. The hunter on the pack must be alert to alterations in their environment, attentive to signs of ice-drift from the land-fast floe. They must listen, for the ice-scape is also a soundscape, and a crunch or a whistle can warn of impending rearrangement. When the pack does move, it can signal disaster, for the hunter might be stranded beyond a widening gap. They might never see shore again.

Hunting at an *allu* requires patience. The hunter might spend several hours locating the breathing hole, and then many more in wait. The sky is smothered, and the air has teeth, and the hunter must stay as still as can be, tilting his will against the elements. He will position himself downwind, his shadow carefully cast away. There is no room for error, for the opportunity when it arises will be fleeting. Long hours of silence, and then a gasp. A second gasp. The seal is in the cupola. *Crack!* The hunter strikes.

This hunter learned to take seals at their breathing holes by imitating the hunting stratagem of the polar bear. In winter, the bear will also seek out an *allu*, locating a flat plane where the ice is thin and the seal's dome is more easily discerned. Having located the site, the bear will deftly dig around the hole, preparing the space. He will take stock of the weather and the light, positioning himself downwind, his shadow cast away. It is a waiting game. 'When stalking seals near their breathing holes, a hunter must imitate the infinite patience of the animal without a shadow. He must enter the spirit of the polar bear,' says Inuit Joseph Susqlak. 'Eskimo people have learned not only *about* animals but also *from* them,' explains anthropologist Richard Nelson.[2]

Nelson tells of a man named Ataaktuk who studied seals so intently he could transform himself into one. Ataaktuk would go hunting in spring, searching for seals basking on the wet, melt-slicked ice. Having spied his prey, he would begin to crawl towards them, in sight but presenting a side view of himself. He would be dressed as a seal, wearing clothing made from sealskin, and he would imitate a seal's movements. Through this mimetic performance Ataaktuk could 'fool the animals into thinking he was one of their own'. When a seal grew suspicious and showed signs of unrest, 'he imitated flippers with his hands and feet, lifted his head high, and scratched the ice with his *azigaun*, a curved wooden handle with four seal claws attached'. Sleeping seals would often scratch the surface of the ice, and this performance reassured the individual that nothing was amiss.

Ataaktuk would crawl closer, and closer, and closer. He knew that he was close enough to strike when he could see the whiskers on the seal's nose.

This mimetic exchange of identities also extended to bear hunting, a dangerous pursuit but one with plentiful rewards. The hunter, in this instance, would seek to transform predator into prey. The ploy would be enacted in the spring, when bears stalked seals on the wet ice, as Ataaktuk did, crawling quietly towards them, moving from cover to cover (sometimes using a paw to conceal their conspicuous black nose). Inuit hunters would trick the predator by pretending to be a basking seal lying atop the ice. They would dress as a seal, recline as a seal, occasionally flap a flipper, enticing the bear to stalk within range.

To hunt bear, one must become a seal. To hunt seal, one must become a bear. To survive in the far north, one must inhabit the skin and instincts of another species. 'A hunter had to know the secrets of whatever animal he would kill,' Nelson explains. 'He would merge his thoughts with those of his prey, so that their minds were one.' Living in this whorl of identities, is it any wonder that the boundaries begin to blur?

Anthropologist Rane Willerslev tells of his mentor, a man named Old Spiridon:

Watching Old Spiridon rocking his body back and forth, I was puzzled whether the figure I saw before me was man or elk. The elk-hide coat worn with its hair outwards, the headgear with its characteristic protruding ears, and the skis covered with an elk's smooth leg skins, so as to sound like the animal when moving in the snow, made him an elk; yet the lower part of his face below the hat, with its human eyes, nose, and mouth, along with the loaded rifle in his hands, made him a man. Thus, it was not that Spiridon had stopped being human. Rather, he had a liminal quality: he was not an elk, and yet he was also not *not* an elk. He was occupying a strange place in between human and nonhuman identities.

Willerslev was living with the Yukaghirs, 'the icy or frozen people', inhabitants of the Upper Kolyma River in Siberia. Over eighteen months, he learned to hunt in the traditional manner, tutored by Old Spiridon and his family. The Yukaghirs are one of the oldest indigenous peoples in north-eastern Asia, and Willerslev entered their world, enduring long hours alone among the trees, 'every sinew straining to distinguish tracks and other signs of prey'. Like the Inuit, the Yukaghirs employ mimesis in the hunt, shifting identities in pursuit of deer, elk, sable and bear.[3]

'Hunters consider it necessary to assume the identity of their prey in order to kill it,' Willerslev explains. 'By means of mimicry, the Yukaghir hunter assumes the viewpoint, senses, and sensibilities of his prey.'

The 'dehumanisation' process begins before the hunter leaves camp for the forest. The hunter will go to the *banya*, the sauna, but instead of bathing with soap, he will wipe his body with dry whisks from birch trees. He says that the elk recognises the attractive smell of birch and does not flee but instead is drawn to approach, lured by the pleasing aroma. Once in the forest, the hunter sheds his language. Talk is discouraged; often no word will be spoken. 'If any sound is made, it will be a sound imitating the animal that they hope to attract.' Cow calls might be voiced to attract bulls; grunts, bugles and barks to arouse the interest of the herd. Finally, he sheds his human appearance. Dressed in furs, his skis wrapped with skins to replicate the sound of the animal when moving over snow, he will begin to stalk elk and move like an elk.[4]

The hunter tracks elk through the forest, searching for hoofprints in the snow, snared branches on the bough, nibbled leaves. When he locates his quarry, his performance grows more elaborate. He begins to imitate the elk's movements, waddling in an elk-like manner. He moves his body from side to side, impersonating the elk's stature and distinct mode of presentation. The ploy piques the animal's curiosity. The hunter approaches, smelling like a tree, talking like an elk, dressed in skins, and moving like the animal's kin, and the elk is 'captured by his mimetic performance'. The elk does not flush, but begins to approach, mirroring the hunter's mimetic movements.

There are dangers in this performance, and they might seem strange to us, for it is said that the hunter risks losing his human identity. 'What we are dealing with is not just some outward mimicry, simulation, or aping, but instead something deeper and more intense,' Willerslev explains. 'If the hunter loses sight of his own human self in this process and surrenders to the single perspective of the animal, he will undergo an irreversible metamorphosis and transform into the animal imitated.'

Tales of metamorphosis abound among the Yukaghirs. One hunter tells such a story, recalling that he spent many hours tracking a herd of reindeer. Night fell, and he had nothing to eat. He was hungry and cold, and he did not sleep. The next morning, he met an old man who gestured for him to follow. The hunter noticed that the man's footprints were those of a reindeer. 'But then I thought I was just hallucinating because I was tired and hungry.' After a long journey, they arrived at a camp, with thirty or more tents. 'The old man took me to his tent. He spoke to his wife by grunting just like a reindeer, and she grunted back.' The woman served the hunter a plate of food, and it was not meat but lichen; he ate it anyway, because he was hungry. When the hunter finally found his way home, his family greeted him with wide-eyed surprise. He could remember being away for only a few days, but he had been in the forest for more than a month. 'It seems that the people I met were reindeer, and I should have killed them, but at that time I did not know.'[5]

The Yukaghirs also tell cautionary tales of hybrid creatures called *syugussuy suroma*, the 'hairy ones' who roam the forest. These creatures are human in appearance, but their bodies are covered in fur, like animals. They live a solitary existence and are said to be hunters who identified too closely with another species, losing sight of their humanity, leaving them stranded in a state of betweenness. The hunter understands that he can only inhabit his prey's perspective for so long before it becomes perilous, and it is vital that a 're-humanisation' ceremony marks his return to the community. This is a ceremony of smoke and story.

Back in the camp, and the air is thick with woodsmoke and tobacco. A joint of meat is roasting over the flames, and a group has returned from the forest. They are sitting by the fire, bathing in the smoke, noisily sharing a meal. During their meal and non-stop afterwards, they talk about the day's hunt. They tell stories, but their stories make little sense. They speak in long elliptical narratives, disjointed phrases and disparate images. People listen, or they don't; they drift in and out. The point is not to tell a coherent tale or to communicate any particular information, but to *speak*, to feel their human voice upon their breath, to taste woodsmoke in their nostrils, meat upon their tongue – for these purge the animal from their mind, helping them to reinhabit their species' identity. 'They come to see that they are neither reindeer nor elk, but rather genuine human persons.'

The difficulty is not over, however, for the hunter's mimetic performance poses an acute *ethical* challenge. Spend many hours thinking elk, talking elk, stalking elk, inhabiting the mind and senses of an elk, and it becomes obvious that the elk is conscious and sentient. It becomes evident that the elk is a *person*, albeit an animal-person, an elk-person. Success in the hunt *requires* that the hunter sees the elk as a person. Without this perception, the hunter will struggle to locate or lure his prey.

The hunter becomes snared in a moral paradox. For the Yukaghirs, killing animals and eating flesh is the very essence of life. Meat is enjoyed and celebrated, and it provides necessary sustenance. But killing and eating animals is also profoundly problematic, for the animals most desirable as food – elk, reindeer, bear – are the ones understood to be most like humans. Eating meat means killing animal-persons, individuals revealed by 'mimetic empathy' to be scarcely different to human persons. 'When killing an elk or a bear, I sometimes feel that I've killed someone human,' one hunter explains. 'But one must banish such thoughts or one would go mad from shame.'

'Killing the animal,' Willerslev reiterates, is 'rather like killing a fellow person'.

And what is it to kill a fellow person, but to commit a murder?

And what is it to eat a fellow person, but to engage in cannibalism?

Hunting strategies rooted in mimetic empathy are employed by many indigenous cultures, not only the Inuit and Yukaghirs, and the possibility of murder and cannibalism arises in many of them.[6]

In the sun-seared Kalahari, San hunters track cheetahs and porcupines across the desert, hoping to steal their kill and eat their meat. 'We put on the cheetah's mind,' one hunter explains. 'When you follow the prints, you see in your mind how the porcupine thinks.' The hunter also seeks kudu and gemsbok, armed with poisoned arrows. When the animal is struck, it can be hours before the poison takes effect, leaving the hunter in long pursuit. Nqate Xqamxebe says that in pursuit, the hunter must inhabit the animal's muscles and mind, imitating the dash and movement of the wounded beast. 'Every animal is like this – you jump when the track shows it jumps.' The mimesis extends to the animal's death. The hunter will attend to his prey, moving as it moves, keening as it cries, participating in the animal's passing.

Anthropologist Louis Liebenberg joined a kudu hunt, tracking the animal through the burning midday heat. 'As we followed the tracks I could visualise the whole event unfolding in front of me.' As the kudu tired, its stride began to grow shorter, and it was running from shade to shade. 'In visualising the kudu I projected myself into its situation,' Liebenberg says. He felt his limbs elongating and his senses reaching into the nerve tissues and tendons of the kudu. 'As if in an almost trancelike state I could not only see how the kudu was leaping from one set of tracks to the next, but in my body I could actually feel how the kudu was moving. In a sense it felt as if I myself actually became the kudu, as if I myself was leaping from one set of tracks to the next.'[7]

Kindred strategies are employed in many hunting cultures. Tom Brown, who was trained in tracking by an Apache elder, says that in the Native American tradition, tracking an animal requires that you 'actually get down and "be" that animal. Listen, see and smell from the animal's point of view. Imagine what predators you might have to fear, and what differences that would make in your movements and activities.' Brown says you can discover a 'tremendous amount' by inhabiting the animal's perspective. 'Adaptations and habits that were once mysteries will suddenly jump into the light of understanding simply because, for a few moments, you had the humility to cast off your human skin.'[8]

In the Amazon, hunters will commonly imitate the vocalisations of birds and alter their body odour and speech to become more attractive to their prey. The Runa of the Ecuadorian Amazon, in keeping with this mimetic tradition, venerate the giant anteater, admiring the way the creature exploits the perspective of ants to feed upon them. When the anteater sticks its tongue into a nest, the ants see the tongue as a branch, and they unsuspectingly climb on. Emulating the ingenious ploy, the Runa hunter will paint his hands purple with crushed fruits when fishing. His hands resemble boulders, and the catfish he seeks fail to notice when he reaches for them from beneath rocks in the river.[9]

The perception that animals are persons is (unsurprisingly) pervasive in indigenous hunting cultures. 'Woolly monkeys, toucans, howler monkeys – all the creatures that we kill in order to eat – are persons, just as we are,' an Achuar hunter in the Amazon explains. This is not an abstract belief, a statement of ideology or principle, but an insight that becomes obvious in the hunt, as the hunter engages with his prey as a thinking, feeling person.[10]

Some Amazonian cultures are 'perspectivist' in their outlook, saying that all animals see themselves as 'human'. Speaking in what seem to be riddles, members of these cultures will tell you that jaguars perceive the blood they drink to be manioc beer, and when the jaguar carries away his prey, it is because he is taking it home for his wife to cook. They say that vultures see the maggots in rotting meat as grilled fish, and that what we perceive to be the stench of rotting carrion, the vulture experiences as the sweet-smelling vapour emanating from a steaming pot of tubers. Other animals are said to live in human societies, with chiefs, shamans, rituals, houses and cultures. 'Although they see jaguars as animals, the Wari' know from their shamans that jaguars see themselves as humans: that is, as people pursuing a full social life and endowed with a human appearance.'[11]

To early anthropologists, these beliefs sounded childlike or superstitious, but contemporary scholars understand that they express a more profound conviction: that humans do not have a privileged perspective on the world; that all animals share a common interiority that is essentially similar to human consciousness; that this consciousness is filtered through each species' sensory apparatus to create a distinct outlook; and that each outlook is as intrinsically valuable as any other. Murder and cannibalism are consequently an ever-present threat, for all animals can be persons, differentiated only by the clothing of their flesh. The hunter is haunted by the 'phantom of cannibalism' and experiences 'real feelings of moral anxiety when killing his prey'.[12]

Hunting societies (and the hunter especially) must go to great lengths to temper the emotional and ethical risks posed by killing and consuming quasi-similar beings. The hunt is often shrouded in taboo, enveloped in narrative and ceremony, and it is often said that the soul of the animal will be reborn in a new body if the right rituals are performed. These rituals help to ease the psychological tensions of the kill, ensuring that consumption does not amount to cannibalism.

Some of the most elaborate rituals have been enacted by the Inuit and other circumpolar peoples upon the killing of a bear. Among the Cree, First Nations peoples of North America, it was customary for the hunters to sit around the carcass immediately after the bear had been killed, sharing a pipe of tobacco. The oldest man in the group would carve the pipe from tree-bark and place it into the bear's mouth, saying, 'My grandfather, I will light your pipe.' The head would then be removed and cooked, and the men would sit in a circle as it was passed, each man striving to take a bite of the bear's flesh without touching the head with his hands. A hunter who was alone would enact a different ritual, cutting off the middle toe and claw of the right forefoot, and handing the token, back at camp, to the person – often his wife – who was to carry the body from the woods. The claw would then be wrapped in cloth, beaded or painted, while the bear would be laid out, like a man, in front of the hunter's wigwam. The men would smoke over the body, and as they smoked, they would refer to the animal as 'black food', while being careful not to point their finger at the deceased. After the bear was butchered, certain parts, including a piece of the heart, were burnt, or 'given to its spirit to eat', while the hunter would eat the remainder. These rituals were enacted out of deference, to encourage the soul of the bear to depart its body. The Naskapi, members of the Cree living in St'aschinuw in northern Quebec and Labrador, would treat the first bear cub killed in the hunting season with especial deference, stripping its skin from its carcass and stuffing its furry pelt with hay, while decorating its head and paws with beads and quills. Its blood, entrails and flesh would be cooked, and everyone would gather for a meal, while 'in the center of the feast the skinny deity is placed, grinning while the drums beat, and the guests devour the flesh in silence'. Among the Montagnais, inhabitants of Innu-assi ('Innu Land') in Quebec and Labrador, a kindred tradition had it that a feast would be held in the bear's honour. A large bowl of hot bear's grease would be passed around, while the bear's head and neck, which had been roasted on a spit, were erected on a stick in front of the chief of the band, who would be required to make a flattering speech.

Among the Inuit of Hudson Bay, a piece of the bear's tongue would be hung in the hut, and knives, saws, drills and other small objects would be attached beside it as presents to the bear's soul. Among the Inuit of Asiatic regions, the bear would be carried into the home, and the head and skin would be left in position for five days and nights during which constant attention would be paid. Men and women would remove their bead necklaces and hang them over the bear's neck. Libations of water and sacrifices of various meats would be offered. The bear would never be left alone, in case they felt lonely. Among the Inuit of southern Greenland, the head of a slain polar bear, having been taken home, would be positioned to face the horizon, so that the bear's soul could find its way back to its tribe. In the Siberian subarctic, hunters would similarly carry the skull home and install it in a place of honour. Friends and family would gather, and a party would be organised in honour of the animal's soul. It was generally considered necessary to consume the entire animal at one sitting so that none of the flesh was wasted, and the feast was conducted in silence, apart from the occasional chanting and drumming of the shaman. The bear's head would be given an honorary position at the feast and provided with a dish of its own meat as an additional token of respect.[13]

In so many ways, the soul of the bear would be placated and encouraged to be born again in a new body. It can't be murder if the animal is reborn. It can't be cannibalism if the soul of the animal is no longer infused in the meat. Or so the hunter tells himself.

One of the most compelling narratives governing the relationship between hunter and prey is voiced by the Tukano, a group of twenty tribes living in the Vaupés territory of the Colombian Amazon. The region takes its name from the Vaupés River, whose gushing falls and rushing rapids – in a land where most transportation is achieved by river – have rendered the area relatively isolated and free from outside interference, at least until recently. The Tukano share their territory with many animals, including rodents (paca, agouti and cavi), monkeys, armadillos, peccary and deer, and birds such as guan, tinamou and toucans (with whom they recognise a common ancestry, hence 'Tukano'). They are hunters and horticulturalists, growing manioc, plantains, peppers, peach palms, tobacco and coca in their gardens.

As in other hunting societies, the Tukano seek to make themselves attractive to their prey. 'A man who prepares himself ritually for the hunt does so in accordance with the animals he wishes to pursue,' anthropologist Gerardo Reichel-Dolmatoff explains. The hunter will observe a strict diet of unseasoned food, devoid of oils and fats. The morning before the hunt, he will drink a large volume of liquid chilli peppers, including through his nostrils, to purge and purify his body, and he will tuck aromatic herbs under his belt, hoping to make himself alluring to the animals of the forest. Odours are important, and the hunter can distinguish diverse species at a distance by their scent, including tapirs, peccaries and deer. He can also discern them by their calls, and he is an expert mimic.[14]

The Tukano tell a vivid and expansive tale of the powers that animate the cosmos. They understand the universe to be formed of an immense circuit of energy that encompasses and flows through the biosphere. The energy floods from the sun into the world, penetrating organic matter, moving between lifeforms, surging around the cosmic coil. But the quantity of energy is finite, and the flow must be carefully managed, or the universe will be thrown out of balance. The Tukano must tend to the balance, attentive to what they eat and how they interact with their environment.

Hunting is the most important and consequential activity, and there are strong taboos governing the treatment of animals and the preparation and consumption of meat. The Tukano hunter knows that each time he kills and consumes an animal, a portion of energy is redirected around the circuit from the animal domain to the human, affecting the overall equilibrium. It is necessary to ensure that human subsistence does not endanger the cohesion of the whole. This means that what is taken must be given back.[15]

It is the role of the shaman to oversee this process of energetic exchange. The shaman acts as the protector of the Tukano's natural resources, mediating between the hunter and his prey, exercising careful control over the tribe's subsistence, dictating which animals may be killed, where, and in what numbers. This ecological governance is enacted with the help of a psychotropic brew called yahé through which the shaman induces an altered state of consciousness and receives 'visions'. These visions come directly from the animals hunted, from the peccary and the armadillo, and from their guardian, a figure known as Vaí-mahsë, the Master of Animals.

Vaí-mahsë (literally, 'Animal-Person') is of singular significance to the Tukano, acting as arbitrator between the human and animal worlds. The Animal-Person is said to be a fierce protector of the forest and its inhabitants, including the animals who live with him in rocky outcrops known as 'hill houses' and in areas of the river known as 'water houses'.

The water houses are found at the bottom of deep pools that are believed to be guarded by giant anacondas. Each house is topped by a spiralling vortex, a whirlpool imagined as a swirl of cosmic and gestational energy. The houses are large, and they are divided into many recesses and chambers, each occupied by schools of fish, scuttling crabs, great snails, coiled river snakes, and other beings. 'Slanting sunrays will penetrate into these depths, illuminating chains of glittering bubbles among which schools of multicoloured fish may be seen flitting by ... Some of these chambers are set with brilliant crystals that glimmer with hidden reflections.' The shaman will visit these water houses under the influence of yahé to barter with Vaí-mahsë for the release of animals to be hunted. 'It is clear that the domains of the Master of Animals are conceived as hallucinatory dimensions,' Reichel-Dolmatoff observes; 'it is the drug experience which provides the atmosphere, both enchanting and frightening, in which these vital creative processes are developing.'[16]

Vaí-mahsë is not known only to the Tukano – kindred figures are found in many indigenous cultures. The Cree say that each animal species possesses a 'chief', including Mistamisk, the great beaver, Mistamōswa, the great moose, and Mistītakōm, the great beetle. The Innu know of at least ten *vai-mahsa*, Animal-Persons, including Papakashtshihk of the caribou, Nisk-napeu of the geese, and Mashkuapeu of the bears. Papakashtshihk, the Caribou-Man, is said to 'live in a cave deep within a hill to which access is gained by a narrow passage'. In this cavern, he dwells with his immense herd. 'The souls of the slaughtered caribou return to the cave, where they are reincorporated into new animals that will be sent out to the hunters on another occasion.'

Among the Campas tribes who live in the rainforests of Peru, the masters of fish include otters, grey herons and egrets – it is they who ensure that the fish swim back up the rivers each year in the spawning season. The swallow-tailed kite is said to be the father of edible insects, and the shaman will pay regular visits to the kite's wife to ask her to allow her children to accompany him to the forest. The shaman will also visit the mistress of peccaries, a being who keeps the forest's peccaries in a garden atop a mountain. The shaman will ask the mistress to part with a member of her herd. When she concedes, she tugs a tuft of bristles from the back of one of her hogs and blows it away, telling the shaman that it will produce many more peccaries, which she will send down to rootle among the trees.

The Inuit say that seals, whales and other sea animals originated from the fingers of Takánâluk, the sea woman. Among the Tunkus, the Samoyeds, the Xant and the Mansi, the whole forest is believed to be animated by a spirit that usually takes the form of a large deer. Among the Chukchees, the master of wild reindeer is called Pičvu'čin. He is described as 'a tiny man, with a sledge made of grass stalks, who sees the mice that pull it as reindeer'. Pičvu'čin lives with his reindeer in an underground den that can be reached by a deep ravine, and it is from here that he sends his herds into the world, if humans have treated reindeer with respect. The Yukaghirs similarly commune with Khoziain, jolly but unreliable beings who spend their time drinking and playing cards, using the animals in their care as stakes. Animals change hands depending on the luck of the game, hence the unpredictability of seasonal migrations.[17]

Vaí-mahsë – in so many guises – embodies the ecological and

ethical demands of the animal world, personifying the requirement that the human community acts with restraint and treats animals with respect. The Tukano understand that no animal may be hunted or consumed without the permission of Vaí-mahsë, and reparations must be made to ensure balance in the energies animating the cosmos.

The loss of balance is experienced as illness. Anthropologist Philip Descola tells of an Achuar hunter named Chumpi whose wife Metekash had been bitten by a lancehead snake. Chumpi was greatly distressed, for he believed the snake had been sent by Jurijri, one of the 'mothers of game' who watch over the lives of forest animals. Chumpi admitted to Descola that the previous day he had taken up a rifle, instead of his usual blowpipe, and had fired at random into a group of woolly monkeys, killing three or four animals and wounding several more. He had brought home three and left one mortally wounded. 'By killing, almost wantonly, more animals than were necessary to provide for his family and by not bothering about the fate of those that he had wounded, Chumpi had transgressed the hunters' ethic and had broken the implicit agreement that linked the Achuar people with the spirits that protected game. Prompt reprisals had duly followed.'[18]

The Tukano are intensely anxious about the possibility of reprisals. They interpret all manner of accidents and illnesses, including falls, cuts, broken limbs, snakebites, painful insect bites, random pains, fevers and dizziness, as of animal origin, wished upon them by the animals they consume. These illnesses and injuries are imagined as thorns, shards of quartz, splinters of hard-wooded trees, and jaguar hairs, shot at the hunter and his family by Vaí-mahsë on behalf of the wronged animal. Premonitions of illness and injury are common, and often arrive as nightmares.

'A greatly feared omen of ill health is when the game animals appear in a hunter's dreams,' Reichel-Dolmatoff explains. 'Animals will also commonly appear in a number of other states and, of course, during narcotic trances induced by hallucino-genic drugs.'[19]

There are striking parallels between the testimonies of slaugh-terhouse workers in contemporary academic literature and the troubled accounts of Tukano hunters. 'Slaughter employees narrated paranoid nightmares and dreams filled with fear and anxiety ... [dreams in which they are] fleeing from vengeful cattle, being confronted by slaughtered cattle who fail to die, seeing animals in pain, fighting with and being watched by animals.' Similarly, the Tukano hunter who kills profligately is plagued by anxiety and disturbing dreams, the belief that 'the animals sent them illnesses, accidents, bad frights, and what was worse, nightmares and visions of monstrous tapirs'. If the hunter kills or consumes more animals than he needs, the animal might 'appear in dreams, in nightmares, or in drug-induced hallucinations'.[20]

To ward off illness and anxiety and ensure the biosphere is kept in energetic balance, the Tukano shaman must make parley with Vaí-mahsë while under the influence of yahé. The shaman drinks the brew, and in trance, enters the water houses and the hill houses where Vaí-mahsë dwells. The latter are domed in shape and formed of hexagonal planes. In these houses dwells the giant prototype of each species, a sort of 'species-soul', along with thousands of somnolent animals, curled in foetal position, regenerating and anticipating birth. If the shaman is successful in his negotiation, then a portion of these animals will be 'woken up' and sent into the forest to live, and these animals may be hunted and eaten. The human community is thus provided with animals to consume, but the arrangement comes at the highest cost. 'The shaman pays with human souls.'

'For every animal given to humans to hunt, a human soul must be given in return, to be transformed into an animal of the same species.' It is those who mistreat animals, who kill carelessly, who eat more meat than they need, who are given over to be reborn. The Tukano ethic is one of 'scrupulous equivalence'; a 'perfectly symmetrical' exchange of human souls and animal flesh.[21]

This exchange forces the community to exercise particular restraint. The hunter must act with supreme care when taking an animal's life. When stalking his quarry, he must be confident that he has followed the right ritual procedures, that his need is true. When the animal spies him in the last, the stakes could not be higher. He must eat meat to survive, but he knows that if he mistreats the animal or consumes more than he needs, he will pay the highest price, his soul given to Vaí-mahsë to be clothed in the scent and pelt of another species, re-born in the body of his prey.

The Inuit have lived in intimacy with the animals of the Arctic, studying them more intensely than any scientist could hope to. Their perception of their environment has been filtered through the senses of these animals. They understood that the thumping and bellowing of walruses warned of shifts in the prevailing wind. They knew that the arrival of white-winged gulls signified the melting of the season's snow. They intuited that squaw ducks in the sky implied weather that would be good for hunting, and when they heard the cries of the loons – their wail, tremolo, yodel and hoot – they knew that the rains would soon begin to fall. 'Volumes could be written on the behavior, ecology, and utilization of arctic animals – polar bear, walrus, bowhead whale, beluga, bearded seal, ringed seal, caribou, musk ox, and others – based entirely on Eskimo knowledge,' Nelson observes. 'I had never experienced anything like the intensity of their relationship to animals.'[22]

Animals provided the raw materials necessary for the Inuit's survival. Caribou provided clothing and food. Their bodies were used for boats and sledges. Their sinew made rope. Their antlers made hooks. Their bones were used as needles. Their tendons were thread. Their blood would dye fabrics. Their skins made tents. Their bladders were used for bags. Even their fat could be chewed to make candles or burned in a stone lamp.

The Inuit have traditionally relied on animals as their primary – or only – source of nutrition. In the summer, they would gather a few plant foods, such as berries, tubers, roots, stems and seaweeds, and they sometimes ate the fermented lichen and grasses found in the stomachs of moose and deer, but for most of the year, animal foods were the only nutrient-dense foods available. Most of the Inuit's calorie requirement was provided by animal fat, including the blubber of whales, seals and caribou. They obtained essential minerals and vitamins from kelp and the oils of fish and sea mammals, including whale skin, and the animals' livers and raw organ meats, seal brain and caribou liver.

Few peoples could say 'meat is necessary' as definitively as the Inuit. The Inuit have needed animal foods to survive, but this necessity has not provided ethical closure. Ask the Inuit whether it is right and good to eat meat, and they will answer strongly in the affirmative. *Yes!* Yet the experience of killing and consuming animals remains fraught with emotional complexity. The mimetic empathy employed in the hunt reveals the prey to be a person – sentient and intentional, if not quite the equivalent of a human person – and killing persons (even animal-persons) is profoundly problematic. As the Inuit shaman Aivilingmiutaq Ivaluardjuk explains: 'The greatest peril of life lies in the fact that human food consists entirely of souls. All the creatures that we have to kill and eat, all those that we have to strike down and destroy to make clothes for ourselves, have souls, like we have.'[23]

The greatest peril of life. The elaborate ceremonies enacted upon the killing of a bear were not performed only out of cultural habit, but psychological necessity. It might be right and reasonable for hunters in circumpolar regions to consume bears, but it is also disturbing, traumatic even, and this potential for psychological unrest evokes a ritual response. Meat might be necessary, but that does not preclude the possibility that it might also be perceived to be murder. Animal foods are nutritious, but omnivory might still amount to cannibalism. The ethical demand penetrates our omnivorous entanglement, an arrow shot through the hunter's web, creating a 'moral paradox at the very centre of their hunting cosmology'.[24]

The Inuit do not believe that a human soul must be donated in return for each animal consumed, as the Tukano do, but reparations are still required. 'Inuit hunting rites and birth rites indicate that souls and flesh, which are so rare and so precious, circulate ceaselessly between different components of the biosphere,' Descola explains; thus 'the remains of the dead are left out for predators; afterbirths are offered to seals, and the souls of the dead sometimes return to the spirit in charge of marine game.'[25]

We might think that these cultural narratives and ritual responses – the Inuit's donation of the dead, the Tukano's yahé ceremony – are alien and rather exotic. We might think that we are altogether more 'modern', but we are susceptible to the same psychological pressures. No less than the Inuit or the Yukaghir, we must make sense of what it means to kill animals, grappling with the question of necessity. No less than the Cree or the Tukano, we are prone to the perception that meat might involve murder. This tension between necessity and murder is the crux of the meat paradox.[26]

In common with these cultures, we tell stories and we enact ceremonies in response – stories that tell us what it means to eat animals; rituals that help us navigate the tension. I went in search of our stories. I went hunting for those rituals.

4

OMNIVORE

John Lewis-Stempel tells of his descent into the underworld. 'The ditch was about eight feet deep – you get a lot of rain on the hills of the Welsh borders – a shadow world of ferns, moss, slime, serpent ivy, slinking water.' The farmer climbed inside, hands gripping at roots, boots sliding in the mud. At the foot of the incline there was a ewe, 'broken, puppet-sprawled'. She was beyond repair, and he realised he had a choice. He could wait for the vet, which would take some time, or he could do what needed to be done. 'I put the 12 bore against the back of her head, pulled the trigger. The blast detached her head. Blood, strangely scarlet and fluorescent, seeped slowly into the water.'

It was then that he realised. 'I believed I had distracted the rest of the flock with a bucket of sheep nuts. Not so.' The flock was watching him. They were standing on the rim of the ditch, peering over. A row of ovine eyes, gazing. 'They then ran in fear to the far end of the field.

'I had not exactly been a hard-hearted, inorganic farmer before that moment but, upon clambering out of the ditch, I was obliged to drop my cognitive dissonance, my objectification of sheep. In a kaleidoscopic moment, I saw that the flock was not a monolithic unit but composed of sub-groups based on friendship and family bonds. One old ewe, Sooty, had movingly gathered her daughter and granddaughter about her.'

Lewis-Stempel describes this as his 'Damascene' moment.

'The flock did not come near me for weeks,' he recalls. This wasn't really a surprise, for sheep have excellent memories; they are sensitive and emotionally intelligent. 'I know because I look into their golden eyes as they die. And I have seen a lot of sheep die.'

The farmer was changed by the experience, as Kumar was changed by his experience trying to herd lambs from his truck at the slaughterhouse, but Lewis-Stempel did not respond as Kumar responded. He did not relinquish his sheep or give up eating meat. 'I realised that I wanted a relationship of compassionate companionship with my flock,' he says. The tenets of this relationship can be expressed in three basic principles:

1. We should eat less meat;
2. The meat we do eat should be sustainable and organic, and nothing less;
3. Farm livestock are not Descartian flesh-robots but sentient creatures deserving of a good life and a good death – which should come only near the end of a natural lifespan.

'Yes, I hold attitudes one would expect from a shrub-drinking hipster outta East London, rather than a fifty-something farmer from the West of England, with a wind-worked face, who has raised livestock for twenty-five years, and whose family have farmed for eight hundred,' but there are proper ways to farm animals and there are improper ways. Industrial animal farming is profoundly improper. 'Raising of livestock in this fashion is not farming, because it abjures any sense of husbandry.'[1]

The word 'husband' once meant 'peasant farmer'. The verb 'to husband' meant 'to manage carefully', with 'animal husbandry' describing a peasant's careful management of their farm animals. 'The essence of husbandry was care,' explains philosopher Bernie

Rollin. 'Humans put animals into the most ideal environment possible for the animals to survive and thrive, the environment for which they had evolved and been selected. In addition, humans provided them with sustenance, water, shelter, protection from predation, such medical attention as was available, help in birthing, food during famine, water during drought, safe surroundings and comfortable appointments.'[2]

This caring management was conceived in the context of an 'ancient contract', as Temple Grandin has called it. The terms of the contract placed duties on both parties. We would provide farm animals with a good life, keeping them healthy and protected from harm, and in return they would 'give us' their bodies as sustenance and materials. Michael Pollan gave voice to this view in *The Omnivore's Dilemma*, in a passage that is worth quoting at length:

> ... domestication took place when a handful of especially opportunistic species discovered, through Darwinian trial and error, that they were more likely to survive and prosper in an alliance with humans than on their own. Humans provided the animals with food and protection in exchange for which the animals provided the humans their milk, eggs, and – yes – their flesh. Both parties were transformed by the new relationship: The animals grew tame and lost their ability to fend for themselves in the wild (natural selection tends to dispense with unneeded traits) and the humans traded their hunter-gatherer ways for the settled lives of agriculturists. (Humans changed biologically, too, evolving such new traits as the ability to digest lactose as adults.) From the animals' point of view the bargain with humanity turned out to be a tremendous success, at least until our own time. Cows, pigs, dogs, cats, and chickens have thrived, while their wild ancestors have languished. (There are ten thousand wolves left in North America and fifty million dogs.)[3]

This notion of a 'bargain' based on mutually beneficial exchange, an 'ancient contract' that both parties have signed up to, is the crux of our cultural narrative. This is the story that we tell to make sense of our consumption of meat. Just as the Tukano speak of a cosmic energy circuit and the Inuit honour the bear's skull, so we tell a story of contractual exchange. Lewis-Stempel's three principles can be read as a commentary on what it might mean to better uphold our side of the bargain.

In Britain, we take our commitments towards other animals very seriously, priding ourselves on being a nation of animal lovers. We adore our pets. We give money to animal charities. David Attenborough is our honorary patron saint. We love animals so much that we would even vote to leave the European Union on their behalf. Thomas Borwick, digital director of the official Vote Leave campaign, which campaigned for the UK to leave the EU, says that in the run-up to the 2016 referendum, the group targeted prospective 'leave' voters with online ads focused on animal suffering and animal rights. These ads suggested that the EU was complicit in animal cruelty, and that Brexit would allow Britain to take back control and treat animals compassionately.

HUNTING WHALES is unnecessary and barbaric! The shipment of whale meat through our ports MUST BE STOPPED! CLICK IF YOU AGREE.

The text was positioned atop an image of a mother whale with her calf. Click on the image and text appeared saying: *'The EU is supporting commercial whaling by forcing us to allow ships carrying whale meat to dock at our ports!'*
Other ads featured graphic images of dead whales.

The EU blocks our ability to speak out and PROTECT polar bears! CLICK TO PROTECT THEM.

The text was positioned atop an image of a mother bear with her two cubs. Click on the image and text appeared saying: *'If we stay in the EU, we will be powerless to increase protection for polar bears.'*

THESE ARE ANIMALS. NOT ENTERTAINMENT.
STOP ANIMAL ABUSE.

This text was positioned atop an image of a bull fight; the bull had been speared and was bleeding as it ran towards the cape of the matador. Click on the image and text appeared explaining that Brexit would help to halt animal cruelty.

These ads didn't need to be completely honest to be effective – they simply needed to appeal to our empathy and our identity as 'animal lovers'. Vote Leave spent more than £2.7 million targeting these ads at groups of prospective voters. The content was segmented, some groups receiving graphic ads featuring mutilated animals while others were sent gentler images of cuddly sheep. There were other ads framed around very different issues, some raising concerns about immigration, others claiming that family budgets and health service funding would be better outside the EU. But of all the ads, those concerning animals and animal rights were the 'most successful', Borwick says. It's not far fetched to ask whether the Brexit vote was ultimately swayed by our love of animals.[4]

In the wake of Brexit, as the UK and US governments began negotiating a trade deal, concerns began to build that such a deal might result in industrially farmed meat (including 'chlorinated chicken') being imported from America and sold in UK supermarkets. The *Mail on Sunday* was one of several papers to run a series of articles exposing the horrors of industrial farming in the US. 'Miserable-looking animals stretch for as far as the eye can see, standing on barren dirt, huddled together under sheets of corrugated iron offering the only shade from the blazing Californian sun. Occasionally there is a plaintive moo, but for the most part the cattle stand silent in their manure-encrusted pens.'[5]

These articles deliberately evoked a sense of abandoned responsibility. The outrage that British people felt at the prospect of American meat arriving on their dinner plates was rooted in the perception that US farming represented a failure in the terms of the contract. 'It's reasonable to assume,' writes cattle rancher Nicolette Hahn Niman, 'that animals would never have opted for such an arrangement if torture had been part of the deal. Stated simply: By raising animals in factory farms, humans are violating their age-old contract with domestic animals.'[6]

It seems obvious that animals wouldn't consent to the worst excesses of factory farming, but it's less obvious (if we pursue the thought experiment) what they *would* consent to. Would a pig agree to life in a 'higher welfare' indoor system, where they were sheltered, routinely fed, but never permitted to feel the sun on their back? How many chickens would agree to live in a shed of 20,000 birds, never knowing what it was to bathe and forage in the dust? How many dairy cows would consent to having their male calves culled soon after birth? How many would agree to be separated from their daughters so that we could drink their milk, as is normal practice even in higher welfare dairy systems? There is a glaring deceit at the heart of our ancient contract narrative – no individual animal has consented to the terms of the deal.

I believe that it's possible for farm animals to be provided with a good life, a life they might agree to, speculative as the idea is. Animal welfare organisation Compassion in World Farming worked with OneKind to conduct an analysis of welfare assurance schemes in England and Scotland and found that organic farming consistently provided the highest potential levels of animal welfare across all species. (Red Tractor 'Assured Food Standards', the UK industry scheme, came bottom of the league table.) Animals on organic farms are genuinely free ranging; they are fed a healthy and natural diet; they often grow more slowly and live fuller lives; and they are spared the routine mutilations of conventional farming. But even in organic, there are difficult questions to be asked, and the most challenging might be: *How long will I live?*[7]

Lewis-Stempel's third tenet – that animals should be provided with a full and natural lifespan – is perhaps the most radical. Yes, we should eat less meat. Yes, we should ensure that our meat is organic and sustainable. But what would it mean to provide farm animals with a full life? Animals are routinely denied such a life, even in higher welfare systems. A pig in the wild might live for five to fifteen years, whereas a pig on an organic farm will typically live for six months. The proposal is fraught with pragmatic and philosophical complexity. How do you define an animal's 'natural' lifespan? How long should a cow be permitted to live? How do you delineate the longevity of a sheep? In the wild, it's normal for weaker animals to be preyed upon (often brutally so) – should we let stronger animals live for longer and eat the weaker? What degree of veterinary care should we invest in keeping an elderly cockerel alive? Given that animals will often produce a surfeit of offspring, an evolutionary adaptation to the likelihood that some will die young, does this mean we should be permitted to eat a percentage of animals at a younger age?

Thorny as the proposal is, there is something in it, I think. There is something in the idea that farm animals should be granted a full life, a natural lifespan, as well as the best living conditions. Is this not the true test of our commitment to the ancient contract? Answer me this. If you were in the animal's position, negotiating the terms of the deal, would you settle for anything less?

Our tale of an ancient contract is a narrative of consent. The animal *agrees* to be eaten. Animals don't literally voice their consent, but we believe the deal to be mutually beneficial. After all, farm animals wouldn't exist if we didn't breed them for consumption. We provide them with a good life, and we ensure they have a swift death. (It's in the contract.) The 'consenting animal' is a favourite trope of the advertising industry. Butter brand Anchor, to name just one example, has spent several decades making ads of dancing and delighted dairy cows: dairy cows celebrating the sale of butter, dairy cows churning butter for human consumption, dairy cows in an impossibly green field frolicking with their calves ('*WE ARE LUCKY COWS!*' a voice in the background chants maniacally). The Anchor cows' consent in these ads is so emphatic, it almost feels disrespectful *not* to eat their butter.[8]

Hunting cultures tell similar tales. The Yukaghirs say that a successful hunt depends on the goodwill of the animal hunted; *tolo'w xanice e'rietum el kude'deti*, they say, 'if the reindeer does not like the hunter, he will not be able to kill it.' Inuit hunters secure the goodwill of their prey by offering seals and whales a drink of fresh water as soon as they are dragged ashore – this is believed to make the animal feel welcome in the human world, encouraging their soul to return to the sea to be born in a new body. Some of the most colourful tales are told by the Cree, who say that prey animals give themselves to be hunted out of generosity. Reindeer (or caribou) are so eager to satisfy human needs, they will even compete with one another to be killed.[9]

The Cree's tale is reinforced by a quirk in the behaviour of hunted reindeer. In the hunt, 'there often comes a critical point when a particular animal becomes immediately aware of your presence. It then does a strange thing. Instead of running away it stands stock still, turns its head and stares you squarely in the face.' Anthropologist Tim Ingold says the behaviour is an adaptation to being hunted by wolves. When the reindeer stops and turns, the pursuing wolf also stops. Both animals take stock of the situation and catch their breath, ready for the ensuing chase. But the adaptation backfires when the reindeer is pursued by a human, for the animal inadvertently provides the hunter with an easy shot. The Cree consequently believe that 'the animal offers itself up, quite intentionally and in the spirit of goodwill or even love towards the hunter'. The meat of caribou is not taken, it is *received*. 'And it is in the moment of encounter, when the animal stands its ground and looks the hunter in the eye, that the offering is made.'[10]

These tales of consent can be deeply entrenched and largely convincing, but they are also precarious and prone to disturbance. What happens when it becomes obvious that the animal does *not* consent to be killed? What happens to the hunter faced with a reindeer who manifestly desires to live? What happens when we are confronted with evidence that farmed animals have not agreed to the terms of the contract? The narrative of consent begins to unravel, and we experience a state of emotional disturbance known to psychologists as 'dissonance'.

The term was coined by Leon Festinger in his 1956 study of the apocalyptic flying saucer cult that coalesced around a Chicago housewife named Marian Keech. Keech had begun receiving messages from a planet named Clarion, from extraterrestrials who warned that the world would be destroyed by a flood shortly before dawn on 21 December 1954. The deluge was nigh, but Keech would be saved. She and her followers, who were called the Seekers, would be taken away in flying saucers. Festinger, intrigued by Keech's prophecy, posed as a believer and infiltrated the group. Several colleagues joined him, and they began taking detailed notes on the anticipated apocalypse. They were interested in how Keech would respond when the flood failed to materialise.

> *Dissonance* and *consonance* are relations among cognitions – that is, among opinions, beliefs, knowledge of the environment, and knowledge of one's own actions and feelings. Two opinions, or beliefs, or items of knowledge are *dissonant* with each other if they do not fit together – that is, if they are inconsistent ... Dissonance produces discomfort and, correspondingly, there will arise pressures to reduce or eliminate the dissonance.

The deluge never came, the skies remained empty, and Festinger watched as Keech and the Seekers concocted elaborate rationalisations to explain away the prophecy, trying to alleviate the dissonance roused by the failure. He observed that the most committed members of the group (those who had given up their homes and jobs) were moved to begin evangelising once it became clear that the flying saucers were not coming. 'When people are committed to a belief and a course of action, clear disconfirming evidence may simply result in deepened conviction and increased proselyting.' Instead of admitting they were wrong, the Seekers recommitted to their worldview, warping their perception of the events that had unfolded, and they then set out to convert others to their cause.[11]

Dissonance theory has been applied to many societal puzzles over the last half-century, but it is only in the past decade that it has been applied to our consumption of meat. It happened almost by accident. Brock Bastian and Steve Loughnan were sharing an office in Melbourne, working on the psychology of dehumanisation, the process by which one person comes to see another as less than human, when one day Bastian unpacked his lunch. It was a ham sandwich. Over a mouthful, he said: 'Isn't it weird that everyone eats animals, but give them a knife and a pig and they would say they couldn't do it?' The observation was obvious, almost banal, but it planted a seed between the two men that blossomed into one of the most important papers in social psychology of the past decade.

It was this paper, published in the journal *Appetite*, that introduced the term 'meat paradox' to describe the contradictions in our relationship with meat. These contradictions derive from our empathy and our eating. We care about animals, we are confronted by ethical demands, and this means we are averse to causing them harm. But we also eat them, and this means causing them harm. The contradiction generates dissonance, 'an unpleasant emotional state that people are motivated to resolve'. The *motivational* character of the state is highly significant. Dissonance can be 'very painful to tolerate', Festinger explains. The meat paradox generates 'a motivational state where people feel the need to resolve the conflict', Bastian tells me.

Our narrative of consent – this tale of an ancient contract – assuages dissonance by reassuring us that animals aren't really harmed for our consumption or killed against their will. Our story tells us that they have consented to their fate, that they desire to be eaten, that their death was part of the deal they struck to enjoy their life. The story allows us to retain an empathetic self-image and uphold our identity as animal lovers, even as we force non-consenting animals to their end. But the story is only partially persuasive. The narrative of consent offers incomplete reassurance, and we are therefore moved to bolster it with supplementary strategies that help keep the dissonance at bay.

The simplest strategy consists in our *detachment* from the processes of meat production. We are removed from the coercion and violence intrinsic to the process of slaughter, and from the restrictive conditions in which many animals are forced to live. We rarely meet the animals we consume. We do not know them as persons or personalities. We do not witness their final moments, and we typically play no part in disassembling their bodies. There are many reasons for this, but our detachment helps to keep the fantasy of consent in place. It's much easier for us to believe that farm animals have agreed to their death if we are never exposed to evidence to the contrary.

It is not only that we are ignorant of the processes of meat production, we are *wilfully* ignorant. 'In several investigations, interviewees explicitly claimed they did not know about farming practices and animal welfare because they wished to remain ignorant,' psychologist Hank Rothgerber observes, 'in some cases, because they knew that such information would make it more emotionally difficult to purchase meat.' Even the most conscientious of us are prone to wilful ignorance. While most of us say that we care about animal welfare, 67 per cent concede that we do not like to think about welfare when we purchase meat. Of those who consider animal welfare to be 'highly important', only about half report thinking about it when buying meat in supermarkets or restaurants.[12]

Several studies have observed our susceptibility to wilful ignorance, among them a 2018 study which found that vegetarians have a more accurate understanding of the conditions typical of industrial animal farming. The study found a gradation in the accuracy of perception extending along the dietary spectrum, with 'unrestricted omnivores' (those who eat lots of meat) holding more inaccurate views than 'flexitarians' (who eat less), and flexitarians holding more inaccurate beliefs than vegetarians. This trend held true regardless of the individual's educational background. Omnivores with more education were equally 'ignorant' as those with less, implying that their beliefs were *motivated*. It's not that we eat lots of industrially farmed meat because we are ignorant of what really happens, rather we are wilfully ignorant *because we eat lots of meat*. When prompted to reflect on the dire conditions in which animals are forced to live, we experience a burgeoning sense of dissonance, and we conjure a falsely positive view. *Life on an industrial farm can't be that bad!*[13]

Our detachment feeds into processes of *dissociation*. Peter Singer made the observation in *Animal Liberation*:

> In general, we are ignorant of the abuse of living creatures that lies behind the food we eat. Buying food in a store or restaurant is the culmination of a long process, of which all but the end product is delicately screened from our eyes. We buy our meat and poultry in neat plastic packages. It hardly bleeds. There is no reason to associate this package with a living, breathing, walking, suffering animal. The very words we use conceal its origins: we eat 'beef', not bull, steer, or cow, and 'pork', not pig.

Singer was writing several decades ago, but researchers have only recently started to empirically investigate how dissociation – the process by which we perceptually divorce meat from its animal origins – shields us from dissonance. The first systematic review of the evidence was published in 2020, examining thirty-three studies, twenty-four of which had been published in the previous five years. 'At the core of the meat paradox is the experience of cognitive dissonance,' the authors write, '... one way to prevent cognitive dissonance from emerging in the first place is to simply dissociate meat from its animal origins.'

In one study, researchers presented volunteers with meat that was either processed or unprocessed and therefore more or less obviously 'from an animal'. They found that processed meat evoked less empathy. When presented with a whole roasted pig, for example, the volunteers reported greater feelings of empathy (and emotional discomfort) when the pig's head remained attached to the body than when the head had been removed. The use of language was also influential. When the word 'harvesting' was used instead of 'slaughtering', it elicited less dissonance, while replacing 'beef' or 'pork' on a restaurant menu with 'cow' or 'pig' increased feelings of empathy, an effect that was enhanced when pictures of the animal also featured on the menu, and this in turn led to an increased appetite for vegetarian dishes.[14]

Several studies have affirmed that, beyond the dissociative effect of meat processing, white meat often evokes fewer animal associations than red meat. In one study, when participants were asked what they understood the word 'meat' to mean, processed meat and white meat such as chicken were hardly thought of as 'meat' at all by some respondents – they were more akin to plants.

Hunting and foraging societies are typically much less detached from the lives and deaths of the animals they consume, but there is evidence that similar strategies of dissociation are employed. Prior to the hunt, for example, it is common for hunters to begin to talk in elliptical terms, eliciting linguistic dissociation. They refrain from referring to the animal by name, using oblique references instead, and they avoid talk of killing. The Achuar speak vaguely of 'going off into the forest', 'walking the dogs' or 'blowing the birds' (for blowpipe hunting). The Innu say they are 'going to search' when they mean to hunt with a rifle or 'going to see' when they mean checking on their traps. The Eveny of Siberia 'use secret language when hunting so that eaves-dropping animals will not recognize their own names'. Similarly, the Yukaghir hunter 'abandons ordinary speech in favour of a special linguistic code'. Allegorical expressions are adopted – elk are referred to as 'the big one' and bears as 'the barefooted one'. The hunter going hunting says, 'I'm going for a walk.' Hunters do not use the word 'kill' but make a downward movement of the hand to indicate the animal falling. The violence of the act, and the hunter's intentions, are removed from view.[15]

These strategies of linguistic dissociation are supported by cooking and preparation processes that further dissociate meat from its animal origins. 'The eaten must be transformed into an object,' Eduardo Kohn explains. 'Processes of desubjectification, such as cooking, are central to this, and the Avila Runa in this regard are like so many other Amazonians in thoroughly boiling their meat and avoiding cooking processes such as roasting that can leave some of the meat raw.'

It is especially important for red meat to be thoroughly cooked prior to consumption. 'The dangers inherent in the different kinds of meat depend very clearly on the size and the amount of blood of the animal,' says Stephen Hugh-Jones, who lived with the Tukano. 'White meat is more harmless than red meat, while that of large land mammals – peccaries, deer, and tapirs – is the strongest and most dangerous of all.' Amazonian attitudes in this regard are linked to the perception that the mind of the animal, its soul or life-force, permeates its blood. The meat remains minded, part of an animal-person, so long as blood remains infused in its tissues.

The Piaroa of the Venezuelan Amazon, in keeping with this tradition, thoroughly cook their meat, purging the mind of the animal from its flesh, and they take additional precautions. 'When shamans ask the masters of large animals for permission to hunt, they are not asking for donations of meat, but rather for donations of plants.' The Piaroa blow invocations over their food, a slab of roasted peccary, and these invocations are said to elicit the animal-to-plant transformation, changing viscera and bone into cassava and plantains. The Barasana, a tribe in the Tukano collective, similarly 'treat the game as though it were a plant', while the Makuna, another Tukano tribe, employ 'food shamanism' to attain a similar result. As they sit to eat, the Makuna 'silently chant and blow spells' over their meal in a ritual designed to 'turn animal-persons into human food'. They recite an incantation that tells of the mythic origin of the species, singing the soul of the animal back to its species-soul to be reborn.[16]

We might not chant incantations over our roast beef or ribeye steak, but our inclination to exclude white meat from the category 'meat' recalls the twisting of taxonomy characteristic of the Piaroa and Barasana, and like the Makuna we seek to expel the mind of the animal from the meat we consume.

Bastian and Loughnan observed the expulsion, convening a study in which volunteers were divided into two groups. Both were asked to complete a series of questionnaires, and one group was given a bowl of nuts to snack on while the other was given a platter of beef. Among the questionnaires were two concerning animals, one that asked about the moral value of twenty-seven animals, and another that asked about the sentience and moral value of a cow. The two groups responded in markedly different ways. The group eating beef rated the cow as being less sentient, less emotionally sensitive and less deserving of moral concern. They also included fewer animals in their circle of moral concern. Crucially, this skew in perception occurred beneath the threshold of conscious thought. They were unaware of what they were doing. They didn't know that they had muted their empathy, denying the mind of the animal they consumed, yet their perception had been altered no less profoundly than that of the Makuna hunter chanting over his meal.[17]

'It is precisely in this moment – when a person is eating or intending to eat – that we would expect the meat paradox to require urgent resolution,' Bastian and Loughnan observe.

It is precisely in this moment – when the animal's body enters our mouth – that our response to the paradox is at its most subtle, its most deceptive, and its most grave.

A Yukaghir hunter is standing over a slain bear. He is panting, his pulse is quick, and his companions are running through the forest towards him. The next few seconds are critically important. Working quickly, the hunters begin to blindfold the bear, croaking all the while like ravens, rasping and squawking, and sometimes flapping their arms. (If no blindfold is available, they will poke out the bear's eyes with sticks, rasping all the while.) Once blindfolded, they begin to process the body, removing the bear's skin and flesh, and as they work, they speak to the bear, saying, 'Big Man! Who did this to you? The one who eats of the willow bushes [the elk] was here.' They try to trick the bear into believing that a raven has pecked out his eyes and stolen his vision. They insinuate that the bear's violent death was caused by the elk – a ruse supported by the fact that the hunters look, move and smell like elk. *Whoever committed this violent act, it surely wasn't a human hunter!*

Deflection rituals of this ilk are found in many cultures. Among the Inuit, for example, tradition had it that when the first seal of the season was killed, the hunter would distribute the meat to each inhabitant of the settlement, thereby sharing culpability around the whole community. The Menomini hunter would take a more direct approach. Speaking to his prey, he would insist that the 'killing was accidental' – there was never any violent intent. Having killed an elk, the Yakaghir hunter would carve a small wooden figure which they would paint with the animal's blood and hang above its body. The figure was said to represent the elk's 'murderer'. The spirit of the elk would smell its blood and would attack the figure, taking revenge, while the hunters could skin and butcher the body in safety.[18]

'This third party blame or "shifting the blame" is an age-old device to distance individuals from the killing of animals and place responsibility elsewhere,' Rothgerber explains, speaking of similar strategies in our society. To experience dissonance, we must perceive that we are responsible for the act in question. If we aren't responsible for an animal's death, then consuming their body is less disturbing, so we pass the buck. Citizens hold farmers responsible for the plight of farmed animals. Farmers point at retailers. Retailers nod towards the government. The government blames the public. Responsibility is shifted amorphously among us, without any single actor feeling the full burden of the animal's violent death.[19]

Crucially, the deflection rituals enacted by the Yukaghirs arise in the context of a narrative of consent and unambiguous nutritional necessity. The community relies on elk and bear meat for sustenance. The hunter knows that killing animals is necessary for their survival. They can take comfort in the understanding that they have been granted permission to make the kill by Khoziain, the Master of Animals. They know their prey has been sent to them for this fate, and they believe that the animal's soul will be reborn in a new body. The killing is perfectly reasonable, required, and entirely justified. No true harm has been done. And yet.

'Virtually all northern hunters are at great pains to employ various tactics of displacement and substitution to cover up the fact that they are the ones responsible for an animal's violent death,' Willerslev observes. 'Why this game of continuous deception? The heart of the matter is that the killing of an animal in the circumpolar north is never an unproblematic act. The reason for this is that notwithstanding hunters' high moral ideals of trust between humans and nonhumans and their elaborate ritual procedures to secure the animals' rebirth, their killings cannot be carried out non-violently and without bloodshed.'[20]

While the Cree conceptualise the relationship between hunter and prey as 'essentially non-violent' – the reindeer giving themselves to the hunter out of generosity – this narrative is contradicted by the bloody reality of the hunt. 'In fact, indigenous hunters know very well that they do not actually hunt the way they say they hunt, making the animal surrender itself through songs, clothing, and eroticism,' Willerslev says. 'This discrepancy between the ideal, in which the docile animal gives itself up to the hunter, and the reality in which animals are manifestly capricious and bent on escape, and in which hunters have to resort to brutality and deceit to bring them down, is a prevalent theme.' The hunter is caught in a 'recurring paradox', torn between a cultural narrative that tells of the animal's consent and the patently obvious fact that the animal *does not consent*. The Cree focus their mythic account – this story of the animal's willing participation in their death – on the final exchange of gaze, when the reindeer stops and turns to look into the eyes of the hunter, because it is in this moment that the potential for dissonance is most acute.[21]

The significance of the animal's gaze is recognised in other hunting societies. Eduardo Kohn recalls that he joined a group of Runa hunters in the Ecuadorian Amazon, among the foothills of the Sumaco volcano. As the party was settling down to sleep under a thatch lean-to, his companion, Juanicu, turned to him and offered some advice. 'Sleep faceup! If a jaguar comes he'll see you can look back at him and he won't bother you. If you sleep facedown he'll think you're *aicha* [prey; literally 'meat' in Quechua] and he'll attack.' The difference between a person and a lump of meat is the ability to look the predator in the eye. 'By returning the feline's gaze, the Runa force jaguars to treat them, in a sense, as interlocutors, that is, as subjects. If, by contrast, the Runa look away, they will be treated as, and may actually become, objects – literally dead meat, *aicha*.'[22]

Vegan activists working with the Save Movement hold vigils at slaughterhouses, stopping trucks as they enter to interact with the animals within. They speak to the animals, look through the bars, offer them water and refreshment, give whatever comfort and acknowledgement can be given. I used to think that this was an oddly futile form of activism, for it does nothing to prevent the animals' deaths, but it is also intensely subversive, for that exchange of gaze has the power to personify. 'Standing alongside the volunteers as the trucks roll up, I can see that there are as many different emotions in the pigs' eyes as there are eyes looking at us. Some are numb or blank or without hope. Some seem to be dissociating themselves from the conditions. Unbelievably, some still appear hopeful and inquisitive and forgiving,' activist and scholar Alex Lockwood recounts.[23]

The Save Movement originated in Toronto, where a group convened by Anita Krajnc began holding regular vigils. Further groups were soon established in Burlington, Melbourne, New York, and then globally. By 2020, there were over nine hundred Save Movement groups in seventy-two countries. 'Toronto Pig Save's goal was to develop a model of resistance against the meat industry and their propaganda by witnessing and putting out stories of the individuality of the animals. The encounters with pigs, cows, chickens, ducks, pigeons, sheep, goats, rabbits, fish and horses at slaughterhouses and live markets bring people face to face with the victims of the meat, dairy and egg industries,' Krajnc explains. 'At vigils, you connect with the animals in a very personal way and an emotional sense.'[24]

This face-to-face encounter, and the personal connection it enjoins, is everything that we typically seek to avoid. Bastian and Loughnan explain that our strategies of detachment, dissociation and deflection are threads in a tightly woven tapestry of denial. These strategies 'operate like a veil ... an imperfect cloak – at times becoming transparent'. The veil becomes transparent when we perceive that an animal has been harmed on our behalf. We dislike such harm, and 'liking meat' while 'disliking the harm caused to animals' is a common expression of the meat paradox. This 'dislike' can be tepid, a pang of unease, but it can also blossom into something altogether more potent and disturbing.

Consider the quandary posed by the bear. Among northern peoples, bears are by far the most problematic animal to kill and consume, hence the deflection rituals enacted upon their death and the ceremonial exertion that accompanies their consumption. Bears can be an important source of nutrition, providing meat and fat in an environment where those commodities are scarce. They offer a thick, furry pelage, and they are among the largest terrestrial mammals available for hunting. But they are also 'person-like' in obvious ways. Bears can stand upright on two legs, walking upright like giant furry people. They are omnivorous. They can swim and climb, while also living on land. They are intelligent, and it is said that they have acted as tutors to human society. Bears will sometimes prey on humans, just as humans will prey on bears, and a skinned bear looks unerringly like a skinned human in the proportions of its body. In Cree, Inuit and Yukaghir societies, despite the elaborate rituals enacted to ensure the rebirth of the bear's soul, despite the permission granted by the Master of Animals and a deep-rooted narrative of consent, despite the necessity of eating and the perpetual risk of hunger, people will commonly refuse to eat the meat of a bear on the grounds that it is too much like human flesh. 'The bear poses more forcefully than any other species the moral paradox of eating beings similar to the self, a dilemma reflected both in those who abstain from its meat and in the particular intensity of its religious celebration.'[25]

Sometimes, no matter how acute one's need, however compelling one's cultural narrative, however precisely one performs the designated rituals, the perception cannot be shaken. Meat is murder. Consumption is cannibalism. The bear demands not to be eaten.

*

The chicken is afforded no such respect. Chickens are the world's most populous farm animal, sitting diametrically opposite the bear in the hierarchy of moral concern. We collectively consume 65 billion of the birds each year, making chicken the world's most popular meat. In the UK, we consume almost a billion chickens annually, and around 95 per cent are members of fast-growing breeds, intensively reared in indoor units. Our tale of an ancient contract is nowhere more dubious, more duplicitous, or more patently betrayed than in industrial chicken farming. John Lewis-Stempel's third principle – that animals should be provided with a full and natural lifespan – is antithetical to everything the poultry industry has spent decades trying to achieve.

For half a century we have been breeding animals for more rapid and corpulent growth, and chickens have suffered some of the worst consequences. Genetics companies have roughly halved the time it takes for a chicken to achieve slaughter weight since the 1950s, shortening the birds' average lifespan at the rate of one day per year. The modern chicken will live for a month and will be killed as an overweight infant, four times larger than a bird in the 1950s. This breeding for intensive growth has resulted in plentiful meat and plentiful suffering.

The chicken's metabolism has been strained to the point of collapse by excessive growth. As energy is diverted into muscle and tissue development, other parts of the body are deprived of energy and oxygen. This puts pressure on the bird's organs, especially the heart and lungs. Sudden death syndrome (a heart attack) is common among chickens and can be triggered by environmental stress or a stressful event, such as when the bird is caught and transported to the slaughterhouse. We don't know the true prevalence of sudden death syndrome, but it's been estimated that heart failure accounts for roughly a third of all mortalities that occur on farms in the UK. The birds that suc-cumb to this condition often have histories of cardiac rhythm disturbances, with an irregular heartbeat detectable in birds as young as seven days of age. Those who don't succumb to a heart attack might suffer ascites, another heart condition that results from the increased metabolic demands of excessively fast growth. Such a rate of growth creates an increased need for oxygen in the bloodstream which can stress the cardiovascular system, resulting in an enlargement of the heart that may cause fluid to leak from the liver and gather in the abdomen of the bird. Roughly 2.4 million chickens are rejected from the food chain in the UK each year as a result of ascites. The condition is deeply unpleasant. In the words of the Royal Society for the Prevention of Cruelty to Animals (RSPCA), ascites 'develops gradually, causing the birds to suffer for an extended period before they die'.[26]

Many chickens also suffer from skeletal developmental disorders such as tibial dyschondroplasia, where the cartilage in the bird's leg and hip develops abnormally and affects their ability to walk. Leg bones can be deformed as the breast fattens, and the bird's immature skeleton collapses under their weight, with microfractures erupting in multiple areas. When these microfractures are colonised by bacteria, it can lead to painful infections and lameness, including a condition called bacterial chondronecrosis with osteomyelitis (BCO). Long periods of sitting – as is common in concentrated confinement in industrial systems – can stunt bone and cartilage development, increasing the risk of BCO. As birds sit in their litter, they become susceptible to hock burn, where ammonia from the faeces of other birds begins to burn through the skin of their legs.

The modern chicken is descended from the red junglefowl, a tropical bird indigenous to the forests of south-east Asia. Shy but sociable, they are bright in plumage, their feathers orange, red, gold, white and metallic green. These wild-ranging chickens, striding through grasses in the foothills of the Himalayas, are a world away from the bird confined on an industrial farm. The junglefowl will live between three and eleven years if given the chance – a lifespan beyond the wildest dreams (or the metabolic capabilities) of a modern meat chicken. Yet the modern chicken – though separated by 7,000 years of breeding – retains facets of their ancestral character and intelligence. Chickens exhibit distinct personalities, even those housed in sheds where they are denied the opportunity to express them. They can recall over one hundred chicken faces and they recognise familiar individuals after weeks of separation. Mother hens are attentive to their young and show signs of empathic distress when their chicks are distressed. Hens and roosters form lasting bonds, and there are anecdotal accounts of hens grieving the loss of a longstanding partner.[27]

KFC UK and Ireland published their first 'Progress Report on Chicken Welfare' in 2020. The fact that KFC published anything about chicken welfare is commendable, though the report is disturbing in its content. As the world's foremost chicken retailer and the UK's favourite fried chicken brand, KFC embodies much that has gone wrong in our relationship with the ancestral junglefowl. Their report says that 97 per cent of the birds in their supply chain are members of fast-growing breeds, at risk of severe health failures and routine suffering. Chickens, the report concedes, are sentient beings, but one in ten birds in KFC's supply chain suffers from hock burn, while one in three suffers footpad dermatitis, a painful condition characterised by lesions on the feet which can result in ulcers that prevent the birds from walking. These welfare failings are so prevalent that in a flock of 10,000 chickens (and many are at least this large), around 400 birds will die or be culled before the end of their thirty-day life, a 4 per cent mortality rate. The British Poultry Council says the average mortality rate for the sector is 2–3 per cent. 'We're proud to be leading the way in our sector,' Paula Mackenzie, managing director of KFC UK & Ireland, declares, apparently without irony, in an introduction to the report. 'We've been on this journey for nearly two decades, which has led us to our well established, already stringent welfare standards.'[28]

Although there are evident parallels in our response to the

meat paradox relative to the hunting societies described here, there are also many differences. Perhaps the most important derives from the mimetic empathy employed in the hunt. While we downplay our estimation of the mind and sentience of the animals we consume, dampening our perception of the animal as a 'person', the hunter is forced into the opposing stance. The prey 'becomes gradually more personlike the closer and more intimately he engages with it'.[29]

In a world of circulating souls, where to be a 'person' is to be coiled in a whorl of rebirth and exchange, the pervasive risks associated with killing are keenly felt, generating strong prohibitions on *unnecessary* consumption. 'Above all, animals are offended by unnecessary killing,' Ingold says of the Cree; killing that does not 'satisfy genuine consumption needs'. The Yukaghir hunter knows that the approval of the Master of Animals 'is best secured by actually needing meat to eat'. Yukaghir hunters will bring provisions for only a few days when going into the forest, so they grow hungry and find themselves in genuine need. 'Ideally people should hunt and eat until all the meat is consumed, and then go hunting again,' with the aim of 'limiting one's killings to an absolute minimum'. Among the Makuna, similarly: 'Fish and game animals can only be caught and killed [to satisfy] immediate family needs ... The rule is mandatory, and transgressions are believed to bring death and disease.' The Inuit ethic may be summarised as: 'Kill only what you need and share it with others.' Necessity might not provide ethical closure, but it is the *very least* that is required.[30]

Such constraints do not exist in our society, at least not in a coherent form. In a 2015 study, Jared Piazza found that 'necessity' was the most common justification offered for the consumption of meat. The belief that 'meat is necessary' was not only widespread, it was correlated with higher levels of consumption of beef, pork, lamb, chicken, fish and seafood. There might be legitimate grounds upon which to assert necessity, but they are restricted in scope and bear scarce resemblance to the way that we eat and farm today. They certainly do not justify the excesses of industrial farming or the abuse of billions of chickens.[31]

I met Charles Way at the Royal Festival Hall on London's South Bank. It was a Thursday afternoon, and the sky was overcast. Tourists were milling along the Thames, and a girl in a green jumper was busking, singing a sad song about a canary and a coal mine which ended in abrupt silence.

'One thing they ask at the job interview is how you would respond if you were at a party and someone asked what you do for a living. You have to be proud to work for KFC, and I am proud.'

As Head of Food Quality Assurance for KFC UK & Ireland, Charles was responsible for elements of KFC's supply chain, overseeing quality standards for production, animal welfare, environmental impact and nutrition. He was friendly, responsive, articulate, and enthusiastic about his work.

'We're a fast-food brand and we sell deep fried chicken,' he said, both hands laid flat upon the table in a gesture of openness, 'and we aim to be better at what we do than anyone else. Some people see us as "industrial food", part of a big American company, but simply by telling the story of who we are and what we do, we can shift some of those perceptions.'

'And what *do* you do?'

'Well, personally, I oversee a team that spends most of its days in factories, making sure that suppliers are producing what they're meant to produce. We have strict quality standards and we're trying to do what's right for our customers, while giving shareholders their returns.'

'What about the chickens?' I asked.

'We're proud of our welfare standards. All our UK chickens are Red Tractor certified, but they're also reared to our own standards which exceed Red Tractor. Lots of our chicken is from Britain, but we also source from Brazil, Thailand and Europe.

We use a lot of white meat, and we take it where we can find it, at the standard we require.'

Charles exuded enthusiasm and talked repeatedly about KFC's desire 'to do the right thing' by being more sustainable.

As we talked, the word 'sustainable' kept getting caught on my tongue. *Sustainable*. What an empty jumble of letters. What a pallid and inadequate concept. The Tukano speak not of sustainability but of *symmetry* – the symmetry of obligations that binds the hunter to their prey. For the Tukano, it is not enough to limit consumption to that which is necessary (though this is absolutely required). The demand still grasps at the hem of the hunter's mind, imprinting the fabric of their perception with the realisation that the bristling peccary is of no less value than the human who consumes them.

The more I think of the Tukano, the more I am impressed by their navigation of the meat paradox. The hunter is not permitted to look away, to deny the possibility that the animal consumed might be an animal-person, scarcely different to a human person. The ethical demand is not denied but affirmed, forcing the hunter to grapple with the terrible realisation that subsistence involves the killing and consumption of quasi-similar beings. The equivalence of human and animal life keeps the antipodes of the paradox – necessity and murder – in creative tension, at the forefront of consciousness. This strikes me as more sophisticated by far than the cascade of evasion and denial that characterises our response.

I think of the Tukano hunter, sweat upon his brow, as he moves between matted vines, steps over scurrying beetles. I think of the energy surging through the cosmic circuit, rushing through stem and seed. I think of his concentration as he stalks his prey, the metaphysical weight upon his shoulders; his understanding that need must be true, his blade quick, or else he will be taken to be clothed in the musk and hide of another body, reborn as the animal he consumes.

'If you knew that you were going to be reborn as a

chicken' – the words were out of my mouth before I knew what I was saying – 'would you really prefer to be born onto a farm in KFC's supply chain, more than on any other farm in the UK?'

Charles frowned at the question and paused before answering. 'Our animal welfare standards are above the industry norm, and we're proud of that,' he said, uncertainly, 'but – when you put it like that – my honest view is that it wouldn't make a world of difference, so no.'

There was a man atop a ladder attaching a light fitting to the ceiling. He was wearing a bright yellow jacket and leather boots.

'Similarly,' I pressed ahead, 'if you knew that you were going to be reborn as a chicken, do you think you would eat less chicken?'

Charles had the look of a man for whom this was not an everyday line of conversation. He opened his mouth to respond, and then closed it again.

I glanced up at the man on the ladder, but he was gone. The ceiling too was gone, and there was nothing above but a slow-turning vortex of feathers.

We remained there, unspeaking, and the silence was pregnant with the possibilities of the meat paradox. We sat quietly, under the watchful and calculating gaze of Vaí-mahsë.

5

HERBIVORE

In March 2019, Gatis Lagzdins and Deonisy Khlebnikov walked into a vegan food market in Soho, London, brandishing two dead squirrels. 'We just want to raise awareness,' Lagzdins said, carcass in hand, 'that veganism equals malnutrition.' The two began to eat the squirrels, tearing at the furry hides with their bare teeth. A crowd of bemused onlookers gathered to watch. 'I just ate the heart,' Lagzdins told them, 'that was pretty good.' But he wasn't going to eat the gall bladder. 'The gall bladder's no use,' he said, showing a glimmer of discernment. There was a plucked bird hanging from his neck by a piece of string. 'We evolved for millions of years on animal products, and so it's a fallacy that we can suddenly eat just plants,' his companion explained. 'There's no one standing up for these facts.'

The pair were found guilty of a public order offence and were fined. 'Deonisy Khlebnikov and Gatis Lagzdins claimed they were against veganism and were raising awareness about the dangers of not eating meat when they publicly consumed raw squirrels,' a spokesperson for the Crown Prosecution Service said. 'But by choosing to do this outside a vegan food stall and continuing with their disgusting and unnecessary behaviour despite requests to stop, including from a parent whose child was upset by their actions, the prosecution was able to demonstrate that they had planned and intended to cause distress to the public.'

It turned out that Lagzdins was a repeat offender. He had been seen earlier in the year at a vegan food festival in Brighton, gnawing on a raw pig's head.[1]

In the garbled commentary that Lagzdins offered to the crowds as he ate his squirrel, he omitted to say where he had procured the animal. Where did the squirrel come from? His demeanour does not suggest 'ethically sourced' would be high on his list of priorities. Did he catch it? How did he kill it? Perhaps he found the squirrel at the side of the road. If the squirrel was roadkill, this raises an interesting question: Could a vegan have stepped forward from the crowd of onlookers and taken a bite? While the circumstances would have discouraged anyone from doing so, the question remains: Can vegans eat roadkill?

This might sound like an odd question, for vegans, by definition, do not eat meat or animal products. But veganism is an intrinsically pragmatic stance. It is defined by the Vegan Society as 'a way of living which seeks to exclude, as far as is possible and practicable, all forms of exploitation of, and cruelty to, animals for food, clothing or any other purpose'. The vegan acts to minimise harm and refrains wherever possible from participating in the exploitation of animals.[2]

If a wild animal has been accidentally killed, might a vegan be permitted to eat their meat? After all, wild meat is nutritious, and the nutrition would otherwise be wasted. The argument might sound facetious – and perhaps it would be, if made in earnest – but philosopher Donald W. Bruckner has indulged it as a thought experiment, arguing that not only *could* a vegan eat roadkill, a vegan *should*, given the opportunity. Bruckner suggests that it would be immoral for them not to.

Most American states allow for the collection of large, intact, fresh and unspoiled animals such as deer, moose and elk (usually in conjunction with some reporting requirements). Bruckner estimates that over two million of these animals (along with many smaller animals) are killed by vehicles each year. If we suppose that all those animals were deer, and 75 per cent of them were suitable for consumption, and 75 per cent of their meat was unspoiled, then on a rough calculation those deer would provide 18,753,209 kilograms of nutritious meat – the equivalent of 80,124 beef cows or 8,268,750 chickens. There are good ecological and ethical reasons to eat this meat. An omnivore would spare the lives of farm animals. A vegan would spare the lives of wild animals killed during crop cultivation while lowering their land-use footprint, without participating in any deliberate harm. A vegan earnestly seeking to minimise the harm they cause to animals would be *morally obligated* to eat the roadkill, Bruckner argues.

Bruckner's argument is playful, not polemical. He isn't trying to persuade vegans to eat roadkill; he's toying with the 'least harm' principle to see where it could lead. He's also trying to tease out the objections that might be voiced in response. One of the most common, he says, concerns the 'ick factor'. 'Collecting and consuming roadkill is disgusting.'[3]

Disgust is a powerful and primal emotion, and it plays a pivotal role in the psychology of meat. Think of it as a 'food-related emotion', says psychologist Paul Rozin. The word means literally 'bad taste' (dis-gust). Rozin defines disgust as 'revulsion at the prospect of oral incorporation of an offensive and contaminating object'. Disgust pertains to revolting things that we might put in our mouth.[4]

Imagine that you are walking through that Soho food market and Lagzdins appears before you, thrusting his half-eaten squirrel carcass towards your mouth. 'Eat it,' he growls. Perhaps you would. More likely, you would feel a strong sense of repulsion. You would want to distance yourself from the offensive object, and from the man stabbing it towards you. Your nose would wrinkle. Your top lip would retract, and your mouth would gape briefly open before firmly closing. This response – the disgust response – is universal, expressed across cultures, and it has deep evolutionary roots.

Those roots reach back to our earliest forays into omnivory. When we began to scavenge animal foods at the fringe of the African savannah, picking at elephant bones, scraping sinew from the femurs of an antelope, the stakes could not have been higher. The meat we sought was energy rich and nutrient dense, but the risk of pathogenic infection was high. We were eating marrow and brains from carcasses that had sometimes been left to bake in the savannah sun, and the ability to discern between the palatable and the rancid was critically important. Our disgust response evolved to help us identify fresh and edible animal foods and reject those that might kill us. These evolutionary pressures are so potent, our capacity for disgust so finely tuned, Rozin says, that *all* animals are potentially disgusting when considered as food.[5]

It is not only animals that we find potentially disgusting. We are also sensitive to bodies more generally, and to the things that come out of them, such as faeces, saliva and mucus. Curiously, these only become disgusting once they are *separated* from the body. I'm not disgusted by the saliva in the mouth of the man sitting opposite me in a coffee shop, but if he begins spitting onto the floor, I might be. Similarly, we might not mind sucking blood from a small cut on our finger, but we would recoil from sucking blood from a used bandage, even if it was our own blood. Tears seem to be the exception to this rule. When we see tears rolling down a cheek, we might experience a range of emotions, but we are unlikely to feel disgusted.

Importantly, disgust is also a *moral emotion*. We are disgusted by animal bodies and bodily secretions, but we are also disgusted by moral violations. This dual faculty – disgust as a physical response and disgust as a moral response – is not just a quirk of the English language. The association holds true in the

French *dégoût*, the German *ekel*, the Russian *otraschenie*, the Spanish *asco*, the Hebrew *go-al*, the Japanese *ken-o*, the Chinese *aw-shin*, and in many other languages. Rozin explains that the two are linked by a process akin to 'preadaptation' in evolutionary biology. Our tongue and teeth evolved for eating, but we now use them for speech and vocalisation. Feathers evolved for thermoregulation, but birds now use them to fly. A system that evolved for one purpose has been pressed into another, novel use. Similarly, feelings of disgust evolved to keep us safe when eating potentially pathogenic animal foods in the African savannah, and these feelings have been pressed into novel uses in a social and moral context.[6]

As a moral emotion, disgust is associated with a distinct 'moral domain' – a way of thinking about morality – and this domain is also rooted in the risk of pathogenic infection. 'Disgust moralizes – that is, amplifies the moral significance of – protecting the purity of the body and soul,' psychologist Elizabeth Horberg explains. 'These values originally related to the evolutionary challenges of avoiding the consumption of toxins, parasites, or bacteria. What began as concerns over purity and contamination of the physical form, however, subsequently extended to include concerns over the purity of the individual's character and social conduct, thus promoting beliefs in the moral value of a physically and mentally pure lifestyle.'[7]

The disgust/purity axis plays an important role in many religious traditions, where the purification of the body is a prerequisite for the purification of the soul. The celibate priest. The kosher feast. Eating and sex are the most tabooed behaviours in many religions (and meat is the focus of the most dietary taboos) because of this concern for bodily and spiritual purity. 'The mouth seems to function as a highly charged border between self and nonself,' Rozin observes. The special role of the mouth derives from a simple anatomical fact: the mouth is the entry point to the gastrointestinal system. In a physiological context, it acts as the gatekeeper to the self. In a psychological context, it acts as the gatekeeper to the soul. We must be very careful which bodies we allow to touch or pass our lips. Kissing and eating are acts of the greatest intimacy.

The intrinsic association between disgust and animal bodies (especially dead animal bodies), and the tendency for disgust to spill over from a physical to a moral response, lends our disgust reaction a heightened significance in contemporary veganism.

Is it permissible for a vegan to eat roadkill? The question has been asked often enough that animal rights organisation People for the Ethical Treatment of Animals (PETA) offers a stock response: 'If people must eat animal carcasses, roadkill is a superior option to the neatly shrink-wrapped plastic packages of meat in the supermarket.' *Carcasses.* Vegan advocacy is replete with terms that conjure vivid (and disgusting) images of animal bodies. Omnivores don't eat meat – they eat corpses, flesh, dismembered body parts. They don't drink milk – they imbibe bovine secretions and congealed mammary fluids. 'Few things make us squirm more than realizing that chicken periods are packed into cartons and sold by the dozen,' PETA says. 'It's one of those things that doesn't seem real, like a scene out of The Exorcist or a Halloween prank gone wrong. But chicken periods are exactly what you're eating every time you fry, scramble, or bake with eggs.'[8]

In the omnivore's parlance, words like 'sausage' and 'bacon' can dissociate meat from its animal origins, muting empathy and reducing dissonance. The meat industry, which wields so much power over our perception through advertisements and marketing, weaponises our susceptibility towards dissociation to keep us inured. But the use of language in vegan advocacy is no less charged with psychological consequence; physical disgust is commonly evoked to engender moral disgust (and vice versa).[9]

There's nothing wrong with this. The disgust/purity axis is part of our moral identity. As omnivores we might be disgusted (physically and morally) by the thought of eating puppies, dolphins, kittens, horses or roadkill squirrels. The blanket application of disgust is more consistent. But disgust and purity must be seen in context. Disgust is only part of our moral identity; its expression is culturally mediated, and it can be pressed towards more or less moral ends. Disgust can be (and has been) exploited to fan the flames of racism and homophobia – its association with the body can lead to prejudices against those with different bodies, or against those who express their sexual identity in different ways. Disgust can play a constructive role in shaping moral attitudes towards meat, but the purity domain can also become imperious, overwhelming the pragmatic core of the vegan project.[10]

One consequence of an overt focus on disgust might be a low retention rate among vegans. A 2015 study found that 84 per cent of vegetarians and vegans commonly lapse from their diet and return to eating animal foods. Philosopher Neil Levy suggests the moralisation of purity might be a contributing factor. 'Seeing a behaviour as a matter of purity encourages an all-or-nothing viewpoint with regard to violations ... If I have fallen off the wagon, I might as well go – or eat – the whole hog. I won't get any less pure; you can't go lower than zero ... Indeed, this kind of logic predicts that people may not feel it worthwhile to return to vegetarianism *at all* after a transgression.'[11]

Disgust can also distort the rational basis of vegan ethics. Veganism, as typically understood within the vegan movement, is an ethical stance opposing the exploitation of animals and promoting their freedom. It is a response to the realisation that meat involves murder, an effort to align one's behaviour with one's values. There are many good reasons to go vegan, and eschewing the consumption of animals is a rational response to the meat paradox, the surest way of removing oneself from the abhorrence of the slaughter line, the omnivore's tangle of dissociation and denial. But 'going vegan' does not provide certain release from the psychological tensions generated by meat. The disgust/purity axis provides one avenue through which those tensions manifest, creating pressures that can edge animal advocacy, in some contexts, into realms of falsehood, delusion and propaganda.

Let's get one thing straight. It is entirely natural for humans to eat meat. We evolved eating meat. We've eaten meat for millions of years. Animal foods helped make us the creatures that we are today. The nutrition provided by foraged and hunted animals fuelled the growth of our brains. The challenge of procuring carcasses in the African savannah propelled our evolution, forcing us into more complex behaviours and more advanced modes of cognition. Our migration across the planet was made possible by our omnivory, as seasonal fluctuations in the availability of plant foods were offset by the perennial availability of edible animals. Eating meat is natural – one hundred per cent so. But that doesn't mean that it is morally right that we eat meat today.

We like to think that it does. 'It's natural' is one of the most popular rationalisations that we cite to justify our consumption. Researchers have found that the more people endorsed the idea that 'eating meat is natural', the more meat they reported eating. But as a moral justification, the reasoning is flawed. We shouldn't arrive at a judgement about what is *right* based on what is *natural*. As moral philosophers have noted, descriptions of what 'is' do not tell us what we 'ought' to do. It might be natural for humans to eat meat, but it might also be 'natural' for adolescent males to act violently towards one another – that doesn't mean it's right for them to do so.[12]

Advocates promoting veganism have pointed out the weakness of the 'it's natural' argument. But some have gone further. Not content with meat being 'natural but nevertheless unethical in a contemporary context', they have suggested that consuming meat is *unnatural*. Humans, they say, are herbivores.

On a webpage titled 'Is It Really Natural? The Truth About Humans and Eating Meat', PETA says, 'a natural human diet is, in fact, vegan.' The article opens with a set of questions: 'Quick test: When you see dead animals on the side of the road, are you tempted to stop and snack on them? Do you daydream about killing cows with your bare hands and eating them raw? If you answered "no" to these questions, then, like it or not, you're an herbivore.' As evidence for the claim, PETA notes that we have short, soft fingernails and small canine teeth. Our stomach acids are weaker than those of carnivorous animals, and our intestines are longer than those of carnivores of a comparable size. 'The good news is that if you want to eat like our ancestors, you still can: Nuts, vegetables, fruit, and legumes are the basis of a healthy vegan lifestyle.'

To substantiate the idea that humans are 'anatomically herbivorous', PETA cites an essay titled 'The Comparative Anatomy of Eating' by medical doctor Milton R. Mills. 'Mammals are anatomically and physiologically adapted to procure and consume particular kinds of diets,' Mills writes. 'Therefore, we can look at mammalian carnivores, herbivores (plant-eaters) and omnivores to see which anatomical and physiological features are associated with each kind of diet. Then we can look at human anatomy and physiology to see in which group we belong.' Mills compares our anatomy to the anatomies of other animals, including omnivorous animals such as bears and raccoons, and concludes that the human body 'is designed for a purely plant-food diet'.[13]

Mills' argument is of dubious validity (for reasons discussed below), but it has struck a chord within the vegan movement, informing advocacy in a variety of contexts. Influencer and campaigner Earthling Ed, for example, addresses the claim that 'eating meat is natural' in his e-book, adroitly pointing out that whether meat is natural is of little significance in an ethical context. But he doesn't stop there. Humans, he says, aren't 'real omnivores'. 'If we were naturally designed to eat meat we would have no objection to killing animals'. Ed cites our 'blunt, ineffective canines' and 'incredibly long intestines' as evidence of our herbivory, and he tees up a thought experiment. Imagine that you are locked in a room with a chicken and an apple. You would eat the apple first, he says, for 'we don't want to ravage animals and tear them apart', whereas we are happy to consume plants.

Mills makes a headline appearance in the 2017 documentary *What the Health?*, written, produced and directed by Kip Andersen and Keegan Kuhn, the team also behind the 2014 film *Cowspiracy*. Billed as 'the health film that health organizations don't want you to see', *What the Health?* follows Andersen as he seeks to expose the relationship between animal foods and chronic disease. It's an endlessly frustrating experience. Andersen does some good work. He raises legitimate concerns regarding zoonotic disease and antimicrobial resistance, implicating animal farming in an escalating threat to human health, and he draws attention to the social and environmental impacts of slurry, produced in prodigious volumes by industrial systems. But segments of *What the Health?* are less than credible, straying from respectable journalism into transparently unscientific anti-meat propaganda.

The film opens with a discussion of the International Agency for Research on Cancer (IARC) and World Health Organization (WHO) classification of processed meat as a class 1 carcinogen, 'alongside tobacco smoking, asbestos and plutonium', and of red meat as a class 2 carcinogen, meaning it's 'probably' carcinogenic to humans. Having grown up eating red and processed meat, Andersen reels from the revelation. 'Was this like I had essentially been smoking my entire childhood?'

Well, no. The IARC classification concerns the *quality of evidence* not the *degree of risk*. Processed meat is categorised as a class 1 carcinogen because we have *good evidence* that processed meat is associated with an increased risk of cancer, just as we have good evidence linking smoking, asbestos and plutonium to cancer. But that doesn't mean processed meat is as carcinogenic as cigarettes. The WHO is explicit in dismissing the comparison. 'Processed meat has been classified in the same category as causes of cancer such as tobacco smoking and asbestos (IARC Group 1, carcinogenic to humans), but this does NOT mean that they are all equally dangerous.'

The science, Andersen explains, has determined that eating 50 grams of processed meat each day is associated with an 18 per cent increased risk of colorectal cancer. This is an accurate statement, but the statistic needs contextualising. Andersen doesn't explain what the figure means. What it *doesn't* mean is that people who eat processed meat have an 18 per cent (almost one in five) chance of getting colorectal cancer, as might be assumed. It *does* mean that the risk of developing colorectal cancer is projected to be 1.18 times higher for those who consume 50 grams of processed meat each day. By contrast, men who smoke cigarettes have roughly twenty times the risk of developing lung cancer as men who do not. Expressed as a percentage, the increase in risk due to smoking is 1900 per cent (compared to 18 per cent for processed meat). Think of it this way. You would have to eat one hundred rashers of bacon every single day for processed meat consumption to equate to the same risk as smoking. The cancer risk of your average Italian carnivore – subsisting on a diet of cold cuts, salami, prosciutto and pancetta – equates to smoking three cigarettes per year.[14]

But Andersen ploughs ahead, revelling in the misleading comparison, presenting his viewers with a series of silly images. *Two children are sitting at the dinner table, while their mother serves cigarettes from a frying pan. Two girls are clutching a hotdog, but a smouldering cigar has taken the place of the meat. A mother is cooking sausages and cigarettes over a flame, while her hungry children look on.* 'If processed meats are labelled the same as cigarettes, how is it even legal for kids to be eating this way?'

There are more subtle confusions in the film, including the persistent leap from 'plants good' to 'meat bad', even though the former does not entail the latter. There is plenty of evidence that a diet rich in plants is associated with good health, but this doesn't mean meat is intrinsically *unhealthy*.

In the context of global nutrition, increasing meat consumption is a priority for many people. Nearly a quarter of all children under the age of five are stunted, and over half are deficient in micronutrients such as iron, vitamin A and zinc, which are vital for healthy development. Anaemia affects one in three women of reproductive age. Billions are malnourished, including many people in the US, where more than one in four children lack calcium, magnesium or vitamin A, and more than one in two are deficient in vitamin D and E. Meat and animal foods typically contain higher concentrations and more bioavailable forms of nutrients commonly lacking in diets, including iron, vitamin A, zinc, calcium, vitamin B12 and high-quality protein. They are the only dietary sources of retinol (preformed vitamin A), which is much more bioavailable than plant sources of vitamin A (carotenoids). Meat is the only source of haem iron, a form of iron that is much more bioavailable than the non-haem iron found in plant foods. Most meat and animal foods also contain 'complete' proteins which include, in accessible form, all nine essential amino acids important for child growth and development, and most (particularly fatty fish) contain essential long-chain omega-3 fatty acids, which have numerous health benefits and are important for infant and child development. Those of us living in affluence with access to a diverse and abundant food supply can subsist healthily with little or no meat in the diet, if our diet is of a high quality, but for billions of people with limited means, eating more meat and animal foods is a nutritional priority. One can recognise this fact and still aspire to a vegan world, but Andersen isn't interested in nuance. Meat and animal foods, he insists, are the primary driver of the modern epidemic of chronic disease, responsible for the tide of obesity, type 2 diabetes, heart disease and cancer that is washing over the Westernised world.[15]

The idea that humans are anatomically herbivorous is the backdrop to Andersen's argument. Humans, he explains, are frugivores (consumers of fruits and fruit-like vegetables and plants). Frugivore jaws can move forwards and back and side-to-side, just like ours, he says. If you compare the teeth of frugivorous and omnivorous animals, ours resemble the former, while true omnivores have stronger stomach acid for digesting meat. 'If humans were indeed true omnivores, we would need to change our physiology and appearance *quite a lot*,' he exclaims, speaking over an animation in which the silhouette of a human body morphs into that of a bear. 'But we fit every requirement of a frugivore. We may behave like omnivores, but anatomically we're frugivores.'

Mills makes an appearance. 'Human beings, unlike bears or raccoons, and to some extent dogs, don't have that mixed anatomy and physiology that you see in the true omnivores, and thus we are not true omnivores,' he declares. 'In humans, the canines have become really small and rounded, and actually function like accessory incisors. They're utterly useless for ripping or tearing anything other than an envelope.' In the spirit of Earthling Ed's 'apple versus chicken' experiment, Mills observes that while the thought of processing fruit in a blender is appealing, the idea of processing a raw fish in a blender is (yes, you guessed it) disgusting.

There are recurring attempts to evoke disgust throughout the film. Milk is described as 'baby calf growth fluid'. Michael Greger, a physician who promotes plant-based diets, describes milk as 'hormonal fluid, packed with sex hormones'. Alan Goldhamer, founder of the TrueNorth Health Centre, warns viewers that cow's milk is filled with pus. 'They actually have laws limiting how much pus you can have in milk and still sell it ... you could think of cheese as coagulated cow pus.' Meat, he says (looking rather pleased with himself), is 'dead, decaying flesh'.

This subtext of disgust betrays the cognitive biases skewing the film's presentation of the science. On the one hand, *What the Health?* is a recruitment video. It is propaganda. The suggestion that we are herbivores adapted for a diet of plants without meat or animal foods is pure chicanery, a deceit designed to draw viewers into the vegan fold. But the narrative also betrays the influence of the purity domain. As meat and animal foods (flesh and secretions) come to be perceived as disgusting, there can arise the desire to purge omnivory from the human story, to purify one's self-image – to become an herbivore.

We are not herbivores, yet neither are we carnivores, as some scholars have claimed. In the sixties, anthropologist and Hollywood screen writer Robert Ardrey popularised the tale of 'Man the Hunter', portraying our species as meat-hungry killers. Ardrey was influenced by archaeologist Raymond Dart, who argued that our ancestors were 'predatory ape-men' who possessed a 'love of flesh'. These ideas have been dismissed by contemporary scholarship, but residues remain, for example among some proponents of 'Paleo' eating, such as Paul Saladino, who advocates a 'nose to tail carnivore diet' as the optimal diet for human health. Saladino warns that plants are toxic, claiming that our early ancestors avoided them wherever possible, just as indigenous peoples do today. This is untrue.[16]

We are not carnivores, and plant consumption has sometimes been underemphasised in the story of our evolution, but evidence of animal consumption is written throughout our bodies and across the archaeological record. It is found in the size of our brains and the shape of our jaws, in the kinetics of our digestive system and the wiring of our metabolism. Our ability to metabolise animal fats, for example, differs markedly from that of our closest living evolutionary relative, the chimpanzee, suggesting a genetic adaptation to meat and animal foods deep in the human lineage. Our guts exhibit preferential absorption of animal haem iron compared to the non-haem iron found in plants. We have a limited capacity to produce taurine, an amino acid important for several metabolic processes, which suggests an evolutionary trajectory in which omnivory reduced the need and capacity of our bodies to synthesise it directly. Uniquely among primates, we have stomach pH values akin to those of carrion feeders, implying a deep history of scavenging, and there are bacteria in our microbiome and parasites inhabiting our gut which suggest humans have been eating animal foods for a very long time. There is also the obvious fact that while vegan diets can be healthy, vegans are prone to deficiencies in key animal-derived nutrients, even with our modern food supply and nutritional knowledge. These deficiencies also appear in the fossil record. Manuel Domínguez-Rodrigo analysed the remains of a young *Homo erectus* dating from 1.5 million years ago and found the child suffered from porotic hyperostosis most likely caused by vitamin B12 deficiency, implying that by this time meat had become so essential to good nutrition that its lack led to harmful pathological conditions.[17]

The human herbivory narrative is contradicted by a compelling body of evidence, but Mills and Andersen are correct in one respect. It is true that we look different to a raccoon or a bear. This is because we *are* different. Our technology has set us apart. Uniquely among omnivorous animals, we process our food extensively before we consume it – and we have done for millions for years. We use tools to slice, grind and mash. We break our food apart before biting it. Natural selection is thrifty. Our nails grew soft and our teeth smaller because, clutching sharpened stones, we no longer needed them for their former function. Our bodies look exactly like those you would expect of a formerly herbivorous, tool-wielding primate, adapted to an eclectic, meat-inclusive diet.

Our use of food-processing technologies also offers insight into the true drivers of our modern epidemic of chronic disease. For millions of years, we have eaten whole foods, plant and animal, which we have processed in various ways, chopping, slicing, boiling, cooking. More recently, we have canned, frozen and fermented our foods. But in the last half century, we have begun eating 'ultra-processed' foods, confections crafted using industrial processes and chemical additives. The proportion of these foods in the diet is closely correlated with rising levels of obesity and chronic disease. Roughly 54 per cent of the food eaten in the UK is ultra-processed (the highest proportion in Europe), and the figure rises to 57 per cent in the US. Research has begun to probe the biological mechanisms underpinning the association, finding that ultra-processed foods can disturb the gut microbiome and possibly the endocrine system, prompting us to overeat, while also typically being calorific and low in essential nutrition. We can be healthy eating lots of plants or on a wholesome diet rich in flesh and secretions, but we will struggle to be healthy on a diet of ultra-processed foods.[18]

The human herbivory fallacy inverts the omnivore's flawed rationalisation. The omnivore who says, 'it's natural!', hoping this provides moral justification, is guilty of leaping from an 'is' to an 'ought'. It is appropriate that the leap is challenged – eating animals is natural, but that doesn't mean that it's morally right in a contemporary context. The animal advocate who proclaims that 'it's unnatural!' is guilty of the same fallacy in reverse – warping what really 'is' to align with the ethical 'ought'.

I don't imagine that many vegans believe we evolved as herbivores. I imagine most would find the question a diversion from the ethical cause. The roots of the vegan project are entirely reasonable, yet these are not fringe ideas. PETA, Earthling Ed and Kip Andersen are not marginal voices. The reimagining of meat, not only as unethical, but as pollution, plutonium, and toxic to our health, runs through the vegan movement, a distorting influence amplified by the purity domain. The reality – that meat is natural, nutritious, and can even be necessary – is rejected because it can arouse dissonance and disgust. The truth – that we are empathetic omnivores, creatures characterised by evolutionary contradiction – is felt to be unpalatable, leaving a foul taste upon the would-be herbivore's tongue.[19]

Our disgust response is associated with a fear of contamination. Imagine that you are working in a restaurant, waiting tables.

As you place a meal before one guest, one of your hairs falls onto the plate. The hair might quickly be removed; it might have only touched the very edge of the meal, but the plate has been contaminated. The guest asks for the meal to be sent back to the kitchen. Once something clean has become defiled, the former purity is not easily recovered. Paul Rozin explains that our fear of contamination had adaptive value in an evolutionary context, protecting us from microbial contamination from raw meat and animal foods, but it continues to shape our outlook today, generating feelings of physical and moral defilement. In some instances, it can instil in us a fear of contamination by death itself.

This fear was observed in a 2017 study exploring how disgust shapes dietary preferences. The study found that some vegans perceive meat to be disgusting because it is felt to contain a contaminating 'essence', the suffering and death endured by the animal remaining infused in its flesh. A kindred effect has been observed among omnivores. In a prior study, researchers found that when samples of meat were paired with descriptions of animals raised on factory farms, they were less appealing than those raised on more humane farms. The meat samples given to both groups were identical, but the meat paired with factory farm descriptions looked, smelled and tasted less pleasant (more disgusting). The mistreatment of the animals had 'contaminated' the meat to such a degree that the basic properties of flavour had been altered, with factory-farmed samples tasting saltier and greasier.[20]

The fear of contamination also seeps into vegan advocacy in some contexts, conjuring images of paradise lost, a pining after a former purity. Such seepage is evident in the account of human evolution offered by Viva!, a vegan campaigning charity specialising in undercover investigations. Over several web pages, Viva! tells the story of our evolution, giving the herbivory narrative thorough treatment. Viva! rightly states that plants were an important part of our ancestral diet, and they acknowledge that our ancestors started hunting and eating animals around 2 million years ago. But the scope and significance of our ancestral omnivory is downplayed, with the development of agriculture marking a decisive turning point. 'The truth is that very little meat was eaten compared to today's consumption,' they write. 'Only when we started farming (hardly natural!) did meat become even a regular part of most human beings' diets.'

This lapse from the 'natural' into the 'unnatural' is a prominent theme, with our pre-agricultural past presented as the more natural state. 'Of all the living primates, humans are the only one to eat large animals, the rest being almost entirely herbivorous. We sprang out of this genetic breeding pool of largely peaceful groups of amiable creatures that lived by eating grasses, leaves, nuts, berries, fruits and roots.' Scarcely removed from these peaceable primates, our early ancestors ate little meat and few animal foods, and we remain 'natural herbivores' today, Viva! says, 'designed to be vegan'.

These claims are difficult to reconcile with the evidence. We cannot say definitively when meat and animal foods became a regular part of our ancestral diet, but even a cautious reading of the science affirms that we were systematically hunting large herbivores half a million years before we began farming. Some early human communities are known to have eaten a diet largely based around animal foods, as revealed by isotopic analysis of their bone collagen. Contrary to Viva!'s tale, the development of agriculture within the past 10,000 years was associated with a *decline* in meat consumption in many contexts. When we began farming – a transition that took many years and was highly varied in its expressions – our diets often became less nutritious, and pathological conditions, including poorer skeletal and dental health, and widespread malnutrition were the result. The archaeological record shows that pre-agricultural hunters were on average six inches taller than their farming descendants in some regions, and this loss of stature was associated with a poorer diet. In the Mediterranean, the use of wheat, rye, and oats as weaning foods, in the absence of animal foods, contributed to infant malnutrition and stunting. As we became reliant on a handful of staple crops, reduced meat consumption led to reduced intake of zinc, vitamin A and vitamin B12, with evidence of nutritional deficiencies in Neolithic remains, including iron deficiencies, and deficiencies in animal-derived amino acids. We were healthier as flesh-eating and wild-foraging hunters, and just as increased consumption of meat and animal foods is a nutritional priority for many people living in food insecurity today, we suffered the consequences as early agriculturalists of the lack of these foods in our diet.[21]

Regardless of the historical accuracy of Viva!'s account, it is the ethical subtext which matters. Viva! proposes that farming marked a decisive turning point in our relationship with animals. 'The farmer owns the creature, controls its life and death – he dominates it and here is where speciesism begins,' they write. 'Only when domestication began did *Homo sapiens* begin to believe that they were the dominating mammal, free to exploit every other living creature.'

The pining after a lost purity plays a role in various religious traditions. In the book of Genesis, the opening book of the Bible, the first humans dwell in the Garden of Eden. They are naked and innocent and close to God. But this paradise wasn't to last. The serpent deceived Eve, and Eve ate the forbidden fruit from the tree at the centre of the garden. Adam also ate the fruit, and they were cast out of Eden as punishment. Catholic doctrine talks of *macula peccati*, the 'stain of original sin'. The contaminating consequences of that first sinful act remain with us today, rendering our species (like the meal with the hair in it) congenitally impure, polluted such that only God's grace can cleanse us. In Viva!'s account, our ejection from the Garden mirrors our lapse into speciesism, the Fall occurring not upon the bite of the apple but upon the yoking of the beast.

Alex is a farmer. He runs a small mixed farm in Wales, producing crops in a rotation with beef cattle and dairy cows. The operation bears resemblance to the peasant farming of the past, though it is rooted in the science of organic and regenerative agriculture. The cows, members of various native breeds, are grass-fed and free ranging, and the dairy cows remain with their calves, day and night, until a natural weaning age. Alex cares for the animals in his keep, and of all these animals, Ned was his favourite. Ned was the first calf born on the farm to be slaughtered for beef. Alex loved Ned, but he drove him to the slaughterhouse, paid for his death, and then sat down to eat his body.

'I loved him. He had a crazy hairdo, was as tall as a racing horse and I used to have to carry him back to the field when he was a calf. I actually miss him. Does that make me a bad person? Does it mean there's something wrong with me? I don't know.'

Alex shared a photograph of the two of them. Ned is a calf, just a few days old, and Alex is clutching him in his arms. Ned used to like to sleep by the front gate during milking, and the other cows, including his mother Mefus, were prone to wandering off without him. Alex is carrying Ned back to the field after one such episode, grinning with affection.

'I can rear an animal with love, and I can kill it. I won't eat meat from an animal constrained on concrete all its life. But I will eat one that's been reared with care and respect. Care for its health and welfare, respect for its needs and desires. For a pig to root the earth, for a cow to wrap its tongue around blades of grass and herbs and to form social bonds.'

I asked Alex whether he said goodbye to Ned or marked his death in any way. Did he treat him any differently to the other animals he had taken to the slaughterhouse?

'I went and had a chat with him, as did the others on the farm (it's a group of six of us running the farm). He was a genuine character and a cow we regarded dearly. I certainly have a different relationship with those that were born here, compared to the ones we bought in as yearlings. I've noticed that clearly.

'The meat from Ned meant more to us, and it felt totally fine talking about him whilst we ate him. It's little things, like every time we get beef back from the butchery, we make a special meal to celebrate it and with some animals it means more than others. Some you bond with more than others. The dairy cows we have the closest relationship with, and we had to cull one a few months ago, and she was a favourite cow, so we made sure we took her for beef for ourselves. We were all a bit sad about it, but all the same enjoyed the beef (well three out of six of us, as the others are veggie!).'

I asked Alex how he could justify killing an animal he professed to care for. Wasn't this even more of a betrayal than killing a wild animal?

'I believe that farming animals is the right thing to do. I believe that ungulates have a part to play in our farming system, a role in the landscape. The romantic vision of hunting, I love, but given human populations and systems, I don't think we're ever returning to the days where the only flesh we eat is wild hunted. Given that ungulates play an important ecological role, I see no problem in manipulating the ecology towards our needs. I would, however, much rather see animals roam over large areas, with shepherds and predators, not fences, as I think we could see improved habitats and ecology. I'm talking about a sort of middle ground between "rewilding" and "farming", maybe more along the lines of how indigenous people of North America manipulated their "wild" landscape. But we're not there in the UK right now. I'd love us to move towards that.'

I put it to Alex that if he really loved Ned, he would have let him live. He would have cared for him, instead of consuming him. How can farmers claim to 'love' their animals if they kill them?

'I was a vegetarian once myself, and not from a farming background, so I have a slightly different perspective on it, and I have friends that are veggie and vegan, including people who live on the farm alongside us. Coming into farming I was probably more judgemental of farmers, and more naive, and since getting to know more farmers, I've realised how many care deeply about their animals, though their hands are often tied by economic constraints.

'Ultimately, I couldn't farm cattle if I thought it was only about producing food or just making money. There has to be a greater purpose to it. I wouldn't say these are just rationalisations for taking animals' lives, though they are the reasons why I'm able to do it. I think I'm talking about some sort of duty to farm these animals, and to do it in as ecological and ethical a way as possible. I can't be entirely sentimental about them. If I were to love Ned so much that I couldn't kill him then we couldn't farm. I suppose I'm saying that I don't love Ned like I love my daughter. Either love is the wrong word, or it needs qualification.'

What are we to make of the farmer who kills and consumes the animal he loves? Does Alex embody our fall into the unnatural contortions of speciesism, or was this an honest effort at reconciling the irreconcilable? Should we interpret Ned's death as betrayal and exploitation, or was this a courageous attempt at balancing pragmatism with care in a world where humans need to eat? However you choose to answer these questions, Viva!'s account is found wanting. While it is likely that farming did alter the terms of our relationship with other species, this was an evolution of a relationship already fraught with contradiction. We were killing and consuming animals long before we began farming, and our empathy is more ancient by far. We distort our own reflection when we deny the roots of our omnivory. We do farmers like Alex a disservice when we ask them to shoulder the burden of Original Sin.[22]

There is more to vegan advocacy than these accounts of human herbivory. I would commend anyone to visit Viva!'s website, read their reports, to seek out Earthling Ed's content, subscribe to his podcasts. The vegan movement is the ally of anyone who opposes the cruelty of industrial animal farming, anyone who desires a more equitable and empathetic society.

But the psychology of meat is complex, capable of skewing thought and behaviour in subtle and significant ways, regardless of our dietary orientation. These tales of herbivory matter, the omnivore's tapestry of evasion and denial matters, for we are careering headlong into an impossible future. We face what scientists have described as a 'planetary emergency', and this emergency is being fuelled by the cognitive complexity of our diets, the drama and dynamics of the meat paradox.

6

EMERGENCY

Each day we wake to a fresh tale of unravelling. The precipitous decline of our pollinators; the calving of ancient ice. Scientists, overwhelmed by the implications of the data, the enormity of the planetary emergency, search for images and concepts that might help non-specialists understand. Think of it this way, they say. If everyone lived as the average European, we would need 2.8 planets to sustain us. If everyone lived as the average American, we would need more than four. Or consider the calendar, they say. By mid-August each year, we have exhausted our planet's resources. We are 'overshooting', and this annual overshoot is propelling us towards social and ecological collapse.

Or think of it like this. There are certain boundaries which demarcate the 'safe operating space' within which our species can thrive. If we live within these planetary boundaries, we should be safe from natural calamity, but transgress them, and we risk tipping the earth system into an altered equilibrium, one more hostile to life and human flourishing. Scientists have identified nine planetary boundaries, and we have already transgressed four, those for climate change, biosphere integrity (or biodiversity), land use change, and the release of reactive nitrogen and phosphorus into the environment. For each of these, we are in dangerous territory, and for each the contribution of our diets is decisive. If we are to resolve the planetary emergency, we will need to change the way we eat.[1]

Each day we wake to the same question, posed on supermarket shelves and restaurant menus, on sandwich packets and in vociferous newspaper headlines. Should we eat animals? Which animals? How many and how often? What role should meat and animal foods play in our diets?

Industrial animal farming is not only cruel, it is wasteful. Globally, roughly 40 per cent of all arable land is used to grow feed crops such as soy and maize, mostly for animals housed in intensive indoor systems. In the UK, roughly 50 per cent of arable land is used for this purpose. These crops consume vast quantities of nitrogen fertiliser and chemical pesticide, and they represent an inefficient way of coaxing nutrition from the land. We could feed ourselves more resourcefully, and within planetary boundaries, if we used more of our arable land to produce plant foods for human consumption.

Scholars have modelled the scenario. Imagine, they say, that we stop competing with animals for food, that we stop feeding these crops to animals. In this scenario, animals might still play an important role in our farming system, but they would be free ranging, with cows and sheep on grasslands and in organic rotations, and chickens and pigs fed on 'leftovers' such as food waste, residues, by-products, and crops unsuited for human consumption. If you think of yourself as an 'ethical omnivore', this might be the scenario you envisage. Imagine a world where animals are no longer confined in cages. Imagine that every cow gets to graze and hoof, enjoying a more natural diet. Imagine pigs that rootle and roam, and chickens that bathe in the dust and grow at a healthier rate. Imagine that we stop felling the Amazon and destroying the Cerrado; that we preserve our planet's riches, provide space for nature to regenerate and resolve the climate crisis. How does that sound? The science is clear. If we farmed like this and shared the produce equitably, there would be much less meat to go around. Many more of us would be vegan. Many would be vegetarian. Animal foods would still be important – contributing to food security and ecological resilience – but the average diet in the UK, Europe and America would need to include 60 to 90 per cent less meat.[2]

To the omnivore, dietary change on this scale might seem daunting or disagreeable. To the vegan, it might sound wholly inadequate. We can quibble about the details later. Resolving the planetary emergency requires that we take a massive step in this direction, as soon as possible. The most urgent and important dietary move any of us can make is to withdraw all custom from industrial animal farming and to buy our food, wherever possible, whether plant or animal, from organic and regenerative farmers. The science is clear that organic and regenerative farming are part of the solution. The science is also clear that dietary change at scale will be needed. Scholars have probed the question from a variety of angles and have repeatedly arrived at the same broad conclusion. We will need to eat less and better meat. Much less. Much better.

One such group of scholars was brought together under the banner of the EAT-Lancet Commission on Food, Planet, Health. The commission was born of a collaboration between the EAT Foundation, a not-for-profit organisation, and *The Lancet*, one of the world's most prestigious medical journals. Made up of thirty-seven scientists and scholars – experts in health, nutrition, sustainability, food systems, economics and political governance, drawn from sixteen countries – the commission spent three years reviewing the evidence. They set out first to define a healthy diet based on the latest evidence, and then to establish how to deliver that diet to a future population of 10 billion (expected mid-century) within planetary boundaries. They published their report in January 2019, presenting 'the first full scientific review of what constitutes a healthy diet from a sustainable food system'.[3]

'The world's diets must change dramatically,' lead author Walter Willett of Harvard University said upon the report's launch. 'More than eight hundred million people have insufficient food, while many more consume an unhealthy diet that contributes to premature death and disease.'

The commission reached an optimistic yet challenging conclusion. Yes, it will be possible to feed everyone a healthy diet, even a massively expanded population, and we can do so within planetary boundaries, but this will require significant changes to the way that we eat, particularly in more affluent countries.

The commission's proposals were presented as a 'reference diet'. If everyone on the planet adopted the reference diet, they said, we could nourish ourselves sustainably. The diet outlined target consumption levels, broken down by food groups, and within each food group, a range was provided. For example, the reference diet recommends the consumption of 250 grams of dairy foods per person per day, but it permits a range of 0–500 grams to allow for differences in personal and cultural preference and need.

The most significant proposals concerned the consumption of animal foods. The commission said diets should include a rich diversity of plants, including lots of pulses, vegetables, fruits and nuts, but only a moderate amount of meat, fish and eggs. 'While meat is an important source of key nutrients including protein, iron and vitamin B12, excess meat consumption can harm our health and the planet. Aim to consume no more than 98 grams of red meat (pork, beef or lamb), 203 grams of poultry and 196 grams of fish per week.' This equates to a small portion of chicken on a couple of days a week, a portion of fish, and a burger once a week or a steak once a month. Compared to the average UK or European diet, this represents a decline in meat consumption of roughly 80 per cent. Compared to the average American diet, it represents a decrease in consumption of approximately 85 per cent.

EAT-Lancet's reference diet was immediately controversial. Food writer Joanna Blythman penned an article describing it as a 'global, one-size-fits-all diet', referring to EAT-Lancet as a 'new form of colonialism in which affluent white people tell everyone from the Inuits of Alaska to the Maasai of Kenya what they all should be eating'. Gian Lorenzo Cornado, Italy's ambassador to the United Nations, similarly outraged, wrote a letter to his fellow ambassadors warning that EAT-Lancet was 'urging for a centralised control of our dietary choices' with the aim of 'the total elimination of consumers' freedom of choice'.

The EAT-Lancet authors were quick to counter the criticism, explaining that they weren't prescribing a diet, but recommending a *dietary pattern*, which could be adapted to diverse cuisines. 'Flexibility to adapt to local diets is inherent in the reference dietary targets,' they said.

> Within these scientific targets ... there is room for a myriad of different food cultures around the world. This includes diets found in Indonesia, Mexico, India, China and across West Africa, and we specifically cited some of these as examples. In fact, traditional diets are not in danger from adoption of the healthy reference dietary targets presented in the EAT-Lancet report, they are in danger from adoption of industrial Western dietary patterns, which is accelerating globally.[4]

It was not an auspicious start, but stronger and far stranger criticisms would be voiced. As the report launched, social media began to fizz with anti-EAT-Lancet sentiment. Legitimate questions about the report's conclusions were interwoven with misinformation and conjecture, and the debate spiralled into one of the most peculiar controversies of the year. As the brouhaha escalated, it became clear that the commission had made a fatal error in the timing of the report's publication. Unfortunately, and by chance, the report had been dropped into the frothing epicentre of the meat debate, bang in the middle of Veganuary.

Veganuary – the calendar month formerly known as 'January' – has become a landmark event in the culture war calendar, an annual exercise in vegan versus omnivore tension. 'Since 2014, Veganuary has inspired and supported more than one million people in 192 countries to try vegan for January and beyond,' the organisation Veganuary UK says. 'We have worked with businesses to drive up vegan food provision in shops and restaurants, and have made veganism more visible and accessible through our work with national and international media.' Cue meat lobby disapproval. 'It's time the livestock sector reclaimed January,' a spokesperson for the Agriculture and Horticulture Development Board (AHDB) grumbles. 'There is a belief that the month is now "owned" by those who follow alternative lifestyle choices and set out to convert others while spreading misinformation and mischief around livestock farming.' Cue the Veganuary retort. 'It's not a surprise to see this meat industry fightback against the growing acceptance and adoption of veganism, but their accusations that we are "spreading misinformation" are completely unfounded ... Unlike the meat industry, we have no vested interest in misleading the public as we gain no personal benefit from the increased adoption of a vegan diet ... It's a shame the meat industry is so selfish and short-sighted.'[5]

The debate is progressively rewriting the calendar. Veganuary (which is also officially 'world carnivore month' and 'organuary', a month dedicated to the consumption of organ meats) is now followed by Februdairy, a campaign launched by an ex-vegan animal scientist in response to Veganuary which promotes milk and dairy consumption throughout the month of February. If you're vegan, however, you might know the month as Februscary (because 'dairy is scary'), an opportunity to counter the industry's pro-dairy campaign by sharing content on social media exposing the hidden harms of dairy farming. And then we're on to Meaty March ...

If Veganuary is controversial, it's partly because it's the largest coordinated global exercise in vegan outreach. In 2019, in what might be the apogee of Veganuary proselytising, a ten-year-old girl named Genesis secured an audience with Pope Francis at the Vatican and offered him a million dollars to go vegan for the month. The Pope might not have converted, but high-profile figures have flocked to the cause. Celebrity ambassadors for Veganuary include Joaquin Phoenix, Paul McCartney, Chris Packham and Alicia Silverstone. Other celebrities reported as being vegan include Zac Efron, Venus Williams, Benedict Cumberbatch, Lewis Hamilton, Bill Clinton, Natalie Portman and Madonna.

The campaign has generated no shortage of media dispute, including lowbrow 'debate' on morning television where guests will be found ruminating on such questions as 'Has Veganuary gone too far – is it time we started sticking up for the meat industry?' Broadcaster Piers Morgan has become the prime pro-vocateur, taking a loud (and often inane) pro-meat, anti-vegan stance. In a characteristically unenlightening segment, Morgan invited onto his show three young activists from animal rights group Direct Action Everywhere. 'Veganism is not about perfec-tion,' one of them patiently explained, 'it's about doing the best that you can.' 'WHAT HAPPENS IN THE JUNGLE?' Morgan shouted, repeatedly bellowing at his young guests, who, he insisted, were 'hypocrites' for eating bread, knowing that insects had been harmed in its production.

The pro-meat kickback against Veganuary is testament to the campaign's success. In its inaugural year in 2014, a modest 3,300 people took part and committed to going vegan for the month. By 2021, that figure had risen to 580,000. People from almost every country in the world had signed up, with North Korea, Vatican City and Eswatini the only countries outstand-ing. The campaign had featured in the mainstream media, including articles in the *New York Times*, *Wall Street Journal*, *The Washington Post*, and on the cover of *The Times* and *New Scientist*. Over 550 new vegan meal options were added to chain menus throughout Veganuary 2020 at major brands including Pizza Hut, Subway and KFC, and over 650 new vegan products were launched in retail outlets across the UK. 'We think it's more of a cultural shift than a trend. It's here to stay,' says Veganuary co-founder Jane Land.[6]

Veganism has so thoroughly penetrated the mainstream in recent years that it's easy to forget that barely a decade ago, it was a fringe movement. Very few people wanted to be vegan, and finding a decent vegan meal in a pub, café or restaurant was a challenge. It's difficult to say exactly when the tide turned, but one unlikely breakthrough occurred on 3 December 2013. It was the night before rapper Jay-Z's forty-fourth birthday, and the man had an important announcement to make.

'You can call it a spiritual and physical cleanse,' Jay-Z wrote in a message posted on his website. 'A 22 Days challenge to go completely vegan, or as I prefer to call it, plant-based!!' Beyoncé would also undertake the challenge, Jay-Z said, and the 22-day duration was significant. 'There's something spiritual to me about it being my 44th birthday, and the serendipity behind the number of days in this challenge; 22 (2+2=4) coupled with the fact that the challenge ends on Christmas day. It just feels right.'

These might sound like the musings of an adolescent pothead, but this was an important moment. Jay-Z's pronouncement marked a shift in our collective consciousness. The vegan movement stepped from the fringe into the centre, evolving into a more diverse and multifaceted form. While ethical concern for animals remained at the core of the movement, veganism would become associated with a broader bundle of concerns, including personal and planetary wellbeing, with a new generation of celebrity and social media influencers set to join the cause. 'The news that Jay-Z and Beyoncé have tried a plant-based diet has sparked a lot of interest and controversy,' Jasmijn de Boo, CEO of the Vegan Society, commented at the end of 2013, a few days before the launch of the inaugural Veganuary. 'It could be said that veganism is at its most popular ever since the coining of the word.'[7]

This cautious acknowledgement of increasing appeal would soon be eclipsed by a surge of global enthusiasm. Between 2014 and 2019, the number of vegans in the UK quadrupled. The number of vegans in America grew by 600 per cent, bringing the total to almost 20 million. In the space of a few years, veganism became an international phenomenon. Google searches for 'veganism' increased sevenfold in the five years between 2014 and 2019. Sales of plant-based meat substitutes grew by 451 per cent across Europe in the same period. UK takeaway service Just Eat reported a 987 per cent increase in demand for meat-free meals in 2018 alone. Pick your country, and the trend was the same. Germany, land of many sausages: a global leader in vegan product innovation. Ireland: a 94 per cent increase in vegan food orders from online takeaways in 2017. Scotland: a 120 per cent rise in demand for vegan haggis. Iceland: named the global epicentre of veganism in 2018. (The UK, Australia and New Zealand topped the table in 2019.) The list goes on.[8]

Public attitudes seemed to be turning squarely against meat. In tandem with the vegan surge, meat-reducing 'flexitarian' diets were also becoming more popular. In 2013, The Food People, a market intelligence agency, predicted that flexitarian eating would be the next national 'mega trend' in the UK. By 2018, this prediction had been realised. A national survey found that one in five people in the UK identified as meat-reducing flexitarians, and one in eight were vegetarian or vegan, meaning one in three people in total were reducing their meat consumption, a percentage that prevailed into 2021.

The meat industry, fearing the changing of the wind, has scrambled to respond. To mark Veganuary in 2021, the AHDB spent £1.5 million identifying members of the British public most inclined to reducing their meat and dairy consumption, targeting them with a marketing campaign designed to increase sales. The trenches have been dug. The lines have been drawn. We must all choose our side, or so we are told. It was into this fractious and polarised atmosphere, in the blustery depths of Veganuary 2019, that the EAT-Lancet report was launched.

The reception that greeted the EAT-Lancet report was so virulent and bizarre that it spawned a spin-off study, published in *The Lancet* several months later. 'Although the report was positively received by established international media outlets such as the *Guardian* and the *New York Times*, it also led to highly polarised debates online including misinformation, conspiracy theories, and personal attacks.' The study's authors analysed a dataset of Twitter activity linked to EAT-Lancet, comprised of 4,278 Twitter users and 8.5 million tweets. 'Our analysis confirms that a digital countermovement managed to organise rapidly, essentially dominating online discussions about the EAT-Lancet report in intriguing and worrying ways.' This countermovement emerged roughly a week before the report was published, with the hashtag #yes2meat used to disseminate pre-emptive criticism.[9]

Investigative science journalist Nina Teicholz contributed to this pre-emptive strike, warning that EAT-Lancet was a ploy to turn the world vegan. '#EATLancet soon coming out with report saying that we should all go vegan,' Teicholz tweeted, two days before the report was published. Joanna Blythman similarly warned of nefarious intent. 'Orchestrated war v meat intensifies tomorrow with launch of Eat-Lancet campaign,' she tweeted.

The suggestion of vegan machination was a recurring theme in the criticism of EAT-Lancet. In an article titled 'Why we should resist the vegan putsch', published the day the report launched, Blythman warned that 'Vegans, about 1% of the population when I last checked, are currently trying to shape the public discourse on food.' EAT-Lancet was at the forefront of this 'anti-animal food putsch', she said, pushing 'a global shift to a "plant-based" diet', a diet that she has described elsewhere as 'quasi-vegan'.[10]

This was a taste of things to come. A few days after Blythman issued her call for 'active resistance' against the so-called putsch, Teicholz announced that an 'examination' of the EAT-Lancet authors revealed that more than 80 per cent of them 'favoured vegetarian/vegan diets' and 'espoused vegetarian views *before* joining the EAT-Lancet project'. Teicholz lists several statements which she says provide incriminating evidence of this pro-vegetarian, pro-vegan bias. They include the following:

Anna Lartey, Director of Nutrition at the Food and Agriculture Organization of the United Nations: 'We must develop the habit of adding more fruits and vegetables to our meal.'

Tim Lang, Professor of Food Policy at City University of London: 'Meat and dairy are as complicated and contentious for environmental analysis as they are for public health nutrition.'

Francesco Branca of the World Health Organization authored a report that said people should 'eat at least 400g (5 portions) of fruit and vegetable a day'.

Corinna Hawkes, Professor of Food Policy at City University of London: 'Everywhere people are consuming too few vegetables, legumes, fish, nuts, seeds and fruits, and too much fat, processed meat, sugary drinks and salt.'

Tara Garnett, Founder and Director of the Food Climate Research Network: 'The current demand for animal products is simply not sustainable and enormous harm is being done in the attempt to meet it. We have to change.'

These are just snippets, but they give a sense of the calibre of evidence upon which Teicholz based her claim. 'This was clearly a highly biased group,' she declared, adding that the

EAT-Lancet authors had engaged in 'inbred conversations' and 'the outcome of their report was therefore inevitably a foregone conclusion'. Blythman echoed the critique, but she added her own spin, claiming not (as Teicholz had) that 80 per cent of the authors 'espoused vegetarian views' (whatever that might mean), but that more than 80 per cent of the EAT-Lancet authors *were* vegetarian or vegan. This was clearly a 'highly partisan' group, she cautioned.[11]

Teicholz announced that the EAT-Lancet report had been funded by the food industry, namely by FReSH, a collaboration of businesses convened by the World Business Council for Sustainable Development, which includes the processed food multinationals Kellogg's, Nestlé and PepsiCo, and the agrichemical giants Syngenta and Bayer (owners of Monsanto). Teicholz shared an image of the brand logos of the FReSH group, which echoed around social media, providing speculative 'proof' of this dastardly interference. As fears of corporate maleficence grew, Blythman stoked the flames, warning that the EAT-Lancet report suggested 'genetically modifying nuts to improve the yield'. The EAT-Lancet report does not suggest the genetic modification of nuts or any other foods, and the FReSH group did not fund the EAT-Lancet report or contribute to its drafting. EAT-Lancet 'was solely funded through the generous support of the Wellcome Trust, which had no role in the writing of the report'.[12]

The rumours became more elaborate. Writing on behalf of the Nutrition Coalition, an American 'non-partisan educational organization', Teicholz published a statement in which she noted that among the report's (alleged) 'corporate funders' in the FReSH group were 'Seven Big Pharma companies, with drugs for many nutrition-related diseases'. Teicholz insinuated (in the absence of any real evidence) that these companies were backing EAT-Lancet because they knew the diet would make people unhealthy and in need of their drugs. 'The pharmaceutical companies profit from selling drugs, insulin, and devices that sick people need. Would these companies be backing EAT if this diet were to genuinely improve health, reduce disease, and thus, shrink their profits? It's hard to imagine.'[13]

Blythman amplified this suspicion of pharmaceutical influence and added a religious overlay. 'The Eat-Lancet report itself was funded by The Wellcome Trust, whose founder, Henry Wellcome, was raised as a Seventh Day Adventist (a Millennialist Christian group) that preaches vegetarianism and shuns red meat. Furthermore, Wellcome made his wealth in the pharmaceutical industry. Cynics would say pharmaceutical companies stand to benefit from illness, not health, while Wellcome comes from a set of values already favourable to vegetarianism.'

Blythman elucidated on the influence of the Seventh Day Adventist Church in an interview on BBC Radio 4. The Adventists, she explained, were 'obsessed with masturbation'. The Adventist Church followed a prophetess named Ellen G. White who had visions and 'proselytised the Garden of Eden diet', which was wholly plant-based. 'Eating meat was seen as a vice and it was seen as stimulating lustful tendencies.' This preoccupation with sexual repression, Blythman says, is at 'the roots of the contemporary plant-based movement'. It's not clear how Blythman thinks this odd history pertains to the Wellcome Trust's funding of the EAT-Lancet report, but she appears to be insinuating that Henry Wellcome's upbringing as an Adventist in the 1850s, which involved a religiously motivated suppression of masturbatory desire, continues to shape the Trust's research agenda today, prompting Wellcome to invest in skewed science favourable towards vegan diets.[14]

Teicholz brought an even wilder speculation to the table. Shortly after the EAT-Lancet report was published, a story made headlines in a number of media outlets warning that women eating a 'ketogenic' low-carb and high-fat diet, which often includes lots of animal foods, are prone to 'irritation and odours in the vaginal area'. The articles quoted experts who warned that a ketogenic diet can cause 'ketocrotch', an odorous 'pH imbalance in the vagina'. Teicholz took to social media to suggest that these tales of 'ketocrotch' might be part of an organised campaign orchestrated by a PR firm also working with the EAT-Lancet Commission, a speculative scenario she described as 'fascinating, scary, illuminating'.[15]

Are you keeping up? The EAT-Lancet report – which ostensibly proposed to establish how we might feed a growing population a healthy diet within planetary boundaries – was actually pseudo-science concocted by a cabal of corrupt vegan academics working with Monsanto and the pharmaceutical industry to force a diet of pesticide-doused junk upon the masses. And at the root of it all? Masturbation! Veganism! Insulin sales! A surprising number of people have drunk from this milkshake of hyperbole (which was mixed by many spoons but frothed most vigorously by Teicholz and Blythman). The words 'EAT-Lancet' can evoke much wailing and gnashing of teeth in some quarters, but largely for spurious reasons.

'This was the work of thirty-seven experts who spent three years looking at the evidence – three years!' Professor Tim Lang, one of the EAT-Lancet authors, told me, his eyes widening at the suggestion of bias. 'Our paper includes more than three hundred references, and there were many we didn't include. It was the most complex piece of statistical modelling I've been involved with. The paper was peer-reviewed – twice – and published in the world's most respected medical journal. It isn't perfect. It doesn't presume to have the final word. But let me be clear: No. Conspiracy.'

Lang was particularly irked by the suggestion of an anti-meat ploy. As a hill farmer in the seventies, he reared sheep and cows in the Forest of Bowland in Lancashire, England. 'I wasn't the only livestock farmer on the commission.'

The EAT-Lancet report is certainly not above criticism. It is appropriate that the study is scrutinised, and cogent critiques have been voiced in relation to the strength of the evidence underpinning the reference diet (including the stringent allowance for red meat) and the social and economic consequences of the dietary transition envisaged. The way the commission launched the report was admittedly problematic. The image of academics flying around the world warning of the climate impacts of our diets, as some EAT-Lancet authors did, is irksome. The EAT Foundation also isn't for everyone. A couple of months after the report was published, I attended their annual 'EAT Forum' in Stockholm, an event which opened with a gaudy onslaught of flashing lights, hyperactive visuals and projections, and EAT founder Gunhild A. Stordalen grinning fervently on stage. It was like trying to watch a TED Talk on LSD.[16]

But the suggestion that EAT-Lancet is a plot hatched by conniving vegan academics to turn the world against meat doesn't stand up to scrutiny. While the report recommends that people in more affluent countries should eat less meat, the authors are clear that many people in the world should eat *more*. It says that increasing the consumption of meat and animal foods is a particular priority among people with inadequate nutrition, including hundreds of millions of people in sub-Saharan Africa and south Asia, where there are high levels of anaemia and stunting, and where 'promotion of animal source foods for children, including livestock products, can improve dietary quality, micronutrient intake, nutrient status, and overall health'.

The EAT-Lancet Commission, when you dig down into the data, recommends a modest 42 per cent decline in the global farm animal population. Figures available on the University of Oxford website reveal the mathematics. The commission calculated the global farm animal population today to be 76 billion. In the 2050 EAT-Lancet scenario, this would decline to 43.7 billion. The global herd of dairy cows would *increase* from 784 million to 789 million. Fish consumption would increase from 118 million tonnes per annum today to 189 million tonnes, a rise of 62 per cent, most of this coming from an expansion of aquaculture (fish farming). Two trillion fish are currently killed for consumption annually. In the EAT-Lancet scenario, this would increase to roughly 3 trillion.

In the future laid out by the EAT-Lancet Commission, we will be farming *more* dairy cows, not fewer. When fish are included in the equation, we will be killing and consuming *more* animals each year than we do today. Most of the animals consumed in the EAT-Lancet scenario (apart from fish) are chickens, and the modelling assumes 'ongoing increases in efficiency and productivity', as one of the authors told me; in other words, these figures assume the continued use of fast-growing and hyper-productive breeds, with all the welfare issues this entails. The more apt criticism of EAT-Lancet is not that it's a covert attempt to turn the world against meat, but that it endorses a scaled-back version of intensive poultry production. Far from being a 'vegan putsch', EAT-Lancet proposes that we feed the world through industrial animal farming.[17]

In an appendix to the report, the authors discuss the scenario described above, where animals are free ranging and fed on 'leftovers'. 'While emissions and overall land use may be high for grazing animals, ruminants can be reared on land unsuited for other food producing purposes and on by-products from crop production,' they write. 'In addition, in mixed farming systems the animals recycle nutrients and re-fertilise soils with their dung, thus fostering a new generation of crops and pasture.' They observe that while these studies make different methodological assumptions, the dietary conclusion they reach is broadly similar. The daily allowance of meat and dairy in a 'leftovers' scenario is roughly 50 grams of meat and 300 grams of milk per person per day, which is comparable to the 43 grams of meat and 250 grams of dairy recommended in EAT-Lancet. In short, whether we feed a growing global population through free-ranging ruminants and organic and regenerative farming, or via a scaled-back version of intensive poultry squeezed within planetary boundaries, our diets will need to change. We will need to eat much less meat.

This is not a vegan conspiracy. At least, I don't think it is. I suppose it could all turn out to be true. Perhaps the EAT-Lancet authors, a group of renowned scientists and scholars, really did collude with a PR agency intent on spreading rumours about smelly vaginas. Perhaps they spent three years plotting how to force the Inuit to eat dehydrated kale. Perhaps within the Wellcome Trust there remains a faction under the sway of an ancient prophetess, a clique of religious extremists preoccupied with promoting a meat-free diet in the hope of stamping out the vice of self-pleasure. Perhaps MORE DAIRY FARMING is what the vegan movement secretly desires, and perhaps this cabal of conniving vegan academics thought that killing tens of billions of animals (plus an extra trillion sea animals) was the obvious next step on the road to animal liberation.

Or perhaps – just perhaps – something else is going on.

Those of us who consume animals are highly sensitive to the ethical critique embodied in those who do not. Put simply, vegans trouble us. In a 2014 study, Hank Rothgerber demonstrated that mere exposure to a strict vegetarian or a vegan – someone we meet at a party, a colleague, or someone we interact with online, for instance – could elicit a reactive response among omnivores, including a heightened commitment to pro-meat justifications.

The study introduced a group of meat-eating volunteers to written descriptions of two people, one a vegetarian, the other eating a gluten-free diet. Those exposed to the vegetarian, when subsequently quizzed, lowered their estimation of animal sentience, denying the emotional similarities between humans and animals, while those exposed to the gluten-free individual did not. Crucially, no proselytising or persuasion was attempted. The volunteers were not encouraged to change their diet; they were simply introduced to someone who chose not to eat animals. 'Vegetarians create in meat eaters emotional states such as anxiety and tension that are associated with the experience of cognitive dissonance,' Rothgerber explains, but 'while vegetarians are generally threatening, they are not all equal in their likelihood of triggering dissonance'.

In a follow-up study, Rothgerber explored how omnivores responded when exposed to individuals exhibiting varying degrees of commitment to vegetarianism, including a 'strict' vegetarian (a vegan) and an 'imposter' who admitted that they sometimes ate meat. 'Exposure to a strict vegetarian led participants to report different consumption patterns than exposure to an imposter,' he explains, with participants reporting eating more vegetarian meals in an average week than those exposed to an imposter. They were also motivated to go on the attack. 'Whenever possible, meat eaters may focus on derogating vegetarians to minimize dissonance, thus eliminating the need to endorse one of the other dissonance reducing strategies.'[18]

Rothgerber's study identified three responses, commonly arising when an omnivore is exposed to a vegan. The omnivore might be moved to denigrate and criticise the individual; or they might misrepresent their consumption by claiming to eat less meat; or they might double down on their pseudo-carnivorous identity, entrenching their commitment to a meat-rich diet. The study has proven to be predictive, for all three responses have become patent in recent years, played out on a societal scale. These responses, it is worth recalling, were elicited by mere exposure to a vegan individual. *Imagine what would happen if there were vegans everywhere!*

When Jay-Z announced his 'spiritual cleanse', catalysing the entry of veganism into the mainstream, the dynamics of the meat paradox were transformed. The strategies of detachment and dissociation that had hitherto kept dissonance at bay for the omnivore majority were punctuated by the ubiquitous presence of individuals voluntarily foregoing animal consumption. Suddenly, there were dissonance triggers everywhere – on restaurant menus and supermarket shelves, on morning television, and in the faces of Hollywood celebrities. A tide of anti-vegan sentiment rose in response.

Jason Hannan calls it 'meatsplaining', the anti-vegan rhetoric commonly expressed by pro-meat proponents as a set of reductive tropes: the idea that vegans are unhealthy in body and mind; that they are ignorant about animals, farming, ecology and nutrition; that vegans have some sort of scheming 'agenda' (whereas the meat industry is free of any such agenda); that vegans are sanctimonious and lack a sense of humour; that they are angry and emotional; that vegans are simultaneously hypersensitive victims yet also tyrannical bullies; and that veganism, because it is inherently extremist, is a threat to social order. In the context of EAT-Lancet, we might add: the idea that vegans are gullibly playing into the hands of the agrochemical and processed food industries; that veganism is shorthand for corporate connivance and the erosion of traditional cultures; and that the vegan movement was born of religious ideology and irrational belief. There are historical precedents for this bias. Vegetarians were persecuted in twelfth-century China and viewed as heretics by the Roman Catholic Church during the Inquisition. Little more than half a century ago, they were characterised as domineering and secretly sadistic, and vegetarianism was proposed as the underlying cause of medical conditions such as stammering.

The reality of anti-vegan discrimination has been substantiated by research. A 2015 study found that vegetarians and vegans – vegans in particular, and male vegans especially – face discrimination on a par with other minorities in Western society. A prior study found that nearly half of all meat eaters held negative views of vegetarians and were inclined to denigrate those of the opposing dietary tribe. These findings cohere with research examining the portrayal of vegans in UK newspapers, with one study finding that most (74 per cent) of the articles that mentioned vegans or veganism were negative in their portrayal, while a handful (20 per cent) were neutral, and only a small number (6 per cent) expressed positive views.[19]

The drive to denigrate vegans is so powerful that the word itself can become an insult. 'People love a good prejudice, and maybe the v of veganism doesn't help – words beginning with v tend to come pre-loaded with moral judgement,' Tara Garnett observes. 'Think virtuous, vicious, vibrant, violent, vivid, vehement, victorious, virulent, vigorous. Vacuous, villainous. Vegan.' One of the most striking features of the EAT-Lancet response was the way the word 'vegan' was used as a slur. EAT-Lancet lead author Walter Willett was described by critics as 'leaning towards veganism', as a 'leader of vegan advocacy' and as 'vegetarian/vegan', even though he is on record saying that he eats meat, fish and animal foods, and he has spent several decades promoting a diet that includes them (albeit with moderate amounts of red meat). Similarly, when Joanna Blythman claimed that 80 per cent of the EAT-Lancet authors were vegetarian or vegan, she appeared to be using the v-word pejoratively. 'Those "37 senior scientists"? More than 80% of them are #vegans or #vegetarians. Might just skew their views, no?'[20]

As well as denigrating vegans, we omnivores have responded to the rise of veganism by misreporting our dietary behaviours. More than a dozen recent studies have found that the phenomenon is rife. A survey of 10,000 Americans found that 60 per cent of vegetarians had eaten meat or seafood within the previous 24 hours. Across several US studies, approximately 7 per cent of people identified as vegetarian, yet when asked about their eating habits, only between 1 and 2.5 per cent ate a vegetarian diet. A similar picture is evident in the UK. A 2018 study found that 3 per cent of British people claimed to be vegan, but a more detailed analysis found that only 0.6 per cent were eating a vegan diet. These findings aren't concerning in themselves, but they illustrate the degree to which our behaviours can become divorced from our self-image, our susceptibility to subtle forms of self-deception. Research is demonstrating that 'perceived behaviour change' is a common strategy adopted in response to the meat paradox.[21]

In one revealing study, Hank Rothgerber told a group of volunteers that they would soon be watching a PETA documentary showing footage of animal abuse in the meat industry. These volunteers reported eating less meat than those in a separate group who were not expecting to watch the documentary. Anticipating dissonance, they were moved to portray themselves as meat-reducing flexitarians. They altered their self-identity, thereby muting the degree to which they felt complicit in the disturbing footage they were about to witness.

Intriguingly, the effect was only observed among female volunteers. Men didn't report eating less. A growing body of evidence suggests that gender is a key predictor of attitudes towards animal consumption, and an important factor in determining an individual's response to the meat paradox. Women often form stronger emotional attachment to animals, perceiving more anthropomorphic similarity between species. They report eating less meat (and this is true across nationalities), and they are more inclined to go vegetarian or vegan. Roughly 85 per cent of participants in Veganuary are women, while in the US, women make up 80 per cent of the vegan community. 'Women display different ways of handling the contradictions instigated by meat consumption than men,' Rothgerber observes. Women are more likely to adopt a meat-free diet, and women who continue to eat meat are more likely to under-report their consumption. The evidence suggests that men are often less apologetic, preferring to reduce dissonance by endorsing pro-meat justifications and by denying the mind and sentience of the animals they consume. In a further twist, those of us most susceptible to this lurch into entrenched carnivory might be those who empathise with animals the most.[22]

Psychologist Andy Martens created a scenario wherein volunteers believed they were killing insects by dropping them through a tube into a coffee grinder. The tube had been designed to protect the bugs from harm, but the participants couldn't see this; they didn't know the insects were being safely secluded in a hidden compartment. Two groups were introduced to the equipment – one group was given a verbal introduction by a researcher, while the other group was told to get 'hands on', dropping an insect into the grinder and turning it on for three seconds. The researcher asked each participant to rate how similar they perceived themselves to be to the bugs prior to commencing the experiment. They were then left alone in a cubicle and told to exterminate the critters. They responded in very different ways. Those who believed they had already killed an insect (during the introduction to the exercise) were more likely to go on to kill a greater number. Crucially, this was only the case for those who perceived some similarity to the bugs. In short, the more the volunteers empathised with the insects, the more disturbed they were by the fact that they had killed one – they experienced dissonance – and they responded to this dissonance by going on to kill *even more insects*. This increased killing made them feel better. When we recognise that we have engaged in a morally troubling behaviour, we sometimes respond by enacting the behaviour *more frequently*, taking comfort in its repetition.

'We can see evidence for this same dynamic in the case of meat eating,' Brock Bastian and Steve Loughnan explain. 'This is perhaps one reason that the consumption of meat has become ritualized and symbolic.' And it perhaps helps explain why the rise of veganism has not translated into reduced meat consumption across the population. Some of us might be eating less, but others are eating more, moved by their empathy into the opposing response.

In 2013, the average person in the UK consumed 78.6 kilograms of meat across the year (including red meat and poultry, but not fish or seafood). By 2017, this had risen to 84.9 kilograms, and the figure rose again in 2018. Plant-based sales rose sharply across the same period – in 2018, the UK launched more vegan food products than any other nation – and one in three of us were claiming to eat less meat, but the average person was eating more meat than a decade previously. The data show that over the period we were all embracing veganism and meat reduction, consumption of lamb declined, but we were eating more beef, more pork, more chicken and more eggs. The latest data (at the time of writing) show a slow decline in retail sales of meat and fish in the year prior to the Covid-19 pandemic, but only 1 per cent of those declines came from households deliberately reducing consumption, the other 99 per cent resulting from people unconsciously buying less meat, perhaps because there were more plant-based products on the shelves competing for their attention. Retail sales of meat and dairy then rose sharply throughout the pandemic.[23]

These contradictory trends were also evident in the US, where veganism has boomed in popularity, and one in four people say they are eating less meat. Despite these overtures to meat reduction, per capita meat consumption (inclusive of red meat, poultry, fish and shellfish) has increased in recent years, rising from 80.5 kilograms in 1970 to 82.1 kilograms in 2014, and then again to a record high of 100.9 kilograms in 2018. Beef consumption peaked in the 1970s and decreased by 0.3 per cent annually from 2000 to 2015, but it began to rise again in 2016 and grew by 3.7 per cent in 2018. Consumption of pork and poultry has more than offset the long-term decline in beef, with poultry consumption more than doubling from 1970 to today.[24]

The same trend has been apparent globally. In Spain, meat consumption rose year-on-year between 2013 and 2017. In Germany, per capita consumption has also increased, reaching a 25-year high in 2016. In response to a 2020 survey, 42 per cent of Germans said they were eating less meat, but the data on actual consumption show no meaningful decline. Consumption has dipped in some countries, including Italy and France, but the overall picture is not one in which Europeans are eating significantly less meat. 'Despite what many consumers claim about their individual habits, plant-based foods are not yet replacing a large amount of meat,' market intelligence group Fi Global observed in July 2020. The pattern has been repeated globally. In the five years from 2013, per capita meat consumption increased in Australia, Brazil, Mexico, Argentina, Russia, Japan, Turkey and Iran, among other nations.[25]

There are different ways of measuring meat consumption, based variously on the weight of animal carcasses, the availability of meat in the system, retail sales data, and self-reported food choices. This lack of consistency makes it difficult to discern the full picture. But it's clear that the explosive rise of veganism, and the concurrent boom in popularity for flexitarian eating, has not translated into a meaningful move away from meat – in some contexts, it has been associated with an *increase* in consumption. The entry of veganism into the mainstream has paradoxically helped to entrench us deeper in an unsustainable dietary niche. We are no closer to resolving the planetary emergency, and the clock is ticking.

Each day we wake to a fresh and heated dispute, the pro- and anti-meat rhetoric rising in volume, the roar of the Veganuary fever season. The dietary tribes have dug their trenches, and from the ditches the loudest voices speak. These voices are rarely the most reasonable, and they are certainly not representative, but they have shaped the societal conversation, often for the worse. Film makers voice vacuously unscientific claims of human herbivory, portraying meat as toxic waste, animal foods as asbestos. Food writers impersonate two-bit conspiracy theorists, mindlessly accusing scholars of complicity in a plant-based ploy simply because they once dared to utter the word 'vegetable'. The vegan movement evolves into a mongrel of animal rights activism and online clamour, its ethical stance distorted by the media into a mush of virtue signalling and celebrity intrigue, while a breed of outraged omnivore rises up in response, pro-meat proponents who, raging against the 'eat less meat' message, come to resemble posturing squirrel eaters in a Soho market, the tip-tapping of their keyboards as they post their latest missive (*'veganism is one part cult, one part eating disorder!'*) scarcely distinguishable from the nibbling of teeth on a raw rodent hide. And while the trenches are dug, the monkey dung flung, the corporate actors behind industrial animal farming rub their hands with glee.

Roughly 99 per cent of animals farmed in the US are reared on intensive 'factory farms' for at least part of their lives. This includes 70.4 per cent of cows, 98.3 per cent of pigs, 99.8 per cent of turkeys, 98.2 per cent of laying hens, and over 99.9 per cent of meat chickens. Globally, over 90 per cent of animals are reared on such farms, including an estimated 74 per cent of birds and mammals, and virtually all farmed fish. Escalating demand for meat and animal foods is fuelling this trend towards intensification, as economies of scale drive consolidation and independent farmers are edged out of the market. Those who farm more ethically and sustainably struggle to make ends meet, while a handful of companies make a killing, figuratively and literally. In the UK, while farming of beef cattle and sheep remains mostly extensive and with better welfare, the trend in pig and chicken farming is towards intensification. Roughly 95 per cent of meat chickens are reared in industrial systems, and intensive pig and poultry units are becoming more common, their numbers increasing by 26 per cent between 2011 and 2017 and by a further 7 per cent between 2017 and 2020. The UK is home to at least 800 farms equivalent to 'Concentrated Animal Feeding Operations' (CAFOs) in the US, defined as a facility with at least 125,000 meat chickens, 82,000 laying hens, 2,500 pigs, 700 dairy cattle or 1,000 cattle. Most are poultry facilities, but there are roughly 190 pig, 21 dairy and 3 intensive beef units. Seven of the ten largest chicken farms in the UK have the capacity to house more than one million birds. The largest pig farm can hold 23,000 pigs while the largest cattle farm can house 3,000 cattle. It is not always the case that 'big' equals 'bad', but this is not the farming system we claim to support, and it is certainly not one that coheres with a resolution to the planetary emergency. In the depths of Veganuary 2021, a survey found that 85 per cent of the British public wanted an 'urgent' ban on factory farming to be implemented, while one in four said they intended to go completely meat-free by the end of the year. Three-quarters of us say we want to do more to support British producers farming to high standards, yet our good intentions are inconsistently translated into action. We do not put our pound in the pocket of the farmer who embodies our values. We remain largely unconscious of the forces shaping our diets, and we are running out of time.[26]

We wake each day to fresh rumours of unravelling, of the threshold crossed, the tipping point reached. Scientists, closer than most to the disturbing implications of the data, focus their efforts on the task they are trained for, amassing an ever greater body of evidence attesting to the causes and consequences of the crisis. Perhaps, they hope, this research will puncture our ennui and animate a response. Perhaps, they think, if we only knew more, we would alter our dietary trajectory. But we are not wholly rational. The more our diets fall under the spotlight, the more dissonance we experience, the less predictable our response. The omnivore's cloak of denial is met by the vegan's resistance to the possibility that animal foods or animal farming might be part of the solution. Ensnared in the paradox, we veer into an impossible tomorrow.

The meat paradox does not explain everything. Our food choices are shaped by habits and tastes, social norms and family histories, marketing and advertisements, politics and economics, and by affluence and convenience – by our spending power and the foods that are available to us. But in the paradox, we find a psychological dynamic which maps onto recent contradictory trends in our diets. The meat paradox helps us understand why the rise of veganism has been correlated with increased meat consumption; why our heartfelt concern for animals is inconsistently expressed and translated into dietary behaviours. The paradox has generated a polarised and fractious atmosphere, wherein the common ground between the would-be ethical omnivore and the pragmatic vegan – the necessary ground – becomes difficult to inhabit. Is there any way to make this ground our home?

To answer this question, we must first ask another. *How did we end up like this?*

7

EVOLUTION

It was dawn and we were nesting in the branches, our bodies reclined, languid in the boughs, when in the distance we heard the snarl of the sabretooth and a mournful wail. Cooing now, chattering, we grasped at one another and hurried towards the kill site, clambering with deft fingers into the trembling canopy. It was hunger that propelled us, the desire to eat and an uncomplicated sense of opportunism. We have no reason to think that we felt any sympathy for the sabretooth's prey. As we looked upon the scene, at the disgorged body of the slain elephant, we might have experienced a range of emotions – anticipation and desire, threat and opportunity, perhaps even veneration and wonder – but we did not feel pity. The meat paradox was yet to evolve, but even here the seeds were being sown.

Zoom out from this scene, withdraw, until the African continent comes into view. Now zoom out further, until you can picture our planet swerving through space. Look closely (very closely) and you will see that the angle of our planet's axis of rotation varies as it orbits the sun. There is 'wobble' in our planet's path, and this tilt and eccentricity has ecological consequences, altering the colour and contour of the seasons, inducing alternating periods of warming and cooling. Lean in, listen closely (very closely) and you will hear the Earth's crust sashay over its mantle, the glide and grind of tectonic plates. This movement also influences our climate: the drift of continents redirecting the flow of the oceans; the rise of mountains rerouting atmospheric circulation patterns. Paleoclimatologists have mapped the periods of climatic variability resulting from the interplay of these planetary forces and have found them to be closely correlated with the appearance and disappearance of hominid species in the archaeological record. Our evolution was sculpted by celestial mechanics and tectonic tension, environmental stresses of planetary origin which created selection pressures for certain traits, inducing extinction and speciation.[1]

The most significant period of climate variability occurred between 2.1 and 1.7 million years ago. It was at this time that we relinquished the arboreal adaptations of our ancestors and took to life in the open. The fossil remains of our ancestors from this period are increasingly associated with antelopes, bovids, zebras, and other animals adapted to the grasslands. This shift in ecological niche, from woodland fringe to savannah scrub, was precipitated by climate-induced thinning of the trees, and (perhaps) by the concurrent demise of the sabretooth. Archaeologist Curtis Marean has suggested that as the tree cover grew sparser, the sabretooth struggled, and the associated loss of scavenging opportunities forced our ancestors to seek alternatives. No longer presented with easy elephant steak, our ancestors 'increasingly utilised more open habitats and would have been forced to confront large predators to gain adequate scavenging returns'.[2]

The savannah was no place for a diminutive primate. We were acutely vulnerable, confronted with carnivorous animals that were swifter and more powerful, creatures honed to their predatory niche over millions of years of natural selection. We were naked apes, dispossessed of the safety of the branches. We did not possess speech and we had no complex technology.

We clutched rudimentary stone tools, and we were armed at best with sticks and stones. We can tell from their gnawed remains that our ancestors were eaten. Primates today are preyed upon by felines, jackals, hyenas, wild dogs, hawks, eagles, owls and bears, and we faced a similar array of predators. 'Unlike the forests, the savannahs of Africa harboured one of the earth's most complex communities of large mammal carnivores. No amount of shouting and limb shaking, baring small canines, or even rock throwing would have driven off a large carnivore once it had learned that it could kill hominids with impunity.' At this point in our evolution, we were 'vulnerable lip-smacking delicacies'.[3]

The peril of our predicament was accentuated by our omnivory. The plant foods and tree fruits that we had eaten in wooded areas were less available in the scrub. We could eat animal foods, but this meant living in proximity to carnivores and competing with other scavengers for remains. The odds were stacked against us. The savannah was vast, and carcasses were few. Modern hyenas are efficient in their scavenging niche, arriving at a kill site within thirty minutes, even at night, and their ancestors would have been similarly adept. Given that predation often occurred at night, it's probable that only a small number of carcasses would have been available for us to eat.

In these challenging conditions, vultures and lions became of totemic significance. Lions were the apex predator, the largest feline of the environment. They would have preyed upon hominids and early humans, but they also provided the best scavenging opportunities. Lions typically do not consume all their prey; they leave behind marrow, brains and scraps. To locate their kills, we would have studied the flight patterns of carrion birds, searching for the circling of vultures, intuiting that when several birds were seen heading in the same direction towards the horizon, this suggested a carcass, even when the kill site was too distant for the birds to be visible gyrating above.[4]

The threat of predation, coupled with the scarcity and

difficulty of obtaining meat and high quality nutrition, meant that competition was fierce, even between hominid and early human species. The archaeological record tells of this competition. Between 1.9 and 1.8 million years ago, there were at least four closely related hominid species living in northern Kenya, a crucible of early human evolution. They were *Homo erectus*, *Homo habilis*, *Paranthropus boisei* and *Homo rudolfensis*. At the end of this period, only one species survived, our ancestors, *Homo erectus*.[5]

We survived (and became human) by learning to live among and through the animals of the savannah. The lion and the vulture were of singular importance, but each species had something to teach us. We observed the way the jackal bristled its coat and stiffened its tail as it prepared to strike. We watched the leopard, ears erect, as it stalked its prey. We studied the signs of attack and the postures and calls that signalled impending threat. The ungulates, suddenly alert, heads raised. The zebras, stamping their forefeet and snorting into the sky. Our ancestors 'lived among a bestiary whose behaviour they knew as well as their own'. Their survival depended on meticulous observation, interpretive skill, and the ability to communicate their experience to others.

This communication was achieved via mimesis. As early humans, we lacked articulate speech – we did not possess words, syntax or sentences – but we could gesture, and we could vocalise; we could use our bodies to enact and perform. 'Acting out the roles of animals is likely to have been a key aspect of early human interactions,' archaeologist Steven Mithen explains. 'Either the mimicking or the more sophisticated mimesis of animal sounds and movements, in order to indicate either what had already been seen or what might be seen in the future.'[6]

Vocal mimesis perhaps arose first. We apprenticed ourselves to the alarm calls of other species, as other animals are known to do. Rhinos, for example, will respond to the alarm calls of oxpecker birds; Diana monkeys to the alarm calls of chimpanzees; ring-tailed lemurs to the alarm calls of Verreaux's sifakas. As we began to interpret the vocalisations and alarm calls of the animals around us, we learned to live beyond the immediacy of our senses. We perceived the meaning of the honks, blabbers and bleats that echoed across the savannah, and then we went further – we began replicating these calls, taking other species' speech onto our tongue.

'As skilful mimics, we first learned to emulate the complex roars, grunts, rhythms, melodies and harmonies that we experienced in our respective habitats,' Bernie Krause, the world's leading expert in natural sound, explains. 'The mimicry helped us to play it safe; there was little room for error in our attunement with life around us ... The soundscapes of the forests and plains signalled where food was (or wasn't) ... the biophonies also served as an aural GPS, signals that guided us to remote locations under the cover of total darkness and through the densest foliage with extraordinary precision.'[7]

Vocal mimesis helped us to communicate in disguise, reducing the risk of being detected while scavenging or foraging. Stalking through long grass, approaching a kill site, we could signal one another, and the hyenas gnawing at the bones would not recognise our approach. Spying a pride of lions on the horizon, we could issue clicks and chirrups as a warning, and the lions would not realise that the voice belonged to a vulnerable primate.

These vocalisations were accompanied by imitative gestures – baring teeth to indicate a predator, flapping arms to suggest a bird – that became more expressive over time. Ronald Englefield has proposed that a 'primitive language of movement' arose prior to articulate speech. In this language, 'Actions of animals may be imitated, either with the whole body or by movements of the arms or fingers ... there may be an attempt to imitate not only the action but the appearance of the animal. And, of course, where animals are concerned, the imitative action can be reinforced by imitative noises.'[8]

Merlin Donald, a cognitive neuroscientist and an expert

on human evolution, has characterised over a million years of our evolution as 'mimetic culture'. This period began with the evolution of *Homo erectus*, and was defined by mimetic enactment, our ancestors harnessing their bodies to imitate animals and performatively represent features of the natural world. Such mimetic communication was essential to our survival. It meant that we could pool our knowledge, share and reflect upon our experiences, and re-present and rehearse scenarios involving humans and animals, including scavenging and hunting. 'Mimetic skill results in the sharing of knowledge, without every member of that group having to reinvent that knowledge,' Donald explains.

Mimetic communication is employed by contemporary hunters, in situations which are broadly analogous to those our early human ancestors would have faced. The !Kung of the Kalahari, for example, stalk their prey in silence and communicate with hand signals, holding two curved fingers erect to signify the curved horns of the hartebeest and a fist with fingers spread wide to signify the broader horns of the wildebeest. Hunters contort their bodies to resemble the animals in question by leaning over, bending their arms and torso, and they call to one another with animal cries. 'When hunters lose sight of one another, they signal each other by prearranged birdlike calls that act as homing signals but do not alarm the animals.'[9]

Back in camp, !Kung hunters talk endlessly about the creatures they encountered during the day's exertions, recounting memorable episodes, sharing knowledge and experiences, and make plans for future expeditions. Archaeologist Derek Hodgson and neuropsychologist Patricia A. Helvenston suggest our early human ancestors would have behaved in a similar manner, conversing and sharing their experiences, communicating via mimesis instead of spoken language:

With the increased development of mimetic culture, shared aspects of the hunt could now be re-presented around the communal hearth. Enhanced voluntary control over emotional expression would have enabled hominins to recreate and re-present emotional hunting situations after the fact (with voluntarily produced vocalisations, gestures and facial expressions) ... the successful hunter, on returning to the campsite, might have re-enacted how animals were stalked and despatched ... Such presentations, accompanied by strong positive affective reactions, would have served to strengthen the social bonds of the participants.[10]

There were other secrets to our survival. We were larger than our hominid predecessors and we lived in bigger groups. We were more sociable and more cooperative, and we could access a more varied diet. We might have been able to group together and launch counterattacks against the predators who would prey on us, and these might have evolved into aggressive scavenging and hunting. But mimesis – including the imitation and enactment of animals – is likely to have been a key element of our behavioural repertoire.

Seen through this lens, the narrative of human evolution is subtly altered. We might think of our ancestors as grunting brutes, savage and ruthless apes. Or we might think of them as burgeoning scientists and engineers, characterised by technical skill and a nascent aptitude for reason. We rarely think of them as they were: prancing as bison and prowling as leopards; cawing as carrion birds and braying as zebras. In the beginning, we flapped our featherless arms. We honked, hooted, puffed, barked and screamed. We danced, taking the rhythms of animal bodies into our own. We became human by mimetically becoming animal, and in these animal enactments we find the roots of our aptitude for empathy, the conception of the meat paradox.

The skull is unique among the bones of the human body in that its growth is not genetically determined but responsive to the expansion of the brain. As the brain grows, it presses against the inside of the skull, imprinting the interior with its shape and form. Such internal casts in the cranial vault are called 'endocasts' and they are discernible in skulls preserved in the archaeological record. These archaic endocasts were formed either by natural processes, as when a skull fills with sediment that solidifies, or by artificial processes, as in the laboratory when cast with latex. Scientists have studied them to understand the external topography of our ancestors' brains.

In 1983, neuro-anthropologist Dean Falk observed a novel imprint pattern on a two-million-year-old hominid endocast. The pattern was absent from earlier hominid skulls but present in later human endocasts, indicating an evolutionary adaptation associated with uniquely human modes of cognition. The elaboration was in the left frontal lobe, in a part of the brain known as Broca's area. Falk initially thought the altered imprint might be associated with a capacity for speech, as Broca's area is known to play a role in speech in modern humans, but Broca's area is now understood to be involved in a broader suite of functions, including as the seat of the mirror neuron system.[11]

Mirror neurons were first observed in macaque monkeys. Researchers studying the macaques' brains noticed a set of neurons that fired both when a movement was made by the monkey and when the monkey observed the same movement made by the researcher. These neurons, located in ventral premotor area F5 in the macaque, were named 'mirror neurons' because of the mirroring effect they implied. Subsequent research has found an analogous system in the human brain, centred upon Broca's area. The human mirror system is thought to underpin our ability to imitate and communicate, with research demonstrating that when we observe the action of another individual, resonances of it ripple through our neural network.

'Watching someone grasping a cup of coffee, biting an apple, or kicking a football activates the same neurons of our brain that would fire if we were doing the same,' neuroscientist Vittorio

Gallese explains. Mirror neurons provide the neural substrate that associates *action observation* with *action execution*, providing the foundation for imitative behaviour. 'The mirror neuron system in humans is directly involved in imitation of simple movements, imitation learning of complex skills, in the perception of communicative actions, and in the detection of action intentions.'[12]

Our ancestors' mimetic skill cannot be explained through mirror neurons alone, for the macaque monkey possesses a mirror system but is not a good imitator or communicator. Neuroscientist Michael Arbib has suggested that the human system underwent progressive stages of elaboration, ultimately enabling mimetic communication, 'a manual-based communication system' among our early human ancestors. Arbib proposes that the evolution of the first early humans 'coincided with the transition from a mirror system used only for action recognition and imitation to a human-like mirror system used for intentional communication'. He describes this gestural communication as 'pantomime'.[13]

Mithen takes a similar view, proposing that the elaboration of Broca's area in early human endocasts indicates an advanced capacity for mimesis, which our ancestors would have employed to imitate and enact animal movements and vocalisations.

A great deal of excitement has surrounded the discovery of the human mirror system. One critic has described mirror neurons as 'the most hyped concept in neuroscience', responding to Vilayanur Subramanian Ramachandran's prediction that 'mirror neurons will do for psychology what DNA did for biology: they will provide a unifying framework and help explain a host of mental abilities that have hitherto remained mysterious and inaccessible to experiments.' Ramachandran has labelled mirror neurons 'Gandhi neurons', suggesting that they are the key to empathetic and compassionate behaviour. This might be an overly bold claim, but it seems that mirror neurons *are* involved in empathy, though they are not the whole story. It also seems that the mirror system plays a critical role in the meat paradox, shaping our empathic response to certain species.[14]

'Why are chickens so far down in the pecking order for moral concern?' asks animal welfare scientist Caroline Spence. 'What is it about our attitude to chickens that encourages us to disregard their widespread maltreatment?'

Chickens are the most consumed animal on the planet, as we have observed. They are intensively reared to the detriment of their wellbeing. They have been mistreated in many cultures for many centuries, and they are exploited in the cruellest way by the billion today. Why don't we care more about chickens? The answer, Spence says, might relate to the functioning of our mirror system. In our relationship with farmed animals, we should 'consider how our own cognitive mechanisms influence our judgements about how intelligent an animal is'.

Research has found that we empathise more readily with phylogenetically similar animals (animals whose bodies resemble ours). We identify more closely with animals such as gorillas, white rhinos and common cranes, than with iguanas, catfish and beetles. A 2018 study found that the more we attend to the anthropomorphic characteristics of animals, the more we care about them. When encouraged to think of animals as 'human-like', we express more moral inclusivity towards them, and we are more concerned about their needs and rights. Similarly, when we see animals in cages and in distress, our bodies react more strongly (for example, by sweating more in empathetic concern) when the animal is phylogenetically similar. The suffering of a monkey elicits a stronger response than the suffering of a pigeon.[15]

These biases are partly shaped by our mirror system. Our mirror neurons, Spence explains, 'are automatically activated when we watch both humans and other animals carry out similar actions to achieve an assumed goal'. They are activated, specifically, by goal-directed behaviour. Researchers have established that when we see a rat reach out to grasp a lump of cheese, our brain is activated using similar mechanisms to those we use to interpret the behaviour of a human performing the same action. This does not mean that we automatically empathise with the rat, but we recognise that the rat is minded and intentional, in the category of beings with whom we might empathise.

'Moving like a chicken might therefore be a major disadvantage when you're being compared to other farmyard inhabitants such as cows or pigs,' Spence says, commenting on this research. 'Despite spending time observing them, it would be harder for our brains to automatically "see" their behaviour and use it as a basis for assuming some semblance of brainpower.'

The movements of a chicken – their strut, cluck, peck and jilt – are so unlike those of a human body that we struggle to recognise their behaviour as goal-directed. Our mirror system is not activated as it might be when we see a chimpanzee reach for a piece of fruit or a dog pawing at our leg, and we are consequently less predisposed to see the chicken as minded and intentional, a being with whom we might empathise.[16]

Fish are at a similar disadvantage. The extraordinary cognitive and emotional capacities of fish have been established by science, but when we see a fish gawping or flapping, gulping or gasping, our empathy is muted, for we struggle to perceive their behaviour as intentional. Their bodies are too alien, their movements too strange, the ribbon of a fish's physique does not stir our mirror system in the same way that a bear pawing through the snow might. (This bias is compounded by our use of language, at least in English. *Fish*. The word is both singular and plural, as though they are all the same, multitudinous and lacking in individuality. The word is both a noun and a verb. A fish. To fish. We go fishing (killing), as though to be hauled from the water, hooked through the face or trawled from the depths has been written into each fish's identity, their meaning and their destiny.)

Why do we eat so many chickens, treating them so poorly? There are many reasons, from the power of the poultry industry to the psychological processes of detachment and dissociation which characterise our response to the meat paradox. But the wiring of our brains also plays a role. This neurological bias against dissimilar bodies perhaps helps to explain why rising levels of public concern for animal welfare have translated into ever-escalating chicken consumption. The more we care about animals, the more we take comfort in swapping red meat for white. Chickens are also the most consumed animal among ex-vegans and ex-vegetarians. We are possessed of an anti-bird (and anti-fish) prejudice, rooted in the functioning of our mirror system, the origins of which return us to the African savannah.

Endocasts also reveal increases in the volume of the brain relative to the body throughout human evolution, a process known as encephalisation. The fossil record shows that in the 7 million years since the human lineage split from that of the chimpanzee, our brains have tripled in size, with most of this growth occurring in the past 2 million years. Our hominid ancestors of 3 million years ago had skulls with internal volumes of between 400 and 550 cubic centimetres (broadly comparable to chimpanzees today). By 1.6 million years ago, *Homo erectus* had evolved a brain with a volume of roughly 900 cubic centimetres. A further growth spurt in the past 500,000 years resulted in modern humans having brain sizes of between 1200 and 1700 cubic centimetres, with an average of 1350.

It is likely that animal foods fuelled this explosive brain growth. The contribution of animal versus plant foods to encephalisation is still being debated, but most scholars agree that it's unlikely the human brain would have evolved had we remained herbivores.

The debate hinges, in part, on whether animal foods were required for the provision of the critical omega-3 fatty acids needed for the development of larger and more complex neural networks. Plants do not produce fatty acids longer than an eighteen-carbon chain, whereas most animals can elongate the chain, producing long-chain varieties. Two long-chain omega-3 fatty acids, eicosapentaenoic acid (EPA) and docosahexaenoic acid (DHA), are critically important for foetal development and human brain functioning, and our bodies cannot produce them directly, meaning a dietary source is needed. EPA and DHA are best consumed in oily fish such as salmon, shellfish, wild game, and grass-fed or organic meat and dairy, but we can also consume their precursor, α-linolenic acid (ALA), in plants such as walnuts, linseed (flax) and green leafy vegetables. ALA can be converted into EPA and then DHA in the human body, but the conversion is inefficient, especially for DHA. Most scholars agree that increased intake of these fatty acids was a key factor in hominid encephalisation – were our ancestors obtaining them from animal foods as EPA and DHA, or were they eating lots of ALA in plants and then converting it?

There are compelling reasons to think that animal foods were the source. Despite the relative abundance of ALA in nature, limited access to preformed DHA and other brain-selective minerals seems to place an important metabolic constraint on brain evolution. Encephalisation among mammals is rare. Only two species have brains that are substantially larger than those of the great apes – humans and dolphins. Dolphins are marine carnivores with a high intake of DHA and other key minerals, while humans are vulnerable to impaired brain development in diets that exclude animal foods and lack these minerals. Iodine deficiency, for example, is present in about 20 per cent of people worldwide, primarily affecting those living away from shores and water sources, without access to fish or seafood. As populations move away from the oceans, they also become more susceptible to depression and other forms of mental ill health. There is a 65-fold higher risk of major depression in the countries with the lowest levels of fish and seafood consumption compared with countries with the highest levels, and a 30-fold higher risk for bipolar disease among those consuming negligible amounts of seafood. These trends betray our ancient evolutionary origins. The first visual and nervous systems evolved in the early proto-ocean, harnessing vitamin A as a photon-sensitive molecule and DHA as the primary fatty acid constituent of the emergent system. Both molecules would have been present in abundance, having been produced by the algae which had dominated the ancient oceans for some 2.5 billion years. DHA has remained the key structural feature of the visual and nervous system throughout the subsequent 600 million years of our evolution. As you read these words, it is DHA which structures your retina, the light-sensitive layer of tissue in your eye which translates the image of the page into electrical neural impulses in the visual cortex; it is DHA which configures the visual cortex and the encompassing cerebral cortex in your brain, where these words come alive with meaning. Research has established that decreased brain DHA levels are associated with an increased corticosterone stress response and depression, as well as developmental issues among infants and cognitive decline among older people. Our sensitivity to DHA depletion attests to the importance of animal foods in the evolution of our brains.

The archaeological record supports the hypothesis that animal foods fuelled encephalisation. The remains of fish have been found at several archaic sites, including Olduvai Gorge in Tanzania, dating to between 1.5 and 2 million years ago. Most were catfish, which were easily accessible in the shallows of lakes and rivers and could be captured with little or no technology. At the Koobi Fora Formation, a site 1.95 million years old in northern Kenya, there is evidence of butchery of both terrestrial and aquatic animals, with hominids at the site scavenging antelope, hippo and rhino carcasses, and foraging aquatic animals such as turtles and fish. With the evolution of our species, the consistent exploitation of fish and seafood becomes more obvious, the consumption of crabs, crayfish, lobsters, mussels, oysters, cockles, pippies, scallops and abalone being evidenced by shell middens. Some scholars believe brains and marrows from terrestrial herbivores were also key. Fossil evidence shows that fatty tissues and organs were being scavenged from large herbivores before the evolution of *Homo erectus*, and modelling has affirmed that these could have provided an adequate source of DHA, alongside iodine and other minerals from fish.[17]

The evolution of larger brains had several important consequences for our evolution, including the requirement for an earlier birth. There is only so large a skull that a woman can fit between her pelvis. Foetal brains are also energetically expensive, placing demands on mothers that become intolerable past a certain point. Our big brains mean that human babies must be born early in their gestation, with brains that are less than 30 per cent of adult brain size. (A human foetus would have to undergo a gestation period of eighteen to twenty-one months instead of the usual nine to be born at a neurological development stage comparable to that of a chimpanzee.) We are consequently born helpless, wholly dependent on our parents, and profoundly vulnerable.[18]

Primate mothers rarely put their babies down, but within a few months, chimpanzee and bonobo babies can cling to their mother's fur as she moves about, freeing her from carrying them directly. Early human mothers would have had a much harder time. Though we are born early, our brains are so large at birth that we are unable to support the weight of our own heads, and we take far longer than other primates to gain control of our posture and locomotion. Our ancestors had relinquished their ancestral body hair, and they had not yet learned to craft slings or carrying devices. Lugging a one-year-old around all day would have been just as physically demanding for a *Homo erectus* mother 500,000 years ago as it would be for a mother today.

The demands of everyday life would have meant that it was sometimes necessary to put the baby down. A mother must sometimes knap a stone, butcher a carcass, pluck some fruit, forage a catfish, or simply have a rest. Early human infants would have disliked this separation no less than modern human or primate infants, who cry and hoot for their mother's attention. Some scholars believe that we evolved a novel mode of communication to manage this separation, 'a disembodied extension of the mother's cradling arms'. Early human mothers substituted for the loss of physical contact when they put their babies down by retaining eye contact, and by singing and voicing prosodic utterances. They learned to communicate in 'motherese'.

Motherese (or 'infant-directed speech') describes the spontaneous way in which parents and caregivers communicate with infants in every human society. Through vocalisations characterised by exaggerated vowels, repetition, alterations in pitch, and a relatively slow tempo, coupled with facial expressions and gestures such as raised eyebrows and smiles, the mother elicits a shared emotional state in her infant. In freeing the mother's hands for other tasks, motherese would have been of survival benefit in the savannah, and it catalysed the evolution of our empathy. In motherese, infant and mother train their attention upon one another, entering 'the temporal world and feeling state of the other'. In our species, this entrainment is progressively extended beyond our mother, as we empathetically enter the feeling states of those around us.[19]

There are two broad dimensions to our faculty for empathy, cognitive and affective, one concerned with thought and the other with feeling. The cognitive dimension allows us to infer the intentions and mental states of others. We note postures, behaviours, tones of voice and other clues, translating them into an understanding of the mind of the other. This dimension is rooted in our mirror system, which helps us recognise intentional and goal-oriented behaviour – the system which evolved to facilitate mimetic communication in the African savannah. The affective dimension of empathy is more immediate. It is spontaneous and involuntary, involving a form of empathic resonance. We participate in the emotions of the other directly; we feel what they feel, reverberating with them; or our emotions are roused in response to theirs. The emotional dimension emerges as mother and infant engage in motherese, engendering in the neonate an attentive regard for their mother's face.

As newborn babies, only minutes old, we recognise and respond to face-like stimuli such as two round blobs over a horizontal line, and we are especially responsive to our mother's face. Given a choice, we will gaze for longer at a picture of our mother than at an image of a female stranger. We also begin to mimic our mother's facial expressions minutes after birth. We are born 'prolific imitators', child psychologist Andrew Meltzoff observes. Within an hour, we begin sticking our tongue out, opening our mouth, puckering our lips and bending our fingers, as we observe the same action in others. This impulse to imitate grows more pronounced through development. After a few months, we will imitate in bodily movements the vocal rhythms of our parents or caregivers, moving our limbs with the cadence and canter of their speech. At nine months old, we become sufficiently adept at imitation to recognise when other people are imitating us: we pay these people more attention, smile at them more frequently, and display 'testing behaviours', acting abnormally to elicit a response.

By the age of two, this impulse to imitate has flourished into a capacity for role play and enactment. We pretend to be a doctor, a horse, a train, this role play contributing to our cognitive development. Imitation 'begets an understanding of other minds', Meltzoff explains. In role play, we are honing our aptitude for perspective taking, imaginatively projecting ourselves into the mind of another. Research has shown that children who engage in role play with their peers are more adept at inferring the psychological states of others, compared to children who engage in solitary play. Four-year-olds who have invented an imaginary character are more skilled at interpreting what other people believe. Autistic children, who characteristically have impairments in understanding other minds and empathy, show earlier deficiencies in imitation and role play.[20]

This role play often involves animals. We play as lions and

bears, we pretend to be sharks and eagles, enacting behaviours and encounters typical of the species. In various hunting cultures, these games have a pedagogical character. Among the Inuit, for example, children will take turns playing as prey or hunter, galumphing as a walrus or squirming as a seal, while another child stalks them. In our society, animal games have been largely displaced by digital games, but residues of animal play are found in 'piggyback' rides, games of 'sardines' or 'leapfrog' or 'bulldog' or 'copycat'. (Parents, meanwhile, engage in gruff nuzzling, growling as bears and providing 'bearhugs'.) Through such role play, we extend our perspective taking beyond our species. We learn to see the world through eyes that are not our own.[21]

Both cognitive and affective aspects of empathy entwine from a young age into an intuitive ethical sense, which is readily extended towards animals. In an elegant display of this ethical sense, several four-year-olds were introduced to a toy bunny in a basket. The psychologist told each child in turn that the bunny was afraid of some animals but not others, and they presented the children with several scenarios. A zebra arrived in the basket and the bunny began trembling with fear. An elephant arrived, and the bunny invited him in. Then the elephant and the zebra both arrived in the basket together, and the bunny trembled with fear again. The children understood the relationships that each animal had with the others. They not only understood that the bunny was afraid of the zebra, they were anxious to help, rushing to remove the offending animal unprompted by the researcher. Both cognitive and affective empathy were engaged, as the children inhabited the perspective of each animal and instinctively 'resonated' with the trembling bunny.[22]

Omnivory fuelled encephalisation. It was animal foods that provided the nutrition and energy for the expansion and increased complexity of our brains. Larger brains forced an earlier birth, and this led to the evolution of motherese, the emotional entrainment which characterises mother–infant relationships. With larger and more complex brains, we imitated our parents and caregivers, we played as animals. As adults we engaged in mimetic communication, bending our bodies to imitate and enact the creatures that lived alongside us in our environment. We are the product of this deep history. We are born into this world primed for imitation and empathy, intuitively mapping our body onto other bodies. We do not need to pretend that we evolved as herbivores to affirm the importance of our empathy. Can you see how deep the roots of the meat paradox reach?

As infants, our participation in the face of the other is immediate. To smile is to feel happy. To feel happy is to smile. We take on the facial expression of our mother, frowning when she frowns, laughing when she laughs, and we feel something of what she feels. 'I live in the facial expression of the other, as I feel him living in mine,' writes philosopher Maurice Merleau-Ponty. As we grow, and consciousness calcifies around us, we come to inhabit an ego, a surer sense of self, but we are never atomised. We remain 'open', our body a bundle of sensing tissue, a fleshed skeleton tuning fork. If killing can be traumatic, even the killing of an animal, it is because we live beyond ourselves, in the face and body of the other. The violence we enact upon them, we enact upon ourselves.

We looked at one another across the stun cage.

Back in the slaughterhouse, and she looked at me as I looked at her.

She was reluctant to step inside, but she braved it, taking a nervous step, a testing hoof to see what might happen. My mirror system stirred, recognising this as an intentional act by a minded being. There were clues in her presentation which betrayed her emotions. The tenseness of her muscles as she paused, uncertain whether to continue. The careful placing of the second hoof. My body was reading these through an inherited faculty, a subtle sense, in a language that I cannot remember having been taught. I watched her eyes explore the metal box, inquisitive and saturated with feeling, and it was obvious that the cow was a qualitatively different entity to the metal bars that surrounded her. I did not need to think these thoughts for their consequence to press upon me. As she looked up and finally stepped inside, my mirror system erupted in a blaze of recognition. She looked at me and I looked at her.

The door slid shut behind her.

The word 'trauma' has both a physiological and a psychological meaning, denoting a violence effected by an external agency, which can be a blow to the head as readily as the shock of emotional bereavement. Trauma is something that comes from outside the self, an interruption that strikes violently and without warning. As we look back at origins of the meat paradox, we see how we came to live beyond the surface of our skin, the primordial importance of the face, and the depth of the predicament we find ourselves in today. The slaughterman bent down, and two million years were folded into two short seconds. He pulled the trigger.

For a while I was unwell. I didn't sleep one night. Some part of me refused. I didn't sleep the next night either. It happened again. I slept one night out of five, and I experienced recurring bouts of insomnia for several months. I didn't know why I wasn't sleeping. I think I was burnt out. I had grown preoccupied with the elaborate funerary rites enacted upon the killing of a bear. I couldn't stop thinking of the ceremonialism of it, the tribute paid. The pipe passed over the body. The beating of the drum. I could see with uneasy clarity that these rituals had been performed not out of cultural habit but psychological necessity. What ritual had I enacted? The slaughterman had carried over her head and hung it upon that hook dangling before me, and I had shot a bolt into her lifeless brain. Something refused sleep.

Something forced me awake. One day, in the middle of it all, I decided to seek out the Lion Man.

I went back to the Natural History Museum. I returned to the Human Evolution gallery, to those stone tools and broken bones. I stood for a while before a butchered rhino skull, 500,000 years old and recovered from Boxgrove in England. I gazed at the Clacton spear, the oldest preserved hunting weapon in the world. I went to find that hybrid statuette, and I returned there repeatedly, drawn by some magnetism to stand in the presence of the *Löwenmensch*.

The people who crafted the statuette are known as the Aurignacians. They lived between 43,000 and 26,000 years ago, and they were like us. They were members of our species, physiologically and psychologically no different to anyone alive today. We picture them stalking bison and aurochs through clumps of pine, clad in furs and clutching spears. We imagine them on the northern plains, tracking deer across the expanse. They were hunters, specks on a vast landscape of deep river valleys, mountains and ice-blown plains. They were also accomplished craftspeople. They used mammoth ivory to carve pendants and figurines, typically portraying the largest and most powerful animals in their environment. Their carvings have a distinctive style, showing obvious facial features such as the mouth, ears and eyes, with the body well represented, but the extremities reduced or omitted. Some bear geometric patterns scratched onto the animal's anatomy: dots, curved lines, zigzags and other motifs. The Lion Man is the earliest of their carvings and displays these geometric patterns, his left arm marked with slanting parallel lines. 'The Lion Man is both an animal and a human at the same time, the earliest known such figure in the world,' anthropologist Brian Fagan writes. 'He epitomizes the fluid boundary that separated the Aurignacians from their prey.'[23]

That boundary has not always been fluid. While our early human ancestors employed mimesis to communicate with one another, imitating and enacting the creatures that inhabited their world, they did not experience the blurring of identity that a modern human might. They did not feel that they were transforming into their prey, as the Yukaghir hunter might when stalking an elk, and they did not perceive the animals they killed to be 'persons', as hunters in many indigenous cultures do today. 'My view of early human mimesis is that it did not involve "thinking animal" in the sense of imagining or believing that they were becoming the animals they were imitating. In this respect, it might have been quite different from the imitation of animals undertaken by modern hunter-gatherers,' Steven Mithen explains. 'My reason for this lies in the structure of their minds.'

Our early human ancestors possessed 'modular' minds, Mithen says. Their thinking was compartmentalised. They were socially intelligent, and skilled at tool making, but their social and technical intelligences evolved as distinct mental modules. Like blades in a Swiss Army knife, one intelligence performed one function and the other intelligence another. They were consequently incapable of harnessing their skill as craftsmen for social expression. They forged stone tools, but they did not make jewellery, body adornments or sculptures, as all modern peoples do. It was not possible for them to do so. Similarly, early humans possessed intimate knowledge of the animals they consumed, including knowledge of their behaviour and anatomies, but they did not use this knowledge to create specialised hunting weapons. They did not create one weapon for an ibex and another for a bison. Modern hunting peoples do exactly this, combining their technical intelligence with their animal intelligence to produce bespoke weaponry.

The modular structure of the early human mind also prohibited them from empathising with their prey. 'In my book *The Prehistory of the Mind*, I argued that it was only with modern humans, *Homo sapiens*, that we began extending human feelings and emotions to animals,' Mithen tells me. 'This was because of a change in cognition that I called "cognitive fluidity". Prior to that and in other types of humans, such as Neanderthals, the human and animal worlds appear to have been much more distinct from each other, and I suspect that animal empathy was lacking.'

Our early human ancestors lived in socially complex groups and it's likely that they were empathetic with one another. They experienced the emotional entrainment characteristic of modern empathy, first in the mother–infant relationship and then with the wider band, and they were adept at perspective-taking, understanding the intentions and mental states of their fellows. But they did not extend these aptitudes outwards, towards other animals. Their mimesis of animals was 'more prosaic in nature: it was concerned with physical imitation alone, as a means to communicate information about the natural world'. Mithen suggests early humans can be characterised as having the capacity for *simile*, they could be 'like' an animal, but not for *metaphor* – they could not 'become' an animal, and, by extension, an animal could not be perceived as a 'person'.

That changed with the evolution of our species, *Homo sapiens*. We evolved a new form of thinking, new neural circuits that added cohesion across cognitive domains. This new form of thought was probably made possible by spoken language. Speech granted us the ability to think in more joined-up and flexible ways, merging one mode of intelligence with another. Our mental modules fused, creating a 'cognitively fluid' mind.[24]

The consequences of this cognitive fluidity are written in the archaeological record. As our species arrives on the scene, we find evidence of jewellery and body adornments, beads and shell necklaces, as our technical intelligence and social intelligence were combined for the first time. We started making complex hunting weapons, fusing our animal intelligence with our technical knowhow. And – crucially – our social and our animal intelligences began to merge. For the first time, we began to intuit human-like thoughts and emotions in the animals we hunted, perceiving 'animal-persons' among the mammoths and reindeer of the tundra. We began to identify more closely with other species. We could not help but do so, for we had been primed by our evolution. For more than a million years, we had bent our bodies into animal forms, taking their calls and cries onto our tongue. We had trained our attention on the creatures that surrounded us, studying them intently. We had enacted animal encounters around the campfire, we had danced as animals, and we had played as animals as children. But now, something extraordinary was afoot. As we stalked bison and danced as reindeer, our minds were filled with intimations of human–animal metamorphoses. As we thrust the spear into the horse's neck, our bodies recoiled in empathic response; we watched the fire dying in the animal's eyes, and we felt the growl of dissonance, the demand reaching out to take hold. It is sometimes said that 'meat made us human'. This is incorrect. *Metaphor* made us human, and our newly evolved aptitude for metaphor transformed our relationship with meat.

The Lion Man is the first known expression of this new mode of metaphorical cognition. In this statuette, we find the earliest material manifestation of the modern mind in full cognitive fluidity, evidence of our ancestors' immersion in the meat paradox. The Lion Man's hybrid form embodies the paradox. Our newfound capacity for empathy with animals had made us the most dangerous predator in the environment, no less than the lion, but it had also rendered us the most conflicted. Now we could inhabit the perspective of our prey, as hunters do today, imaginatively projecting ourselves into the skin of the creature we hunted, becoming bison, becoming bear, but the same act of empathic projection brought the personhood of our prey into view, in all its ethical consequence.[25]

Plagued by a nascent sense of dissonance, disturbed by the abrupt and bewildering perception that meat might involve murder, torn between our omnivory and our empathy, we sought release. We told stories which helped us make sense of the new and catastrophic rift that had opened in our consciousness. We devised rituals that helped to assuage the ache and tension of our unprecedented evolutionary predicament. We began to craft images. We started to create art.

The Lion Man is the earliest known representational sculpture in the archaeological report, among the very first works of art. He is far from the last. Shortly after crafting the Lion Man, the Aurignacians began to paint and draw upon rock surfaces. They entered remote caverns, clutching tallow lamps and skins of ink, intent on leaving their mark upon the walls. For tens of thousands of years, our ancestors painted animals in the darkness of caves, moved by the meat paradox to mount a ritual and artistic response. I needed to see them.

8

CAVE

'We do not know what these markings mean, but they are found in great numbers, in hundreds of caves, often in proximity to the animals.'

Our guide had paused beside a panel daubed in red and black. He gestured and we peered, and by criss-crossing torchlight we saw them. The markings had been carefully arranged. There were two horizontal rows of black dots. Several claviform (club-shaped) figures. A vertical line of red dashes, which resembled a crudely drawn spine. Four lines slashed across the centre of the arrangement, like the clawing of a bear.

'The same markings are found again and again,' our guide said. 'The same figures and the same forms. We do not know what they represent.'

We were a long way from daylight, a long walk from the mouth of the cave, from the tang of pine and the splash of the Vicdessos River, sinuous in the valley below. This was Grotte de Niaux, a cave-complex cut into the northern foothills of the Pyrenees in the Ariège *département* of south-western France, and we were half a kilometre deep.

'Once you are in, you cannot return,' our guide had warned

us before we stepped inside, 'not until the journey is complete. Some of it will be challenging. The cave is more than two kilometres long, and there are many branching chambers and paths that lead away in different directions. Please do not stray from the path. Please do not touch the walls.'

We entered through an angular tunnel carved into the rear of a high cavern; single file, slow descent. The air that rose from the chamber below was cold and odourless and mute, a gulp of darkness.

The interior of the cave was immediately disorienting. The walls and ceilings were stacked at unlikely angles, their surfaces glinting with calcite, deposits of speleothem that erupted periodically into cones and pendants, ribbons and mounds, stalagmites and stalactites. Alien architectures. We walked on, and it felt like being slowly swallowed. Down the oesophagus, a black tunnel slicked with rivulets of trickling water, along emptied riverbeds, through a narrow aperture cut through ancient roof fall, towards the cave's vital organs.

'It seems that these paintings were placed here for a reason,' our guide said, as we gazed at the perplexing figures. 'We do not know what that reason was, but the markings perhaps signify that we will soon arrive at the main chamber.'

Niaux is famed for its paintings and drawings, which were crafted in the Upper Palaeolithic between 12,000 and 14,000 years ago. The images adorning its walls are ancient, but there are far older paintings in other caves. Our ancestors began painting in caves across Europe almost 40,000 years ago, and they maintained the tradition for close to 30,000 years.

'There is no greater archaeological enigma than the subterranean art of Upper Palaeolithic western Europe,' one scholar observes. 'Anyone who has crouched and crawled underground along a narrow, absolutely dark passage for more than a kilometre, slid along mud banks and waded through dark lakes and hidden rivers to be confronted, at the end of such a hazardous journey, by a painting of an extinct woolly mammoth or a powerful, hunched bison will never be quite the same again. Muddied and exhausted, the explorer will be gazing at the limitless *terra incognita* of the human mind.'

These images are important, but we cannot know for certain what they mean. Palaeolithic art signals the 'Big Bang' of human cultural evolution, Steven Mithen explains, our first full out-pouring of artistic and symbolic expression. The artworks are widely recognised as marking a 'coming of age' moment in the story of our species, evidence of full psychological and cultural maturity, but what are we to make of these strange creations? Why paint in the darkness of a cave?[1]

The motivation clearly had something to do with animals. Animals are the primary and often sole focus of Palaeolithic art. Across the full span of the European tradition, we know of thousands of animals in some two hundred caves, but there is not a single image that can be identified as portraying a mountain or a river, a tree or a man-made structure, a scene of domestic life, such a childbirth, a feast or a battle, or a celestial body, such as the sun, moon or stars. Human depictions are rare and are typically partial. There are several hybrid figures. Mostly, our ancestors painted large herbivores: bison, horse, aurochs, deer. They painted them fervently and with great devotion, overlaying one image atop another. They painted them with hallucinatory intensity or with naturalistic realism, and often with both. They etched crude figurines, and they collaborated to paint sophisti-cated murals that betray a fine-tuned aesthetic sensibility. 'We have learned nothing in twelve thousand years,' Pablo Picasso declared, upon departing from the cave at Lascaux.

The geometric markings often appear beside the animals or overlaying them. The same figures, again and again. Dots and dashes, zigzags and claviforms, grids and undulating lines. There are more than one hundred animals in Niaux, and a similar number of geometric markings. They appear to be strategi-cally arranged, positioned opposite one another, beside notable natural features, or framing the animal compositions. These markings have baffled cave art scholars. Why paint angular patterns beside images of mammoths and reindeer? Were these markings a primitive alphabet, incipient language? Were they symbolic? How was it possible that individuals living thousands of years apart, in different cultures, speaking different tongues, painted the same abstract forms upon distant cave walls?

'What do *you* think the markings mean?' someone asked.

Our guide was silent for a moment.

The walls leant in.

'The urge to make images seems to be a human universal,' he said. 'That is all I know.'

I grew up, as all children do, surrounded by images of animals. There were cartoon critters: Tom and Jerry, Bugs Bunny; stuffed animals – chimpanzees and koalas; animals in books – Peter Rabbit and Squirrel Nutkin; animated creatures – Baloo and Shere Khan; animals for breakfast, tigers on cereal packets; talking purple dinosaurs on the television; puppets and animatronics – Yoda and Ludo. But among all these, one image struck me with distinct resonance. It was an unusual image, more compelling than the others.

We attended church each Sunday, the whole family, the same church. It was a Victorian structure, I believe, though a chapel had been on the site for at least 700 years and had been updated over the centuries. Nave and aisle. Tower and steeple. I remember the wooden beams and the high rafters, the pipe organ and the colourful windows. On the reverse of the chancel arch, half hidden from view, there was a faded painting of a pelican.

The pelican had been painted in gold upon a red background. She was perched on her nest, and her feathered neck was bent, her wings spread. Her head was haloed, and she was pecking at a wound in her side. She was opening her flesh with her great, pointed beak. Three chicks were in the nest below, gazing up at her, their wings spread, mouths ajar. The pelican was feeding her chicks from her body. Blood dripped from the wound into their reaching mouths.

In the *Physiologus*, a Christian text written in the second century by an unknown author in Alexandria in Egypt, the pelican is presented as an allegory for Jesus' crucifixion, recalling the Last Supper where he shared wine with his followers, and his subsequent wounding by a Roman spear upon the cross – his blood poured out to provide spiritual sustenance for believers.

Centuries later, the image took on an altered meaning among the alchemists, those oddball scholars of mind and metal. The pelican lent its name to a circulatory distillation vessel in the alchemists' laboratory. The vessel had long, curving side-arms which fed condensed vapours back into the body of the vessel as it was heated over a flame – the side-arms recalling the neck of the bird bent towards its body. The alchemists thought of the pelican as both allegory and apparatus. The circling of vapour within the vessel was at once a chemical process and a process of the soul. The steam that rose and condensed in the throat of the pelican was purified – as emotions were refined by the process – and these waters would *drip, drip, drip* back into the body of the vessel, the anatomy of the alchemist.

Beneath these layers of meaning and association, there was perhaps a naturalistic observation. When pelicans feed their young, they will sometimes press their bills onto their chests to empty their throat pouches of food. When they do, it can look as though they are stabbing themselves.

'Come,' our guide said. 'We are almost there.'

It was a few days before Christmas, 1994. Three speleologists with an interest in archaeology – Jean-Marie Chauvet, Éliette Brunel Deschamps and Christian Hillaire – had crawled into a fissure in the Cirque d'Estre gorge, close to the Ardèche River in France. The opening was slight, measuring a mere thirty centimetres by eighty, and on the far side there was a narrow vestibule. The vestibule was unremarkable, but the explorers noticed a breeze emanating from a blocked duct at the rear of the space. They pulled the boulders away and discovered a vast chamber below. Having climbed down, they found evidence of animal habitation, including calcified bones and teeth, and depressions in the floor where bears had nested and hibernated. Suddenly Deschamps cried out. She had spied two red lines daubed across the wall. 'They have been here,' she called.

'We found ourselves in front of a rock wall covered entirely with red ochre drawings,' Chauvet remembers. 'The panel contained a mammoth with a long trunk, then a lion with red dots spattered around its snout in an arc, like drops of blood. We crouched on our heels, gazing at the cave wall, mute with stupefaction.'

They found further evidence of human activity deeper in the cave. Footprints on the floor, intact and undisturbed after so many years. Hearths that looked as though they had been extinguished only hours previously. Chauvet recalls that the three were 'seized by a strange feeling. Everything was so beautiful, so fresh, almost too much so. Time was abolished, as if tens of thousands of years that separated us from the producers of these paintings no longer existed.' In one chamber, they found a slab of rock hauled into the centre of the space. The skull of a cave bear had been placed upon it, as though upon an altar, its canine teeth hooked over the edge. More than thirty calcite-covered bear skulls had been arranged around the slab in deliberate configuration.

There were more than four hundred paintings and engravings spread over six chambers throughout the cave. Ghostly bears. A panther. Wild horses. An owl with head turned. Two rhinos with butting horns. Hoofing stags and ethereal mammoths. Some of the paintings were lavish in their detail. One panel showed an arrangement of nine lions and a reindeer beside a herd of seventeen rhinos. Another depicted a pride of sixteen lions in rapt pursuit of seven bison. Not far from the lions, on a rock protruding from the ceiling, there was a figure that appeared to be a human–bison hybrid. Scattering the walls, overlaying the animals, were geometric patterns and abstract forms.[2]

This was not the first painted cave to be discovered, but Chauvet (as the cave was named) was remarkable. The images were works of 'aesthetic mastery' and they were unusual in their focus. While large herbivores were the subject in most caves, the artists in Chauvet were preoccupied with powerful and dangerous animals, painting bears and rhinos, and seventy-five felines. 'Some of the lion paintings are very anthropomorphic, with a nose and human profile showing an empathy between the artists and these carnivores,' says Jean-Michel Geneste, the scientific director of the cave. 'They are painted completely differently from other animals in Chauvet.'[3]

The images were crafted across a 10,000-year period, with the oldest dating from 37,000 years ago. They were created by the Aurignacians, the people of the Lion Man.

Jean Clottes, an archaeology expert in the French Ministry of Culture, was called upon to verify the images, arriving a few days after their discovery. He was not disappointed. 'These were hidden masterpieces that nobody had laid eyes on for thousands and thousands of years, and I was the first specialist to see them,' he recalls. 'I had tears in my eyes.'

Clottes had recently begun working with archaeologist David Lewis-Williams, an expert in the rock art of the San people in southern Africa. Lewis-Williams had ventured a novel interpretation of Palaeolithic art, and the interpretation had captured Clottes' imagination. In 1996, two years after the discovery of Chauvet, the two scholars published the fruit of their collaboration, *The Shamans of Prehistory: Trance and Magic in the Painted Caves*. The key to understanding these ancient animal images, they said, lay in the geometric markings that so commonly accompanied them on the cave walls.[4]

Their interpretation had been inspired by Gerardo Reichel-Dolmatoff, the Colombian anthropologist who lived with the Tukano in the Amazon, participating in their yahé ceremony. Yahé is the Tukano's psychedelic brew, produced by simmering bundles of fresh *Banisteriopsis caapi* vine with the leaves of several other plants containing psychoactive molecules. *Banisteriopsis caapi* had been 'discovered' and named by British botanist Richard Spruce as he travelled through the Tukano's territory in 1853. (Spruce dutifully shipped a sample home to the Royal Botanic Gardens at Kew in London.) The name is taken from the Tukano, *caapi* deriving from *gahpí*, meaning 'placenta' or 'womb'. In Tukano, *yaheáse* means 'to ascend' or 'to levitate', with the name yahé alluding to the experience of ascending into a womb-like space. (Elsewhere in the Amazon, and more commonly in English, the brew is called ayahuasca, a Quechua word meaning 'vine of the soul'.)

Yahé elicits powerful physiological and psychological responses, including vomiting and 'visions' of great cultural significance to the Tukano. '[Yahé] visions are very colourful,' Reichel-Dolmatoff reports:

> After an initial tremor and the sensation of rushing winds, the drug produces a state of drowsiness during which the person concentrates with half-closed eyes on the luminous flashes and streaks which appear in his visual field. This first stage is characterised by the appearance of small, star-shaped or flower-shaped elements which flicker and float brilliantly against a dark background, in kaleidoscopic patterns ... Grid patterns, hexagons, zigzag lines and undulating lines, rapidly vibrating lines, eye-shaped motifs, many-coloured concentric circles or chains of dots slowly float by, combining and recombining in ever new patterns and changing colours.

As the experience intensifies, these geometric figures are transformed into 'iconic' images of great cultural significance to the Tukano, including animals, spirits and ancestors. 'This is a highly emotion-charged stage.' As the patterns evolve into more elaborate imagery, pent-up memories and emotions are released through the vision.[5]

The Tukano paint the geometric patterns perceived in the

first stage of their yahé ceremony on fabrics and rock faces, and they carve them onto their houses. Reichel-Dolmatoff collated these patterns, drawing them on numbered cards and consulting the Tukano. 'It soon became clear that the drawings contained individual variations of some twenty well-defined design motifs.' Reichel-Dolmatoff realised he had seen these motifs before. The Tukano's designs mirrored those drawn by volunteers dosed with LSD and psilocybin. They also mirrored those drawn by volunteers subject to electrical stimulation of the brain by researcher Max Knoll.[6]

These geometric forms are understood by scientists today to be 'entoptic phenomena', entoptic meaning 'originating inside the eye'. In normal circumstances, when light strikes the retina, cells called photoreceptors turn the light into electrical signals that fizzle through the optic nerve to the visual cortex in the brain, where they are turned into images. *We look. We see.* But in an altered state of consciousness – induced by drinking yahé, taking LSD or psilocybin, or via electrical stimulation of the brain in the laboratory – the perception can be reversed. The electrical signals fizzling into the visual cortex of the brain are *themselves* experienced as a visual percept. 'People in this condition are seeing the structure of their own brains,' Lewis-Williams explains.[7]

Lewis-Williams compared the Tukano's designs with the geometric markings found in Palaeolithic caves. They matched. The Tukano and the Palaeolithic artists were painting the same forms, the same recurring motifs. This led Lewis-Williams to a bold conclusion, which Clottes endorsed. Our ancestors – those who painted in caves – were tripping.

Clottes and Lewis-Williams propose that our ancestors entered caves to deliberately induce altered states of consciousness, intent on painting their visions upon the cave walls. 'In the first, or lightest, stage of trance people "see" geometric forms, such as dots, zigzags, grids, sets of parallel lines, nested curves, and meandering lines,' they explain. As the altered state deepens, these geometric forms evolve into iconic images of lions, bears, bison and deer. 'In a second stage recognized by the Tukano there is a diminution of these patterns and the slow formation of larger images,' they observe. 'They now perceive recognizable shapes of people, animals, and strange monsters.'

The Tukano's yahé visions revealed the neuropsychological context in which Palaeolithic art was created, the association between this ancient imagery and the functioning of the human nervous system. The Tukano might also help us understand the motivation of the image-makers. Our ancestors ventured into the darkness of the cave, Clottes and Lewis-Williams suggest, because, like the Tukano, they knew that the otherworld perceptible in the altered state was the realm of animal powers. They went to negotiate with those powers. They went seeking an encounter with Vaí-mahsë, the Master of Animals.

It was October and it was raining. Poet Clayton Eshleman and his wife Caryl were returning to their rented accommodation, a small stone cottage situated at the end of a dirt road near Les Eyzies in Dordogne, France. Through the blurred windscreen, they saw a young couple huddled at the side of the road. Hitchhikers. Eshleman steered the car to a halt and beckoned to them. *Gosh, thank you. Look at this rain! How fortuitous.* The hitchhikers clambered in, grinning, and voicing their thanks. It transpired that they were staying at a property a few kilometres away. The two couples were to be neighbours, for a few days at least. They decided to spend some time together.

The following afternoon the four set out into the woods, intent on foraging wild mushrooms. The day was clear, shafts of light spilled through the branches, and for several hours they walked here and there, eyes trained upon the scattered leaves and lichen below. It was good foraging. Cèpe after cèpe was added to their haul. Enjoying each other's company, they decided to dine together.

As they returned to the car, they passed a farmer on his tractor, and stopped him to ask about the cèpes. While the others showed the farmer the mushrooms – and learnt that over half were faux cèpes, inedible and poisonous – Eshleman turned back, retracing his steps to a scene just passed. 'Next to several large, mostly eaten *Amanita muscaria* were three field slugs, vibrating on their backs.' *Amanita muscaria* is a poisonous, psychedelic mushroom, containing the psychoactive compounds muscimol and ibotenic acid. 'There was no way to tell whether the slugs were in agony or ecstasy.'

A poem began to form in Eshleman's mind:

> *Three inch caramel-coloured field slug*
> *on its back, vibrating*
> *by the scraps of a big Amanita muscaria.*
> *It has eaten more than its size*
> *and now its true size in visionary trance*
> *makes me sad of my size –*
> *I can never eat enough of a higher order*
> *to trick the interior leper to the door,*
> *banish him – but what would remain if I were to*
> *become pure?*[8]

The poem edged into dark terrain, conjuring troubling imagery, and Eshleman was disturbed by his words, so much so that he decided not to show the poem to Caryl, who normally read everything he wrote. 'I sensed that I was moving towards something that would hurt me, not out of self-destructiveness, but as if I had been moved "on track" towards a harmed and initiated state.'

Eshleman had been on the verge of this initiated state for several years. His preoccupation with the painted caves had grown increasingly intense. He realised that no poet had ever steeped themselves in the imagery of the Palaeolithic. Archaeologists had studied the walls. Writers had put words to paper. Academics had proposed clever explanations. But no poet had committed their craft to the task. Eshleman was seeking 'saturation', hoping to enter the mind and imagination of the image-makers. He knew the endeavour was not without risk. 'Several people, including James Hillman, had warned me: You must be very careful when you are trying to induct prehistoric archetypes.' Hillman, the protégé of Carl Jung, had warned Eshleman that his quest might expose him to chaotic forces. The warning proved to be prescient.

'It's getting late.'

The fire was smouldering in the hearth, and the wine had all been drunk. The two couples had cooked and eaten together, talking and laughing as they dined on the edible cèpes.

'May I give you a ride home?'

The hitchhikers gladly accepted Eshleman's offer.

Back at their cottage, the young couple invited the poet to join them for a final glass of brandy. They said they would be leaving the next day. They also said there was a cave on the property, and they invited Eshleman to explore it with them.

Eshleman paused, brandy in hand. He had told the young couple of his fascination for painted caves, his preoccupation with Palaeolithic imagery. But he was only really interested in *painted* caves, not in caves per se. He politely declined.

They were insistent. They cajoled and corralled him.

And so, Eshleman recounts, 'a little after midnight, with one flashlight between us, we walked into the woods and crawled down a more-or-less vertical cave, perhaps fifty yards deep, consisting of three chambers with two bottleneck passageways.'

Eshleman and the hitchhikers were underground, submerged in a hollow of soil, root and rock. 'There was really nothing to see in the cave,' Eshleman recalls, 'and an hour later we emerged, covered with mud.'

As Eshleman climbed out, pulling himself up through the last bottleneck, he felt a sharp sensation in his left ankle. It had been twisted in a crevice. 'But the sensation was of having been bitten.'

Eshleman was limping and in pain. He was struggling to walk, and he faced a dilemma. He had no way of contacting Caryl, for there were no phones. He might have asked the couple whether he could stay, but he felt increasingly uncomfortable with the man. 'While we were having our brandy, he pointed out a wood mask lodged in the loft window of a barn facing the house. He said it was the devil's mask, and then went on to talk about how much he hated his father. I was his father's age.'

Eshleman decided to return to Caryl. He limped to his car, started the engine, and began driving along the winding, single-lane road that led back to the cottage.

His ankle was throbbing; the night was thick.

Eshleman was part-way home, taking a wide curve, when a bolt of pain shot up his leg. His foot pressed to the floorboard in spasm. The car veered out of control, swerved into a ditch and smashed into a boulder. His ankle was broken in three places.

He was trapped.

He couldn't walk. He couldn't extract the car from the ditch.

'Until the next morning, when I figured I would be discovered by a local farmer, there was nothing to do but stay in the car and try to make sense out of what had happened.'

It began to rain. Lightning split the sky.

The idea that a poet should seek 'saturation' had been voiced by Charles Olsen in a 1955 letter to the young poet Ed Dorn. 'Best thing to do is *dig one thing or place or man* until you yourself know more abt [sic] that than is possible to any other man. It doesn't matter whether it's Barbed Wire or Pemmican or Paterson or Iowa. But *exhaust* it. Saturate it. Bear it.' Eshleman was not the first poet or artist to visit the caves. Pablo Picasso had entered the caves at Altamira and Lascaux. T.S. Eliot had visited a cave in the Pyrenees, coming away with the impression that 'art never improves'. Georges Bataille had come closest to a 'saturation job' in his 1955 work, *Lascaux, or the Birth of Art*, which explored themes of identity and transgression.

Eshleman was following in the footsteps of these artists, but his concern was different. 'Eshleman is obsessed with nothing less than the advent of "that catastrophic miracle called consciousness," the mysterious, mournful separation of the human from the animal.'[9]

Eshleman first discerned the outline of this 'catastrophic miracle' as he sheltered in his car and nursed his broken bones. He realised that he was stepping over the threshold. He was entering the 'harmed and initiated state' that he had intimated would befall him.

He reflected on the trail of events. He had fantasised about slugs poisoned by psychedelic mushrooms, vibrating in agony or ecstasy. 'As if following an occult recipe, I then ate possibly poisonous mushrooms and crawled to the bottom of a "wild" cave, which clawed out at me as I attempted to emerge.' He emerged, covered with mud as the slime of the agitated slug, limping and injured by his initiation, now quivering beneath a storm. But he returned with insight. 'After my accident, I began to see prehistoric psychic activity as a swamplike churning in which creative and destructive forces were entwined.' This churning was 'activated by the much earlier catastrophic separation between animal and hominid' that inspired our ancestors to paint upon the walls of the cave.

This was the insight that Eshleman carried back over the initiatory threshold. Cave art, he said, had been created in response to a 'crisis' in our ancestors' relationship with the animals around them, a crisis born of 'the empirical daytime world of hunting and surviving'. Our ancestors felt 'a profound bond' with the animals they hunted, an emotional and spiritual attachment, but they also killed these animals; they ate them and used their bodies as clothing, tools and weapons. 'Under such circumstances, it would seem that a terrible need welled up in Cro-Magnon to somehow deal with sensations that were internally tearing him apart.' The caves 'presented themselves as a kind of primordial laboratory' in which the artist could engage these fraught emotions, allowing them to be dramatised, alchemised, processed and expressed.[10]

Our ancestors had been immersed in the meat paradox.

These paintings were their response.

It was not far to the main chamber.

Our guide led us from the Panel of the Markings to the Great Crossroads, a spacious cavity in which the tunnel branched. We followed the largest branch, ascending a trail that led over dunes of ash-coloured silt, a subterranean sandscape hundreds of metres from the sunlit surface. The trail led up into a vast rotunda, and this was it: 'flesh-creeping immensity'. Le Salon Noir. The Black Chamber.[11]

The dimensions of the space were impossible to discern in the darkness, but it seemed expansive; breathing came more easily, and our footfall landed more brightly. As our torches probed the gloom, the walls began to take form. They were folded into smooth, curved apses, and as our eyes adjusted, we saw them, painted across the apses. Animals.

Bison. Horses. Ibex. Deer. There were dozens of them.

Our guide gathered us before the first panel, and our torches were extinguished. Our eyes fixed upon his beam, and he began to move it back and forth, mimicking the swaying of a tallow lamp. This was how the image-makers would have seen their creations, not as static images under the glare of an electric bulb, but in motion, animated. There were two large bison facing to the right. The one in front had an arrow-like sign marked on his body, as though speared. Beneath this bison was an ibex facing to the left. There was also a horse, its chest drawn with a single line. The horse's head was part formed by cracks and reliefs in the wall, suggesting the artist had perceived the animal to be pregnant within the stone surface.

We do not know who crafted these images. We do not know their name, what they looked like, who they cared for, where they were born or how they died. But we know they were a member of a small band who spent the summer months on the northern plains, the vast steppe that extended from England across Eurasia and into Alaska. On the steppe they hunted woolly rhinos, horses, bison and saiga antelope, and they lived among wolves, lions, cheetahs, hyenas and bears. These animals were their life, the focus of their storytelling and subsistence. They gazed at mammoths as they migrated the plains, trailed by flocks of arctic ptarmigan. They studied the darkening of the reindeer's pelt, measuring the movement of the seasons. The steppe was cold, windswept and hostile. Grasses thrived but trees were scarce. Hunting was arduous and the winter was savage. When the cold winds arrived, they migrated south, towards the coniferous forests and temperate valleys below, and it is here, on the southern border of the steppe, that we find their painted caves.

They would have arrived in Vicdessos Valley as the season turned, as ibex descended into the valleys to rut and salmon ascended the rivers, prompted by the first frost to return to their breeding grounds to spawn. Their habitation site was situated opposite Niaux, on the far side of the valley. La Vache, as the site is called, was frequented over many generations. Archaeologists have unearthed 142,000 animal remains at the site. These suggest that the community subsisted primarily on ibex throughout the winter, also hunting reindeer, chamois, game birds, and the occasional fox, hare, wild boar, wolverine, squirrel and vole. When spring came, the pace of life quickened. Deciduous trees burst into green and the melting snow swelled the rivers. They began to hunt the red deer who fed on grass shoots in the surrounding clearings; the aurochs who grazed ankle deep in water meadows. The reindeer would soon begin their migration north, and the community prepared to follow.

They painted the animals that they hunted, though not always and not consistently. While a handful of caves, such as Chauvet, are decorated with predatory and dangerous animals, most are decorated with animals that were killed and consumed. Where birds are depicted, they are typically game species with substantial meat, such as waterfowl and grouse. When fish are painted, they are species that are good to eat, such as salmon. (A trout is engraved into the floor at the entrance to the Salon Noir.) Images of birds and fish are rare, however. The most common images are of large herbivores, cold-hardy and adapted to harsh conditions, the focus of the hunt on the northern steppe. The animals on the walls of Niaux were all hunted: ibex in the surrounding valleys; horse and bison on the northern plains in the summer months.

The image-makers would have employed mimetic empathy in the hunt, just as indigenous peoples do today. 'Large-mammal anatomy is close enough to our own that once you have worked out the evolutionary analogies, you can imaginatively inhabit an animal, getting a bodily sense of their being,' ethologist and cave art expert R. Dale Guthrie explains. Palaeolithic hunters would have spent many hours studying the movements and behaviour of their prey, imaginatively projecting themselves into the skin and senses of the animals they pursued. 'This deep involvement with other large mammals informs and animates Palaeolithic art.'[12]

Many paintings attest to the artists' intimate knowledge of animal behaviour and anatomy. Among more abstract and hallucinatory images, there are animals drawn with careful regard to realism. The size and shape of antlers reveal the age and sex of a deer. Aurochs are shown grazing and reclining, chewing the cud. Reindeer are depicted with swollen bellies, displaying the fat deposits that would see them through winter, testament to the importance of late-summer hunts ahead of the scarce season ahead. 'In the art we see that they observed how different animals fed, drank, nursed, knelt, slept, rested, defecated, fought, moved, groomed, courted, copulated, and retched to death on lung blood. The biological content of the drawings gives us a new comprehension of late Palaeolithic intellect.'

We can see from these images that woolly rhinos, woolly mammoths, steppe bison, reindeer, cave bears and northern lions looked different to their living analogues. Mammoths, for example, had a 'handlike' trunk tip unlike the trunk tip of African elephants, and this is reflected in Palaeolithic art. Cave bears had a sharper forehead step than contemporary bears, and larger, looser lips, adapted for plant feeding. Palaeolithic lions had smaller ears than those of living lions, an adaptation to colder conditions. The horns of woolly rhinos differ from those of living rhinos, the woolly beast possessing a nasal horn that was long and flattened laterally. These features can all be seen in the art.

The naturalistic detail in the images was affirmed by a group of indigenous hunters – two Inuit and one Cree, elders in their communities – who were taken to visit several Palaeolithic caves under the guidance of prehistorians. Though they were confronted with images of animals that are not found in the far north, such as ibex, they consistently recognised nuances of age, sex and behaviour in the paintings. They perceived the animals to be 'real', recognising the naturalistic detail that spoke of the animals' lives and deaths.[13]

Images of hunting and death recur throughout the full span of Palaeolithic art, and across its full geographic range, though these images are relatively rare. Around 15 per cent of all large ungulates painted in caves are speared and bleeding, mostly horses and bison. Injured animals make up roughly a quarter of the images in Niaux. These images are also rich in naturalistic detail. Spears are positioned in the animal as the hunter would strike in real life, thrust through the ribcage into the heart or penetrating the thorax. Wounded animals are shown with blood spurting from their snout and nostrils; projectiles slicing their thoracic cavity. These images are realistic, but they do not revel in the violence they depict, and they do not seem to be vicious in intent.[14]

'Look at this ibex.'

We had moved onto the next panel, and our guide was pointing.

'Look at the care with which the animal has been drawn.'

The ibex was perfect. That is the only word for it. Its deft, expressive eye. The detail of its horns. Its textured coat. Those precise hooves.

'This would have been drawn from memory, of course. The artist knew this animal intimately, as well as he knew himself.' The guide paused a moment, and then added: 'There is no reason to think that a man painted this image. We know that women also frequented the galleries and they are just as likely to be responsible for the images on the walls. Perhaps it was a "she".'

Eshleman named one of his poems 'Permanent Shadow', recalling the shadows that were blasted into the walls during the atomic bombing of Hiroshima. (The atomic explosion was so intense that while people were vaporised, their shadows remained, etched onto walls and into pavements.) The poem is set in Lascaux, a cave famed for its elaborate depictions of bulls, stags and aurochs. It plays on two meanings of the verb 'to fell', which means both 'to kill' and 'to sew into position' when stitching a fabric. It is from the French *abattre*, 'to fell' ('to kill'), that we derive the word abattoir. The cave wall, in Eshleman's mind, becomes an animal hide sewn into position, adorned with images of felled animals. The cave

> *ceases merely to be stone hiding,*
> *but turns in the very word abattoir,*
> *felling or hide of the cave, its fell,*
> *herd pouring across a wall turned hide*[15]

In Eshleman's imagination, human consciousness is presented as an atomic blast, the evolution of the modern mind an eruption of light and heat of such intensity that these images were fixed onto the cave wall, permanent shadows that betray our psychological state at that moment in time – silhouettes cast by the emotional complexity of the meat paradox.

If the Palaeolithic artists were inducing altered states of consciousness, how were they doing it? They weren't drinking yahé, for the brew is of Amazonian origin and its ingredients could not be procured in Europe. They might have been eating psychotropic mushrooms. More than thirty such species were growing in Europe during the Palaeolithic, sprouting from the dung of wild herbivores, where our ancestors would certainly have encountered them. *Psilocybe semilanceata* is touted as the most likely candidate by mycologists with an interest in Palaeolithic art. But it needn't have been mushrooms. Other psychotropic plants growing in Europe at the time include members of the *Solanaceae* family, such as datura, mandrake, henbane and belladonna. Scholars have also noted that manganese dioxide, the black pigment commonly used as paint (and employed to paint the animals in the Salon Noir), can have hallucinogenic effects when held in the mouth. In some caves, the artists would blow paint from their mouths onto the wall. Was it the ink?

'The use of hallucinogens is in fact one of humankind's most widespread practices,' Clottes and Lewis-Williams observe. 'Everywhere, people in small-scale societies have remarkable knowledge of plants and their psychotropic properties, and this was almost certainly the case in the Upper Palaeolithic. But, as we have noted, drugs are not essential for entry into an altered state.'[16]

The sensory deprivation of the cave would have sufficed. Experiments with sensory deprivation have shown that darkness and isolation can induce powerful alterations in consciousness, including visual and auditory hallucinations. Eshleman recalls such an experience, reporting that after thirty minutes alone in a deep cave, staring into the dark, 'pinpoints of light appeared like a fine snowfall.'

Inching along walls and through tunnels, sometimes on my knees or waddling, occasionally on my belly, the cave and my mind became a synaesthetic 'salad' of splitting overlays. Sensations and associations amassed and crumbled, bent and extended, died and then flashed again, in ways that made me feel I was being processed through them, rather than the other way around. Standing before large compositions in which the realistic, the fantastic, and the unreadable are in overlapping juxtaposition, I have felt myself drawn into a vortex of shifting planes which afford no place for a perspective or a terminal.

Spend enough time alone in the dark, and the cave becomes a 'living power', Eshleman warned, and this power can sometimes engender something even more peculiar, 'an unstable fusion between a person and the cave itself'.[17]

Barbara MacLeod experienced this unexpected fusion. It was November 1972, and MacLeod had set out to spend forty-eight hours, without lights or watches, an hour's scramble from the entrance of an unnamed cave in Belize. She was joined by her companion Kim. They had nothing with them but water, ponchos and sleeping bags, carried into the cave with the help of a friend, who was instructed to return two days later when their vigil was complete. MacLeod sat in darkness and silence and she observed how the darkness and the silence fell upon her.

The most striking feature of the early phase, beginning within some four hours, was synaesthesia. While we were in total silence but for the sounds we ourselves made, the cave occasionally yielded a murmur – a drip plunking into some distant pool. This triggered a brilliant geometric pattern before my eyes (open or closed) much like the visual displays produced by psychedelic drugs (with which I had been familiar for eight years).

These patterns appeared for only a fraction of a second but sometimes occurred 'in rapid-fire sequence', and were accompanied by 'the dredging up of early material' including childhood memories.

One day in, MacLeod and her companion began to experience aural hallucinations. They heard 'unexplainable' sounds including 'a small bell tinkling' and 'a series of howls coming from the direction of the entrance'. MacLeod knew that they were too deep into the cave to hear anything from the outside world.

My disordered mind grappled with explanations ... a dog at the entrance in pursuit of game? No, the entrance was too far away. Another small entrance hitherto unsuspected? A possibility. The Maya K'ank'in dog, who guides the souls of the dead on the first leg of the journey into the underworld? A possibility, as good as any other ... Now I knew I had crossed a discriminatory threshold, beyond which supernatural explanations worked as well as any other.

MacLeod recalled that in the Mayan tradition, apprentice shamans would be left alone for hours in the Blank'anche cave, near the Mayan temple complex Chichen-Itza in the Yucatan peninsula. They would sit in darkness and silence and wait for the arrival of a distinct chill. Upon feeling this tremor, they would hear noises rising from the water pooled in the cave, 'as if something was moving on its surface'. These noises were believed to be the movement of the Balames, underwater jaguar spirits, which were said to dwell in the darkness. MacLeod did not encounter a jaguar, but sometime later she found that she was suddenly cold. She felt a distinct chill, even though the cave maintained a consistent temperature, which was not especially cold. MacLeod's companion was shivering. He climbed into his sleeping bag and wrapped the other sleeping bag around him as a blanket. 'I felt his chill as an energy field, and my trembling was that of fear.'

MacLeod realised they were not alone. 'There was something

else in here with us,' she recalls. 'Neither of us could speak for several minutes, and during this time I had an image of the "presence" as an amoeba-like consciousness which *was* the cave.' MacLeod felt herself extended throughout the cave, along its corridors, 'everywhere in it all at once'. The amoeba-like consciousness, she later reflected, had invited her to enter 'into a relationship'. It had issued her an invitation: apprenticeship.[18]

I found what I was looking for.

It was the most complex panel in the Black Chamber, and to my eyes the most beautiful. There were eight bison and two ibex arranged around the dorsal line of a horse. The panel was the work of a single artist, and the animals had been skilfully depicted. She – at least, I thought it was a she – was in the corner of the arrangement. A bison, her horns, mane and hump deftly drawn. Two spears were piercing her side and she appeared to be dying. The head of a smaller, much younger bison had been drawn before hers. A cow and her calf? A few feet from the scene there were geometric figures dashed across the wall.

I looked at the bison on the cave wall, and she gazed back.

I looked at the cow across the stun cage, and she gazed back.

Our ancestors painted animals in caves for so long it confounds comprehension. The span of time separating the oldest images in Niaux from the most recent is longer than the full span of Christianity. The span of time separating the oldest images in Chauvet from the most recent is more than double the time separating us from the construction of the Great Pyramids at Giza in Egypt. Our ancestors painted animals in these caves for thirty millennia, for more than a thousand generations, in a continuous, unbroken tradition. Whatever motivated the creation of these images was enduring and evidently important. That something perhaps still speaks to us today.

Scholars have observed that Palaeolithic artists would sometimes carry animal remains into the caves with them, the teeth of horses and the bones of bears, to insert into the cave wall. 'In these instances, one may possibly discern some sort of restitution ritual: two-way traffic between this world and the spirit world.' This restitution ritual, Clottes and Lewis-Williams suggest, might have been performed to appease a figure akin to Vaí-mahsë. The Lion Man, they propose, was perhaps a 'manifestation' of this figure, the earliest known depiction of the Master of Animals.[19]

Other scholars have suggested that the Lion Man might have been a shaman in trance, an elder of the community entering an altered state. The geometric markings etched into the Lion Man's arm mirror the entoptic images painted on cave walls. The figure's hands and feet are transforming into paws, and they are extended. 'The posture of the "lion-human", and the way in which its "feet" are carved, gives the distinct impression that it is "hovering" or "suspended" above the ground. A sense of floating is yet another widely reported hallucinatory experience of altered states.' The Lion Man's intent stare, these scholars say, tells of the poise required of the individual who seeks to parley with the animal powers; the courage demanded of him who would stand face-to-face with Vaí-mahsë.[20]

'Gather round,' our guide said.

He said it too soon. I could have stayed with that bison for hours.

'Here, in the centre.'

I was reluctant to leave the image, but it was OK, for the cave had one more secret to reveal.

'We're going to try something unexpected. On the count of three, we will extinguish all the lights. Are you ready?'

We gathered in the centre of the rotunda. I could still sense her from the far side of the chamber, her gaze beneath the vessel and the vapours rising.

'One. Two. Three.'

drip, drip, drip

Darkness.

9

CATHARSIS

Fwoosh. Gume struck a match and his face was fleetingly illuminated, amber upon his brow, green fire in his eyes. He was holding a thick cigar rolled with *mapacho* tobacco. He held the match to the cigar's tip, and he began to puff.

Puff. Puff. Puff. He inhaled three times and blew smoke over his hands and his arms.

Puff. Puff. Puff. He drew on the cigar and exhaled over his chest and his legs.

Shadows danced from wall to ceiling. There was a fire burning in the hearth, and ripples of warmth were filling the space. We were in a remote cabin, high in the mountains, and the sun was setting.

Gume had taken the dusk as his cue. He was humming now, and whistling, still drawing on his *mapacho* cigar. In his hand there was a bottle of thick, brown yahé.

Puff. Puff. Puff. He drew on the cigar and he blew smoke over the bottle. He began to sing, soft-spoken, an incantation –

Cielo, cielo ayahuasca ...

His words were smokesong, the movement of ocean currents and the chirruping of birds. He sang to the yahé, and these words (he later told me), which moved in and out of Spanish and several native Amazonian dialects, had been taught to him *by* the yahé. These songs, which he called *icaros*, had been imparted to him by the *Banisteriopsis caapi* vine, and by his mentor, a man named Julio.

Julio did not want to lose his leg. That was how it all began.

Julio Llerena Pinedo was born in 1916 in Pucallpa on the Ucayali River. Pucallpa is now a city, but it was then a small jungle town surrounded by tousled vegetation. Julio had grown up in the traditional manner, paddling the river in his dugout canoe, fishing and keeping a smallholding. His friends tell contradictory tales of his injury and its consequence. Some say he was wounded in the war with Ecuador and doctors told him that one of his legs needed to be amputated from the knee down. Others say that he was bitten by a viper and was warned that if he went to hospital, he would lose his leg to its venom. Either way, his leg was injured, and his injury led him to consult a *curandero*, a healer who worked with plants. One thing led to another. Julio was healed, and he retreated to the forest to study plant medicine.

He built a small house in an isolated area, as was the tradition. But Julio's apprenticeship was unorthodox, for he had no mentor, no tutor but the plants themselves. With only trees and vines to guide him, he tried to remember the permutation of ingredients the *curandero* had employed in his healing. 'I was there for a long time,' he recalls. 'First, I learned how to make ayahuasca. Then I learned about the spirits in the trees and began to make tea from their barks and roots. I made friends with *lupuna* and *catawa* and *chiric sanango* and a lot of others. It took months, but it was the only way I knew because I had no teacher, no maestro teaching me.'

Over an intense half-year period, Julio studied the medicinal possibilities of the rainforest, taking yahé as his tutor. This might sound strange to us, but it is common fare in the Amazon. It is normal to believe that plants and other organisms might teach us, if only we would lower our voices and open our ears.

It seems that Amazonian peoples have been drinking yahé for at least a millennium. A 2019 chemical analysis of organic residues found in a thousand-year-old ritual bundle recovered from the Andean highlands bordering the Amazon found traces of both β-carboline alkaloids and dimethyltryptamine (DMT), the two primary ingredients in the brew. Both are required. DMT is a potent psychedelic, but when consumed orally, the molecule is rendered inactive by enzymes in the digestive tract. In yahé, the DMT provided by psychotropic plants such as *Psychotria viridis* interacts with the β-carboline alkaloids provided by the *Banisteriopsis caapi* vine. The alkaloids prevent the breakdown of DMT in the digestive tract, allowing the molecule to activate the central nervous system. This biochemical interaction is not easily attained. It requires lengthy and precise preparations. How and why communities in remote parts of the Amazon learned to prepare the brew, choosing the correct combination of ingredients from among tens of thousands of plants, is unknown. But for Julio the answer was simple – the plants taught the method.[1]

In keeping with this notion of vegetal communication, the Tukano say they drink yahé to commune with the roots, rhizomes, shrubs and creatures that co-habit their territory. 'Plants and animals tell the visionary how they want to be treated and protected,' Reichel-Dolmatoff explains; 'how they suffer from carelessness, overhunting, the cutting down of trees, the abuse of fish poisons, the destructiveness of firearms.' For the Tukano, drinking yahé 'is a lesson in ecology, in the sense that it gives nature a chance to voice its complaints and demands in unmistakable terms'.

These demands often concern the proper treatment of animals, and the need to achieve dietary balance by curtailing the consumption of meat. Animals, 'when seen during a narcotic trance, will communicate with the visionary: they will speak to him in a language he can understand and will explain to him the rules by which they must be treated in ordinary reality'. The shaman will help to incite and interpret these visions, explaining how they relate to past and future hunts, and their significance for the hunter's relationship with Vaí-mahsë.

Vaí-mahsë is latent in every yahé quest. The Tukano understand that illness results from imbalance, and imbalances are caused by the mistreatment of animals or careless consumption. When such mistreatment occurs, the animal might seek revenge, asking Vaí-mahsë to send anxiety or disease, perceived as tiny darts which puncture the hunter's flesh. The shaman can typically intuit the onset of such an illness before it manifests, for a man who has killed wantonly will appear in the shaman's trance in the shape of the wronged species. The image will be accompanied by a certain luminosity, a particular quality of light, which imparts the meaning of the vision. Once the vision has been received, the shaman will suggest the appropriate reparation ritual, angled towards the rebalancing of the human and animal communities.[2]

Julio was not of the Tukano, but his practice was based on a similar conception of energetic and ecological balance. In time, he became an adept healer in the *vegetalista* tradition, a term which distinguishes non-tribal yahé practitioners from their tribal counterparts. He moved from Pucallpa to Auchyacu, where the rainforest meets the eastern slopes of the Andes, and he started a family. Journalist Peter Gorman, who was friends with Julio, says:

He was the local doctor on the river on which he lived ... Auchyacu means Indian Water, and the river was periodically inhabited by the indigenous Matses, most of whom live further east, on several rivers near the Brazilian border. But they, like everyone else who lived on the Auchyacu, and many from further away, trusted Julio to fix their babies' tummies, mend broken legs, eliminate the venom from poisonous snake bites, find their lost souls, repair their broken marriages, clean ugliness and hatred from their hearts.[3]

Gume's parents took him to Julio when he was a child. The eldest son of Roldan and Gertrudes Galindo, Gume was born on the Ucuyali River, a tributary of the Amazon, near the village of Jenaro Herrera, and he had fallen sick. He had grown feverish and weak, and his parents feared he might die. Julio agreed to drink yahé to assess Gume's condition. It was good news, he said, having arrived at his prognosis. Julio reassured Gume's parents that their son would live, he would be healthy, and more – one day, he would grow up to become an adept yahé practitioner.

It took many years for the premonition to be realised. It was not until he was a teenager that Gume sat in on a yahé ceremony. He did not drink the brew, but he nevertheless felt its effects. 'I was thirteen years old and more interested in football and girls than anything else,' he says, grinning, 'but I felt *mareado*, even without drinking. That is when I knew that this was important.' The word *mareado* means 'dizzy', but in colloquial use it describes the experience of being under the influence of yahé. Gume sought out Julio and became his apprentice. He practised with him until his tutor's death in 2007, at the age of ninety-one.

Gume was still puffing on his *mapacho* cigar.

The moon was rising, and the night was calm.

He was sitting in the centre of the space, amid a fragile assembly of bare-beamed walls and slanting rafters. We were above the treeline, and from the door of the cabin you could look down onto the groves of conifers that thronged the slopes below, and up, in the opposite direction, towards Ranrapalca and Tsurup, two peaks that seemed almost within touching distance. A wide plain opened out between, scattered with barbed shrubs and great granite boulders, rucking into an intermontane valley, an hour's walk away. The sky above was empty and everywhere, streaked with the Milky Way by night and brushed with the condors who rose each day with dawn.

In its iron coffin it dwells
among the rusty stones
feeding on horseshoes.

In Pablo Neruda's imagination, the Andean condor nests in iron, hungering for the metallic tang of raw meat. The bird, the vulture indigenous to these mountains, 'pecks at the sky's zinc, waiting for a sign of blood', and when it strikes, it is with elemental violence. 'The black cyclone planes down' and 'blood-stained cacti' are left in its wake. I thought of Neruda's poem that afternoon as the storm spilled over the mountain. They were the largest hail stones I had ever seen; great fists of ice that thrashed the grasses and pummelled the earth. We huddled in a doorway, delighted and disturbed. Gume was deep in a game of chess – he spent most days deep in a game of chess – but he paused to frown into the hail. The sky cleared as quickly as it had darkened, and a rainbow appeared, a flush of light on the tail feathers of the furore. The smell of ozone and the vulture satiated. Enskyment.[4]

Gume was holding a cup of yahé to his lips.

He was singing still, crouching over a piece of patterned fabric spread across the floor between us.

On the fabric there was a jaguar skull, bleached white and snarling.

Beside the jaguar skull were two vulture feathers.

Gume poured a second cup, filled to the brim, and he handed it to me.

Standing above the skull was a statuette, roughly thirty centimetres tall. The statuette depicted a human–feline hybrid, humanoid and jaguar, reminiscent of the Lion Man.

Gume bent down and blew over the hybrid. I watched smoke curl about its grimacing jaw, its folded form.

I took the cup. I drank my fill.

*

Life in the high mountains is tough and subsistence is challenging. The first indigenous peoples to settle here survived by hunting the wild camelids – vicuña, guanco and deer – which grazed the *páramo* and the *puna*, the high-altitude plains. In time, they began herding, domesticating llamas and alpacas around 5,000 years ago. Agriculture was more difficult to establish. The mountain soils are thin and immature, and the conditions are unforgiving, but Andean peoples nevertheless learned to draw food from the land, dividing the terrain into discrete zones of production. The *puna*, the high grassland, was for grazing and hunting. The steep slopes and hollows of the *suni* (3,200–4,000 metres) would grow tubers, including potatoes and oca, quinoa, and lupines such as tarwi and broad beans. The lower slopes in the *quechua* zone (2,300–3,200 metres) were frost-free and could take maize, squash and vegetables; and the lowest, *yunga* zone (1,000–2,300 metres) would grow valued crops such as chili pepper, coca, avocado and fruits. In some areas, these zones are all within a day's journey, but they are often distant enough that trade and migration are required. It was on one of these ancient trade routes that the temple was constructed.

Chavín de Huántar was seemingly designed to withhold its secrets, repelling casual approach. The temple was built in a narrow valley on the Mosna River, at an elevation of 3,180 metres. It was an out-of-the-way spot, high in the Cordillera Blanca, enclosed by sharp inclines, rugged cliffs and glaciated peaks. Unlike other ancient temples, Chavín did not aspire to be admired from a distance; it did not announce its importance or invite veneration. The only approach was via a trail that led to the western face of the edifice where there were no visible entrances. The walls were four storeys high, built of monumental stone blocks, and they offered neither windows nor doors. Huge carved heads studded the exterior, monstrous hybrids with gargantuan jaws and protruding teeth. Their contorted expressions seemed to grimace a warning. *Beware what lies within.*

Scholars are still trying to decipher the significance of the site. Peruvian archaeologist Julio C. Tello pioneered the excavation of the ruins, publishing his findings in several papers between the 1940s and the 1960s. Tello believed that Chavín was the centre of an ancient empire, the birthplace of Andean civilisation, the matrix out of which all later Peruvian cultures developed. Contemporary scholarship largely affirms this view. At its peak, Chavín exerted a sphere of influence – identifiable by a distinctive artistic style – over more than 200,000 square kilometres. The temple was built almost 3,000 years ago and it endured for close to a millennium, longer than the Roman Empire. But Chavín was not an empire, and this is where the mystery deepens. It was not a city or a state. The temple was constructed without slavery or coercion. There is no evidence of a military support base and scant sign of a religious or political hierarchy. The temple could not defend itself or spread its influence by force. Yet its influence prevailed, century after century.[5]

Clues as to what took place here are found in the temple's architecture, and in the carvings and artworks adorning its walls. The temple was U-shaped in design, a pyramidal structure enclosing a square court and a circular sunken plaza. The walls of the court were decorated with friezes and sculptures, mostly depicting animals, plus humans and animals in various stages of fusion and transformation. Smaller cloisters were arranged on raised platforms surrounding the court, and some of these offered doors which opened onto the temple interior. Inside, there was something extraordinary. A honeycomb. A labyrinth of narrow passageways that split and branched at right-angles, occasionally opening out into reclusive chambers.

I visited Chavín and entered the labyrinth. I stepped down into those tunnels and felt the abrupt dislocation that was the purpose of their design. The labyrinth permitted no sources of natural light. The angular turns were seemingly intended to induce disorientation and sensory deprivation among those who ventured inside. *The Gallery of the Madmen. The Gallery of the Offerings. The Gallery of the Labyrinths. The Gallery of the*

Bats. Much of the labyrinth remains unexplored, having been buried beneath the mountain or intentionally sealed in antiquity, but those galleries and chambers which have been unearthed have been evocatively named. Within these dark passages, archaeologists have found a horde of ancient artefacts including hollow bones and ritual trays – snuffing apparatus.

Snuffs containing DMT are inhaled throughout the Amazon. The Tukano are among the cultures who partake of them, inhaling a powder formed of the ground inner bark of the *Virola theiodora* tree. Other tribal groups are known to inhale snuffs made from the seeds of *Anadenanthera peregrina*. The practice appears to be ancient. Pipes made of puma bone recovered from the JuJuy Province in Argentina, found to contain traces of DMT derived from *Anadenanthera peregrina*, have been dated to more than 4,000 years ago. It's likely that these snuffs would have been inhaled in a ceremonial context, for the effects are immediate and ferocious. While yahé comes on relatively slowly, taking thirty to sixty minutes to take hold and persisting in full intensity for several hours, the inhalation of DMT elicits a sudden and overwhelming alteration of consciousness. Among the Tukano, such snuffs are primarily used in the shaman's arduous apprenticeship. Reichel-Dolmatoff explains:

> The apprentice and his teachers must retire to a remote spot in the forest where they go to live in a temporary shelter, a hut that contains only the barest essentials: a few hammocks, a hearth, some cooking vessels. The small group of men will live in isolation for several months, subsisting on some boiled manioc starch, but little else. At night they will sing and dance, under the influence of different narcotic drugs, and after about two months they will barely be able to walk and then will spend most of the time in their hammocks, their prostrate emaciated bodies convulsed, their faces contorted, their hoarse voices chanting endlessly to the rhythm of their gourd rattles.[6]

The Tukano mix their tree bark residue with white powder shaved from a stalactite procured from a cave in their territory (believed to be the abode of Vaí-mahsë), and they inhale it through a hollow harpy eagle bone. In the blizzard that ensues, it is said that they encounter the animals who will act as their future avatars – the harpy eagle, the jaguar and the anaconda. These animals are the apex predators in the Amazon, the harpy eagle ruling the skies, the jaguar the forests, the anaconda the rivers. They are of mythic significance to many Amazonian cultures, and, curiously, they are the animals most prominently carved onto the walls and friezes of Chavín de Huántar.

The prominence of these animals in Chavín's iconography has puzzled archaeologists, for they are neither local to the site nor indigenous to the highlands. Subsequent Andean traditions would emphasise more local fauna, such as the llama, the deer, the fox and the hummingbird, but these animals are conspicuously absent from Chavín's bestiary. Carved into the temple walls are sneering felines, some fused with raptorial birds, snakes writhing as whiskers. There are eagles with recursive beaks, their wings spread wide, human feet below sprouting tufts of feathers. Some of the figures have eyes that roll to the back of the head and mucus streaming from their nostrils, as happens when the harsh DMT snuff is inhaled. They are often depicted atop swirling designs which heave hypnotically from the stone, yet the images are also realistic, attentive to anatomical detail. The portrayal of the jaguar – its ears, maw and lithe physique – suggests a first-hand knowledge of the creature.

The primacy of the jaguar in the temple's iconography was affirmed by the discovery in 1972 of a towering statue secluded in a restrictive cruciform chamber at the very centre of the labyrinth. Known as the Lanzón, the figure is upward standing, 4.5 metres tall, with the hands and arms of a human, the large upper incisors and snarling mouth of a jaguar, and a column of fanged feline heads worn as a headdress. At once ferocious and harmonious, the Lanzón seems to embody a sense of strenuous balance which perhaps extended throughout the temple. Think of the temple's architecture as 'a physical expression of the ideology', scholar Richard Burger suggests, the U-shape design 'a metaphor for the mediation of dual opposing forces, represented by the right and left wings'. The Lanzón was positioned in the centre of these opposing wings, facing east along the axis of the temple towards the rising sun. Its right arm was raised towards the sky, while its left arm was lowered. The figure points to the above and the below, embodying an intimation of the cosmic harmony which was surely the concern of the Chavín ritual.[7]

The jaguar is a beautiful beast. Its eyes are golden. The dark rosettes which pattern its pelt are shaped as butterflies, and in the Amazon, as in so many cultures, the butterfly is associated with *psyche*, the soul. Conservation science knows the soul-garnished feline as a keystone species, the apex predator, shaping savannah and forest ecologies by modulating herbivore populations. In the Cerrado, where soy crops and cattle grazing have swallowed so much native vegetation, the jaguar has been edged into precipitous decline, and its demise has catalysed a trophic cascade of loss, diminishing the richness and abundance of the biome. We are losing this precious savannah because our appetite for industrially farmed meat and unsustainable beef cannot be satiated. *Panthera onca* holds the land in balance, even as our appetite tips it into disarray. As the jaguar is edged into oblivion, the world unravels in its wake.

The artists at Chavín might not have known the jaguar as a 'keystone species' but they understood its ecological importance, they were familiar with the cat's golden gaze, and they intuited that the temple was situated at an epicentre of biological diversity. From the threshold of Chavín, you can travel to a hundred different worlds. The Cordillera Blanca boasts some of the tallest peaks in Peru, ice-capped giants, and there are trails that lead through these peaks into almost every landscape imaginable. In the west, these trails lead to the shores of the Pacific Ocean, passing through montane grasslands and temperate valleys, and down into a coastal plain so arid that it receives less rainfall than the Sahara or Gobi Deserts. In the east, they lead through lush pasture, prairie and tundra into steaming, steep-sloped cloud forests, and then down into the heat and tangle of the Amazon. There is nowhere else on the planet where such contrasting environments are found in such proximity. This coincidence of dissimilar habitats is unique in the biosphere.

The Lanzón was the axis about which so many worlds turned. The temple was positioned midway between the coast and the tropics, and it attracted visitors from both. Built on one of the few snow-free routes that allowed passage over the Cordillera Blanca, the temple marked a natural gateway, and fishermen came from the Pacific, foragers arrived from the jungle. It was an arduous six-day journey from the Amazon, a treacherous ascent up the Marañón River, and the journey from the coast was no less difficult. But they came, these travellers and pilgrims, these traders and seekers, and Chavín became a site of uniquely rich cultural exchange. Hordes of pink *Spondylus* shells have been found at the temple, carried from the ocean. The snuffs derived from the forest, and the animal imagery also rose from the east. Chavín de Huántar began as a public centre constructed by and for the surrounding rural population, but it was infused from the beginning with the dreams and mythology of the rainforest. At Chavín, a society of farmers entered the mindscape of the hunter. An agricultural people engaged in an exchange of ideas and images with those who inhabited wildly different worlds. That was why it appealed to me. That was why I went.

Our cabin was a few kilometres from the temple, situated at a modestly higher elevation of 3,700 metres. I spent eight days and eight nights there, and I remember them brightly. Slow mornings on the veranda with a panoramic view of the mountains. Skies clear, and the day fresh. The mornings were good, the afternoons heavier. A storm would typically break late in the day, lashing the slopes and clearing before sundown. The afternoons were also weighted with hunger and trepidation. It is unwise to drink yahé on a full stomach, so we enjoyed a light lunch and then ate nothing until morning. Gume recommended a restrictive diet, in keeping with his Amazonian heritage. Salt, sugar, spices, pork, oil, black tea, and coffee were prohibited. Eggs were permitted, as were quinoa, cauliflower, carrots, broccoli, beetroot, potato, freshwater trout, rice, yucca, plantains, cucumber and coconut. When I departed, it was on the understanding that I was to eat no honey for the next twenty-four hours and no fish that had teeth for at least a week. I was to eat no pork, duck, alligator, piranha or venison for six months. If possible, I should never eat those animals again.

Gume was a slight figure, handsome and kindly. He was quiet during the days but came alive at night when the sun sank and the yahé took hold. I later learned that he was homesick, at least some of the time. The peoples of the mountains differ in temperament from those of the forest. The jungle is promiscuous, brimming with a sense of fecundity which infuses the indigenous population with a flirtatious and playful spirit. In the high mountains, where the conditions were cold and harsh, the mentality was very different. The people were less playful and more severe, and Gume perhaps felt out of place.

But he came, as so many had come before, travelling from the east. He came because to drink yahé in the mountains was a different endeavour to drinking yahé in the rainforest. The energies in the mountains were clearer, Gume said. The rarefied atmosphere, the stellar reaches, the snow and ice and endless sky, combined to induce an experience of a markedly different quality to that roused by the seething abundance of the Amazon. Yet the rainforest was incipient in the brew. As Gume sang his *icaros*, he shook a *shacapa*, a leaf-bundle rattle that sounded like tree branches rustling in the wind, the rhythmic stride of paws over a litter of dried leaves.

After about half an hour, I began to feel the yahé working upon me.

Gume was standing over the Lanzón, singing still.

In Tukano, the words for 'shaman' and 'jaguar' are the same, *yee*. Makuna shamans say they are allied to jaguars and refer to themselves and all predatory animals under a kindred term, *yai*. To the west, in the Ecuadorian Amazon, the Runa people speak of *runa-pumas*, human-jaguars (*runa* in Quechua means 'human' and *puma* means 'jaguar') which appear in yahé visions to commune with the elders. Among the Huaorani, also of the Ecuadorian Amazon, shamans are said to be *menera*, 'parents of jaguars', chosen to be adoptive fathers by a jaguar spirit that manifests in their dreams. Vaí-mahsë took many forms among the Tukano, but among the animals of the rainforest, he was perceived to be a jaguar. We do not know who or what the Lanzón was, but this human–jaguar hybrid, like the Lion Man, perhaps embodied both the elder in their transformed state and the powers of the animal world. The Tukano shaman would drink yahé to take on the jaguar's form, slipping into the cat's skin to commune with those powers, to speak with Vaí-mahsë, feline to feline.[8]

Gume's voice was louder now, and the heat was rising.

Coils of energy at the base of my spine. I felt nauseous.

Gume had placed a rock crystal beside the jaguar skull. The skull had a broad brow, and the crystal threw refracted light onto its surface, as the fire seared in the hearth. The hexagonal shape of the crystal is of great significance to the Tukano. The world, they insist, is hexagonal in form. The headwaters and mouths of rivers are enclosed in hexagons. Their territory is bounded by a hexagon, by six anacondas lying outstretched, mouth in tail. The human heart is hexagonal, as is the womb, the brain. There are hexagons everywhere if you know where to look. They are in a honeycomb, on a tortoiseshell, in the segmentation of a palm trunk, the skin of pineapple, in spiders' webs, the pattern of a snake's skin. The Tukano believe that hexagonal rock crystals contain the concentrated energy of the sun, the full spectrum of colours, of which they recognise thirty. This spectrum is associated with the colours seen under yahé, the rainbow patterns perceptible on the shimmer of a waterfall, the light glinting on the scales of a fish as it leaps from the river. These rock crystals are also associated with Vaí-mahsë, and are referred to as *yeea vii*, 'house of the jaguar'.

When the shaman drinks yahé, he imaginatively enters the rock crystal, the jaguar house, to stand before the Master of Animals. The interior is conceived as a womb, or a beehive, or a cloud of many-coloured butterflies fluttering within a geode, a circular space that is domed and hollow. The inside surface of the space is said to be coated with a drusy crust of innumerable minute, inward-projecting crystals. In each tiny shard resides the soul of an animal, somnolent and anticipating birth.

The Tukano will tell you that the night sky is also a hexagonal crystal, and when the shaman enters *yeea vii* they are standing in the centre of the cosmos. This journey into the house of the jaguar is also a journey into a human brain, for its hemispheric structure mirrors the night sky split by the Milky Way. The hemispheres of the brain are said to be divided by a great fissure, a deep riverbed, a depression formed in the beginning of time by the cosmic anaconda. Energy streams from the sun through the fissure, pulsing in synchrony to the human heartbeat and the stars throbbing above. Vaí-mahsë traverses the above, watching over the interactions between humans and animals, and the Tukano know the Milky Way as *vaí-mahsë maá*, the Trail of the Master of Animals. Vaí-mahsë is personified, but ultimately conceived as an immediate force of nature, the demands of the animal world streaked across the cosmos as the meat paradox is painted across the human brain.

The walls were swaying.

The Lanzón seemed taller now.

It felt as though the yahé was penetrating every cell in my

body. My vision had come alive with spots and splashes, dancing and shimmering. They were pollen and seed, sand and smoke, the sediment of star dust, threads and feathers, microbes and mitochondria. Patterns rising through the night. The same patterns painted on the walls of the cave.

'Gather round,' our guide said. 'Here, in the centre.'

Back in Niaux, and we had gathered in the middle of the rotunda.

'On the count of three, we will extinguish all the lights. Are you ready?'

One. Two. Three.

Darkness.

'Now,' our guide said, 'who knows how to sing?'

No one spoke.

'Aaaaaaaaaaaaaah.'

Our guide sang a single, clear note. His voice was a morning bell, rich and clean and resonant. It filled the space, reverberating from the vaulted ceiling to the apses of the walls.

'Can you hear that, the quality of the sound? It seems that the animals have been positioned on the walls of the Salon Noir not only for aesthetic reasons but for acoustic purposes. They were painted here because of how the walls *sound*. It is the same in other caves.'

Scholars in the fields of acoustics and archaeology have been examining the sound qualities of the painted caves for several decades, and there is compelling evidence that images were sometimes positioned where there was an acoustic response. Some scholars believe the image-makers might have been choosing where to paint by listening for echoes, reverberations and resonances, using these to navigate in the dark. Others say that certain animals, such as horses and bison, might have been positioned where echoes most resembled the sound of galloping hooves or animal cries. Iegor Reznikoff found that 90 per cent of the images in Niaux, most of them in the Salon Noir, were positioned in resonant locations such as these.[9]

Steven Mithen imagines the scene. There is an artist and his young apprentice. They are deep in the cave and working the walls. 'The artist is an old but sprightly man with long grey hair, naked but with painted flesh. He is part of a community who live by reindeer hunting on the tundra of southern France.' Surrounding them are lumps of red ochre; some have been crushed to a powder and mixed with water from puddles on the cave floor. There are also sticks of charcoal and hairbrushes, the artist's paraphernalia. 'There is a sweet smell in the air: herbs are smouldering upon a fire. Every few moments the artist kneels and inhales deeply to refresh the vision within his mind.'

The artist has painted two horses; 'he takes mouthfuls of paint and spits it through a leather stencil to make circles on the wall. His breath is the key ingredient to make the horses come alive.' He works tirelessly, 'pausing only to change his pigment or his stencil, to switch a brush or sponge, to replenish the fat within his lamps and intoxicate his mind. He talks and sings to the horses, he drops to all fours and then rears like a stallion.' The old man finally completes the work. 'As he comes to an end, the artist is physically exhausted and mentally drained.'[10]

In Mithen's scene, image-making becomes a multisensory activity that engages the whole body. The artist mimetically becomes the animal he seeks to portray, while the burning of aromatic herbs and the artist's breath conjure the animal to life, perhaps to speak or respond. The Tukano say that animals speak to them directly in their yahé visions. Similarly, Lewis-Williams writes, 'we must allow that the painted and engraved animals of Upper Palaeolithic art probably also "spoke" to people in auditory hallucinations.' The artists might have evoked such hallucinations by imitating animal calls, or these hallucinations might have arisen unbidden, induced by the sensory deprivation of the cave.

In Lascaux, there is a painting known as the Roaring Stag.

The image shows the neck, head and back of a large black stag, and its mouth is open and baying. Stags are known to lift their heads and roar in this posture during the rutting season at the end of winter. 'That the stag is emitting a sound was probably significant in terms of multisensory experiences in the cave: sound is implied by the image,' Lewis-Williams writes. 'Perhaps people participating in rituals imitated the roaring sound; some may have interpreted their aural hallucinations as the roaring of stags.'[11]

There is evidence of music-making and dance in the caves. Flutes formed of swan bones and bear femurs have been unearthed, the earliest from the Swabian Jura, the region of the Lion Man, and they are of a similar age. One fine specimen was crafted of the wing bone of a griffon vulture, bored with five finger holes and a mouthpiece. There is also evidence of dance. In the cave at Tuc d'Audobert, beyond a maze of tight and difficult passages, one finds 'the startling footprints of ancient dancers in bare feet and the models of copulating bisons, in clay on the floor'. The size and shape of the footprints indicate that the dancers moved in a circle; one of them might have been a teenage boy or girl. 'The unusual position of the foot suggests that the youth was imitating in a dance the movements of the hoofed animal.'[12]

The San people, Lewis-Williams recalls, would enter altered states of consciousness following long, repetitive rhythmic dances that lasted for many hours. They would report aural hallucinations, as well as bodily transformations, and they painted their experiences on rock surfaces and cave walls. Aural hallucinations are often experienced at the onset of an altered state, with many cultures reporting a buzzing or humming sound, which is sometimes interpreted as a swarm of bees. The San experience these aural hallucinations in tandem with entoptic phenomena, leading them to believe that the geometric patterns they perceive in trance are bees swarming over a honeycomb.

The Tukano are similarly sensitive to sounds, saying that the background noise of the rainforest can both evoke and represent the altered state induced by yahé. 'All sounds are coded and are thought to transmit precise messages,' Reichel-Dolmatoff explains. 'The principal and most permanent sounds are those made by insects ... The continuous buzzing and whizzing of cicadas is interpreted by the Indians as a chant, *dári dári dári nyiiiiii*; while others sing, *dári dári dári yoooooooo*, referring to *dári* energies, and the verb *yorí*, to carry, to be charged with. "The insects sing to the energies", say the Indians.' The Tukano use the verb ~*menyahári* to portray the state of mind induced by the chanting of insects and the drinking of their psychotropic brew. The verb designates the act of jumping from a tree into a pool. 'The underlying idea is that of changing from one dimension to another.' It is used in other contexts to denote the shaman's transformation into a jaguar (*yee ~menyahári*) or the experience of being 'permeated' by the energies of the rainforest, the dimension of Vaí-mahsë (*Vaí mahsë turí ~menyahári*). These overlapping meanings imply that even in mundane situations, everyday sounds such as the thrumming of cicadas have the potential to elicit a shift in perception; voices implicit in the hubbub of the daylight world speaking beneath the normal frequency of human hearing, singing to the energies that animate the cosmos. 'The insect song has turned into a jaguar's growl,' the Tukano explain, 'and thence into nature's fertility.'[13]

It seems that sound was also important at Chavín, with auditory hallucinations deliberately induced by the design of the labyrinth. Archaeologists have discovered a series of ducts and tunnels laced throughout the structure. These were constructed to divert water from the river above through its interior, ostensibly helping to aerate its corridors and keep them from flooding, but this flow might also have served an acoustic function. The sound of water draining through the labyrinth would have been distorted and amplified, the resulting sound reverberating through its chambers and onto the plazas and terraces below. The sound was that of 'pulsating applause' or the purring of a feline. To the pilgrim, their mind primed by images of human–feline metamorphosis, it would have sounded as though the temple was an enormous jaguar, stretching and awakening.[14]

Researchers investigating the science of altered states suggest that our perception is shaped by the interplay of 'bottom-up' sensory inputs and 'top-down' expectations derived from prior experiences. When the 'bottom-up' inputs are cut off, as in the darkness of the cave, or become disordered, as when psychedelics are consumed, the mind imposes 'top-down' meaning upon the disorder. The confusion is folded into familiar or exotic forms, manifesting as visual and auditory hallucinations. Researchers have observed that reports of a 'presence' are common among those subject to sensory deprivation and extended isolation, a hallucination perhaps prompted by a strong 'top-down' expectation of other people. We are born into an interpersonal world, and the same empathic openness which makes us responsive to others generates the expectation of an 'other' when all sensory inputs are removed. In the caves and at Chavín, it seems that art and ritual were used to prime the mind for the expectation of *animal* presences. Curiously, where images of felines appear in the caves, they are typically in the most distant, difficult and isolated recesses, those most plausibly used to induce an altered state. This might suggest that the presence evoked was often felt to be powerful and predatory, an 'other' akin to a lion or a jaguar.[15]

More curious still, contemporary science is affirming that the disordered perception characteristic of altered states may be of *therapeutic* value, at least in some contexts. After decades in a legal hinterland, scientists have begun to employ psychedelics in clinical trials as putative treatments for anxiety, depression, 'existential distress' resulting from a terminal diagnosis, alcoholism and addiction. The trials are still in their infancy, but the early results have been positive, suggesting that psychedelics might be of therapeutic potential, if used appropriately.[16]

Neuroscientist Robin Carhart-Harris says this potential

might derive from the ability of psychedelics to disrupt negative patterns of thought and behaviour, introducing 'entropy' or disorder into the brain activity upon which they rest. This is partly through their interaction with receptors in the serotonin system known as 5-HT2AR. 'Psychedelic therapy harnesses a therapeutic window opened up by the brain via the effects of the drugs to facilitate insight and emotional release and, with psychotherapeutic support, a subsequent healthy revision of outlook and lifestyle.'[17]

Think of it as metallurgy. 'One may think of enhancing 5-HT2AR signalling as analogous to increasing the temperature (or excitability) of the brain,' Carhart-Harris theorises. 'Extending this analogy to the process of annealing (i.e. whereby a metal is heated to make it more malleable) – one may think of 5-HT2AR signalling as functioning to induce an entropic state characterised by enhanced flexibility and malleability during which work can be done that, upon cooling, may leave a lasting change.'

The Tukano shaman provides no direct analogue for the modern psychotherapist, but the shaman, in a kindred manner, harnesses the disordered brain patterns elicited by yahé to release psychological tensions, including those associated with the hunt. The Tukano will drink yahé in 'an enriched environment' in which the shaman progressively exposes participants to vocal and instrumental music, bright colours, different odours and subtle changes in light. The aim is to induce states of consciousness in which the dissonance of the meat paradox is both evoked and released.

The Tukano shaman acts as metallurgist, heating the material of the mind to impress upon the community the ontological equivalence between humans and animals, the reality of Vaímahsë. The pervasive anxiety the Tukano feel about the risk of reprisals is deliberately cultivated by the shaman. It is desirable that the hunter, as he approaches the tufted peccary, understands that someday their positions might be reversed. It is appropriate that the child, as they sit down to consume a platter of monkey flesh, believes that excessive consumption comes at the highest cost. The yahé ceremony entrenches the community's commitment to the 'perfectly symmetrical' exchange of animal bodies and human souls, but it also provides release when the emotional tensions become overwhelming.

'Emotionally, the hunt is a focus of many expectations and fears, gratifications and anxieties,' Reichel-Dolmatoff writes. When these fears and anxieties become too acute, some individuals might fall sick. The hunter is plagued by nightmares, troubling visions in which they are confronted by the accusing eyes of their victim. In the depths of the yahé ritual, the shaman will sometimes conjure a vulture, carrion birds which swoop down to cleanse the body, consuming the 'rotten matter' that penetrates the hunter's flesh, the tiny darts hurled by Vaí-mahsë. The vulture arrives in psychotropic squall, claws and wings, its hooked beak deftly pulling darts from the body, engendering emotional release. 'Much of this is irrational,' Reichel-Dolmatoff concedes, 'but the [yahé] ceremony seems to provide people with an important catharsis, not accessible in other states.'[18]

It was perhaps this catharsis that our ancestors sought in the darkness of the cave. The dissonance of the hunt, the trauma of killing quasi-similar beings, aroused a response. This response was enacted via story and ritual in the daylight world, but in moments of crisis, it required an extraordinary journey into the earth. An act of restitution, as teeth and bones were pushed into the cave wall. The release of animal images from pent-up depths, as a group danced and sang and imitated animal cries. We carried our dreams of swooning mammoths into the dark. We painted the image of cow and calf upon a remote stone surface, and we sat in silence and listened for their response. Selected individuals, perhaps elders, carrying the burden on behalf of the community, ventured into the deepest recesses, harnessing sensory isolation to heat the pathways of the mind. The cave was our laboratory, the darkness our catalyst and flame.

10

FUTURES

It felt like a hood had been thrown over my head, like a heavy material had been draped over me. It was stifling; I could hardly breathe. I felt helpless, flushed with futility and dread, as if I was losing my foothold and slipping into a terrible and terrifying *un*reality. It came in waves, this feeling, and I was dizzy. I wanted to reach out and grasp the person next to me, ground myself by holding onto them, but I didn't. I was sitting next to Caroline Lucas, Member of Parliament for Brighton Pavilion, the former leader of the Green Party, whom I admire greatly, and I didn't want to startle her.

I had been late arriving.

The queue to enter Portcullis House had been longer than usual, and we stood patiently in a slow-shuffling line, waiting to be admitted. There were tourists and taxis. Long boats on the River Thames and pigeons pecking at crisp packets. A troupe of pro-Brexit demonstrators had paraded past, twenty of them or thereabouts. They were on their way, presumably, to the Palace of Westminster on the far side of Parliament Square to complain about something or other. They were holding the English flag aloft, the red cross of Saint George, proud and bright in the morning sun, and they were trying to chant in unison –

What do we want? BREXIT!
When do we want it? NOW!

– but they kept getting the words muddled –

Who do we want? NOW!
When do we what it? BREXIT!

The security guard finally beckoned me in. I placed my bag on the scanner and walked through the metal detector. 'Wear this,' he said, handing me a laminated ID. And then on, through the sliding glass doors, up the stairs overlooking the atrium where MPs and their advisors drink coffee, plot and ploy (an underground tunnel leads beneath the square to the Palace of Westminster where the House of Commons and House of Lords sit), and then along a narrow corridor to the briefing room door.

I arrived just as Chris Stark, CEO of the Climate Change Committee, was taking the stage. The Climate Change Committee is the independent body established to advise the UK government on its legal duties with respect to the climate crisis, including those pertaining to the Climate Change Act 2008, which committed the UK to an 80 per cent decline in greenhouse gas emissions by 2050. The Act was overwritten in 2019 when Parliament set a legally binding target to cut greenhouse gas emissions to 'net zero' by 2050. I had been invited, along with various politicians and scientists, policy makers and campaigners, to the parliamentary launch of the Climate Change Committee's annual progress report. Stark was explaining how the UK was getting on in reducing emissions and adapting to future warming.

It wasn't good news. Of the twenty-five policy actions the committee had recommended a year before, only one had been implemented in full, and ten had not shown even partial progress. The government was failing so comprehensively in its legal obligations that Lord Deben, chair of the committee, had suggested that ministers could be sued in court. In a comment issued to journalists that morning, Deben had compared the UK's response to the climate crisis to *Dad's Army*, a 1970s sitcom set in the Second World War in which a group of hapless characters struggle to organise the Home Guard in the face of imminent invasion from the Nazis. The comment captured the headlines, but it was an unfortunate comparison, for it made the government's failings seem almost endearing, and distracted from the real news of the day, the bombshell that Stark was about to drop on stage.

'We are already seeing the impacts of a global temperature rise of just one degree Celsius,' Stark said, 'and these impacts are significant. The Paris Agreement sets the target of keeping warming below two degrees, ideally below one point five. We are a long way from achieving that. Current global commitments only give us a fifty per cent chance of staying within three degrees of warming. Although the UK is committed to working for global action towards one point five degrees, it is prudent to plan for a higher warming scenario. The Climate Change Committee is therefore recommending today that the UK government puts adaptation strategies in place for a four-degree rise in global temperatures.'

It was then that the hood was pulled over me, that I felt that flood of futility and inchoate dread. *Four degrees!* This man in smart shoes and a sensible shirt was recommending that the UK government should formally begin preparing for a rise of 4 °C (7.2 °F) in global temperatures. It was madness.

Of course, the recommendation was entirely reasonable. Global emissions continue to track the scenario labelled 'RCP8.5' by the Intergovernmental Panel on Climate Change (IPCC), which would lead to a rise in global temperatures of between 2.6 °C and 4.8 °C by the end of this century. Although climate policies have the potential to bend the curve, they need to be implemented and enacted, and that's not happening anywhere near fast enough. We are plausibly on course for 4 °C global heating in just a few decades.[1]

It might not sound like much, but each degree of warming embodies a heightened risk of ecological and social collapse. A 4 °C rise in global temperatures would render our planet unrecognisable and profoundly hostile to human civilisation. Picture the scene. The glaciers that feed many of Asia's rivers have melted. Drought and heatwaves scorch the planet's breadbaskets where most of the world's food is produced. Widespread and recurring crop failures have left billions struggling with hunger. Humidity and heat stress have made parts of the equatorial belt of the planet biologically uninhabitable. India, Pakistan and Bangladesh no longer exist as social or political entities, forcing a large proportion of the global population to become climate refugees. We are a species in retreat, societies shifting to high-latitude areas where agriculture is still possible, such as Canada, Siberia, Scandinavia and Alaska in the northern hemisphere, and New Zealand, Tasmania, western Antarctica and Patagonia in the south. The Sahara Desert has expanded into Europe, swallowing the Mediterranean, drying rivers including the Danube and the Rhine, devastating Europe's food system. As Europe succumbs to desertification, malaria, dengue, yellow fever and Zika arrive from the south. On the other side of the Atlantic, America is smothered by dust storms in its southern and western states, harvests are collapsing and cattle dying from heat stress and thirst, while national parks burn to the ground. One in three humans is without access to fresh water, but salt waters are rising. Sea levels are already two metres higher, displacing hundreds of millions of people from coastal areas, leaving dozens of cities cowering behind sea walls vulnerable to the next storm. Having passed the tipping points for the Greenland and West Antarctic ice sheets, an ice-free world is now all but guaranteed, with at least ten metres of future sea-level rise locked in. The planet is blanketed in smoky haze as vast forest fires accelerate the catastrophic dieback of the Amazon rainforest, triggering an abrupt mass extinction event. The oceans are transformed; coral reefs, home to a quarter of all fish species, have died, along with a large proportion of shellfish and plankton, wiped out by rising acidity and algal blooms that starve the waters of oxygen. Without prey, larger sea life, including most whales, face extinction. The Arctic permafrost has melted, releasing billions of tonnes of carbon dioxide and methane in a positive feedback. With the summer ice also gone, and the sun shining upon the darker open waters, the warming of the planet is set to accelerate. Floods carry away towns and villages. Tropical cyclones devastate coastal cities, and with national infrastructure collapsing, even in affluent nations, the survivors are left to fend for themselves. Mass migrations put a strain on borders and exacerbate the crises of hunger and food insecurity. The planet is so transformed by megadroughts and altered precipitation, there is barely enough food to feed *half* the planet's population, let alone the 10 billion expected at the end of this century.[2]

To paint such a picture might seem perverse – a 'doomer' fantasy of a worst-case future – but this is the task the Climate Change Committee has set the UK government. This is what a sober reading of the science says a 4 °C heated world looks like. This is the world the committee has tasked our political leaders with preparing to inhabit. How do you even begin?

A seam of mind-bending unreality runs through the climate crisis. We are *choosing* to bring this world into being, even today. Such a world is already on the horizon, and for all the political posturing of recent years, we are nowhere near a resolution. Anyone can jack DMT into their nervous system and watch the world come apart, but to look our collective trajectory in the eye, to behold the causes and the consequences of the climate crisis, and to understand how little time we have, is to be faced with true madness. How can we prepare to live in such a world? Is it possible to face up to the prospect without being overwhelmed by sadness or paralysed by fear?

And it is worse than that, for if we bring such a world into being, there is every chance that the crisis will not end there. On the Climate Change Committee's own estimation, 4 °C of global heating means stepping over an 'extreme danger threshold' beyond which lie irreversible tipping points in the climate system, feedback loops that would lock us into further warming, from 6 °C to 8 °C and on to the precipice of extinction. On our current emissions trajectory, 4 °C of heating, or its threshold, could be realised within the lifetimes of children and young adults alive today. We are careering headlong into an impossible future, and the meat paradox is fuelling the dietary excesses that exacerbate the crisis. In a horrible irony, our appetite for industrially farmed meat is propelling us into a *post-agricultural world*.[3]

The human story has been impelled by climate change from the beginning. It was a shift in the global climate that forced us from the trees into the open savannah, triggering our evolution from hominid to early human around 2 million years ago. For 97 per cent of our history, we have lived as hunters and foragers, and it was a further change in the global climate that made farming possible. In the Holocene, a geological epoch that began around 12,000 years ago, an unprecedented combination of climate stability and warm temperatures enabled increased dependence on wild grains in several parts of the world. Over the next several millennia, this growing dependence led to agriculture, large-scale societies, and civilisation. The rest, as they say, is history. But our farming days might be numbered. The Holocene is ending, and agriculture could end with it.

Within a few years, atmospheric carbon dioxide is set to exceed a concentration of 427 parts per million. This hasn't occurred since the mid-Pliocene warming period over 3 million years ago, when temperatures were 3–4 °C hotter than today and sea levels were 20 metres higher. By about 2025, our atmosphere is likely to have carbon dioxide concentrations not experienced since the Middle Miocene Climatic Optimum, 15 million years ago, around the time our pre-hominid ancestors diverged from the lineage of the orangutan. 'With the future climate instability already locked into the system by recent human activity we will most likely return to the climate volatility of the Pleistocene,' Professor John Gowdy explains. 'Agriculture was impossible in the past because of climate/weather instability and it is likely to again be impossible if similar conditions return.'[4]

In a provocative paper, 'Our hunter-gatherer future: Climate change, agriculture and uncivilization', published in the journal *Futures* in 2020, Gowdy suggests that we are on the cusp of a post-agricultural age. The global food system is not about to collapse, not in the immediate future, but when we look beyond the end of this century, two centuries from now, we are looking into a world of instability and climate variability such that farming might be impossible. Gowdy does not speculate as to whether this post-agricultural age will arrive following the abrupt collapse of our civilisation, or following a slower and more deliberate transition, but either would be catastrophic for most people. 'It may be unlikely, but if the effects of climate change are gradual enough, a soft landing to a non-agricultural economy may be possible.' Gowdy's vision might be disturbing or unusual, but his reframing of the crisis deserves consideration. Climate change narratives often fail to look beyond the end of this century, as though '4 °C by 2100' is the end of the story. The story does not end with this century, and a planet heated by 4 °C might simply be a stepping stone to something else. If we should strive to curtail global heating, Gowdy says, it is partly because, in this post-agricultural world, every fraction of a degree matters. Our descendants will be able to live more easily on a planet heated by 5 °C than on one that has heated by 6 °C. We are not simply fighting for the survival of our society, but for a world in which our hunter-gatherer grandchildren can thrive.

The images on the walls of Niaux were painted upon the

brink of the Holocene, as the world began to warm and the climate stabilised. It would be several millennia before the hunting life patterns of our ancestors would give way to settlement and agriculture, but the world was already changing. The artists at Niaux were among the last practitioners of a tradition that had endured for a thousand generations, reaching back through Chauvet to the crafting of the Lion Man. Throughout this time, the climate had oscillated between bitter cold and more temperate and humid periods. During the last glacial maximum (the 'peak' of the last Ice Age), around 20,000 years ago, Europe was locked in extreme cold. Iceberg-strewn waters lapped upon the shores of France and Spain, and polar bears swam in the River Thames. A glacier filled the Vicdessos Valley, walls of ice rising above the entrance to the cave. In the millennia that followed, the northern ice sheets would contract and the glacier would retreat, carving the V-shaped vale that can be seen beneath Niaux today. Remnants of the receding glacier were still in the valley when the artists first entered the cave. Lush shoots of pine, spruce and herbage were rising from the land that had been cleared, grazed by ibex in winter and early spring. It was these animals that drew the community here, the focus of their subsistence and the inspiration for their art.

It is a strange thing to stand before their images today, these charcoal outlines and painted animals. Palaeolithic art does something peculiar to the perception of time. The expanse of the past opens out while drawing near, and the future is felt bearing down at breakneck speed. The glacier gripping the valley is gone, and a few decades from now, it will be desert winds that rise from the south, Saharan airstreams licking the mouth of the cave. These images might outlive us. Perhaps they will be discovered several centuries from now by our hunting and foraging descendants. The Vicdessos Valley is poised between ice and fire, as we all are. These images speak of the past in the present, and the possibility of our ancient futures.[5]

Gowdy's vision is not wholly negative. 'In the long run, the vision of returning to a hunting and gathering way of life is wildly optimistic compared to the technological dystopias envisioned by many science fiction authors and social philosophers. Every characteristic that defines us as a species – compassion for unrelated others, intelligence, foresight and curiosity – evolved in the Pleistocene.'

As we look towards this post-agricultural world, we might learn how to live by attending to the societies that still survive in autonomy and sufficiency today. 'In view of the looming social and environmental changes we face, this makes it even more important to support and protect the world's remaining indigenous cultures that still have the ability to live beyond the confines of modern civilization.' If I have been drawn back repeatedly to the Inuit and the Tukano, the Yukaghirs and the Cree, it is perhaps for this reason. These peoples might seem like a vestige of our past, but they are as contemporary as anyone alive today, and they might tell us something of what it means to live in the world soon to come. The Climate Change Committee has asked the UK government to prepare for a 4 °C heated planet, and that is a world in which this hunter-gatherer future is uncomfortably plausible.

Of course, there is one further detail to be added to this dire account. A footnote to supplement this vision of post-agricultural subsistence and civilisational collapse.

It doesn't have to be like this.

Peter was just a boy when his father accidentally purchased an industrial pig farm. British Field Products, his father's company, had set up shop in an abandoned airfield. The family were living in the old control tower, above the factory where grass and alfalfa were dried and processed into pellets. It was the years following the Second World War, and the government was looking to increase the UK's self-sufficiency in food. British Field Products found a niche in the post-war market, selling their pellets as animal feed, helping to reduce British farmers' reliance on imported fishmeal. As the business grew, Peter's father began buying up the surrounding farmland. He needed more grass and alfalfa for processing. He didn't realise that one of the farms included an intensive pig unit.

Peter remembers stepping inside. 'We walked in through the door, dad and I, and the smell and the noise were unbelievable. My father had a very sensitive nose, and he took a couple of steps inside and then marched out and said: "we're selling this – we're not having it."'

The memory 'struck, very strongly in my mind', Peter says. Decades later, as policy director for the Soil Association, Peter would lead a successful campaign to oppose the planning application for an industrial pig farm at Foston in Derbyshire, England. The childhood memory of that place, 'the stench of ammonia and darkness and horror', still moved him.

Many of Peter's childhood memories were of animals. The Norfolk countryside of the fifties and sixties was teeming with wildlife, especially birds. 'I remember standing in the garden and watching lapwings flying over back to the coast. The whole sky would be full of them.' There were tree sparrows and skylarks, curlews and corn buntings, yellowhammers and partridges, and a pair of turtle doves, migratory birds who would arrive from sub-Saharan Africa each year to breed. Peter learned to anticipate their arrival, a blur of blue-grey in sudden flight across a field at the northern end of the farm.

If Peter was attentive towards the animals of his Norfolk environs, it was partly because he was trying to shoot them. 'If you're hunting something, you're very conscious of what's there,' he explains. Peter shot pheasants and partridges from a young age, and he went beagling, hunting hares on foot with a pack of dogs. His grandfather, a poet and devoted fox hunter, had risen to the rank of Master of the Fox Hounds, but Peter never enjoyed hunting on horseback, and in time he would renounce blood sports. 'I saw a lot of hares being killed, so when I turned against hunting, I could see through the specious arguments of the hunting lobby.' The idea that hunting was humane, an ancient and honourable practice, a way of forging a 'spiritual' connection to the British countryside, was, in Peter's estimation, 'bullshit'.

The move from hunter to anti-hunting campaigner was one of several swerves in Peter's life. Born Peter Robert Henry Mond, Peter succeeded to the title of 4th Baron Melchett upon his father's death in 1973. The peerage had originally been granted to his great-grandfather, Sir Alfred Mond, one of the founders of Imperial Chemical Industries, the largest chemical manufacturer in the UK. Peter's father, Julian, had also been an industrialist, chairing the British Steel Corporation, and Peter could easily have followed his father into a career in industry, but he chose a different path.

That path is too rich to tell in its entirety, though I would like very much to try. I would like to tell you about Peter's political career, how he became the youngest government minister in modern times (pipped only by William Pitt the Younger); about his achievements as minister for state in two Labour governments, and how he sat on the front bench of the opposition in the Lords. I would like to tell you about his maiden speech in the House of Lords, when he spoke out against the cruelty of keeping animals in captivity in zoos. ('It was the 1970s, and everyone thought going to London Zoo was wonderful,' he remembers. 'I felt quite sick the whole time I was there.') I would like to tell you about his political legacy, which was both environmental and cultural; his role in delivering the Wildlife and Countryside Act 1981, the UK's first major piece of environmental legislation; and about the time he became the government minister responsible for the UK's free party and festival scene.

(OK, I'll tell you about that one. It was the early 1970s, the years following the legendary Woodstock Festival held in 1969 on Max Yasgur's dairy farm in Bethel, New York, and a festival scene had sprung up in the UK. Parties were being convened in Windsor Great Park, much to the disapproval of the local residents, and Thames Valley Police had begun to employ extreme violence to disperse the revellers. Someone was going to get killed. Peter was invited to chair a parliamentary committee investigating festivals and free parties. 'I was young and liberal, and I had long hair,' he recalls. He took it upon himself to find an alternative venue for the Windsor contingent. In an extraordinary scene, which has surely never been repeated, a government minister was to be found poring over maps of military airbases, searching for sites where free parties could be held without fear of police violence. Peter moved the Windsor party to an airbase at Watchfield. 'It wasn't a very attractive site for a festival, but at least it kept the police from killing someone.' Under Peter's guidance, the committee concluded that parties and festivals were *a good thing* and they recommended avenues of appeal for organisers. Michael Eavis, the founder of Glastonbury Festival, says that without Peter's work on the committee, Glastonbury Festival wouldn't exist today. But I digress.)

There is more, so much more. I would like to tell you about how Peter joined Greenpeace, first as chair and then as executive director, and about the anti-nuclear protests that helped land him the role, the work of the Snowball group, on whose behalf Peter was arrested for attempted criminal damage. I would like to tell you about the evolution of environmental activism in the 1980s, and how Peter, fresh out of government, brought acumen and political savvy to an energetic but unruly movement; the inflatable boats that he sent to intercept whaling vessels, the activists who put their bodies in the way of the harpoon; the oil installations occupied on Peter's watch, the water cannons that tried to sweep the intruders from the decks. I would like to tell you about how Peter went fishing – literally – for nuclear submarines, sending tugs with nets to catch subs on manoeuvre off the coast of Scotland; his fear that Greenpeace's assets would be seized in response; the time the secret service infiltrated the organisation in France, forcing the chapter to close; the occasion that government agents broke into a car to steal plans of an upcoming protest; and the events that prompted the Ministry of Defence to raid Peter's office.

(OK, another digression. It was 1995, and Greenpeace had reason to believe the UK government was failing to comply with its obligations under the international Nuclear Non-Proliferation Treaty. To force the issue, a troop of activists occupied two nuclear facilities at Sellafield and Aldermaston, pouring six tonnes of cement into a pipe discharging waste from Aldermaston into the Thames, forcing a halt to the production of weapons-grade plutonium. The government was furious. Shortly after the action, Greenpeace's offices were raided by the Ministry of Defence (MOD), and files and videos were seized as evidence. There is archive footage of the ensuing press conference. 'No, we've never been raided before,' Peter says, faced with a wall of journalists. 'I think the MOD have obviously felt under unprecedented pressure and have probably made unprecedented fools of themselves.' As the government pored over the files, searching for evidence to pin charges on the activists involved, Peter wrote an open letter to Malcolm Rifkind, Secretary of State for Defence:

> I guess all military (and naval) commanders look a bit silly sometimes. And the same goes for government ministers. But silly and cowardly in combination is demeaning for any minister and, I'd have thought, especially inappropriate for the Secretary of State for Defence. So, after trawling through our records, if you are going to try to scapegoat a few individuals, my message to you is this: Greenpeace does not hide behind the actions of individual activists. Greenpeace is its activists. And Greenpeace actions are performed by and on behalf of its 400,000 supporters. As executive director, I take responsibility for Greenpeace. If you want to attack Greenpeace, Malcolm, here I am, ready when you are.

Rifkind didn't take up the invitation, but the pursuit of legal action was dropped. 'The shit hit the fan quite a lot in the nineties,' John Sauven, one of the activists involved, now executive director of Greenpeace UK, remembers. 'The government was really pissed off. A lot of us faced quite long stretches in Her Majesty's prison. But we slept easy because Peter was at the helm, and when faced with extreme adversity, he never blinked first.')

I would like to tell you about Peter's time at the Soil Association, the campaigns he led against pesticides, and his role in tackling the overuse of antibiotics in industrial animal farming. I would like to tell you about his collaboration with a dinner lady named Jeanette Orrey, how they sparked a revolution in school food, improving the meals served to millions of children today. And the prelude to it all, Greenpeace's campaign against genetically modified foods. Peter leading a dawn raid on a field of genetically modified maize. The farmers who arrived, knives in hand, and began slashing at Greenpeace's banners. The shouts of 'Melshit! Melshit!' that could be heard, hurled at the 4th Baron Melchett, as they drove tractors at Peter and his colleagues in an apparent attempt to kill them. The police who were forced to intervene; how one thing can lead to another. 'Much to our annoyance, the night before we were about to go on a family holiday, we learnt that he had been refused bail and sent to a Norwich prison,' Peter's daughter Jessie remembers. I would like to tell you about the trial, the toll it took on Peter and the protesters; the newspaper headlines ('Peter Melchett – Vandal or Visionary?'); how the president of the National Farmers' Union demanded to see Peter locked up, describing the jury's not guilty decision as 'perverse'. I would like to tell you about all this, and so much more. But instead, I will tell you about those turtle doves – where they went, why they came back, and what it meant to Peter.

Peter's life was profoundly influenced by two books (as lives are prone to be, when the right books come along). They were Peter Singer's *Animal Liberation* and Rachel Carson's *Silent Spring*. One was the founding text of the animal rights movement, the other the founding text of the environmental movement. Peter walked both paths, embodying the tensions and contradictions that ensued.

The importance of Carson's *Silent Spring* can hardly be overstated. Serialised in successive issues of the *New Yorker* during the summer of 1962 and published as a book later the same year, *Silent Spring* marked the birth of the modern environmental movement. Carson gave voice to a simple yet vital ecological insight: that everything in nature is related to everything else. She explained how the use of chemical pesticides had killed insects, eroded wildlife and undermined the biological complexity in which our lives, our health and our food system are embedded. A 'chemical barrage has been hurled against the fabric of life – a fabric on the one hand delicate and destructible, on the other miraculously tough and resilient, and capable of striking back in unexpected ways'. Her writing blended scientific acumen with an unapologetic love of the living world, and it opened Peter's eyes.

'I remember as a child there was a farm field at the end of the garden – walk into the field in winter, and the whole field would take off in flight, there were so many seed-eating birds on the winter stubble. I remember watching the tree sparrows and the skylarks, the sky full of lapwings. Now if you see a flock of ten, it feels like a privilege.'

Peter had witnessed the abrupt decline in the wildlife of his native Norfolk throughout the sixties and seventies. 'I was acutely aware, partly because I was shooting and hunting, of the numbers.' The corn buntings were in decline. The yellow-hammers had fallen silent. The hares were fewer. The turtle doves had all but disappeared (turtle doves are now the UK's fastest declining bird species, on the verge of extinction). The gamekeepers working the shoots told him the birds were dying because of the weather, or because it was a 'bad year'. Peter realised they hadn't a clue. When he read *Silent Spring*, he understood that the birds were being poisoned and were starving, insecticides killing the insects they fed on, intensive farming disrupting their habitats.

Peter began to convert the family farm to organic shortly before he joined the Soil Association. But to farm organically, he needed to farm animals. And this posed a quandary, for he was a vegetarian.

Peter had been turned on to animal rights by Peter Singer's *Animal Liberation* in the early 1980s. As minister of state, he had been responsible for health policy in Northern Ireland, and in this capacity he had visited hospitals where terminally ill children were cared for, and psychiatric wards where the most vulnerable adults were tended and protected. Why should we treat animals with any less empathy? Peter was persuaded by Singer's reasoning. He gave up meat and became a lifelong advocate for animal rights.

But he was also committed to conservation. Together with his partner Cass, he had purchased an area of marshland on the coast, not far from the farm, which provided a habitat for countless birds, including several rare species. 'We kept cattle on the farm because we needed cows to graze the grazing marsh,' he explains; 'without them hundreds of thousands of ducks and geese and other birds wouldn't have a suitable habitat.'

He also began farming pigs. 'We needed something to bring nutrients back onto the farm. The pigs provide phosphate and potassium, which we need to grow crops and avoid digging up the Atlas Mountains in Morocco, which is where mined phosphate comes from.' After trying a few breeds, Peter landed on the Tamworth, a native breed that is closely related to its wild ancestors, the wild boar.

'I learned a huge amount,' he says of the pigs. 'I learned that sows are social animals who like living, nesting and rearing young together. If families of four or five sows are brought up together, and if they have a reasonable amount of space and a good healthy diet, including food from grass and soil they can root in, they will not fight or injure each other. In these conditions, the pigs can happily live in a manner similar to how wild boars live. But to rear pigs like this, you need a breed which has lost less of the resilient wild boar characteristics and is still able to mother and care for their young. We are talking about a very different approach from any indoor or intensive system.'

This negotiation between ecology and ethics was not straightforward. Peter recalls 'agonising' over the decision, but he understood that it was a necessary arrangement, for without the pigs, the farm would be reliant on industrial inputs and fossil fuel fertilisers – and Peter understood better than most the folly of such reliance.

Peter was intimately acquainted with the mendacity of the fossil fuel industry. He had seen the way oil companies would search for loopholes in environmental legislation, expanding extraction into ecologically vulnerable areas. He had witnessed their disregard for the oceans, their willingness to cause irreversible damage in pursuit of profits. He had grappled with the industry, taking ten oil companies and the UK government to court, and sending activists to occupy oil rigs, including Brent Spar, a rig that Shell was intending to dump in the North Sea. There is a wonderful scene in Parliament from the days following the campaign's success, when Shell was forced to abandon their plan. Prime Minister John Major is excellently irate. 'I *deeply* regret Shell's decision to cave in to *misguided* pressure from *environmental* groups,' he grumbles, while rows of dusty Conservative MPs groan their flaccid support.

Peter had also taken on the phosphate industry, responsible for the manufacture of agricultural phosphate fertilisers, leading an action against a factory in Cumbria that was dumping industrial waste into the Irish sea. Greenpeace activists had blocked the pipe, attaching a steel plate to its end, halting the effluence, but this had landed them in a perilous legal situation. Peter met with the directors of the phosphate company, and in a game of charm and brinkmanship, he talked them down. With characteristic defence and warmth, he had befriended them while subtly threatening further action, which would include sending Greenpeace's ship the *Rainbow Warrior* to the island where the phosphate was being mined. The charges were dropped, and the company agreed to stop discharging into the ocean.

Peter converted his farm to organic because he wanted to take a stand against the GM industry, and because he loved wildlife and understood the harms caused by pesticides. But he also recognised the benefit – and necessity – of moving away from fossil fuel fertilisers and industrially processed phosphate. The organic alternative meant farming with animals. His idealism was tempered by his pragmatism, and he became the most unlikely of things, a vegetarian animal farmer.

In this hybrid identity, Peter was following in the footsteps of Lady Eve Balfour, who founded the Soil Association in 1946. Balfour was the first woman to study agriculture at an English university and the author of *The Living Soil*, a work that remains strikingly contemporary in its insight into the interdependence of human and ecological health. Balfour wanted to know why some people were healthy and others were not. She surveyed the ethnographic evidence, the accounts of indigenous peoples who 'still enjoy an exceptional measure of health'. What these peoples had in common, she observed, was not race, colour or creed; and it was not the environment in which they lived, for 'there could hardly be greater contrasts than between the plains and hills of rural China or the prairies of North America and the precipitous mountain crags of the northern provinces of India, or than between the frozen north and the luxuriant warmth of Tristan de Cunha'. Nor was it diet – at least not in the obvious sense – for their diets ranged from the mostly plant-based, as among the Hunza, to the almost purely carnivorous, as among the Eskimos. What mattered, Balfour perceived, was the *quality* of the diet. These peoples all ate 'whole' diets, formed of natural and unprocessed foods, and these foods were provided by a system in which all the wastes of the community were returned to the land from which they came. 'There is a complete and continuous transference of health from a fertile soil, through plant and/or animal to man, and back to the soil again. The whole carcass, the whole grain, the whole fruit or vegetable, these things from their source, and that source a fertile soil.' Balfour included the Eskimos in her analysis, the Inuit who returned bladders and bodies to the sea, an ecology of flesh. 'For the sea too is a "soil" in this sense, supporting its teeming population by means of the rule of return – the everlasting cycle of life and decay.' We can be healthy on all manner of diets, she concluded, if the diet is minimally processed and of a high quality, and if it is provided by an organic or cyclical farming system.

Balfour was a lifelong vegetarian, though not an entirely strict one. She stopped eating meat on compassionate grounds having witnessed the violence of a pheasant shoot as a young girl. Yet she recognised that animals were an integral component of this cyclical farming system, that the return of nutrients and life to the soil, which engendered a healthy land, healthy food and healthy people, often required grazing and browsing animals. She chose not to eat meat, but she pioneered an understanding of 'the vital relationships between soil, plant, animal and man', laying the foundations for the organic movement, which still aspires today to balance the ethical and the ecological, our commitments to animals with our biotic entanglement, and which holds so many of the answers to the climate crisis.

'I think it's right to be a vegetarian, but I don't think the whole world has to be vegetarian,' Peter said at one time. 'And perhaps I wouldn't have been, if I had been an organic farmer at the time that I read *Animal Liberation*; I don't know. What I do know is that all of us will need to eat less meat in the future. We can't tackle climate change and live on this planet if we all eat as much as we do in the UK or North America, at least not fairly or equitably.

'I met Peter Singer once,' he added, a wry smile in his voice.

'He gave a talk, and afterwards I went to find him, and I introduced myself. I told him that I became vegetarian after reading *Animal Liberation*. I told him I found the work very influential. But I said I'm now an organic farmer, and that means I farm pigs and cows.'

Singer replied to this: 'Oh, I think you're quite right – climate change is such a huge threat, I think we all have to farm more organically, that's the priority!'

I worked with Peter for the last five years of his life. We collaborated closely on a Soil Association campaign called Out to Lunch, which worked to improve the food served in popular restaurant chains and visitor attractions. Peter acted as a mentor of sorts, and we achieved a great deal. We got organic on the menu at more than a dozen of the UK's largest chains, including JD Wetherspoon and Harvester. The number of chains serving sustainable fish trebled under our watch. We removed two hundred tonnes of sugar from children's menus, and we put more than ten million additional portions of veg on plates. It wasn't just the two of us, there were many others, but it was me and Peter on the front line, faced with the angry CEOs whose brand we had criticised in the national press; sat in boardrooms faced with rows of glaring eyes, PR gurus gurning. Peter usually managed to arrive ten minutes late, leaving me to sweat it alone.

Peter died as this book was approaching full gestation. Though his death was not unexpected, it still came as a shock, a gut-punch of loss. In the months that followed, I found myself searching his life, as though looking for something, I didn't know what. I was looking for reassurance, I suppose. I was searching for a reason to believe that we might yet find our way through this mess, this crisis that promises to consume us. I must tell you this. I did not find it. There was no reassurance to be found. It would be tempting to read Peter's life as a tale of environmental optimism, a story of the campaigner who takes on the powers of industry and ecological degradation and wins, but that would be trite. Peter's achievements were many and significant, but the legacy of the environmental movement is failure. More than half a century after *Silent Spring*, the fabric of life is unravelling as never before. After decades of environmental campaigning, here we are, staring down the barrel of this century. David has slain Goliath in skirmish after skirmish, but Goliath (it turns out) is a many-headed hydra, and with each head lopped, another rises in its place. It is now so late in the day, and the odds are stacked squarely against us. The weight and momentum behind this monster is simply too much. I can reach no other conclusion. I would not bet on a happy ending.

But then I think of those turtle doves, their wings arched over open reaches of shore and desert; the grace of their flight as the sand and seas roil below. I think of their path over savannah and forest, the towns and cities of Morocco and the Mediterranean, the curve of the earth beneath their gaze, and the clarity and intensity of their will. I think of the distance they travelled to arrive on these shores. Britain, an expanse of concrete and ryegrass, field boundaries and suburban sprawl. I think of their swiftness as they traversed the land, the myriad places they might have chosen to alight. I think of the improbability of their arrival back in that field, after so many years.

'The very first year we stopped using sprays – weed killers and insecticides – the turtle doves returned. They came back to the very same field. I always remembered as a child seeing a pair flying across this field, which is at the northern end of the farm. It happened the first year we went organic. I was walking up the green lane, and I saw this pair of birds flying across in front of me, and I had a flashback. They had returned! It was an amazing thing.'

We don't know how they do it, these birds. We don't know how they find their way from Senegal to Norfolk, across thousands of miles of shifting terrain. We are yet to unravel the secrets of the turtle doves' navigation. Scientists used to believe they employed astronavigation, taking measurements from celestial bodies, using the azimuthal position of the sun and stars to determine their direction of travel. Windblown almanac. Avian astrolabe. This might be part of the answer, but it cannot be the whole story, for one would need a map as well as a compass to find the way. The map might have been provided by magneto-reception, clusters of neurons in the birds' brains connected to concentrated iron particles in their beaks, guiding them through our planet's magnetosphere, head as rudder, wings as sails set against solar winds. Perhaps they tacked from landmark to landmark, drawn by field lines that flexed and expanded with the changing latitude. Or perhaps it was the olfactory sense that guided them, a map of vapours and scent trails, airborne molecules and chemosensory instinct, for we know that doves deprived of their ability to smell cannot navigate.

Scientists now believe they might have cracked it. The most convincing hypothesis says the turtle dove is sensitive to infra-sound, capable of hearing low-frequency acoustic waves that undulate beneath the range of human hearing. The science of infrasonics says these sounds are generated by deep ocean swells reverberating into the land and sky. They are also produced by weather patterns and avalanches, by lightning storms and the calving of icebergs, by aurorae and meteor showers, overlapping layers interacting with nearly everything in the living world, from tree stumps to the frothing of wave tips, river boulders to the weft and warp of the Earth's crust, conjuring a choral landscape in the bird's brain which guides them on their way. Perhaps it is all these in concert. A symphony of synaesthetic intelligence, overlaid aptitudes luring their bodies back to this corner of the land, a blur of blue-grey in sudden flight across a field at the northern end of the farm, inciting a rush of joy and wonder and remembering in the farmer's brain. Somehow word had reached Africa that Peter had converted his farm to organic. The old breeding grounds were good again. Is this poetry or science speaking?

We might think of the turtle doves' return to that field in purely scientific terms, events dictated by the laws of season and chem-istry, instinct and biological programming. Perhaps the absence of weed killers had allowed the fumitory to flourish, providing the birds' preferred breeding habitat, and perhaps, by chance, two birds had spied this while on the wing to who-knows-where. Probably, this is true. But in the sheer unlikeliness of their return we might discern something more, coded language spoken in voices that fall below the normal range of human hearing. I hear them sometimes, those voices, in rare and treasured moments. I heard them as I stepped from Portcullis House into Parliament Square, still shellshocked from the Climate Change Committee's briefing. I was drenched from head to toe, dripping with futility, but the world was turning still. There were tourists on the banks of the Thames and taxis rushing past; the bustle and business of the city. There was a man hawking watches, and those factions were still protesting outside the doors of Parliament, voices shrill and banners aloft. I sat on a bench amid the pigeons and stared into the concrete. I rested my head in my hands and gazed blankly into a sandwich wrapper below, and that was when it happened. It was as entirely surprising to me as it would have been to you. Pulsating applause, rising up and through. The mantra of frogs in the midnight pond. The tarmac chanting as cicadas in the jungle dusk. They were the same voices that I heard deep in the night, through the rhythm of Gume's rattle and the pattern of his song. The same voices that guided that small-bodied bird – *turr turr turr* – to the field where the farmer waited. Reach out with that subtle sense. Reach far. Reach into the wings of the dove as it drums upon the skin of space, become that feather–bone bundle, pulsing, sky-thrown and fleet, and you will hear them too. The infrasonics of the ten thousand things. The hum beneath the hubbub. Lower your voice, for they are speaking. Tune your ear, for they are less indifferent than we have been led to believe. The coded language of iguana and earthworm, spindrift and fever tree. The whole churning lot of them, urging us in a single breath, a plea and an invitation. *Defy the odds.*

*

We arrived at the Natural History Museum.

It was a Tuesday, and the wind was blustering down Exhibition Road from Hyde Park.

For once, Peter wasn't late. I saw him hurrying from the tube, his shirt untucked, his waterproof flapping in the wind. He was clutching his phone in his left hand, a backpack slung over his shoulder, and his hair was tousled. 'Hello,' he said in a gruff voice, grinning. 'This should be interesting.'

We were greeted at reception. They were expecting us. The administrative assistant led us past an arrangement of hominid skulls, beyond a colossal *Stegosaurus* skeleton, among moon rocks and rare metals, through an apothecary of fluorescent minerals and glowing vials, into the hidden bowels of the institution. We were taken beyond the public galleries, along strip lit corridors, up flights of stairs and through swipe-card security doors, to a remote corner of the museum, a claustrophobic room with plastic chairs and a single small window.

There were two seats arranged on one side of the table, a row of frowning faces on the other.

It was awkward.

I'd made a nuisance of myself. The newspapers had been involved. Headlines splashed. The morning television pundits had caught on, bright-eyed and twitching with caffeine. I had spoken to prime-time radio, babbling disc-jockeys and opinionated callers. The museum's administration was (shall we say) *displeased*. Heated phone calls had been exchanged, irate voices seething as the story dropped. I sent combative emails in response, threatening further action unless the menu was improved.

The museum restaurant had been forced to close while the menu was rebranded and redesigned. One senior individual sitting at the table later confided in me that they had almost lost their job. Peter and I had been through this routine a dozen times before with other restaurants and businesses, but on this occasion the atmosphere was especially tense. Opposite us were senior directors from the museum and their catering outfit, those responsible for the museum's food, the head of PR, and the head chef from the restaurant. Peter's reputation usually preceded him; they were eyeing us like a bomb had just walked in.

Stand up. Sit down. Stunted smile. Forced greetings.

We sat down.

The sound of chair legs scraping.

No one said anything.

The restaurant's new menu was open on the table between us. It was much improved. They had done a good job. There were now more meat-free options, including vegan options for the first time. There was higher welfare and British meat on the menu, and the museum had, for the first time, made a public commitment to sourcing only sustainable fish. Information about the provenance and sustainability of the ingredients had been added to the menu, and in the conversation that followed, the museum would commit to reviewing their sourcing policies in relation to soy and feed crops. (The Natural History Museum, with its catering partner Benugo, now serves some of the best food of any attraction in the UK.)

We knew about these changes before we arrived. We had seen the new menu, and we were pleased with their response. We had come to make peace.

But we weren't going to tell them that, at least not immediately.

We looked at one another.

Someone opened their mouth to speak, and then closed it again.

I glanced over at Peter. He was grinning; he was in his element.

Beyond the door, down the stairs, through a labyrinth of corridors, in the corner of the Human Evolution gallery, a human–feline statuette stared out from a glass case.

Leon Festinger's seminal work *A Theory of Cognitive Dissonance* was published in 1957, a year after his monograph on Marian Keech and her apocalyptic flying saucer cult. The book sparked 'a revolution that revitalized social psychology and changed it forever'. Elliot Aronson remembers, 'I first read Festinger's book in the form of a pre-publication carbon copy that he thrust into my hands (rather disdainfully!) after I told him I was trying to decide whether to enrol in his graduate seminar. Reading that manuscript was something of an epiphany for me. It was (and still is) the single most exciting book I have ever read in all of psychology.'

In the decades since, dissonance theory has been applied to many societal puzzles, advancing our understanding of multiple domains of thought and behaviour, from food phobias to gambling, colour preferences to safer sex, paranoias to religious proselytising, and it is now poised to transform our understanding of our relationship with meat, revealing the hidden dynamics of dietary change.

Aronson was Festinger's student. He spent years working with the architect of dissonance theory, and he went on to voice a revised conception. While Festinger had focused on inconsistency between cognitions (I care about animals; animals are harmed to provide my meat), Aronson reframed dissonance theory around the question of *identity*. We do not experience dissonance simply because cognitive contradictions make us uncomfortable, but because some contradictions disturb our narrative of identity, creating a rupture in the story of the self. Dissonance arises 'when an important element of the self-concept is threatened, typically when a person performs a behaviour that is inconsistent with his or her sense of self'. It is that sense of self – as an ethical omnivore or a committed vegan – which is punctuated by the meat paradox.[6]

Some of the most insightful research into the meat paradox has reflected Aronson's concern with personal identity. When we under-report how much meat we consume, when we say we are vegetarian even when we are not, when we tell others that we only eat higher welfare animals even though this is untrue, and when we rage against the opposing dietary tribe, it is because we are trying to maintain a cohesive self-image in the face of contradictory evidence. Similarly, when we concoct tales of human herbivory, cleaving to the delusion that our species is anatomically 'vegan by design', it is because we are trying to cultivate a self-image that aligns with the ethical demand.

The meat paradox holds us in its grasp, conjuring these elaborate cascades of deflection and denial, fuelling this fractious societal debate, because our narratives of identity – omnivore and vegan – are often inadequate to the task that is put to them. The perception that 'meat involves murder' has no place in the omnivore's tale. The stories that we tell as meat eaters do not help us make sense of the emotions that arise (that might arise) as we stand in the slaughterhouse. There is nothing in this narrative of an 'ancient contract' to affirm that killing animals for food might be irretrievably wrong, acutely disturbing, or even traumatic. Inversely, the perception that 'meat can be necessary' has an ambivalent place in the vegan narrative, at least as it is expressed in the mainstream. The stories that we commonly tell as vegans are often in denial of the fact that meat and animal foods can be nutritious or beneficial, perhaps integral to a sustainable farming system. The dissonance generated by the paradox is too potent to be processed.

We are living in the consequences of these failed narratives, ensnared in a dynamic that is fuelling excessive consumption and cultural polarisation, propelling us towards ecological collapse.

Every society must find a way of navigating the contradictions inherent in the human condition. I have returned repeatedly to the Tukano because I find their navigation of the meat paradox to be singularly sophisticated. The paradox is not a peripheral concern to the Tukano; it is the central concern of their culture. How to align subsistence with the demands of the animal world. How to procure nutrition without causing environmental degradation. How to manage the emotional tensions of the hunt, the ethical burden incurred by the killing of quasi-similar beings. How to maintain, in Reichel-Dolmatoff's words, 'ecological and psychological equilibria' as an empathetic and meat-hungry omnivore.[7]

The Tukano's most prized cultural narratives and rituals have evolved in response. The extraordinary weighting of human and animal life, expressed as an ethic of 'scrupulous equivalence', trains the mind of the hunter upon the question of necessity. The fear of reprisals at the hands of Vaí-mahsë forces the community to grapple to keep the world in poise. 'We may call the Master of Animals a creature of the imagination, a focus of primitive superstitions,' Reichel-Dolmatoff observes, 'but on a deeper level, what we call superstition is based upon sound observation, on hard biological facts.' The Tukano know that human life can only be sustained by killing. They know our carnivorous appetite can degrade the biosphere and disturb the equilibrium of the mind. They perceive that remedial action is necessary.

Reichel-Dolmatoff describes Vaí-mahsë as 'a projection of man's conscience'. The word 'projection' is surely misplaced, for Vaí-mahsë embodies a power immanent within the forest, an intelligence born of the more-than-human world. The figure might seem to us a projection but the Tukano say he is the Master of Animals, voicing the demands of the animal world as they press upon the human community from without. These are difficult ideas for us to entertain, for we like to think of our species as the sole arbiter of ethical conduct, but if we put aside our pretensions, if we have the humility to take the Tukano at their word, there is something significant we might learn.

The Tukano's use of yahé to commune with the animal world might strike us as fantastical, but who are we to judge? The idea that an ancient society built a temple that purred like a jaguar, that our ancestors sought altered states in the darkness of the cave, might sound like mumbo-jumbo, but what do we know? For all our technological wizardry, we are rupturing the fabric of life. For all our purported rationality, we are eating our way to extinction. For all our scientific wisdom, we are emotionally stunted and alienated from ourselves. One in five adults in the UK has considered taking their own life. Twenty per cent of the population. We sanction alcohol, a drug incalculably more destructive than the psilocybin we prohibit. Too many of us are anxious, lonely or uncertain. We have fallen out of psychological and ecological equilibria, and we stand, chicken nugget in hand, swaying over the precipice.

I am not of the Tukano. I cannot speak for them, or for any indigenous peoples. I have offered only a partial (and inevitably flawed) presentation of their culture. I have attended to these societies which differ from ours not because I think that we should ape them. I do not think we should borrow or appropriate their ideas, though there is certainly a great deal that we might learn from them. We live in different worlds, yet when we look towards these cultures, we might perceive that we are looking into a mirror of sorts. We are looking at fellow humans, no less contemporary than we are, who navigate the meat paradox, each in their own way. The mirror can only provide a blurry image, but we might catch a glimpse of ourselves, see what we are relative to who they are, and perhaps perceive what we are lacking.

Veganism is sometimes said to be a modern aberration, our disconnect from the natural world tipping us into a syrupy and sentimental moral stance without precedent in the human story. But the emotions and motivations that animate the vegan movement are not new. Veganism comes adorned with all the baubles and twinkling lights of social media and modernity, but it is industrial animal farming, and not our ethical concern for animals, that is the aberration. The meat paradox is as old as the painted caves, and the roots of the vegan project reach back to the origins of our species, to the stirring of our empathy as it was first extended towards animals. Look beyond our society, and there is no culture in which the consumption of animals is unproblematic. Observe the hunter in the Kalahari keening over his prey. The Cree who declines the platter of barbecued bear. There is no culture in which plant foods are problematic in the same way. There is no equivalent figure to Vaí-mahsë governing the consumption of fruits and vegetables among the Tukano.

Veganism might even be said to be implicit in the hunter's ethic. *Kill only what you need*. The Inuit or Yukaghir living by this refrain arguably has far more in common with the modern vegan than the average omnivore. Veganism has emerged in our culture as a corrective, a riposte to our transparently inadequate pretence at 'ethical omnivory', an expression of our evolved empathy, a rational response to the exploitation of animals and the peril of the planetary emergency. Yet the fact remains that we are not herbivores. We are not frugivorous by evolutionary design, as some would have you believe. Many of us can subsist on a plant-based diet, but there are ecological and nutritional barriers to a world in which no animals are consumed, and they are not trivial. The designation 'ethical omnivore' might be often misplaced, rarely attained, perhaps duplicitous even in the best circumstances, but we are not excused from the predicament into which we have landed. We are confronted with the same task that is set before every society, that of finding a route through, of telling a tale capable of containing the contradiction, of locating an image to anchor the paradox.

In the opening pages of this book I quoted Aldous Huxley, who observed, 'In the history of science the collector of specimens preceded the zoologist and followed the exponents of natural theology and magic.' The collector, Huxley explained, was not yet a student of animal behaviour. 'His primary concern was to make a census, to catch, kill, stuff, and describe as many kinds of beasts as he could lay his hands on.' Huxley was not speaking of Sir Hans Sloane or the explorers and collectors whose work was on display at the Natural History Museum. These words are from the opening paragraphs to *Heaven and Hell*, an essay published as a sequel to *The Doors of Perception*, Huxley's renowned account of his experience on mescaline. Huxley was reaching for a metaphor to describe the remoter regions of the human psyche, the unexplored vistas of the mind. He continues:

Like the earth of a hundred years ago, our mind still has its darkest Africas, its unmapped Borneos and Amazonian basins. In relation to the fauna of these regions we are not yet zoologists, we are mere naturalists and collectors of specimens. The fact is unfortunate; but we have to accept it, we have to make the best of it. However lowly, the work of the collector must be done, before we can proceed to the higher scientific tasks of classification, analysis, experiment, and theory making. Like the giraffe and the duck-billed platypus, the creatures inhabiting these remoter regions of the mind are exceedingly improbable. Nevertheless they exist, they are facts of observation; and as such, they cannot be ignored by anyone who is honestly trying to understand the world in which he lives.[8]

For many years, collectors of specimens have amassed tales of our contradictory relationship with animals. We have observed that one society consumes one animal species while another consumes another. We have seen that one culture's pet is another culture's deity. We have puzzled over the fact that what disgusts one man might be dinner and delight to another. Scholars have observed the extraordinary reach of our empathy, and the paradoxical depths of our disregard. But it is only in the last decade that we have proceeded to the higher scientific task of theory making, becoming more than collectors of specimens. Steve Loughnan and Brock Bastian were the first zoologists of the meat paradox, the first to translate our consumption of meat into the language of dissonance theory, unveiling the cognitive dynamics which skew our thought and perception in so many surprising ways. We now study the behaviour of the beast. We have the creature squarely in view.[9]

Throughout these pages, we have been stalking an improbable animal, a hybrid, part human and part lion. We have been on the trail of a hominoid feline conjured into life in the Upper Palaeolithic. The Lion Man *is* the meat paradox. Its hybrid body contains the contradictions in our nature.

As a human transforming into a lion, the Lion Man is an image of humankind as flesh eater, of our species as predator and hunter, as we have been for over a million years. His hybrid body tells of our evolution from plant-eating primate to meat-hungry hominid, our ascent up the scavenging hierarchy, our position alongside the carnivore guild. We became as lions, but we are not lions. We are not carnivores. The Lion Man also embodies the fantasy that we are no different to a predatory feline; the delusion that we are obedient to instinct, held in appetite's thrall. We long for meat to be denuded of complexity, free from emotional conflict and ethical contradiction. This cannot be.

The Lion Man embodies the empathy intrinsic to our nature, our ability to project ourselves beyond our skin into the mind and senses of another. This figure is every bison, every horse, every cow, every mammoth, every pig and every chicken that has roused our dissonance, all those whose life we have taken and whose gaze we have denied. Carved into a mammoth's tusk 40,000 years ago, the statuette tells of the evolution of the modern mind, the cognitive aptitudes which first emerged in our species, simultaneously making us the most dangerous predator on the planet and the most conflicted.

As Vaí-mahsë – the Master of Animals in human-feline form – the Lion Man embodies the demands of the animal world, the capacity of those whom we consume to prey upon us with the perception of personhood, to impose moral obligations which we cannot control and sometimes cannot respect. We are held in the claws of incongruity, mauled by the gaze of the other. This statuette is the earliest material manifestation of the meat paradox, and it speaks of our earliest response. The stories we began to tell. The rituals we sought to enact. This crisis, which we are still struggling to resolve.

The Lion Man is a hybrid, as surely as you are. We have been tracking this unlikely beast through so many pages, across millions of years of evolution, through the contours of the contemporary meat debate, into alien cultures and through our own, into the pathways of your body and the landscapes of your mind. The Lion Man is the meat paradox, incipient and breathing within you, his left arm scored with geometric forms, his paws suspended three inches from the ground. He stirs, and perhaps the rift is not unbridgeable. His eyes open, and that which tears us apart may yet be held together. Shoulders broadening. Jaw bristling. There is so much more that we could be.

AFTERWORD

In 1996, anthropologist Stephen Hugh-Jones published a paper titled *Bonnes raisons ou mauvaise conscience? De l'ambivalence de certains Amazoniens envers la consommation de viande*. Hugh-Jones had been living among the Tukano, with the Barasana and Makuna in the Colombian Amazon. Notwithstanding the dizzying differences between our culture and theirs, he said, there were evident parallels in how we managed the emotional tensions roused by the consumption of meat.

The Tukano, he observed, perceived a moral hierarchy in the animals they consumed, mirroring the hierarchy found in Europe, large mammals typically being of highest concern. Through the craft of 'food shamanism', the Tukano would lower their meat dishes down the hierarchy, transforming mammal flesh into fish and plants, which were much less disturbing to consume. So compelling was the effect that many members of the tribe viewed themselves as vegetarians, despite frequently consuming the meat of large herbivores. Recalling the testimonies of French slaughterhouse workers, Hugh-Jones suggested that similar efforts to assuage the dissonance of meat might be found in our society. Such a comparison, he said, would be ripe for further study.

The paper drew criticism. The slaughterhouse worker and the hunter inhabited wildly different worlds, critics said. To be a 'person', 'animal' or 'human' meant something wholly different in the 'animist' ontology of the Amazon, compared to the 'naturalist' outlook of the West. We should be careful not to project the mindset of the animal rights activist onto the indigenous hunter.

Hugh-Jones responded in a postscript to the paper. Of course, he said, we must respect difference and refrain from conflating indigenous worldviews with the Western but let us not lose sight of the common ground. An overt focus on the conceptual orders of 'animism' and 'naturalism' can make non-Western societies 'look stranger and more exotic than they actually are', crafting a 'monolithic opposition between Western culture and tribal peoples' which obscures our shared humanity. In virtue of this humanity, and regardless of our cosmological or conceptual framework, we encounter animals as breathing beings, embodied, and imbued with intentionality and sentience. This in an encounter 'between living organisms, and not between collective abstractions', and the empathy awoken by such an encounter is 'arguably a human universal'.

Are we so different, after all? Amazonian hunters, Hugh-Jones recalls, would tell him that 'the compassion they sometimes feel for animals comes through the exchange of glances' – through the eye contact which engenders intimacy, evoking a sense of ethical obligation. I am not of the Tukano, and I cannot speak for them. I am not of the Upper Palaeolithic, yet my consciousness is filtered through the same physiology and neural apparatus as the artist drawing a black bison upon the wall of the cave. Were we not carved, for all our dazzling diversity, along a common evolutionary curve? What if we stopped measuring the distance between us and attended instead to the aptitudes and experiences, the empathy and paradox, which draw us closer together?

ACKNOWLEDGEMENTS

Thanks are due to the scholars and the scientists, the farmers and the activists, the ancestors and the poets. Boundless gratitude to the illustrator, the incomparable Bethan McFadden (www.bethanmcfadden.com). For comments on segments of the draft manuscript, thanks to James Rucker, Alex Lockwood, Brock Bastian, Hank Rothgerber, Frédéric Leroy, Tara Garnett, Alex Heffron and Diana Hawdon. Deepest thanks to Cass Wedd and Chris Rose. For doing extraordinary work in extraordinary times, a sweeping bow of respect to everyone at the Soil Association. Heartfelt appreciation to Joanna Lewis for every opportunity. For words of guidance and encouragement along the way, thanks to Jay Griffiths and Paul Kingsnorth. For words of light and fire, cedar tree and the firm, humble thanks to Annie Dillard. Sincere gratitude to my agent Zoe Ross for seeing the potential when this book was still feral in spirit and form. To Richard Beswick for steadfast support. To Olivia Davies and everyone at United Agents. To Nithya Rae, Steve Gove and the team at Little, Brown. To Claiborne Hancock, Jessica Case and everyone at Pegasus Books.

Lashings of love to the unruly ones.

And to Odin, maestro and mentor, bearded traveller and example to us all.

BIBLIOGRAPHY

Aaltola, E. (2018), *Varieties of Empathy: Moral Psychology and Animal Ethics* (London and New York: Rowman & Littlefield).

Aaltola, E. (2019), 'The Meat Paradox, Omnivore's Akrasia, and Animal Ethics', *Animals*, 9(12): 1125.

Académie Royale de Médecine de Belgique (ARMB) (2018), 'Régimes végétariens et végétaliens administrés aux enfants et adolescents'.

Acari, P. (2020), *Making Sense of 'Food' Animals: A Critical Exploration of the Persistence of 'Meat'* (Singapore: Palgrave Macmillan).

Adams, C. J. (1990), *The Sexual Politics of Meat: A Feminist-Vegetarian Critical Theory* (New York: Continuum; reprint edition, 1999).

Adams, C. J. (2001), *Living Among Meat Eaters: the Vegetarian's Survival Handbook* (New York: Three Rivers Press).

Adams, C. J., Gruen, L., eds. (2014), *Ecofeminism: Feminist Intersections with Other Animals and the Earth* (New York & London: Bloomsbury).

Adesogan, A. T., Havelaar, A. H., McKune, S. L., Eilitta, M., Dahl, G. E. (2020), 'Animal source foods: Sustainability problem or malnutrition and sustainability solution? Perspective matters', *Global Food Security*, 25: 100325.

Agam, A., Barkai, R. (2015), 'Not the brain alone: The

nutritional potential of elephant heads in Paleolithic sites', *Quaternary International*, 406.

Agam, A., Barkai, R. (2018), 'Elephant and Mammoth Hunting during the Paleolithic: A Review of the Relevant Archaeological, Ethnographic and Ethno-Historical Records', *Quaternary*, 1(1): 3.

Agurell, S., Holmstedt, B., Lindgren, J. E., Schultes, R. E. (1969), 'Alkaloids in certain species of Virola and other South American plants of ethnopharmacologic interest', *Acta Chemica Scandinavia*, 23(3): 903–16.

Ahmed, A. A. Q., Odelade, K. A., Babalola, O. O. (2019), 'Microbial Inoculants for Improving Carbon Sequestration in Agroecosystems to Mitigate Climate Change', in *Handbook of Climate Change Resilience*, ed. F.W. Leal (Berlin Springer).

Aiello, L. (1997), 'Brains and guts in human evolution: The Expensive Tissue Hypothesis', *Brazilian Journal of Genetics*, 20(1).

Aiello, L., Wheeler, P. (1995), 'The Expensive-Tissue Hypothesis: The Brain and the Digestive System in Human and Primate Evolution', *Current Anthropology*, 36(2): 199–221.

Allen, M. R., Shine, K. P., Fuglestvedt, J. S., Miller, R.J., Frame, D. J., Macey, A. H. (2018), 'A solution to the misrepresentations of CO2-equivalent emissions of short-lived climate pollutants under ambitious mitigation', *npj Climate and Atmospheric Science*, 1: 16.

Allès, B., Baudry, J., Méjean, C., Touvier, M., Péneau, S., Hercberg, S., Kesse-Guyot, E. (2017), 'Comparison of Sociodemographic and Nutritional Characteristics between Self-Reported Vegetarians, Vegans, and Meat-Eaters from the NutriNet-Santé Study', *Nutrients*, 9(9): 1023.

Alvaro, C. (2020), *Raw Veganism: The Philosophy of the Human Diet* (London and New York: Routledge).

Amato, K. R., Yeoman, C. J., Cerda, G., Schmitt, C. A.,

Cramer, J. D., Miller, M. E. B., Gomez, A., Turner, T. R., Wilson, B. A., Stumpf, R. M., Nelson, K. E., White, B. A., Knight, R., Leigh, S. R. (2015), 'Variable responses of human and non-human primate gut microbiomes to a Western diet', *Microbiome*, 3: 53.

Amiot, C. E., Sukhanova, K., Greenaway, K. H., Bastian, B. (2015), 'Towards a psychology of human-animal relations', *Psychological Bulletin*, 141(1): 6–47.

Amiot, C. E., Bastian, B. (2017), 'Solidarity with Animals: Assessing a Relevant Dimension of Social Identification with Animals', *PLoS ONE*, 12(1): e0168184.

Anderson, E. C., Barrett, L.F. (2016), 'Affective Beliefs Influence the Experience of Eating Meat', *PLoS ONE*, 11(8): e0160424.

Anderson, J. J., Darwis, N. D. M., Mackay, D. F., Celis-Morales, C. A., Lyall, D. M., Sattar, N., Gill, J. M. R., Pell, J.P. (2018), 'Red and processed meat consumption and breast cancer: UK Biobank cohort study and meta-analysis', *European Journal of Cancer*, 90: 73–82.

Ang, C-S., Chan, N-N., Singh, L. (2019), 'A comparison study of meat eaters and non-meat eaters on mind attribution and moral disengagement of animals', *Appetite*, 136: 80–5.

Angel, L. (1984), 'Health as a crucial factor in the changes from hunting to developed farming in the Eastern Mediterranean', in *Paleopathology at the Origins of Agriculture*, eds. M. N. Cohen, G. Armelagos (New York: Academic Press).

Appleby, P., Roddam, A., Allen, N., Key, T. (2007), 'Comparative fracture risk in vegetarians and nonvegetarians in EPIC-Oxford', *European Journal of Clinical Nutrition*, 61(12): 1400–06.

Araújo, A. M., Carvalho, F., Bastos, M. L., Guedes de Pinho, P., Carvalho, M. (2015), 'The hallucinogenic world of tryptamines: an updated review', *Archives of Toxicology*, 89(8): 1151–73.

Arbib, M. A. (2000), 'The Mirror System, Imitation, and the Evolution of Language, in *Imitation in Animals and Artifacts*, eds. C. Nehaniv, K. Dautenhahn (Cambridge, MA: MIT Press).

Archer, E., Lavie, C.J. (2019), 'Healthy diets and sustainable food systems', *The Lancet*, 394(10194): 214–15.

Århem, K. (1996), 'The cosmic food web: human-nature relatedness in the Northwest Amazon', in *Nature and Society: Anthropological Perspectives*, eds. P. Descola, G. Pálsson (London and New York: Routledge).

Aronson, E. (1999), 'Dissonance, Hypocrisy, and the Self-Concept', in *Cognitive Dissonance: Progress on a pivotal theory in social psychology*, eds. E. Harmon-Jones, J. Mills (Washington, DC: American Psychological Association).

Ashfin, A., et al. (2019), 'Health effects of dietary risks in 195 countries, 1990–2017: a systematic analysis for the Global Burden of Disease Study 2017', *The Lancet*, 393(10184): 1958–72.

Astrup, A., Geiker, N. R. W., Magkos, F. (2019), 'Effects of Full-Fat and Fermented Dairy Products on Cardiometabolic Disease: Food Is More Than the Sum of Its Parts', *Advances in Nutrition*, 10(5): 924S–930S.

Atterton, P. (2011), 'Levinas and Our Moral Responsibility Toward Other Animals', *Inquiry*, 54(6): 633–49.

Aubert, P-M., Schwoob, M-H., Poux, X. (2019), 'Agroecology and carbon neutrality: what are the issues?', IDDRI.

Avnon, T., Paz Dubinsky, E., Lavie, I., Bashi, T. B-M., Anbar, R., Yogev, Y. (2020), 'The impact of a vegan diet on pregnancy outcomes', *Journal of Perinatology*.

Bahn, P. (2001), 'Save the last trance for me: An assessment of the misuses of shamanism in rock art studies', in *The Concept of Shamanism: Uses and Abuses*, eds. H. Francfort, R. Hamayon, P. Bahn (Budapest: Akademiai Kiado).

Bajželj, B., Richards, K. S., Allwood, J. M., Smith, P., Dennis, J., Curmi, E., Gilligan, C. (2014), 'Importance of food-demand management for climate mitigation', *Nature Climate Change*, 4: 924–9.

Bakaloudi, D. R., Halloran, A., Rippin, H. L., Oikonomidou, A. C., Dardavesis, T. I., Williams, J., Wickramasinghe, K., Breda, J., Chourdakis, M. (2020, in press), 'Intake and adequacy of the vegan diet. A systematic review of the evidence', *Clinical Nutrition*.

Baldassarre, M. E., Panza, R., Farella, I., Posa, D., Capozza, M., Mauro, A. D., Laforgia, N. (2020), 'Vegetarian and Vegan Weaning of the Infant: How Common and How Evidence-Based? A Population-Based Survey and Narrative Review', *International Journal of Environmental Research and Public Health*, 17(13): 4835.

Baldridge, A. S., Huffman, M. D., Taylor, F., Xavier, D., Bright, B., Van Horn, L. V., Neal, B., Dunford, E. (2019), 'The Healthfulness of the US Packaged Food and Beverage Supply: A Cross-Sectional Study', *Nutrients*, 11: 1704.

Balfour, E. B. (1943), *The Living Soil* (London: Faber & Faber).

Balter, V., Braga, J., Télouk, P., Thackeray, J. F. (2012), 'Evidence for dietary change but not landscape use in South African early hominins', *Nature*, 489: 558–60.

Banta, J. E., Lee, J. W., Hodgkin, G., Yi, Z., Fanica, A., Sabate, J. (2018), 'The global influence of the Seventh-Day Adventist Church on diet', *Religions*, 9: 251.

Barabási, A-L., Menichetti, G., Loscalzo, J. (2020), 'The unmapped chemical complexity of our diet', *Nature Food*, 1: 33–7.

Baran, B. E., Rogelberg, S. G., Clausen, T. (2016), 'Routinized killing of animals: Going beyond dirty work and prestige to understand the well-being of slaughterhouse workers', *Organization*, 23(3): 351–69.

Barański, M., Średnicka-Tober, D., Volakakis, N., Seal, C., Sanderson, R., Stewart, G., Benbrook, C., Biavati, B., Markellou, E., Giotis, C., Gromadzka-Ostowska, J.,

Rembialkowska, E., Skwarlo-Sonta, K., Tahvonen, R., Janovska, D., Niggli, U., Nicot, P., Leifert, C. (2014), 'Higher antioxidant and lower cadmium concentrations and lower incidence of pesticide residues in organically grown crops: A systematic literature review and meta-analyses', *British Journal of Nutrition*, 112(5): 794–811.

Barbosa, P. C., Mizumoto, S., Bogenschutz, M. P., Strassman, R.J. (2012), 'Health status of ayahuasca users', *Drug Testing and Analysis*, 4(7–8): 601–9.

Bar-On, Y. M., Phillips, R., Milo, R. (2018), 'The biomass distribution on Earth', *Proceedings of the National Academy of Sciences*, 115(25): 6506–11.

Bastian, B., Loughnan, S. (2017), 'Resolving the Meat Paradox', *Personality and Social Psychology Review*, 21(3): 278–299.

Bastian, B., Amiot, C. E. (2020), 'The animal in me', in *Why We Love and Exploit Animals*, eds. K. Dhont, G. Hodson (London & New York: Routledge).

Bastian, B., Loughnan, S., Haslam, N., Radke, H. R. M. (2012), 'Don't Mind Meat? The Denial of Mind to Animals Used for Human Consumption', *Personality and Social Psychology Bulletin*, 38(2): 247–56.

Beasley, D. E., Koltz, A. M., Lambert, J. E., Fierer, N., Dunn, R. R. (2015), 'The Evolution of Stomach Acidity and Its Relevance to the Human Microbiome', *PLoS ONE*, 10(7): e0134116.

Becker, E., Lawrence, N. S. (2021, in press), 'Meat disgust is negatively associated with meat intake – evidence from a cross-sectional and longitudinal study', *Appetite*: 105299.

Bellah, R. N. (2011), *Religion in Human Evolution: From the Palaeolithic to the Axial Age* (Cambridge, MA and London: Harvard University Press).

Ben-Dor, M., Barkai, R. (2020), 'The importance of large prey animals during the Pleistocene and the implications of their extinction on the use of dietary ethnographic analogies', *Journal of Anthropological Archaeology*, 59: 101192.

Ben-Dor, M., Gopher, A., Hershkovitz, I., Barkai, R. (2011), 'Man the Fat Hunter: The Demise of *Homo erectus* and the Emergence of a New Hominin Lineage in the Middle Pleistocene (ca. 400 kyr) Levant', *PLoS ONE*, 6(12): e28689.

Bengtsson, J., Ahnstrom, J., Weibukk, A.-C. (2005), 'The effects of organic agriculture on biodiversity and abundance: a meta-analysis', *Journal of Applied Ecology*, 42: 261–9.

Bennett, C. E., Thomas, R., Williams, M., Zalasiewicz, J., Edgeworth, M., Miller, H., Coles, B., Foster, A., Burton, E. J., Marume, U. (2018), 'The broiler chicken as a signal of a human reconfigured biosphere', *Royal Society Open Science*, 5: 180325.

Benningstad, N. C. G., Kunst, J.R. (2020), 'Dissociating meat from its animal origins: A systematic literature review', *Appetite*, 147: 104554.

Bentham, J. (1789), *An Introduction to the Principles of Morals and Legislation* (Dover Publications, 2007).

Benton, T. G, Bieg, C., Harwatt, H., Pudasaini, R., Wellesley, L. (2021), 'Food system impacts on biodiversity loss: Three levers for food system transformation in support of nature', Chatham House, Energy, Environment and Resources Programme.

Bentsen, H. (2017), 'Dietary polyunsaturated fatty acids, brain function and mental health', *Microbial Ecology in Health and Disease*, 28(1).

Berger, J. (1980), 'Why Look at Animals?', in *About Looking* (New York: Pantheon).

Berry, S. E., Valdes, A. M., Drew, D. A. et al. (2020), 'Human postprandial responses to food and potential for precision nutrition', *Nature Medicine*, 26: 964–73.

Berson, J. (2019), *The Meat Question: Animals, Humans, and the Deep History of Food* (Cambridge, MA: MIT Press).

Bhat, Z. F., Kumar, S., Bhat, H. F. (2015), 'Bioactive peptides of animal origin: a review', *Journal of Food Science Technology*, 52: 5377–92.

Bilewicz, M., Imhoff, R., Drogosz, M. (2011), 'The humanity of what we eat: Conceptions of human uniqueness among vegetarians and omnivores', *European Journal of Social Psychology*, 41: 201–9.

Binford, L. R. (1987), 'Were There Elephant Hunters at Torralba?', in *The Evolution of Human Hunting*, eds. M. H. Nitecki, D. V. Nitecki (Boston, MA: Springer).

Binford, L. R. (1985), 'Human ancestors: Changing views of their behavior', *Journal of Anthropological Archaeology*, 4(4): 292–327.

Bird-David, N. (2003), 'Tribal metaphorization of human-nature relatedness: a comparative analysis', in *Environmentalism*, ed. K. Milton (London: Routledge).

BirdLife International and Vulture Conservation Foundation (2014), 'Ban veterinary diclofenac, Technical summary', BirdLife International.

Blum, W., Zechmeister-Boltenstern, S., Keiblinger, K. (2019), 'Does Soil Contribute to the Human Gut Microbiome?', *Microorganisms*, 7: 1–16.

Bocherens, H., Drucker, D. G., Billiou, D., Patou-Mathis, M., Vandermeersch, B. (2005), 'Isotopic evidence for diet and subsistence pattern of the Saint-Césaire I Neanderthal: review and use of a multi-source mixing model', *Journal of Human Evolution*, 49(1): 71–87.

Bogenschutz, M.P., Forcehimes, A.A., Pommy, J. A., Wilcox, C. E., Barbosa, P., Strassman, R. J. (2015), 'Psilocybin-assisted treatment for alcohol dependence: a proof-of-concept study', *Journal of Psychopharmacology*, 29: 289e299.

Bottomley, E., Loughnan, S. (2017), 'Chickening out of change: Will knowing more about thinking chickens change public perceptions?', *Animal Sentience*, 058.

Bouvard, V., Loomis, D., Guyton, K. Z., Grosse, Y., Ghissassi, F. E., Benbrahim-Tallaa, L., Guha, N., Mattock, H., Straif, K., on behalf of the International Agency for Research on Cancer (IARC) Monograph Working Group (2015), 'Carcinogenicity of consumption of red and processed meat', *The Lancet Oncology*, 16(16): 1599–1600.

Bova, S., Rosenthal, Y., Liu, Z. et al. (2021), 'Seasonal origin of the thermal maxima at the Holocene and the last interglacial', *Nature*, 589: 548–53.

Bradbury, J. (2011), 'Docosahexaenoic acid (DHA): an ancient nutrient for the modern human brain', *Nutrients*, 3(5): 529–54.

Bradshaw, C. J. A., Ehrlich, P. R., Beattie, A., Ceballos, G., Crist, E., Diamond J., Dirzo, R., Ehrlich, A. H., Harte, J., Harte, M. E., Pyke, G., Raven, P. H., Ripple, W. J., Saltré, F., Turnbull, C., Wackernagel, M., Blumstein, D.T. (2021), 'Underestimating the Challenges of Avoiding a Ghastly Future', *Frontiers in Conservation Science*, 1.

Brander, M. (2003), *Eve Balfour: The Founder of the Soil Association and the Voice of the Organic Movement* (East Lothian: The Gleneil Press).

Bratanova, B., Loughnan, S., Bastian, B. (2011), 'The effect of categorization as food on the perceived moral standing of animals', *Appetite*, 57: 193–6.

Braun, D. R., Harris, J. W. K., Levin, N. E., McCoy, J. T., Herries, A. I. R., Bamford, M. K., Bishop, L. C., Richmond, B. G., Kibunjia, M. (2010), 'Early hominin diet included diverse terrestrial and aquatic animals 1.95 Ma in East Turkana, Kenya', *Proceedings of the National Academy of Sciences*, 107(22): 10002–10007.

Brenna, J. T. (2002), 'Efficiency of conversion of alpha-linolenic acid to long chain n-3 fatty acids in man', *Current Opinion in Clinical Nutrition & Metabolic Care*, 5(2): 127–32.

Brenna, J. T., Carlson, S. E. (2014), 'Docosahexaenoic acid

and human brain development: evidence that a dietary supply is needed for optimal development', *Journal of Human Evolution*, 77: 99–106.

Brenna, J. T., Salem Jr, N., Sinclair, A. J., Cunnane, S.C. (2009), 'α-Linolenic acid supplementation and conversion to n-3 long-chain polyunsaturated fatty acids in humans', *Prostaglandins, Leukotrienes and Essential Fatty Acids*, 80(2): 85–91.

Brightman, R. A. (1993), *Grateful Prey: Rock Cree Human-Animal Relationships* (Berkeley, CA: University of California Press).

Briske, D., Bestelmeyer, B., Brown, J., Fuhlendorf, S., Polley, H. (2013), 'The Savory Method Can Not Green Deserts or Reverse Climate Change', *Rangelands*, 35: 72–4.

British Dietetics Association (BDA) and The Vegan Society (2017), 'Memorandum of Understanding between the British Dietetic Association and The Vegan Society'.

Broadhurst, C. L., Wang, Y., Crawford, M. A., Cunnane, S. C., Parkington, J. E., Schmidt, W. F. (2002), 'Brain-specific lipids from marine, lacustrine, or terrestrial food resources: potential impact on early African Homo sapiens', *Comparative Biochemistry and Physiology Part B: Biochemistry and Molecular Biology*, 131(4): 653–73.

Brosnan, M. E., Brosnan, J. T. (2016), 'The role of dietary creatine', *Amino Acids*, 48: 1785–91.

Brown, T. (1983), *Tom Brown's Field Guide to Nature Observation and Tracking* (New York: Berkley Books).

Bruckner, D. W. (2016), 'Strict Vegetarianism is Immoral', in *The Moral Complexities of Eating Meat*, eds. B. Bramble, B. Fischer (Oxford: Oxford University Press).

Bucher, T., Collins, C., Rollo, M. E., McCaffrey, T. A., De Vlieger, N., Van der Bend, D., Truby, H., Perez-Cueto, F. J. A. (2016), 'Nudging Consumers towards Healthier Choices: A Systematic Review of Positional Influences on Food Choice', *British Journal of Nutrition*, 115: 2252–63.

Bulliet, R. W. (2005), *Hunters, Herders, and Hamburgers* (New York: Columbia University Press).

Bunn, H. T., Kroll, E. M. (1986), 'Systematic Butchery by Plio/Pleistocene Hominids at Olduvai Gorge, Tanzania', *Current Anthropology*, 27(5): 431–52.

Bunn, H. T., Pickering, T., Domínguez-Rodrigo, M. (2017), 'How Meat Made us Human: Archaeological Evidence of the Diet and Foraging Capabilities of Early Pleistocene Homo in East Africa', in *The Oxford Handbook of the Archaeology of Diet*, eds. J. Lee-Thorp, M. A. Katzenberg (Oxford: Oxford Handbooks Online).

Burdge, G. C. (2006), 'Metabolism of alpha-linolenic acid in humans', *Prostaglandins, Leukotrienes & Essential Fatty Acids*, 75(3): 161–8.

Burdge, G. C., Calder, P. C. (2005), 'Conversion of alpha-linolenic acid to longer-chain polyunsaturated fatty acids in human adults', *Reproduction Nutrition Development*, 45(5): 581–97.

Burdge, G. C., Tan, S., Henry, C. (2017), 'Long-chain n-3 PUFA in vegetarian women: A metabolic perspective', *Journal of Nutritional Science*, 6: E58.

Burger, R. L. (1992), *Chavín and the Origins of Andean Civilization* (London: Thames and Hudson).

Burke, K. D., Williams, J. W., Chandler, M. A., Haywood, A. M., Lunt, D. J., Otto-Bliesner, B. L. (2018), 'Pliocene and Eocene provide best analogs for near-future climates', *Proceedings of the National Academy of Sciences*, 115 (52): 13288–93.

Carhart-Harris, R., Nutt, D. (2017), 'Serotonin and brain function: a tale of two receptors', *Journal of Psychopharmacology*, 31(9): 1091–1120.

Carhart-Harris, R. L., Bolstridge, M., Day, C. M. J., Rucker, J., Watts, R., Erritzoe, D. E., Kaelen, M., Giribaldi, B., Bloomfield, M., Pilling, S., Rickard, J. A., Forbes, B., Feilding, A., Taylor, D., Curran, H. V., Nutt, D.

J. (2017), 'Psilocybin with psychological support for treatment-resistant depression: six-month follow-up', *Psychopharmacology* (Berl), 29: 1e10.

Carlson, B. A., Kingston, J. D. (2007), 'Docosahexaenoic acid, the aquatic diet, and hominin encephalization: difficulties in establishing evolutionary links', *American Journal of Human Biology*, 19(1): 132–41.

Carson, R. (1962), *Silent Spring* (Boston: Houghton Mifflin).

Carter, J., Jones, A., O'Brien, M., Ratner, J., Wuerthner, G. (2014), 'Holistic Management: Misinformation on the Science of Grazed Ecosystems', *International Journal of Biodiversity*, 2014: 163431.

Castro, M. M., Camacho, F. R. C., Ceriani, F., Fares, N., Herrera, T. I., Ferreira, C. V., Arocena, E., Girona, A., Cavalleri, F., Colistro, V., Borbonet, D. (2020), 'Relationship Between Maternal Meat Consumption During Pregnancy and Umbilical Cord Ferritin Concentration', PREPRINT (Version 1) available at Research Square.

Chamorro, R., Gonzalez, M. F., Aliaga, R., Gengler, V., Balladares, C., Barrera, C., Bascuñan, K. A., Bazinet, R. P., Valenzuela, R. (2020), 'Diet, Plasma, Erythrocytes, and Spermatozoa Fatty Acid Composition Changes in Young Vegan Men', *Lipids*, 55: 639–48.

Chang, C. Y., Ke, D. S., Chen, J. Y. (2009), 'Essential fatty acids and human brain', *Acta Neurology Taiwanica*, 18(4): 231–41.

Charles HRH The Prince of Wales, Juniper, T., Skelly, I. (2010), 'Harmony: A New Way of Looking at Our World' (London: HarperCollins e-books).

Chi, T., Gold, J. A. (2020), 'A review of emerging therapeutic potential of psychedelic drugs in the treatment of psychiatric illnesses', *Journal of Neurological Sciences*, 15 (411): 116715.

Clark, M. A., Domingo, N. G. G., Colgan, K., Thakrar, S. K.,

Tilman, D., Lynch, J., Azevedo, I. L., Hill, J.D. (2020), 'Global food system emissions could preclude achieving the 1.5° and 2°C climate change targets', *Science*, 370 (6517): 705–8.

Clarys, P., Deliens, T., Huybrechts, I., Deriemaeker, P., Vanaelst, B., De Keyzer, W., Hebbelinck, M., Mullie, P. (2014), 'Comparison of nutritional quality of the vegan, vegetarian, semi-vegetarian, pesco-vegetarian and omnivorous diet', *Nutrients*, 6 (3):1318–32.

Clottes, J. (2010), *Cave Art* (New York: Phaidon Press).

Clottes, J. (2016), *What is Palaeolithic Art? Cave Paintings and the Dawn of Human Creativity* (Chicago and London: University of Chicago Press).

Clottes, J., Lewis-Williams, J. D. (1998), *The Shamans of Prehistory: Trance and Magic in the Painted Caves* (New York: Harry N. Abrams).

Coeckelbergh, M., Gunkel, D. J. (2014), 'Facing Animals: A Relational, Other-Oriented Approach to Moral Standing', *Journal of Agricultural and Environmental Ethics*, 27: 715–33.

Cofnas, N. (2019), 'Is vegetarianism healthy for children?', *Critical Reviews in Food Science and Nutrition*, 59(13): 2052–60.

Cohen, M., Crane-Kramer, G., eds. (2007), *Ancient Health: Skeletal Indicators of Agricultural and Economic Intensification* (Gainesville: University Press of Florida).

Cole, J. (1998), *About Face* (Cambridge, MA and London: MIT Press).

Cole, M., Morgan, K. (2011), 'Vegaphobia: derogatory discourses of veganism and the reproduction of speciesism in UK national newspapers', *The British Journal of Sociology*, 62 (1): 134–53.

Cole, M., Stewart, K. (2014), *Our Children and Other Animals: The Cultural Construction of Human-Animal Relations in Childhood* (London: Routledge).

Cole, M., Stewart, K. (2020), 'The distance between us', The Open University: https://www.open.edu/openlearn/history-the-arts/philosophy/the-distance-between-us [accessed January 2021].

Coletta, J. M., Bell, S. J., Roman, A. S. (2010), 'Omega-3 Fatty acids and pregnancy', *Reviews in Obstetrics & Gynecology*, 3 (4): 163–71.

Colley, C., Wasley, A. (2020), 'Industrial-sized pig and chicken farming continuing to rise in UK', *Guardian*: https://www.theguardian.com/environment/2020/apr/07/industrial-sized-pig-and-chicken-farming-continuing-to-rise-in-uk [accessed January 2021].

Compassion in World Farming and OneKind (2012), 'Farm Assurance Schemes & Animal Welfare: How the standards compare', Compassion in World Farming.

Conard, N. J. (2003), 'Palaeolithic ivory sculptures from southwestern Germany and the origins of figurative art', *Nature*, 426: 830–2.

Conneller, C. (2004), 'Becoming deer: Corporeal transformations at Star Carr', *Archaeological Dialogues*, 11(1): 37–56.

Coolidge, F., Wynne, T. (2006), 'The effects of the tree-to-ground sleep transition in the evolution of cognition in early Homo', *Before Farming*, 4: 1–18.

Cooper, J., Lombardi, R., Boardman, D., Carliell-Marquet, C. (2011), 'The future distribution and production of global phosphate rock reserves', *Resources, Conservation and Recycling*, 57: 78–86.

Cooper, J., Reed, E. Y., Hörtenhuber, S., Lindenthal, T., Loes, A-K., Mader, P., Magid, J., Oberson, A., Kolbe, H., Moller, K. (2018), 'Phosphorus availability on many organically managed farms in Europe', *Nutrient Cycling in Agroecosystems*, 110: 227–39.

Cordain, L., Miller, J. B., Eaton, S. B., Mann, N., Holt, S. H., Speth, J.D. (2000), 'Plant-animal subsistence ratios and macronutrient energy estimations in worldwide hunter-gatherer diets', *The American Journal of Clinical Nutrition*, 71(3): 682–92.

Cordain, L., Watkins, B., Mann, N. (2001), 'Fatty Acid Composition and Energy Density of Foods Available to African Hominids', *World Review of Nutrition and Dietetics*, 90: 144–61.

Cordell, D., White, S. (2011), 'Peak Phosphorus: Clarifying the Key Issues of a Vigorous Debate about Long-Term Phosphorus Security', *Sustainability*, 3: 2027–49.

Craig, W. J. (2009), 'Health effects of vegan diets', *The American Journal of Clinical Nutrition*, 89(5): 1627S–1633S.

Crawford M. A., Wang, Y., Lehane, C., Ghebremeskel, K. (2010), 'Fatty Acid Ratios in Free-Living and Domestic Animals', in *Modern Dietary Fat Intakes in Disease Promotion, Nutrition and Health*, eds. De Meester, F., Zibadi, S., Watson, R. (Totowa, NJ: Humana Press).

Critchley, S. (2007), *Infinitely Demanding: Ethics of Commitment, Politics of Resistance* (London and New York: Verso).

Crittenden, A. N., Schnorr, S. L. (2017), 'Current views on hunter-gatherer nutrition and the evolution of the human diet', *American Journal of Physical Anthropology*, 162: 84–109.

Crowe, F., Steur, M., Allen, N., Appleby, P., Travis, R., Key, T. (2011), 'Plasma concentrations of 25-hydroxyvitamin D in meat eaters, fish eaters, vegetarians and vegans: Results from the EPIC-Oxford study', *Public Health Nutrition*, 14(2): 340–6.

Crowe, J. (2008), 'Levinasian Ethics and Animal Rights', *Windsor Yearbook of Access to Justice*, 26(2): 313–28.

Cunnane, S. C., Crawford, M. A. (2003), 'Survival of the fattest: fat babies were the key to evolution of the large human brain', *Comparative Biochemistry and*

Physiology – Part A: Molecular & Integrative Physiology 136(1) (2003): 17–26.

Cunnane, S. C., Plourde, M., Stewart, K., Crawford, M. A. (2007), 'Docosahexaenoic acid and shore-based diets in hominin encephalization: A rebuttal', *American Journal of Human Biology*, 19: 578–81.

Cuthbert, R., Green, R. E., Ranade, S., Saravanan, S., Pain, D. J., Prakash, V., Cunningham, A. A. (2006), 'Rapid population declines of Egyptian vulture (*Neophron percnopterus*) and red-headed vulture (*Sarcogyps calvus*) in India', *Animal Conservation*, 9: 349–54.

Davey, G. K., Spencer, E. A., Appleby, P. N., Allen, N. E., Knox, K. H., Key, T. J. (2003), 'EPIC-Oxford: lifestyle characteristics and nutrient intakes in a cohort of 33 883 meat-eaters and 31 546 non meat-eaters in the UK', *Public Health Nutrition*, 6(3): 259–69.

Davies, M., Wasley, A. (2017), 'Intensive farming in the UK, by numbers', The Bureau of Investigative Journalism: https://www.thebureauinvestigates.com/stories/2017-07-17/intensive-numbers-of-intensive-farming [accessed January 2021].

Davis, W. (1997), *One River: Explorations and Discoveries in the Amazon Rain Forest* (New York: Simon & Schuster).

De Backer, C. J. S., Hudders, L. (2015), 'Meat morals: relationship between meat consumption consumer attitudes towards human and animal welfare and moral behavior', *Meat Science*, 99: 68–74.

de la Vega, E., Chalk, T. B., Wilson, P. A., Bysani, R. P., Foster, G. L. (2020), 'Atmospheric CO2 during the Mid-Piacenzian Warm Period and the M2 glaciation', *Scientific Reports*, 10: 11002.

De Schutter, O. (2014), 'Report of the Special Rapporteur on the right to food, Final report: The transformative potential of the right to food (A/HRC/25/57)', United Nations, General Assembly, Human Rights Council.

Dennell, R. (1997), 'Life at the sharp end: The world's oldest spears', *Nature*, 385: 767–8.

Descola, P. (2005), *Beyond Nature and Culture* (Paris: Editions Gallimard).

Dillard, J. (2007), 'A Slaughterhouse Nightmare: Psychological Harm Suffered by Slaughterhouse Employees and the Possibility of Redress through Legal Reform', *Georgetown Journal on Poverty Law and Policy*.

Dineva, M., Rayman, M., Bath, S. (2020), 'Iodine status of consumers of milk-alternative drinks v. cows' milk: Data from the UK National Diet and Nutrition Survey', *British Journal of Nutrition*, 1–9.

Dinu, M., Abbate, R., Gensini, G. F., Casini, A., Sofi, F. (2017), 'Vegetarian, vegan diets and multiple health outcomes: A systematic review with meta-analysis of observational studies', *Critical Reviews in Food Science and Nutrition*, 57(17): 3640–9.

Domínguez-Rodrigo, M., Pickering, T. R. (2017), 'The meat of the matter: an evolutionary perspective on human carnivory', *Azania: Archaeological Research in Africa* 52(1): 4–32.

Domínguez-Rodrigo, M., Pickering, T. R., Diez-Martín, F., Mabulla, A., Musiba, C., Trancho, G., Banquedano, E., Bunn, H. T., Barboni, D., Santonja, M., Uribelarrea, D., Ashley, G.M., Martinez-Avila, M., Barbasa, R., Gidna, A., Yravedra, J., Arriaza, C. (2012), 'Earliest Porotic Hyperostosis on a 1.5-Million-Year-Old Hominin, Olduvai Gorge, Tanzania', *PLoS ONE*, 7(10): e46414.

Domínguez-Rodrigo, M., Pickering, T. R., Semaw, S., Rogers, M. J. (2005), 'Cutmarked bones from Pliocene archaeological sites at Gona, Afar, Ethiopia: implications for the function of the world's oldest stone tools', *Journal of Human Evolution*, 48(2): 109–21.

Donald, M. (1991), *Origins of the Modern Mind: Three Stages in the Evolution of Culture and Cognition* (Cambridge MA: Harvard University Press, 1991).

Donald, M. (2001), *A Mind So Rare: The Evolution of Human Consciousness* (New York: W.W. Norton).

Donovan, J. (1990), 'Animal Rights and Feminist Theory', *Signs: Journal of Women in Culture and Society*, 15(2).

Donovan, J. (1996), 'Attention to Suffering: Sympathy as a Basis for Ethical Treatment of Animals', *Journal of Social Philosophy*, 27(1).

Donovan, J., Adams, C. J., eds. (2007), *The Feminist Care Tradition in Animal Ethics* (New York: Columbia University Press).

Dorovskikh, A. (2015), 'Killing for a Living: Psychological and Physiological Effects of Alienation of Food Production on Slaughterhouse Workers', Undergraduate Honors Thesis, University of Colorado Boulder.

dos Santos, R. G. (2013), 'Safety and side effects of ayahuasca in humans – an overview focusing on developmental toxicology', *Journal of Psychoactive Drugs* 45(1): 68–78.

Dowsett, E., Semmler, C., Bray, H., Ankeny, R. A., Chur-Hansen, A. (2018), 'Neutralising the meat paradox: Cognitive dissonance, gender, and eating animals', *Appetite*, 123: 280–8.

Dowson, T. A., Porr, M. (2004), 'Special Objects – Special Creatures: Shamanic Imagery and the Aurignacian Art of South-West Germany', in *The Archaeology of Shamanism*, ed. N. S. Price (London: Routledge).

Dutkiewicz, J., Rosenberg, G. (2021), 'The Sadism of Eating Real Meat Over Lab Meat', *The New Republic*: https://newrepublic.com/article/161452/sadism-eating-real-meat-lab-meat [accessed February 2021].

Dutkiewicz, J., Specht, L. (2020), 'Let's Rebuild the Broken Meat Industry – Without Animals', *WIRED*: https://www.wired.com/story/opinion-lets-rebuild-the-broken-meat-industry-without-animals/ [accessed January 2021].

Eating Better (2018), 'Principles for eating meat and dairy more sustainably: the "less and better" approach', Eating Better.

Eating Better (2020), 'We need to talk about chicken', Eating Better.

Eaton, S. B., Konner, M. K. (1985), 'Palaeolithic Nutrition: A Consideration of its Nature and Current Implications', *The New England Journal of Medicine*, 312: 283–9.

Eaton, S. B., Shostak, M., Konner, M. (1988), *The Paleolithic Prescription: A Program of Diet and Exercise and a Design for Living* (New York: HarperCollins).

Eaton, S. B., Sinclair, A. J., Cordain, L., Mann, N. J. (1998), 'Dietary intake of long-chain polyunsaturated fatty acids during the Paleolithic', in *The Return of ω3 Fatty Acids into the Food Supply, vol. I: Land-Based Animal Food Products and Their Health Effects*, ed. A.P. Simpoulos (Basel: Karger).

Ebinger-Rist, N., Wolf, S., Wehrberger, K., Kind, C-J. (2018), 'L'homme-lion d'Hohlenstein – Stadel', *L'Anthropologie*, 122(3): 415–36.

Edelglass, W., Hatley, J., Diehm, C. (2012), *Facing Nature: Levinas and Environmental Thought* (Pittsburgh: Duquesne University Press).

Efeca, on behalf of the UK Roundtable on Sustainable Soya (2020), 'UK Roundtable on Sustainable Soya: Annual progress report, 2019', Efeca.

Eisler, M. C., Lee, M. R. F., Tarlton, J. F., Martin, G. B., Beddington, J., Dungait, J. A. J., Greathead, H., Liu, J., Mathew, S., Miller, H., Misselbrook, T., Murray, P., Vinod, V. K., Van Saun, R., Winter, M. (2014), 'Agriculture: Steps to sustainable livestock', *Nature News*.

Eisnitz, G. (1997), *Slaughterhouse: The Shocking Story of Greed, Neglect, and Inhumane Treatment inside the U.S. Meat Industry* (New York: Prometheus Books).

El Zaatari, S., Grine, F. E., Ungar, P. S., Hublin, J-J. (2011), 'Ecogeographic variation in Neandertal dietary habits: Evidence from occlusal molar microwear texture analysis', *Journal of Human Evolution*, 61(4): 411–24.

Eldridge, J. J., Gluck, J. P. (1996), 'Gender Differences in Attitudes Toward Animal Research', *Ethics & Behavior*, 6(3): 239–56.

Elizabeth, L., Machado, P., Zinöcker, M., Baker, P., Lawrence, M. (2020), 'Ultra-Processed Foods and Health Outcomes: A Narrative Review', *Nutrients*, 12(7): 1955.

Ellis, E. C., Gauthier, N., et al. (2021), 'People have shaped most of terrestrial nature for at least 12,000 years', *Proceedings of the National Academy of Sciences*, 188(17): e2023483118.

Elorinne, A. L., Alfthan, G., Erlund, I., Kivimäki, H., Paju, A., et al. (2016), 'Food and Nutrient Intake and Nutritional Status of Finnish Vegans and Non-Vegetarians', *PLoS ONE*, 11(2): e0148235.

Englefield, F. R. H. (1977), *Language: Its Origin and Relation to Thought* (London: Pemberton Publishing).

Erb, K. H., Lauk, C., Kastner, T., Mayer, A., Theurl, M. C., Haberl, H. (2016), 'Exploring the biophysical option space for feeding the world without deforestation', *Nature Communications*, 7: 11382.

Eshelman, C. (2003), *Juniper Fuse: Upper Paleolithic Imagination and the Construction of the Underworld* (Middletown, CT: Wesleyan University Press).

European Commission (2020), 'Farm to Fork Strategy – for a fair, healthy and environmentally-friendly food system', European Commission.

Fagan, B. (2010), *Cro-Magnon: How the Ice-Age Gave Birth to the First Modern Humans* (New York and London: Bloomsbury).

Fairlie, S. (2010), *Meat: A Benign Extravagance* (East Meon: Permanent Publications).

Faith, J. T., Rowan, J., Du, A. (2019), 'Early hominins evolved within non-analog ecosystems', *Proceedings of the National Academy of Sciences*, 116(43): 21478–83.

Falk, D. (1983), 'Cerebral cortices of East African early hominids', *Science*, 221: 1072–4.

Falk, D. (2014), 'Interpreting sulci on hominin endocasts: old hypotheses and new findings', *Frontiers in Human Neuroscience*, 8: 134.

Falk, D., Redmond, J. C., Guyer, J., Conroy, C., Recheis, W., Weber, G. W., Seidler, H. (2000), 'Early hominid brain evolution: a new look at old endocasts', *Journal of Human Evolution*, 38(5): 695–717.

FAO (2011), 'World Livestock 2011 – Livestock in food security' (Rome: Food and Agriculture Organization of the United Nations).

FAO (2018), 'World Livestock: Transforming the livestock sector through the Sustainable Development Goals' (Rome: Food and Agriculture Organization of the United Nations).

Faurby, S., Silvestro, D., Werdelin, L., Antonelli, A. (2020), 'Brain expansion in early hominins predicts carnivore extinctions in East Africa', *Ecology Letters*, 23: 537–44.

Fazenda, B. (2017), 'Cave acoustics in prehistory: Exploring the association of Palaeolithic visual motifs and acoustic response', *The Journal of the Acoustical Society of America*, 142(3): 1332–49.

Feedback (2020a), 'It's Big Livestock versus the Planet: A case to cut off meat and dairy corporations' financial fodder' (London: Feedback Global).

Feedback (2020b), 'Butchering the Planet: The big-name financiers bankrolling livestock corporations and climate change' (London: Feedback Global).

Ferraro, J. V., Plummer, T. W., Pobiner, B. L., Oliver, J. S., Bishop, L. C., Braun, D. R., Ditchfield, P. W., Seaman III, J. W., Binetti, K. M., Seaman Jr, J. W., Hertel, F., Potts, R. (2013), 'Earliest Archaeological Evidence of Persistent Hominin Carnivory', *PLoS ONE*, 8(4): e62174.

Ferreiro, S. R., López, A. M., Villares, J. M. M. (2020), 'Recomendaciones del Comité de Nutrición y Lactancia

Materna de la Asociación Española de Pediatría sobre las dietas vegetarianas', *Anales de Pediatria*, 92(5): 306. e1–306.e6.

Fessler, D. M. T., Arguello, A. P., Mekdara, J. M., Macias, R. (2003), 'Disgust sensitivity and meat consumption: a test of an emotivist account of moral vegetarianism', *Appetite*, 41(1): 31–41.

Festinger, L. (1957), *A Theory of Cognitive Dissonance* (Stanford, CA: Stanford University Press).

Festinger, L., Riechen, H., Schachter, S. (1956), *When Prophecy Fails: A Social and Psychological Study of a Modern Group That Predicted the Destruction of the World* (Minneapolis, MN: University of Minnesota Press).

First Steps Nutrition Trust (2020), 'Eating well: vegan infants and under-5s', First Steps Nutrition Trust.

Fitzgerald, A. J. (2010), 'A Social History of the Slaughterhouse: From Inception to Contemporary Implications', *Human Ecology Review*, 17(1): 58–69.

Fließbach, A., Oberholzer, H. R., Gunst, L., Mäder, P. (2007), 'Soil organic matter and biological soil quality indicators after 21 years of organic and conventional farming', *Agriculture, Ecosystem and Environment*, 118: 273–84.

Food, Farming and Countryside Commission (2019), 'Our Future in the Land', FFCC.

Food, Farming and Countryside Commission (2021), 'Farming for Change', FFCC.

Frazer, J. G. (1890), *The Golden Bough: A Study in Comparative Religion* (London: Macmillan and Co.).

Frehner, A., Muller, A., Schader, C., De Boer, I. J. M., Van Zanten, H. H. E. (2020), 'Methodological choices drive differences in environmentally-friendly dietary solutions', *Global Food Security*, 24: 100333.

Gallese, V. (2005), '"Being Like Me": Self-Other Identity, Mirror Neurones, and Empathy', in *Perspective on Imitation, From Neuroscience to Social Science*, Volume

1, *Mechanisms of Imitation and Imitation in Animals*, eds. S. Hurley, N. Chater (Cambridge, MA: MIT Press).

Gallese, V. (2009), 'Mirror Neurons, Embodied Simulation, and the Neural Basis of Social Identification', *Psychoanalytic Dialogues*, 19(5): 519–36.

Garcia, D., Galaz, V., Daume, S. (2019), 'EATLancet vs yes2meat: the digital backlash to the planetary health diet', *The Lancet*, 394(10215): 2153–4.

Gardner, C. J., Wordley, C. F. R. (2019), 'Scientists must act on our own warnings to humanity', *Nature Ecology and Evolution*, 3(9): 1271–2.

Garnett, T. (2019), 'Has veganism become a dirty word?' Food Climate Research Network: https://tabledebates.org/blog/has-veganism-become-dirty-word [accessed January 2021].

Garnett, T., Godde, C., Muller, A., Röös, E., Smith, P., de Boer, I., zu Ermgassen, E., Herrero, M., van Middelaar, C., Schader, C., Van Zanten, H. (2017), 'Grazed and confused? Ruminating on cattle, grazing systems, methane, nitrous oxide, the soil carbon sequestration question – and what it all means for greenhouse gas emissions', Food Climate Research Network, Oxford Martin Programme on the Future of Food, Environmental Change Institute, University of Oxford.

Garrels, S. (2004), *Imitation, Mirror Neurons, and Mimetic Desire: Convergent Support for the Work of Rene Girard* (Pasadena: Fuller Theological Seminary).

Gasser, P., Kirchner, K., Passie, T. (2015), 'LSD-assisted psychotherapy for anxiety associated with a life-threatening disease: a qualitative study of acute and sustained subjective effects', *Journal of Psychopharmacology*, 29: 57e68.

Gattinger, A., Muller, A., Haeni, M., Skinner, C., Fliessbach, A., Buchmann, N., Mäder, P., Stolze, M., Smith, P., El-Hage Scialabba, N., Niggli, U. (2012), 'Top soil carbon stocks under organic farming', *Proceedings of the National Academy of Sciences*, 109(44): 18226–31.

Gerber, P. J., Steinfeld, H., Henderson, B., Mottet, A., Opio, C., Dijkman, J., Falcucci, A., Tempio, G. (2013), 'Tackling climate change through livestock – A global assessment of emissions and mitigation opportunities' (Rome: Food and Agriculture Organization of the United Nations).

Gerster, H. (1998), 'Can adults adequately convert alpha-linolenic acid (18:3n-3) to eicosapentaenoic acid (20:5n-3) and docosahexaenoic acid (22:6n-3)?', *International Journal for Vitamin and Nutrition Research*, 68(3): 159–73.

Ghabbour, E. A., Davies, G., Misiewicz, T., Alami, R. A., Askounis, E. M., Cuozzo, N. P., Filice, A. J., Haskell, J. M., Moy, A. K., Roach, A. C., Shade, J. (2017), 'National Comparison of the Total and Sequestered Organic Matter Contents of Conventional and Organic Farm Soils', in *Advances in Agronomy*, vol. 146, ed. D.L. Sparks (Amsterdam: Academic Press).

Ghodsi, R., Kheirouri, S. (2018), 'Carnosine and advanced glycation end products: a systematic review', *Amino Acids*, 50: 1177–86.

Gill, E. (2010), 'Lady Eve Balfour and the British organic food and farming movement', PhD thesis, Department of History & Welsh History, Aberystwyth University.

Gilligan, C. (1982), *In a Different Voice: Psychological Theory and Women's Development* (Cambridge, MA: Harvard University Press).

Gilsing, A. M., Crowe, F. L., Lloyd-Wright, Z., Sanders, T. A., Appleby, P. N., Allen, N. E., Key, T. J. (2010), 'Serum concentrations of vitamin B12 and folate in British male omnivores, vegetarians and vegans: results from a cross-sectional analysis of the EPIC-Oxford cohort study', *European Journal of Clinical Nutrition*, 64(9): 933–9.

Goldman, A. I. (2005), 'Imitation, Mind Reading, and

Simulation', in *Perspectives on Imitation: From Neuroscience to Social Science*, Volume 2, *Imitation, Human Development, and Culture*, eds. S. Hurley, N. Chater (Cambridge, MA and London: MIT Press).

Gopnik, A. (1998), *The Philosophical Baby: What Children's Minds Tell Us About Truth, Love, and the Meaning of Life* (Cambridge, MA: MIT Press).

Gorman, P. (2010), *Ayahuasca in My Blood: 25 Years of Medicine Dreaming* (Lulu.com).

Gossard, M., York, R. (2003), 'Social Structural Influences on Meat Consumption', *Human Ecology Review*, 10.

Gowdy, J. (2020), 'Our hunter-gatherer future: Climate change, agriculture and uncivilization', *Futures*, 115: 102488.

Grady, W. (1997), *Vultures: Nature's Ghastly Gourmet* (San Francisco: Sierra Club Books).

GRAIN and the Institute for Agriculture and Trade Policy (IATP) (2018), 'Emissions impossible: How big meat and dairy are heating up the planet', GRAIN and IATP.

Green, R. E., Donázar, J. A., Sánchez-Zapata, J. A., Margalida, A. (2016), 'Potential threat to Eurasian griffon vultures in Spain from veterinary use of the drug diclofenac', *Journal of Applied Ecology*, 53: 993–1003.

Greenpeace (2020), 'Winging It: How the UK's Chicken Habit Is Fuelling the Climate and Nature Emergency', Greenpeace UK.

Griffiths, B., Morgan, G. (2018), 'Supermarkets use "fake farms" on labels to lure customers into buying own-brand chicken', the *Sun*: https://www.thesun.co.uk/money/6995299/fake-farms-labels-supermarket-investigation/ [accessed January 2021].

Griffiths, R. R., Johnson, M. W., Carducci, M. A., Umbricht, A., Richards, W. A., Richards, B. D., Cosimano, M. P., Klinedinst, M. A. (2016), 'Psilocybin produces substantial and sustained decreases in depression and anxiety in patients with life-threatening cancer: a randomized double-blind trial', *Journal of Psychopharmacology*, 30: 1181e1197.

Griffiths, R. R., Richards, W. A., McCann, U., Jesse, R. (2006), 'Psilocybin can occasion mystical-type experiences having substantial and sustained personal meaning and spiritual significance', *Psychopharmacology* (Berl), 187(3): 268–83.

Gruen, L. (1993), 'Dismantling Oppression: An Analysis of the Connection Between Women and Animals', in *Ecofeminism: Women, Animals, Nature*, ed. G. Gaard, (Philadelphia: Temple University Press).

Gruen, L. (1994), 'Towards an Ecofeminist Moral Epistemology', in *Ecological Feminism*, ed. K. J. Warren (New York: Routledge).

Gruen, L. (2015), *Entangled Empathy: An Alternative Ethic for our Relationship with Animals* (New York: Lantern Books).

Gruen, L., Jones, R. C. (2016), 'Veganism as an Aspiration', in *The Moral Complexities of Eating Meat*, eds. B. Bramble, B. Fischer (Oxford: Oxford University Press).

Guan, L., Miao, P. (2020), 'The effects of taurine supplementation on obesity, blood pressure and lipid profile: A meta-analysis of randomized controlled trials', *European Journal of Pharmacology*, 885: 173533.

Guesnet, P., Alessandri, J-M. (2011), 'Docosahexaenoic acid (DHA) and the developing central nervous system (CNS) – Implications for dietary recommendations', *Biochimie*, 93(1): 7–12.

Guiot, J., Cramer, W. (2016), 'Climate change: The 2015 Paris Agreement thresholds and Mediterranean basin ecosystems', *Science, American Association for the Advancement of Science*, 354(6311): 465–8.

Gupta, S. (2016), 'Brain food: Clever eating', *Nature*, 531: S12–S13.

Guthrie, R. D. (2006), *The Nature of Palaeolithic Art* (Chicago: University of Chicago Press).

Haddad, L. (2019), 'The EAT Lancet Report: landmarks, signposts and omissions', Global Alliance for Improved Nutrition (GAIN): https://www.gainhealth.org/media/news/eat-lancet-report-landmarks-signposts-and-omissions [accessed January 2021].

Hagstrum, J. T. (2013), 'Atmospheric propagation modeling indicates homing pigeons use loft-specific infrasonic "map" cues', *Journal of Experimental Biology*, 216: 687–99.

Haider, L. M., Schwingshackl, L., Hoffmann, G., Ekmekcioglu, C. (2018), 'The effect of vegetarian diets on iron status in adults: A systematic review and meta-analysis', *Critical Reviews in Food Science and Nutrition*, 58(8): 1359–74.

Haidt, J. (2003), 'The Moral Emotions', in *Handbook of Affective Sciences*, eds. R. J. Davidson, K. R. Scherer, H. H. Goldsmith (Oxford: Oxford University Press).

Hallowell, A. I. (1926), *Bear Ceremonialism in the Northern Hemisphere* (University of Pennsylvania).

Hammer, J. (2015), 'Finally, the Beauty of France's Chauvet Cave Makes its Grand Public Debut', *Smithsonian Magazine*: https://www.smithsonianmag.com/history/france-chauvet-cave-makes-grand-debut-180954582/ [accessed January 2021].

Hancock, G. (2005), *Supernatural: Meetings with the Ancient Teachers of Mankind* (London: Century).

Hannah, J. (2020), *Meatsplaining: The Animal Agriculture Industry and the Rhetoric of Denial* (Sydney: Sydney University Press).

Harris, W. S., Tintle, N. L., Imamura, F. et al. (2021), 'Blood n-3 fatty acid levels and total and cause-specific mortality from 17 prospective studies', *Nature Communications*, 12: 2329.

Hart, D., Sussman, R. W. (2005), *Man the Hunted: Primates,*

Predators, and Human Evolution (Cambridge, MA: Westview Press).

Hawkes, J. (2013), 'How Has the Human Brain Evolved?', *Scientific American*: https://www.scientificamerican.com/article/how-has-human-brain-evolved/ [accessed January 2021].

Heller, M., Keoleian, G., Rose, D. (2020), 'Implications of Future US Diet Scenarios on Greenhouse Gas Emissions', Center for Sustainable Systems, University of Michigan.

Hendricks, P. S., Thorne, C. B., Clark, C. B., Coombs, D. W., Johnson, M. W. (2015), 'Classic psychedelic use is associated with reduced psychological distress and suicidality in the United States adult population', *Learning Disability Quarterly*, 29(3): 67–79.

Hendrickson, M. K., Howard, P. H., Miller, E. M., Constance, D. H. (2020), 'The Food System: Concentration and its Impacts', Family Farm Action Alliance.

Henneberg, M., Sarafis, V., Mathers, K. (1998), 'Human adaptations to meat eating', *Human Evolution*, 13: 229–34.

Henry, A. G., Brooks, A. S., Piperno, D. R. (2014), 'Plant foods and the dietary ecology of Neanderthals and early modern humans', *Journal of Human Evolution*, 69: 44–54.

Henry, R. C., Alexander, P., Rabin, S., Anthoni, P., Rounsevell, M. D. A., Arneth, A. (2019), 'The role of global dietary transitions for safeguarding biodiversity', *Global Environmental Change*, 58: 101956.

Herzog, H. (2010), *Some We Love, Some We Hate, Some We Eat: Why It's So Hard to Think Straight About Animals* (New York: HarperCollins).

Hestermann, N., Le Yaouanq, Y., Treich, N. (2019), 'An Economic Model of the Meat Paradox', Rationality and Competition Discussion Paper 164, CRC TRR 190 Rationality and Competition.

Hirvonen, K., Bai, Y., Headey, D., Masters, W. A. (2020), 'Cost and Affordability of the EAT-Lancet Diet in 159 Countries', *The Lancet Global Health*, 8(1): e59–e66.

Hodgson, D., Helvenston, P. (2006), 'The emergence of the representation of animals in palaeoart: Insights from evolution and the cognitive, limbic and visual systems of the human brain', *Rock Art Research*, 23: 3–40.

Hoogland, C. T., de Boer, J., Boersema, J. J. (2005), 'Transparency of the meat chain in the light of food culture and history', *Appetite*, 45(1): 15–23.

Ho-Pham, L. T., Nguyen, N. D., Nguyen, T. V. (2009), 'Effect of vegetarian diets on bone mineral density: a Bayesian meta-analysis', *The American Journal of Clinical Nutrition*, 90(4): 943–50.

Hopwood, C.J., Bleidorn, W., Schwaba, T., Chen, S. (2020), 'Health, environmental, and animal rights motives for vegetarian eating', *PloS ONE*, 15(4): e0230609.

Horberg, E. J., Oveis, C., Keltner, D., Cohen, A.B. (2009), 'Disgust and the moralization of purity', *Journal of Personality and Social Psychology*, 97(6): 963–76.

Horrocks, L. A., Yeo, Y. K. (1999), 'Health benefits of docosahexaenoic acid (DHA)', *Pharmacological Research*, 40(3): 211–25.

Hou, Y., Yin, Y., Wu, G. (2015), 'Dietary essentiality of "nutritionally non-essential amino acids" for animals and humans', *Experimental Biology and Medicine*, 240(8): 997–1007.

Hovinen, T., Korkalo, L., Freese, R., Skaffari, E., Isohanni, P., Niemi, M., Nevalainen, J., Gylling, H., Zamboni, N., Erkkola, M., Suomalainen, A. (2021), 'Vegan diet in young children remodels metabolism and challenges the statuses of essential nutrients', *EMBO Molecular Medicine*: e13492.

Huang, J., Liao, L. M., Weinstein, S. J., Sinha, R., Graubard, B.I., Albanes, D. (2020), 'Association Between Plant and

Animal Protein Intake and Overall and Cause-Specific Mortality', *JAMA Internal Medicine*, 180(9): 1173–84.

Hughes, T., 'The Jaguar' (1957), in *The Hawk in the Rain* (London: Faber & Faber).

Hugh-Jones, S. (1996), 'Bonnes raisons ou mauvaise conscience? De l'ambivalence de certains Amazoniens envers la consommation de viande', *Terrain*, 26: 123–48.

Hurtado, S., Tresserra-Rimbau, A., Vallverdú-Queralt, A., Lamuela-Raventós, R.M. (2017), 'Organic food and the impact on human health', *Critical Reviews in Food Science and Nutrition*, 59: 1–11.

Huxley, A. (1956), *The Doors of Perception and Heaven and Hell* (New York: Harper & Brothers; London: HarperCollins, reprint edition 1977).

IAASTD (2009), 'Agriculture at a Crossroads – Global Report', International Assessment of Agricultural Knowledge, Science and Technology for Development.

IFOAM and FIBL (2016), 'Organic Farming, Climate Change Mitigation and Beyond: Reducing the Environmental Impacts of EU Agriculture', IFOAM.

Ingold, T. (1994), 'From Trust to Domination: an alternative history of human-animal relations', in *Animals and Human Society: Changing perspectives*, eds. A. Manning, J. Serpell (London: Routledge).

Ingold, T. (1998), 'Culture, nature, environment: steps to an ecology of life', in *Mind, Brain and Environment: The Linacre Lectures 1995–96*, ed. B. Cartledge (Oxford: Oxford University Press).

Ingrid, T. (2019), 'WHO pulls support from initiative promoting global move to plant-based foods', *British Medical Journal*, 365: l1700.

Innis, S. M. (2008), 'Dietary omega 3 fatty acids and the developing brain', *Brain Research*, 1237: 35–43.

Intergovernmental Panel on Climate Change (IPCC) (2014), 'Climate Change 2014: Synthesis Report, Contribution of Working Groups I, II and III to the Fifth Assessment Report of the Intergovernmental Panel on Climate Change', eds. Pachauri, R. K., Meyer, L. A.

Intergovernmental Panel on Climate Change (IPCC) (2019a), 'Food Security', in *Climate Change and Land: an IPCC special report on climate change, desertification, land degradation, sustainable land management, food security, and greenhouse gas fluxes in terrestrial ecosystems*', eds. P. R. Shukla, J. Skea, E. C. Buendia, V. Masson-Delmotte, H-O. Pörtner, D. C. Roberts, P. Zhai, R. Slade, S. Connors, R. van Diemen, M. Ferrat, E. Haughey, S. Haughey, S. Neogi, M. Pathak, J. Petzold, J. Portugal Pereira, P. Vyas, E. Huntley, K. Kissick, M. Belkacemi, J. Malley.

Intergovernmental Panel on Climate Change (IPCC) (2019b), 'Summary for Policymakers', in *Climate Change and Land: an IPCC special report on climate change, desertification, land degradation, sustainable land management, food security, and greenhouse gas fluxes in terrestrial ecosystems*, eds. P. R. Shukla, J. Skea, E. C. Buendia, V. Masson-Delmotte, H-O. Pörtner, D. C. Roberts, P. Zhai, R. Slade, S. Connors, R. van Diemen, M. Ferrat, E. Haughey, Haughey, S. Haughey, S. Neogi, M. Pathak, J. Petzold, J. Portugal Pereira, P. Vyas, E. Huntley, K. Kissick, M. Belkacemi, J. Malley.

Intergovernmental Science-Policy Platform on Biodiversity and Ecosystem Services (IPBES) (2019), 'Report of the Plenary of the Intergovernmental Science-Policy Platform on Biodiversity and Ecosystem Services on the work of its seventh session, Addendum, Summary for policymakers of the global assessment report on biodiversity and ecosystem services of the Intergovernmental Science-Policy Platform on Biodiversity and Ecosystem Services' (Bonn: IPBES secretariat).

Intergovernmental Science-Policy Platform on Biodiversity and

Ecosystem Services (IPBES) (2020), 'Workshop Report on Biodiversity and Pandemics of the Intergovernmental Platform on Biodiversity and Ecosystem Services', Daszak, P., das Neves, C., Amuasi, J., Hayman, D., Kuiken, T., Roche, B., Zambrana-Torrelio, C., Buss, P., Dundarova, H., Feferholtz, Y., Foldvari, G., Igbinosa, E., Junglen, S., Liu, Q., Suzan, G., Uhart, M., Wannous, C., Woolaston, K., Mosig Reidl, P., O'Brien, K., Pascual, U., Stoett, P., Li, H., Ngo, H.T., (Bonn: IPBES secretariat).

Ison, S. H., Rutherford, K. M. D. (2014), 'Attitudes of farmers and veterinarians towards pain and the use of pain relief in pigs', *The Veterinary Journal*, 202(3): 622–7.

Janssen, M., Busch, C., Rödiger, M., Hamm, U. (2016), 'Motives of consumers following a vegan diet and their attitudes towards animal agriculture', *Appetite* 105: 643–51.

Jarrett, C. B. (2012), 'Mirror neurons: the most hyped concept in Neuroscience?', *Psychology Today*: http://www.psychologytoday.com/blog/brain-myths/201212/mirror-neurons-the-most-hyped-concept-in-neuroscience [accessed January 2021].

Jay, M. (2005), 'Enter the Jaguar': https://mikejay.net/enter-the-jaguar/ [accessed January 2021].

Jay, M. (2019), *Mescaline: A Global History of the First Psychedelic* (New Haven and London: Yale University Press).

Jeffers, R., 'Vulture' (1963), in *Selected Poems: Robinson Jeffers* (Manchester: Carcanet Press, 1987).

Jepson, P., Blythe, C. (2020), *Rewilding: The radical new science of ecological recovery* (London: Icon Books).

Jochelson, W. (1926), *The Yukaghir and the Yukaghized Tungus*, ed. Boas, F. (New York: American Museum of Natural History).

Johnson, M. W., Garcia-Romeu, A., Cosimano, M. P., Griffiths, R. R. (2014), 'Pilot study of the 5-HT2AR agonist psilocybin in the treatment of tobacco addiction', *Journal of Psychopharmacology*, 28: 983e992.

Joordens, J. C., Kuipers, R. S., Wanink, J. H., Muskiet, F. A. (2014), 'A fish is not a fish: patterns in fatty acid composition of aquatic food may have had implications for hominin evolution', *Journal of Human Evolution*, 77: 107–16.

Joy, M. (2010), *Why We Love Dogs, Eat Pigs, and Wear Cows: An Introduction to Carnism* (San Francisco: Conari Press).

Katz, D. L. (2019), 'Plant-Based Diets for Reversing Disease and Saving the Planet: Past, Present, and Future', *Advances in Nutrition*, 10(4): S304–S307.

Kaviani, M., Shaw, K., Chilibeck, P. D. (2020), 'Benefits of Creatine Supplementation for Vegetarians Compared to Omnivorous Athletes: A Systematic Review', *International Journal of Environmental Research and Public Health*, 17(9): 3041.

Kelloway, C., Miller, S. (2020), 'Food and Power: Addressing Monopolization in America's Food System', The Open Market Institute.

Kelly, R. L. (1995), *The Foraging Spectrum: Diversity In Hunter-Gatherer Lifeways* (Washington, DC: Smithsonian Institution Press).

Kennedy, G. E. (2005), 'From the ape's dilemma to the weanling's dilemma: early weaning and its evolutionary context', *Journal of Human Evolution*, 48(2): 123–45.

KFC UK and Ireland(2020), 'Annual Report on Chicken Welfare: July 2020', KFC UK and Ireland.

Kheel, M. (1985), 'The Liberation of Nature: A Circular Affair', *Environmental Ethics*, 7(2).

Kim, B., Neff, R., Santo, R., Vigorito, J. (2015), 'The Importance of Reducing Animal Product Consumption and Wasted Food in Mitigating Catastrophic Climate Change', John Hopkins Centre for a Livable Future.

Kim, H., Caulfield, L. E., Garcia-Larsen, V., Steffen, L. M., Coresh, J., Rebholz, C. M. (2019), 'Plant-Based Diets Are Associated with a Lower Risk of Incident Cardiovascular Disease, Cardiovascular Disease Mortality, and All-Cause Mortality in a General Population of Middle-Aged Adults', *Journal of the American Heart Association*, 8.

Kind, C-J., Ebinger-Rist, N., Wolf, S., Beutelspacher, T., Wehrberger, K. (2014), 'The smile of the Lion Man: Recent excavations in Stadel Cave (Baden-Württemberg, southwestern Germany) and the restoration of the famous Upper Palaeolithic figurine', *Quartär*, 61: 129–45.

King, B. J. (2017), *Personalities on the Plate: The Lives and Minds of Animals We Eat* (Chicago: University of Chicago Press).

Kinsbourne, M. (2005), 'Imitation as Entrainment: Brain Mechanisms and Social Consequences', in *Perspectives on Imitation: From Neuroscience to Social Science*, Volume 2, *Imitation, Human Development, and Culture*, eds. S. Hurley, N. Chater (Cambridge, MA and London: MIT Press).

Knight, J. (2012), 'The Anonymity of the Hunt', *Current Anthropology*, 53(3): 334–55.

Knight, S., Vrij, A., Cherryman, J., Nunkoosing, N. (2004), 'Attitudes towards animal use and belief in animal mind', *Anthrozoös*, 17(1): 43–62.

Koch, P. L., Barnosky, A. D. (2006), 'Late Quaternary Extinctions: State of the Debate', *Annual Review of Ecology, Evolution, and Systematics*, 37: 215–50.

Koebnick, C., Hoffmann, I., Dagnelie, P. C., Heins, U. A., Wickramasinghe, S. N., Ratnayaka, I. D., Gruendel, S., Lindemans, J., Leitzmann, C. (2004), 'Long-Term Ovo-Lacto Vegetarian Diet Impairs Vitamin B-12 Status in Pregnant Women', *The Journal of Nutrition*, 134(12): 3319–26.

Koeth, R., Wang, Z., Levison, B., Buffa, J. A., Org, E.,

Sheehy, B. T., Britt, E. B., Fu, X., Wu, Y., Li, L., Smith, J. D., DiDonato, J. A., Chen, J., Li, H., Wu, G. D., Lewis, J. D., Warrier, M., Brown, J. M., Krauss, R. M., Tang, W. H. W., Bushman, F. D., Lusis, A. J., Hazen, S. L. (2013), 'Intestinal microbiota metabolism of L-carnitine, a nutrient in red meat, promotes atherosclerosis', *Nature Medicine*, 19: 576–85.

Kohn, E. (2007), 'How dogs dream: Amazonian natures and the politics of transspecies engagement', *American Ethnologist*, 34(1): 3–24.

Kohn, E. (2013), *How Forests Think: Toward an Anthropology Beyond the Human* (Berkeley: University of California Press).

Kornsteiner, M., Singer, I., Elmadfa, I. (2008), 'Very low n-3 long-chain polyunsaturated fatty acid status in Austrian vegetarians and vegans', *Annals of Nutrition and Metabolism*, 52(1): 37–47.

Kothapalli, K. S., Ye, K., Gadgil, M. S., Carlson, S. E., O'Brien, K. O., Zhang, J. Y., Park, H. G., Ojukwu, K., Zou, J., Hyon, S. S., Joshi, K. S., Gu, Z., Keinan, A., Brenna, J. T. (2016), 'Positive Selection on a Regulatory Insertion-Deletion Polymorphism in FADS2 Influences Apparent Endogenous Synthesis of Arachidonic Acid', *Molecular Biology and Evolution*, 33(7): 1726–39.

Krajnc, A. (2020), 'The Save Movement: Bearing witness to suffering animals worldwide', in *Meatsplaining: The Animal Agriculture Industry and the Rhetoric of Denial*, ed. J. Hannah (Sydney: Sydney University Press).

Krause, B. (2013), *The Great Animal Orchestra: Finding the Origins of Music in the World's Wild Places* (Boston: Back Bay Books; reprint edition).

Krause, B. (2015), *Voices of the Wild: Animal Songs, Human Din, and the Call to Save Natural Soundscapes* (New Haven: Yale University Press).

Kristensen, N. B., Madsen, M. L., Hansen, T. H., Allin,

K. H., Hoppe, C., Fagt, S., Lausten, M. S., Gobel, R. J., Vestergaard, H., Hansen, T., Pedersen, O. (2015), 'Intake of macro- and micronutrients in Danish vegans', *Nutrition Journal*, 14: 115.

Kristensen, T. S. (1991), 'Sickness absence and work strain among Danish slaughterhouse workers: An analysis of absence from work regarded as coping behaviour', *Social Science and Medicine*, 32(1): 15–27.

Kruger, C., Zhou, Y. (2018), 'Red meat and colon cancer: A review of mechanistic evidence for heme in the context of risk assessment methodology', *Food and Chemical Toxicology*, 118: 131–53.

Kubberød, E., Ueland, Ø., Tronstad, Å., Risvik, E. (2002), 'Attitudes towards meat and meat-eating among adolescents in Norway: a qualitative study', *Appetite*, 38(1): 53–62.

Kunst, J. R., Haugestad, C. A. P. (2018), 'The effects of dissociation on willingness to eat meat are moderated by exposure to unprocessed meat: A cross-cultural demonstration', *Appetite*, 120: 356–66.

Kunst, J. R., Hohle, S. M. (2016), 'Meat eaters by dissociation: How we present, prepare and talk about meat increases willingness to eat meat by reducing empathy and disgust', *Appetite*, 105: 758–74.

Laidlaw, S. A., Shultz, T. D., Cecchino, T. J., Kopple, J. D. (1988), 'Plasma and urine taurine levels in vegans', *The American Journal of Clinical Nutrition*, 47(4): 660–3.

Lambert, P. M. (2009), 'Health versus Fitness: Competing Themes in the Origins and Spread of Agriculture?', *Current Anthropology*, 50(5): 603–8.

Lampkin, N. (2020), 'Potential contribution of organic farming and growing to ELM', English Organic Forum.

Landfald, B., Valeur, J., Berstad, A., Raa, J. (2017), 'Microbial trimethylamine-N-oxide as a disease marker: something fishy?', *Microbial Ecology in Health and Disease*, 28: 1.

Lane, K., Derbyshire, E., Li, W., Brennan, C. (2014), 'Bioavailability and potential uses of vegetarian sources of omega-3 fatty acids: a review of the literature', *Critical Reviews in Food Science and Nutrition*, 54(5): 572–9.

Langdon, J. H. (2006), 'Has an aquatic diet been necessary for hominin brain evolution and functional development?', *British Journal of Nutrition*, 96(1): 7–17.

Larsen, C. K. (1995), 'Biological Changes in Human Populations with Agriculture', *Annual Review of Anthropology*, 24(1): 185–213.

Larsen, C. K. (2006), 'The agricultural revolution as environmental catastrophe: Implications for health and lifestyle in the Holocene', *Quaternary International*, 150(1): 12–20.

Latham, K. J. (2013), 'Human Health and the Neolithic Revolution: an Overview of Impacts of the Agricultural Transition on Oral Health, Epidemiology, and the Human Body', *Nebraska Anthropologist*, 187.

Laugrand, F., Oosten, J. (2015), *Hunters, Predators and Prey: Inuit Perceptions of Animals* (Oxford: Berghahn Books).

Le Barre, W. (1970), *The Ghost Dance: The Origins of Religion* (London: Allen & Unwin).

Le, L. T., Sabaté, J. (2014), 'Beyond meatless, the health effects of vegan diets: findings from the Adventist cohorts', *Nutrients*, 6(6): 2131–47.

Lee, R. B. (1979), *The !Kung San: Men, Women, and Work in a Foraging Society* (Cambridge: Cambridge University Press).

Leenaert, T. (2017), *How to Create a Vegan World: A Pragmatic Approach* (New York: Lantern Books).

Leinonen, I., Iannetta, P. P. M., Rees, R. M., Wendy, R., Christine, W., Barnes, A. P. (2019), 'Lysine Supply Is a Critical Factor in Achieving Sustainable Global Protein Economy', *Frontiers in Sustainable Food Systems*, 3.

Leopold, A. (1949), *A Sand County Almanac: And Sketches Here and There* (Oxford: Oxford University Press).

Leroi-Gourhan, A. (1982), *The Dawn of European Art: An Introduction to Palaeolithic Cave Painting* (Cambridge: Cambridge University Press).

Leroy, F., Cofnas, N. (2020), 'Should dietary guidelines recommend low red meat intake?', *Critical Reviews in Food Science and Nutrition*, 60(16): 2763–72.

Leung, A. M., LaMar, A., He, X., Braverman, L. E., Pearce, E. N. (2011), 'Iodine Status and Thyroid Function of Boston-Area Vegetarians and Vegans', *The Journal of Clinical Endocrinology and Metabolism*, 96(8): E1303–E1307.

Levinas, E. (1961), *Totality and Infinity* (The Hague: Martinus Nijhoff).

Levinas, E. (1974), *Otherwise than Being* (The Hague: Martinus Nijhoff).

Levinas, E., Wright, T., Hughes, P., Ainley, A. (1988), 'The Paradox of Morality: An Interview with Emmanuel Levinas', in *The Provocation of Levinas: Rethinking the Other*, eds. R. Bernasconi, D. Wood (London: Routledge).

Levy, N. (2016), 'Vegetarianism: Towards Ideological Impurity', in *The Moral Complexities of Eating Meat*, eds. B. Bramble, B. Fischer (Oxford: Oxford University Press).

Lewis-Williams, J. (2004), 'Neuropsychology and Upper Paleolithic art: Observations on the progress of altered states of consciousness', *Cambridge Archaeological Journal*, 14(1): 107–11.

Lewis-Williams, J. D. (2002), *The Mind in the Cave: Consciousness and the Origins of Art* (London: Thames & Hudson).

Lewis-Williams, J. D., Dowson, T. A. (1988), 'The Signs of All Times: Entoptic Phenomena in Upper Palaeolithic Art', *Current Anthropology*, 29(2): 201–45.

Liang, Y., Zhan, J., Liu, D., Luo, M., Han, J., Liu, X., Liu, C.,

Cheng, Z., Zhou, Z., Wang, P. (2019), 'Organophosphorus pesticide chlorpyrifos intake promotes obesity and insulin resistance through impacting gut and gut microbiota', *Microbiome*, 7: 19.

Liebenberg, L. (2013), *The Origin of Science: On the Evolutionary Roots of Science and its Implications for Self-Education and Citizen Science* (Cape Town: Cybertracker).

Liebhardt, W. (2003), 'The performance of organic and conventional cropping systems in an extreme climate year', *American Journal of Alternative Agriculture*, 18(3): 146–54.

Linzey, A., Linzey, C., eds. (2019), *Ethical Vegetarianism and Veganism* (London: Routledge).

Lippi, M. M., Foggi, B., Aranguren, B., Ronchitelli, A., Revedin, A. (2015), 'Multistep food plant processing at Grotta Paglicci', *Proceedings of the National Academy of Sciences*, 112(39): 12075–80.

Lockwood, A. (2016), *The Pig in Thin Air* (New York: Lantern Books).

Lonsdale, S. (1981), *Animals and the Origins of Dance* (New York: Thames & Hudson).

Lopez, B. (1978), *Of Wolves and Men* (New York: Simon & Schuster).

Lori, M., Symnaczik, S., Mäder, P., De Deyn, G., Gattinger, A. (2017), 'Organic farming enhances soil microbial abundance and activity – A meta-analysis and meta-regression', *PLoS ONE*, 12(7): e0180442.

Lotter, D., Seidel, R., Liebhardt, W. (2003), 'The performance of organic and conventional cropping systems in an extreme climate year', *American Journal of Alternative Agriculture*, 18(3): 146–54.

Loughnan, S., Davies, T. (2020), 'The meat paradox', in *Why We Love and Exploit Animals*, eds. K. Dhont, G. Hodson (London and New York: Routledge).

Loughnan, S., Haslam, N., Bastian, B. (2010), 'The role of meat consumption in the denial of moral status and mind to meat animals', *Appetite*, 55: 156–9.

Lund, A. M. (2019), 'Questions about a vegan diet should be included in differential diagnostics of neurologically abnormal infants with failure to thrive', *Acta Paediatrica*, 108: 1377–9.

Lynas, M. (2020), *Our Final Warning: Six Degrees of Climate Emergency* (London: HarperCollins).

Machovina, B., Feeley, K. J., Ripple, W. J. (2015), 'Biodiversity conservation: The key is reducing meat consumption', *Science of the Total Environment*, 536: 419–31.

MacInnis, C. C., Hodson, G. (2017), 'It ain't easy eating greens: Evidence of bias toward vegetarians and vegans from both source and target', *Group Processes and Intergroup Relations*, 20(6): 721–44.

MacNair, R. M. (2002), *Perpetration-Induced Traumatic Stress: The Psychological Consequences of Killing* (Westport, CT: Praeger Publishers/Greenwood Publishing).

Magkos, F., Tetens, I., Bügel, S., Felby, C., Schacht, S., Hill, J., Ravussin, E., Astrup, A. (2019), 'A Perspective on the Transition to Plant-Based Diets: A Diet Change May Attenuate Climate Change, but Can It Also Attenuate Obesity and Chronic Disease Risk?', *Advances in Nutrition*.

Mann, F. D. (1998), 'Animal Fat and Cholesterol May Have Helped Primitive Man Evolve a Large Brain', *Perspectives in Biology and Medicine*, 41(3): 417–25.

Mann, N. (2007), 'Meat in the human diet: An anthropological perspective', *Nutrition and Dietetics*, 64: S102–S107.

Marean, C. W. (1989), 'Sabertooth cats and their relevance for early hominid diet and evolution', *Journal of Human Evolution*, 18(6): 559–82.

Marean, C. W., Ehrhardt, C. L. (1995), 'Paleoanthropological and paleoecological implications of the taphonomy of a sabertooth's den', *Journal of Human Evolution*, 29(6): 515–47.

Margulis, S. (2004), 'Causes of Deforestation of the Brazilian Amazon', World Bank Working Paper No. 22 (Washington, DC: World Bank).

Markandya, A., Taylor, T., Longo, A., Murty, M., Murty, S., Dhavala, K. (2008), 'Counting the cost of vulture decline: An appraisal of the human health and other benefits of vultures in India', *Ecological Economics*, 67(2): 194–204.

Marshall, L. (1976), *The !Kung of Nyae Nyae* (Cambridge, MA and London: Harvard University Press).

Martin, R. C., Lynch, D. H., Frick, B., van Straaten, P. (2007), 'Phosphorus status on Canadian organic farms', *Journal of the Science of Food and Agriculture*, 87: 2737–40.

Maslin, M. (2017), *The Cradle of Humanity: How the Changing Landscape of Africa Made Us So Smart* (Oxford: Oxford University Press).

McAfee, A. J., McSorley, E. M., Cuskelly, G. J., Moss, B. W., Wallace, J. M. W., Bonham, M. P., Fearon, A. M. (2010), 'Red meat consumption: An overview of the risks and benefits', *Meat Science*, 84(1): 1–13.

McCarty, M. F. (2004), 'A taurine-supplemented vegan diet may blunt the contribution of neutrophil activation to acute coronary events', *Medical Hypotheses*, 63(3): 419–25.

McCorriston, J., Hole, F. (1991), 'The Ecology of Seasonal Stress and the Origins of Agriculture in the Near East', *American Anthropologist*, 93(1): 46–69.

McGilchrist, I. (2009), *The Master and His Emissary: The Divided Brain and the Making of the Western World* (New Haven & London: Yale University Press).

McKenna, D., Callaway, J., Gro, C. (1998), 'The Scientific Investigation of Ayahuasca: A Review of Past and Current Research', *The Heffter Review of Psychedelic Research*, 1.

McPherron, S. P., Alemseged, Z., Marean, C. W., Wynn, J. G., Reed, D., Geraads, D., Bobe, R., Béarat, H. A. (2010), 'Evidence for stone-tool-assisted consumption of animal tissues before 3.39 million years ago at Dikika, Ethiopia', *Nature*, 466: 857–60.

McWilliams, J. (2015), *The Modern Savage: Our Unthinking Decision to Eat Animals* (New York: Thomas Dunne Books).

Meena, R. S., Kumar, S., Datta, R., Lal, R., Vijayakumar, V., Brtnicky, M., Sharma, M. P., Yadav, G. S., Jhariya, M. K., Jangir, C. K., Pathan, S. I., Dokulilova, T., Pecina, V., Marfo, T. D. (2020), 'Impact of Agrochemicals on Soil Microbiota and Management: A Review', *Land*, 9(2): 34.

Mejborn, H., Møller, S. P., Thygesen, L. C., Biltoft-Jensen, A. (2021), 'Dietary Intake of Red Meat, Processed Meat, and Poultry and Risk of Colorectal Cancer and All-Cause Mortality in the Context of Dietary Guideline Compliance', *Nutrients*, 13: 32.

Melamed, Y., Kislev, M. E., Geffen, E., Lev-Yadun, S., Goren-Inbar, N. (2016), 'The plant component of an Acheulian diet at Gesher Benot Ya'aqov, Israel', *Proceedings of the National Academy of Sciences*, 113(51): 14674–9.

Melina, V., Craig, W., Levin, S. (2016), 'Position of the Academy of Nutrition and Dietetics: Vegetarian Diets', *Journal of the Academy of Nutrition and Dietetics*, 116(12): 1970–80.

Mellars, P. (1996), *The Neanderthal Legacy* (Princeton, NJ: Princeton University Press).

Meltzoff, A. N. (2004), 'The Human infant as Homo imitans', in *Social Learning*, eds. T. R. Zentall, B. G. J. Galef (Hillsdale, MI: Lawrence Erlbaum Associates).

Meltzoff, A. N. (2005), 'Imitation and Other Minds: The "Like Me" Hypothesis', in *Perspectives on Imitation: From Neuroscience to Social Science*, Volume 2, *Imitation, Human Development, and Culture*, eds. S.

Hurley, N. Chater (Cambridge, MA and London: MIT Press).

Mercader, J. (2009), 'Mozambican grass seed consumption during the Middle Stone Age', *Science*, 326(5960): 1680–3.

Mercader, J., Bennett, T., Raja, M. (2008), 'Middle Stone Age starch acquisition in the Niassa Rift, Mozambique', *Quaternary Research*, 70(2): 283–300.

Miele, J., Tingley, L., Kimball, R., Broida, J. (1993), 'Personality Differences between Pro- and Antivivisectionists', *Society and Animals*, 1(2): 129–44.

Mighty Earth (2020), 'The Mighty Earth Soy and Cattle Deforestation Tracker: Recommendations for retailers to tackle deforestation and clearance linked to agribusiness traders in Brazil', Mighty Earth.

Miller, M. J., Albarracin-Jordan, J., Moore, C., Capriles, J. M. (2019), 'Chemical evidence for the use of multiple psychotropic plants in a 1,000-year-old ritual bundle from South America', *Proceedings of the National Academy of Sciences of the United States of America*, 116(23): 11207–12.

Milton, K. (1984), 'The role of food processing factors in primate food choice', in *Adaptations for Foraging in Non-Human Primates: Contributions to an Organismal Biology of Prosimians, Monkeys and Apes*, eds. P. S. Rodman, J. G. H. Cant (New York: Columbia University Press).

Milton, K. (1999), 'A hypothesis to explain the role of meat-eating in human evolution', *Evolutionary Anthropology*, 8: 11–21.

Milton, K. (2000), 'Hunter-gatherer diets – a different perspective', *The American Journal of Clinical Nutrition*, 71(3): 665–7.

Milton, K. (2003), 'The critical role played by animal source foods in human (Homo) evolution', *The Journal of Nutrition*, 733(11): 3886S–3892S.

Minson, J. A., Monin, B. (2012), 'Do-Gooder Derogation: Disparaging Morally Motivated Minorities to Defuse Anticipated Reproach', *Social Psychological and Personality Science*, 3(2): 200–7.

Mithen, S. (1996), *The Prehistory of the Mind: A Search for the Origins of Art, Religion, and Science* (London: Thames & Hudson).

Mithen, S. (1998), 'The origins of anthropomorphic thinking', *Journal of the Royal Anthropological Institute*, 4(1): 129–32.

Mithen, S. (1999), 'Symbolism and the Supernatural', in *The Evolution of Culture*, eds. R. Dunbar, C. Knight, C. Power (Edinburgh: Edinburgh University Press).

Mithen, S. (2003), *After the Ice: A Global Human History, 20,000–5000 BC* (London: Orion).

Mithen, S. (2005), *The Singing Neanderthals* (London: Weidenfeld & Nicolson).

Miyagawa, S., Berwick, R., Okanoya, K. (2013), 'The Emergence of Hierarchical Structure in Human Language', *Frontiers in Psychology*, 4.

Molloy, A. M. (2004), 'Genetic Variation and Nutritional Requirements', *World Review of Nutrition and Dietetics*, 93: 153–63.

Monteiro, C. A., Cannon, G., Lawrence, M., Costa Louzada, M. L., Pereira Machado, P. (2019b), 'Ultra-processed foods, diet quality, and health using the NOVA classification system' (Rome: FAO).

Monteiro, C. A., Cannon, G., Levy, R. B., Moubarac, J. C., Louzada, M. L., Rauber, F., Khandpur, N., Cediel, G., Neri, D., Martinez-Steele, E., Baraldi, L. G., Jaime, P. C. (2019a), 'Ultra-processed foods: what they are and how to identify them', *Public Health Nutrition*, 22(5): 936–41.

Monteiro, C. A., Moubarac, J. C., Levy, R. B., Canella, D. S., Louzada, M. L. D. C., Cannon, G. (2018), 'Household availability of ultra-processed foods and obesity in nineteen European countries', *Public Health Nutrition*, 21(1): 18–26.

Monteiro, C. A., Pfeiler, T. M., Patterson, M. D., Milburn, M.A. (2017), 'The Carnism Inventory: Measuring the ideology of eating animals', *Appetite*, 113: 51–62.

Mora, C., Tittensor, D. P., Adl, S., Simpson, A. G. B., Worm, B. (2011), 'How Many Species Are There on Earth and in the Ocean?', *PLoS Biology*, 9(8): e1001127.

Morales-Garcia, J. A., Calleja-Conde, J., Lopez-Moreno, J. A., Alonso-Gil, S., Sanz-SanCriostobal, M., Riba, J., Perez-Castillo, A. (2020), 'N,N-dimethyltryptamine compound found in the hallucinogenic tea ayahuasca, regulates adult neurogenesis in vitro and in vivo', *Translational Psychiatry*, 10(331).

Moyer, J., Smith, A., Rui, Y., Hayden, J. (2020), 'Regenerative agriculture and the soil carbon solution', Rodale Institute.

Mozaffarian, D. (2019), 'Dairy Foods, Obesity, and Metabolic Health: The Role of the Food Matrix Compared with Single Nutrients', *Advances in Nutrition*, 10(5): 917S–923S.

Muller, A., Schader, C., El-Hage Scialabba, N., Bruggemann, J., Isensee, A., Erb, K-H., Smith, P., Klocke, P., Leiber, F., Stolze, M., Niggli, U. (2017), 'Strategies for feeding the world more sustainably with organic agriculture', *Nature Communications*, 8: 1290.

Mun, J. G., Legette, L. L., Ikonte, C. J., Mitmesser, S.H. (2019), 'Choline and DHA in Maternal and Infant Nutrition: Synergistic Implications in Brain and Eye Health', *Nutrients*, 11: 1125.

Murdock, G. P. (1967), 'Ethnographic Atlas: A Summary', *Ethnology*, 6(2): 109–236.

Murphy, J. (2014), 'Eshleman's Caves', in *Clayton Eshleman: The Whole Art*, ed. S. Kendall (Boston: Black Widow Press).

Nagel, T. (1974), 'What is it like to be a bat?', *Philosophical Review*, 83: 435–50.

Naghshi, S., Sadeghi, O., Willett, W. C., Esmaillzadeh, A. (2020), 'Dietary intake of total, animal, and plant proteins and risk of all cause, cardiovascular, and cancer mortality: systematic review and dose-response meta-analysis of prospective cohort studies', British Medical Journal, 370: m2412.

Navarrete, A., Schaik, C., Isler, K. (2011), 'Energetics and the evolution of human brain size', Nature, 480: 91–3.

Neal, A. L., Bacq-Labreuil, A., Zhang, X., Clark, I. M., Coleman, K., Mooney, S. J., Ritz, K., Crawford, J. W. (2020), 'Soil as an extended composite phenotype of the microbial metagenome', Scientific Reports, 10: 10649.

Nelson, R. K. (1980), Shadow of the hunter: Stories of Eskimo Life (Chicago: University of Chicago Press).

Nelson, R. K. (1993), 'Searching for the Lost Arrow: Physical and Spiritual Ecology in the Hunter's World', in The Biophilia Hypothesis, eds. S. R. Kellert, E. O. Wilson (Washington: Island Press).

Neruda, P. (1989), 'Andean Condor (Vultur gryphus)', in Art of Birds (Austin: University of Texas Press).

Niemyjska, A., Cantarero, K., Byrka, K., Bilewicz, M. (2018), 'Too humanlike to increase my appetite: Disposition to anthropomorphize animals relates to decreased meat consumption through empathic concern', Appetite, 127: 21–7.

Niman, N. (2014), Defending Beef: The Case for Sustainable Meat Production (Vermont: Chelsea Green).

Nordborg, M., Röös, E. (2016), 'Holistic management – a critical review of Allan Savory's grazing method', SLU/EPOK – Centre for Organic Food & Farming & Chalmers.

Nordhagen, S., Beal, T., Haddad, L. (2020), 'The role of animal-source foods in healthy, sustainable, and equitable food systems', GAIN Discussion Paper No. 5.

Nutt, D., Erritzoe, D., Carhart-Harris, R. (2020), 'Psychedelic Psychiatry's Brave New World', Cell, 181(1): 24–8.

Onwezen, M. C., van der Weele, C. N. (2016), 'When indifference is ambivalence: Strategic ignorance about meat consumption', *Food Quality and Preference*, 52: 96–105.

Orlich, M. J., Singh, P. N., Sabaté, J., Jaceldo-Siegl, K., Fan, J., Knutsen, S., Beeson, W. L., Fraser, G. E. (2013), 'Vegetarian dietary patterns and mortality in Adventist Health Study 2', *JAMA Internal Medicine*, 173(13): 1230–8.

Osório, F. de. L., Sanches, R. F., Macedo, L. R., Santos, R. G., Maia-de-Oliveira, J. P., Wichert-Ana, L., Araujo, D. B., Riba, J., Crippa, J. A., Hallak, J. E. (2015), 'Antidepressant effects of a single dose of ayahuasca in patients with recurrent depression: a preliminary report', *Brazilian Journal of Psychiatry*, 37(1): 13–20.

Pachirat, T. (2011), *Industrialized Slaughter and the Politics of Sight* (New Haven and London: Yale University Press).

Pailhaugue, N. (1998), 'Faune et saisons d'occupation de la salle Monique au Magdalénien Pyrénéen, Grotte de la Vache (Alliat, Ariège, France), trans. Don Hitchcock, *Quaternaire*, 9(4): 385–400.

Pante, M. C., Njau, J. K., Hensley-Marschand, B., Keevil, T. L., Martín-Ramos, C., Peters, R. F., de la Torre, I. (2018), 'The carnivorous feeding behavior of early Homo at HWK EE, Bed II, Olduvai Gorge, Tanzania', *Journal of Human Evolution*, 120: 215–35.

Papandreou, C., Moré, M., Bellamine, A. (2020), 'Trimethylamine N-Oxide in Relation to Cardiometabolic Health-Cause or Effect?', *Nutrients*, 12(5): 1330.

Parkinson, J. (2018), 'Revisiting the hunting-versus-scavenging debate at FLK Zinj: A GIS spatial analysis of bone surface modifications produced by hominins and carnivores in the FLK 22 assemblage, Olduvai Gorge, Tanzania', *Palaeogeography, Palaeoclimatology, Palaeoecology*, 511: 29–51.

Parodi, P. W. (2009), 'Has the association between saturated fatty acids, serum cholesterol and coronary heart disease been over emphasized?', *International Dairy Journal*, 19(6–7): 345–61.

Paulson, I., Auer, N. E. (1964), 'The Animal Guardian: A Critical and Synthetic Review', *History of Religions*, 3(2): 202–19.

Peden, R. S. E., Camerlink, I., Boyle, L. A., Loughnan, S., Akaichi, F., Turner, S. P. (2020), 'Belief in Pigs' Capacity to Suffer: An Assessment of Pig Farmers, Veterinarians, Students, and Citizens', *Anthrozoös*, 33(1): 21–36.

Perkins, J. M., Subramanian, S. V., Smith, G. D., Özaltin, E. (2016), 'Adult height, nutrition, and population health', *Nutrition Reviews*, 74(3): 149–65.

Perpich, D. (2008), *The Ethics of Emmanuel Levinas* (Stanford, CA: Stanford University Press).

Piazza, J., Ruby, M. B., Loughnan, S., Luong, M., Kulik, J., Watkins, H. M., Seigerman, M. (2015), 'Rationalising meat consumption: The 4Ns', *Appetite*, 91: 114–128.

Pieper, M., Michalke, A., Gaugler, T. (2020), 'Calculation of external climate costs for food highlights inadequate pricing of animal products', *Nature Communications*, 11: 6117.

Pilloud, M. A., Haddow, S. D., Knüsel, C. J., Larsen, C. S. (2016), 'A bioarchaeological and forensic re-assessment of vulture defleshing and mortuary practices at Neolithic Çatalhöyük', *Journal of Archaeological Science: Reports*, 10: 735–43.

Plummer, T. (2004), 'Flaked stones and old bones: Biological and cultural evolution at the dawn of technology', *American Journal of Physical Anthropology*, 125: 118–64.

Pobiner, B. (2013), 'Evidence for Meat-Eating by Early Humans', *Nature Education Knowledge*, 4(6): 1.

Pochettino, M. L., Cortella, A. R., Ruiz, M. (1999), 'Hallucinogenic snuff from Northwestern Argentina: Microscopical identification of anadenanthera colubrina

294 THE MEAT PARADOX

var. cebil (fabaceae) in powdered archaeological material', *Economic Botany*, 53: 127–32.

Pollan, M. (2006), *The Omnivore's Dilemma: A Natural History of Four Meals* (New York: The Penguin Press).

Pollan, M. (2018), *How to Change Your Mind: What the New Science of Psychedelics Teaches Us About Consciousness, Dying, Addiction, Depression, and Transcendence* (London: Penguin Books).

Ponte, P. I., Alves, S. P., Bessa, R. J., Ferreira, L. M., Gama, L. T., Brás, J. L., Fontes, C. M., Prates, J. A. (2008), 'Influence of pasture intake on the fatty acid composition, and cholesterol, tocopherols, and tocotrienols content in meat from free-range broilers', *Poultry Science*, 87(1): 80–8.

Poore, J., Nemecek, T. (2018), 'Reducing food's environmental impacts through producers and consumers', *Science*, 360(6392): 987–92.

Poux, X., Aubert, P-M. (2019), 'An agroecological Europe in 2050: multifunctional agriculture for healthy eating, Findings from the Ten Years For Agroecology (TYFA) modelling exercise', IDDRI.

Prakash, V., Bishwakarma, M. C., Chaudhary, A., Cuthbert, R., Dave, R., Kulkarni, M., Kumar, S., Paudel, K., Ranade, S., Shringarpure, R., Green, R. E. (2012), 'The population decline of Gyps vultures in India and Nepal has slowed since veterinary use of diclofenac was banned', *PloS ONE*, 7(11): e49118.

Prakash, V., Galligan, T., Chakraborty, S., Dave, R., Kulkarni, M., Prakash, N., Shringarpure, R. N., Ranade, S. P. (2019), 'Recent changes in populations of Critically Endangered Gyps vultures in India', *Bird Conservation International*, 29(1): 55–70.

Prakash, V., Pain, D. J., Cunningham, A. A., Donald, P. F., Prakash, N., Verma, A., Gargi, R., Sivakumar, S., Rahmani, A.R. (2003), 'Catastrophic collapse of Indian white-backed Gyps bengalensis and long-billed Gyps indicus vulture populations', *Biological Conservation*, 109(3): 381–90.

Pribac, T. B. (2021), *Enter the Animal: Cross-species perspectives on grief and spirituality* (Sydney: Sydney University Press).

Purcell, N. (2011), 'Cruel Intimacies and Risky Relationships: Accounting for Suffering in Industrial Livestock Production', *Society and Animals*, 19(1): 59–81.

Rashid, S., Meier, V., Patrick, H. (2020), 'Review of Vitamin B12 deficiency in pregnancy a diagnosis not to miss as veganism and vegetarianism become more prevalent', *European Journal of Haematology*, Accepted Author Manuscript.

Rauber, F., Steele, E. M., Louzada, M. L. da C., Millett, C., Monteiro, C. A., Levy, R. B. (2020), 'Ultraprocessed food consumption and indicators of obesity in the United Kingdom population (2008–2016)', *PLoS ONE*, 15(5): e0232676.

Rausch, L. L., Gibbs, H. K., Schelly, I., Brandão Jr, A., Morton, D. C., Filho, A. C., Strassburg, B., Walker, N., Noojipady, P., Barreto, P., Meyer, D. (2019), 'Soy expansion in Brazil's Cerrado', *Conservation Letters*, 12: e12671.

Regan, T. (1983), *The Case for Animal Rights* (Berkeley: University of California Press).

Regan, T. (1985), 'The Case for Animal Rights', in *In Defense of Animals*, ed. P. Singer (New York: Blackwell).

Reichel-Dolmatoff, G. (1975), *The Shaman and the Jaguar: A Study of Narcotic Drugs Among the Indians of Colombia* (Philadelphia: Temple University Press).

Reichel-Dolmatoff, G. (1996), *The Forest Within: World-View of the Tukano Amazonian Indians* (Totnes, Devon: Themis Press, in association with the COAMA Programme, Colombia and the Gaia Foundation, London).

Reichel-Dolmatoff, G. (1997), *Rainforest Shamans: essays on the Tukano Indians of the Northwest Amazon* (Totnes, Devon: Themis Press, in association with the COAMA Programme, Colombia and the Gaia Foundation, London).

Reshef, H., Barkai, R. (2015), 'A taste of an elephant: The probable role of elephant meat in Paleolithic diet preferences', *Quaternary International*, 379: 28–34.

Rewilding Europe (2015), 'Natural Grazing: Practices in the rewilding of cattle and horses', Rewilding Europe.

Reznikoff, I., Dauvois, M. (1988), 'The sound dimension of painted caves', *Bulletin de la Société Préhistorique Française*, 85(8): 238–46.

Richards, M. P., Trinkaus, E. (2009), 'Isotopic evidence for the diets of European Neanderthals and early modern humans', *Proceedings of the National Academy of Sciences*, 106(38): 16034–9.

Richardson, K. (2018), 'Livestock and the boundaries of our planet', in *Farming, Food and Nature: Respecting Animals, People and the Environment*, eds. J. D'Silva, C. McKenna (London: Routledge).

Richter, M., Boeing, H., Grünewald-Funk, D., Heseker, H., Kroke, A., Leschik-Bonnet, E., Oberritter, H., Strohm, D., Watzl, B. (2016), 'Vegan diet. Position of the German Nutrition Society (DGE)', *Ernahrungs Umschau*, 63(04): 92–102. Erratum in 63(05): M262.

Ripple, W. J., Wolf, C., Newsome, T. M., Barnard, P., Moomaw, W. R. (2020), '11,258 scientist signatories from 153 countries, Corrigendum: World Scientists' Warning of a Climate Emergency', *BioScience*, 70(1): 100.

Ripple, W. J., Wolf, C., Newsome, T. M., Betts, M. G., Ceballos, G., Courchamp, F., Hayward, M. W., Van Valkenburgh, B. V., Wallack, A. D., Worm, B. (2019), 'Are we eating the world's megafauna to extinction?', *Conservation Letters*, 12: e12627.

Ripps, H., Shen, W. (2012), 'Review: taurine: a "very essential" amino acid', *Molecular Vision*, 18: 2673–86.

Rizzolatti, G., Arbib, M.A. (1998), 'Language within our grasp', *Trends in Neurosciences*, 21(5): 188–94.

Rizzolatti, G., Camarda, R., Fogassi, L., Gentilucci, M., Luppino, G., Matelli, M. (1988), 'Functional organization of inferior area 6 in the macaque monkey', *Experimental Brain Research*, 71: 491–507.

Roberts, M., Parfitt, S. (1999), *Boxgrove: A Middle Pleistocene hominid site at Eartham Quarry, Boxgrove, West Sussex* (London: English Heritage).

Rodgers, D., Wolf, R. (2020), *Sacred Cow: The Case For (Better) Meat* (Dallas: BenBella Books).

Rogerson, D. (2017), 'Vegan diets: practical advice for athletes and exercisers', *Journal of the International Society of Sports Nutrition*, 14: 36.

Rollin, B. E. (2002), 'An ethicist's commentary on equating productivity and welfare', *The Canadian Veterinary Journal*, 43(2): 83.

Röös, E., Bajželj, B., Smith, P., Patel, M., Little, D., Garnett, T. (2017), 'Greedy or needy? Land use and climate impacts of food in 2050 under different potential livestock futures', *Global Environmental Change*, 47: 1–12.

Rosell, M. S., Lloyd-Wright, Z., Appleby, P. N., Sanders, T. A., Allen, N. E., Key, T. J. (2005), 'Long-chain n-3 polyunsaturated fatty acids in plasma in British meat-eating, vegetarian, and vegan men', *American Journal of Clinical Nutrition*, 82(2): 327–34.

Ross, S., Bossis, A., Guss, J., Agin-Liebes, G., Malone, T., Cohen, B., Mennenga, S. E., Belser, A., Kalliontzi, K., Babb, J., Su, Z., Corby, P., Schmidt, B. L. (2016), 'Rapid and sustained symptom reduction following psilocybin treatment for anxiety and depression in patients with life-threatening cancer: a randomized controlled trial', *Journal of Psychopharmacology*, 30: 1165–e1180.

Rothgerber, H. (2013), 'Real Men Don't Eat (Vegetable) Quiche: Masculinity and the Justification of Meat Consumption', *Psychology of Men and Masculinity*, 14(4): 363–75.

Rothgerber, H. (2014), 'Efforts to overcome vegetarian-induced dissonance among meat eaters', *Appetite*, 79: 32–41.

Rothgerber, H. (2015), 'Can you have your meat and eat it too? Conscientious omnivores, vegetarians, and adherence to diet', *Appetite*, 84: 196–203.

Rothgerber, H. (2019), 'But I Don't Eat that Much Meat', *Society and Animals*, 27(2): 150–73.

Rothgerber, H. (2020a), 'Meat-related cognitive dissonance: A conceptual framework for understanding how meat eaters reduce negative arousal from eating animals', *Appetite*, 146: 104511.

Rothgerber, H. (2020b), 'How we love and hurt animals: Considering cognitive dissonance in young meat eaters', in *Why We Love and Exploit Animals*, eds. K. Dhont, G. Hodson (London and New York: Routledge).

Rowntree, J. E., Stanley, P. L., Maciel, I. C. F., Thorbecke, M., Rosenzweig, S. T., Hancock, D. W., Guzman, A., Raven, M. R. (2020), 'Ecosystem Impacts and Productive Capacity of a Multi-Species Pastured Livestock System', *Frontiers in Sustainable Food Systems*, 4: 232.

Royal Society for the Prevention of Cruelty to Animals (RSPCA) (2020), 'Eat, Sit, Suffer, Repeat: The Life of a Typical Meat Chicken', RSPCA.

Rozin, P., Fallon, A.E. (1987), 'A perspective on disgust', *Psychological Review*, 94(1), 23–41.

Rozin, P., Haidt, J., McCauley, C. R. (2008), 'Disgust', in *Handbook of Emotions*, 3rd edn, eds. M. Lewis, J.M. Haviland-Jones, L.F. Barrett (New York: Guilford Press).

Rucker, J. J. H., Iliff, J., Nutt, D. J. (2018), 'Psychiatry and the psychedelic drugs. Past, present and future', *Neuropharmacology*, 142: 200–18.

Rucker, J. J. H., Jelen, L. A., Flynn, S., Frowde, K. D., Young, A. H. (2016), 'Psychedelics in the treatment of unipolar mood disorders: a systematic review', *Journal of Psychopharmacology*, 30: 1220–9.

Safina, C. (2015), *Beyond Words: What Animals Think and Feel* (New York: Henry Holt & Co.).

Sahnouni, M., Rosell, J., van der Made, J., Vergès, J.M., Ollé, A., Kandi, N., Harichane, Z., Derradji, A., Medig, M. (2013), 'The first evidence of cut marks and usewear traces from the Plio-Pleistocene locality of El-Kherba (Ain Hanech), Algeria: implications for early hominin subsistence activities circa 1.8 Ma', *Journal of Human Evolution*, 64(2): 137–50.

Sakkas, H., Bozidis, P., Touzios, C., Kolios, D., Athanasiou, G., Athanasopoulou, E., Gerou, I., Gartzonika, C. (2020), 'Nutritional Status and the Influence of the Vegan Diet on the Gut Microbiota and Human Health', *Medicina* (Kaunas, Lithuania), 56(2): 88.

Saladino, P. (2020), *The Carnivore Code: Unlocking the Secrets to Optimal Health by Returning to Our Ancestral Diet* (New York: HMH Books).

Sanches, R. F., de Lima Osório, F., Dos Santos, R.G., Macedo, L. R., Maia-de-Oliveira, J. P., Wichert-Ana, L., de Araujo, D. B., Riba, J., Crippa, J. A., Hallak, J.E. (2016), 'Antidepressant Effects of a Single Dose of Ayahuasca in Patients With Recurrent Depression: A SPECT Study', *Journal of Clinical Psychopharmacology*, 36(1): 77–81.

Sanders, J., Hess, J., eds. (2019), 'Leistungen des ökologischen Landbaus für Umwelt und Gesellschaft' ('Performance of organic farming for environment and society'), Thünen Report 65, Thünen-Institut, Braunschweig.

Sanders, T. A. B. (2009), 'DHA status of vegetarians', *Prostaglandins, Leukotrienes and Essential Fatty Acids*, 81(2): 137–41.

Santo, R. E., Kim, B. F., Goldman, S. E., Dutkiewicz, J., Biehl, E. M. B., Bloem, M. W., Neff, R. A., Nachman,

K. E. (2020), 'Considering Plant-Based Meat Substitutes and Cell-Based Meats: A Public Health and Food Systems Perspective', *Frontiers in Sustainable Food Systems*, 4.

Schader, C., Muller, A., El-Hage Scialabba, N., Hecht, J., Isensee, A., Erb, K.-H., Smith, P., Makkar, H. P. S., Klocke, K., Leiber, F., Schwegler, P., Stolze, M., Niggli, U. (2015), 'Impacts of feeding less food-competing feedstuffs to livestock on global food system sustainability', *Journal of the Royal Society Interface*, 12(113).

Schenberg, E. E. (2020), 'Psychedelic-Assisted Psychotherapy: A Paradigm Shift in Psychiatric Research and Development', *Frontiers in Pharmacology*, 9: 733.

Schmutz, U., Foresi, L. (2017), 'Vegan organic horticulture: Standards, challenges, socio-economics and impact on global food security', *Acta Horticulturae*, 1164: 475–84.

Schultes, R. E., Hofmann, A., Rätsch, C. (1992), *Plants of the Gods: Their sacred, healing, and hallucinogenic powers* (Rochester: Healing Arts Press).

Schwalm, C. R., Glendon, S., Duffy, P. B. (2020), 'RCP8.5 tracks cumulative CO2 emissions', *Proceedings of the National Academy of Sciences*, 117(33): 19656–7.

Scientific Advisory Committee on Nutrition (SACN) (2019), *Saturated fats and health: SACN report*, SACN.

Sebastiani, G., Herranz Barbero, A., Borrás-Novell, C., Alsina Casanova, M., Aldecoa-Bilbao, V., Andreu-Fernández, V., Pascual Tutusaus, M., Ferrero Martínez, S., Gómez Roig, M. D., García-Algar, O. (2019), 'The Effects of Vegetarian and Vegan Diet during Pregnancy on the Health of Mothers and Offspring', *Nutrients*, 11: 557.

Senthong, V., Wang, Z., Li, X.S., Fan, Y., Wu, Y., Tang, W. H. W., Hazen, S. L. (2016), 'Intestinal Microbiota-Generated Metabolite Trimethylamine-N-Oxide and 5-Year Mortality Risk in Stable Coronary Artery Disease: The Contributory Role of Intestinal Microbiota in a COURAGE-Like Patient

Cohort', *Journal of the American Heart Association*, 5(6): e002816.

Serpell, J. (1986), *In the Company of Animals: A Study of Human-animal Relationships* (Oxford: Basil Blackwell).

Shahidi, F., Ambigaipalan, P. (2018), 'Omega-3 Polyunsaturated Fatty Acids and Their Health Benefits', *Annual Review of Food Science and Technology*, 9(1): 345–81.

Shanon, B. (2010), *The Antipodes of the Mind: Charting the phenomenology of the ayahuasca experience* (Oxford: Oxford University Press).

Shapiro, P. (2018), *Clean Meat: How Growing Meat Without Animals Will Revolutionize Dinner and the World* (New York: Gallery Books).

Sheldrake, M. (2020), 'The "enigma" of Richard Schultes, Amazonian hallucinogenic plants, and the limits of ethnobotany', *Social Studies of Science*, 50(3): 345–76.

Sherwood, S. C., Webb, M. J., Annan, J. D., Armour, K. C., Forster, P. M., Hargreaves, J. C., Hegerl, G., Klein, S. A., Marvel, K. D., Rohling, E. J., Watanabe, M., Andrews, T., Braconnot, P., Bretherton, C. S., Foster, G. L., Hausfather, Z., von der Heydt, A. S., Knutti, R., Mauritsen, T., Norris, J. R., Proistosescu, C., Rugenstein, M., Schmidt, G. A., Tokarska, K. B., Zelinka, M. D. (2020), 'An assessment of Earth's climate sensitivity using multiple lines of evidence', *Reviews of Geophysics*, 58: e2019RG000678.

Shotwell, A. (2016), *Against Purity: Living Ethically in Compromised Times* (Minneapolis and London: University of Minnesota Press).

Singer, P. (1975), *Animal Liberation: A New Ethics for Our Treatment of Animals* (New York: Random House).

Sistiaga, A., Husain, F., Uribelarrea, D., Martín-Perea, D. M., Ferland, T., Freeman, K. H., Diez-Martín, F., Baquedano, E., Mabulla, A., Domínguez-Rodrigo, M., Summons, R. E. (2020), 'Microbial biomarkers reveal a hydrothermally active landscape at Olduvai Gorge at the dawn of the

Acheulean, 1.7 Ma', *Proceedings of the National Academy of Sciences*, 117(40): 24720–8.

Smaje, C. (2020), *A Small Farm Future* (Vermont and London: Chelsea Green).

Smil, V. (2013), *Should We Eat Meat? Evolution and Consequences of Modern Carnivory* (Chichester: Wiley-Blackwell).

Smith, J. (2018), 'The role of livestock in developing countries', in *Farming, Food and Nature: Respecting Animals, People and the Environment*, eds. J. D'Silva, C. McKenna (London: Routledge).

Sobal, J. (2005), 'Men, Meat, and Marriage: Models of Masculinity', *Explorations in the History and Culture of Human Nourishment*, 13(1–2): 135–58.

Soil Association (2010), 'A rock and a hard place: Peak phosphorus and the threat to our food security' (Bristol: Soil Association).

Soil Association (2020a), 'Ultra-processed foods: The case for re-balancing the UK diet' (Bristol: Soil Association).

Soil Association (2020b), 'Fixing Nitrogen: The challenge for climate, nature and health' (Bristol: Soil Association).

Soulier, M-C., Morin, E. (2016), 'Cutmark data and their implications for the planning depth of Late Pleistocene societies', *Journal of Human Evolution*, 97: 37–57.

Sözmen, B. (2015), 'Relations and Moral Obligations towards Other Animals', *Relations*, 3: 179–93.

Spector, T. (2015), *The Diet Myth: The Real Science Behind What We Eat* (London: Weidenfeld & Nicolson).

Spector, T. (2020), *Spoon-Fed: Why Almost Everything We've Been Told About Food Is Wrong* (London: Jonathan Cape).

Spence, C. (2017), 'Why aren't we more outraged about eating chicken?', *The Conversation*: https://theconversation.com/why-arent-we-more-outraged-about-eating-chicken-82284 [accessed November 2020].

Spence, C., Osman, M., McElligott, A. G. (2017), 'Theory of

Animal Mind: Human Nature or Experimental Artefact?', *Trends in Cognitive Sciences*, 21(5): 333–43.

Sponheimer, M., Lee-Thorp, J. A. (1999), 'Isotopic evidence for the diet of an early hominid, Australopithecus africanus', *Science*, 283(5400): 368–70.

Sprague, M., Dick, J., Tocher, D. (2016), 'Impact of sustainable feeds on omega-3 long-chain fatty acid levels in farmed Atlantic salmon, 2006–2015', *Scientific Reports*, 6: 21892.

Springmann, M., Wiebe, K., Mason-D'Croz, D., Sulser, T. B., Rayner, M., Scarborough, P. (2018), 'Health and nutritional aspects of sustainable diet strategies and their association with environmental impacts: a global modelling analysis with country-level detail', *The Lancet Planetary Health*, 2(10): e451–e461.

Średnicka-Tober, D., Barański, M., Seal, C., Sanderson, R., Benbrook, C., Steinshamn, H., Gromadzka-Ostrowska, J., Rembiałkowska, E., Skwarło-Sońta, K., Eyre, M., Cozzi, G., Krogh Larsen, M., Jordon, T., Niggli, U., Sakowski, T., Calder, P. C., Burdge, G. C., Sotiraki, S., Stefanakis, A., Yolcu, H., Stergiadis, S., Chatzidimitriou, E., Butler, G., Stewart, G., Leifert, C. (2016a), 'Composition differences between organic and conventional meat: a systematic literature review and meta-analysis', *British Journal of Nutrition*, 115(6): 994–1011.

Średnicka-Tober, D., Barański, M., Seal, C., Sanderson, R., Benbrook, C., Steinshamn, H., Gromadzka-Ostrowska, J., Rembialkowska, E., Skwarlo-Sonta, K., Eyre, M. Cozzi, G., Larsen, M. K., Jordon, T., Niggil, U., Sakowski, T., Calder, P. C., Burdge, G. C., Sotiraki, S., Stefanakis, A., Stergiadis, S., Yolcu, H., Chatzidimitriou, E., Butler, G., Stewart, G., Leifert, C. (2016b), 'Higher PUFA and n-3 PUFA, conjugated linoleic acid, α-tocopherol and iron, but lower iodine and selenium concentrations in organic milk: A systematic literature review and meta- and redundancy analyses', *British Journal of Nutrition*, 115(6): 1043–60.

Stallwood, K. (2014), *Growl: Life Lessons, Hard Truths, and Bold Strategies from an Animal Advocate* (New York: Lantern Books).

Stanley, P. L., Rowntree, J. E., Beede, D. K., DeLonge, M. S., Hamm, M. W. (2018), 'Impacts of soil carbon sequestration on life cycle greenhouse gas emissions in Midwestern USA beef finishing systems', *Agricultural Systems*, 162: 249–58.

Starkovich, B. M., Conard, N. J. (2015), 'Bone taphonomy of the Schöningen "Spear Horizon South" and its implications for site formation and hominin meat provisioning', *Journal of Human Evolution*, 89: 154–71.

Steele, T. S. (2010), 'A unique hominin menu dated to 1.95 million years ago', *Proceedings of the National Academy of Sciences*, 107(24): 10771–2.

Stewart, K. (1994), 'Early hominid utilization of fish resources and implications for seasonality and behavior', *Journal of Human Evolution*, 27: 229–245.

Stiner, M. C. (2002), 'Carnivory, Coevolution, and the Geographic Spread of the Genus Homo', *Journal of Archaeological Research*, 10: 1–63.

Stringer, C. (2011), *The Origin of Our Species* (London: Penguin Books).

Stull, D. D., Broadway, M. J. (2004), *Slaughterhouse Blues: The Meat and Poultry Industry in North America* (Belmont, CA: Thomson/Wadsworth).

Sutton, M., Howard, C. M., Erisman, J. W., Billen, G., Bleeker, A., Grennfelt, P., van Grinsven, H., Grizzetti, B., eds. (2011), *The European Nitrogen Assessment: Sources, Effects and Policy Perspectives* (Cambridge: Cambridge University Press).

Syromyatnikov, M. Y., Isuwa, M. M., Savinkova, O. V., Derevshchikova, M. I., Popov, V. N. (2020), 'The Effect of Pesticides on the Microbiome of Animals', *Agriculture*, 10(3): 79.

Tang, G. (2010), 'Bioconversion of dietary provitamin A carotenoids to vitamin A in humans', *American Journal of Clinical Nutrition*, 91(5): 1468S–1473S.

Taussig, M. (1993), *Mimesis and Alterity: A Particular History of the Senses* (New York & London: Routledge).

Tello, J. C. (1942), 'Discovery of the Chavín Culture in Peru', *American Antiquity*, 9(1): 35–66.

Testoni, I., Ghellar, T., Rodelli, M., De Cataldo, L., Zamperini, A. (2017), 'Representations of Death Among Italian Vegetarians: An Ethnographic Research on Environment, Disgust and Transcendence', *European Journal of Psychology*, 13(3): 378–95.

Thieme, H. (1997), 'Lower Palaeolithic hunting spears from Germany', *Nature*, 385: 807–10.

Thomas, D. (2007), 'The mineral depletion of foods available to us as a nation (1940–2002) – a review of the 6th Edition of McCance and Widdowson', *Nutrition and Health*, 19(1–2): 21–55.

Thompson, E. (2001), 'Empathy and Consciousness', in *Between Ourselves: Second-person issues in the study of consciousness*, ed. E. Thompson, *Journal of Consciousness Studies*, 8 (5–7).

Thompson, J. C., Carvalho, S., Marean, C. W., Alemseged, Z. (2019), 'Origins of the Human Predatory Pattern: The Transition to Large-Animal Exploitation by Early Hominins', *Current Anthropology*, 60(1): 1–23.

Thorning, T. K., Bertram, H. C., Bonjour, J-P., de Groot, L., Dupont, D., Feeney, E., Ipsen, R., Lecerf, J. M., Mackie, A., McKinley, M. C., Michalski, M-C., Rémond, D., Risérus, U., Soedamah-Muthu, S. S., Tholstrup, T., Weaver, C., Astrup, A., Givens, I. (2017), 'Whole dairy matrix or single nutrients in assessment of health effects: current evidence and knowledge gaps', *The American Journal of Clinical Nutrition*, 105(5): 1033–45.

Tian, Q., Hilton, D., Becker, M. (2016), 'Confronting the

meat paradox in different cultural contexts: Reactions among Chinese and French participants', *Appetite*, 96: 187–94.

Timmers, J. F. (2018), 'Protected Cerrado and sustainable diets: complementary pathways towards a more conscious appetite', in *Farming, Food and Nature: Respecting Animals, People and the Environment*, eds. J. D'Silva, C. McKenna (London: Routledge).

Tirado, R., Thompson, K. F., Miller, K. A., Johnston, P. (2018), 'Less is more: Reducing meat and dairy for a healthier life and planet – Scientific background on the Greenpeace vision of the meat and dairy system towards 2050', Greenpeace Research Laboratories Technical Report (Review).

Tomasello, M. (1999), *The Cultural Origins of Human Cognition* (Cambridge, MA: Harvard University Press).

Tomova, A., Bukovsky, I., Rembert, E., Yonas, W., Alwarith, J., Barnard, N. D., Kahleova, H. (2019), 'The Effects of Vegetarian and Vegan Diets on Gut Microbiota', *Frontiers in Nutrition*, 6(47).

Tong, T. Y. N., Appleby, P. N., Armstrong, M. E. G., Fensom, G. K., Knuppel, A., Papier, K., Perez-Cornago, A., Travis, R. C., Key, T. J. (2020), 'Vegetarian and vegan diets and risks of total and site-specific fractures: results from the prospective EPIC-Oxford study', *BMC Medicine*, 18: 353.

Tong, T. Y. N., Appleby, P. N., Bradbury, K. E., Perez-Cornago, A., Travis, R. C., Robert, C., et al. (2019), 'Risks of ischaemic heart disease and stroke in meat eaters, fish eaters, and vegetarians over 18 years of follow-up: results from the prospective EPIC-Oxford study', *British Medical Journal*, 366: l4897.

Tree, I. (2018), *Wilding: The Return of Nature to a British Farm* (London: Picador).

Tubb, C., Seba, T. (2019), 'Rethinking Food and Agriculture 2020-2030 The Second Domestication of Plants and

Animals, the Disruption of the Cow, and the Collapse of Industrial Livestock Farming', RethinkX.

Tuck, S. L., Winqvist, C., Mota, F., Ahnström, J., Turnbull, L. A., Bengtsson, J. (2014), 'Land-use intensity and the effects of organic farming on biodiversity: a hierarchical meta-analysis', *Journal of Applied Ecology*, 51: 746–55.

Tudge, C. (2008), 'Enlightened Agriculture and the new agrarianism', in *The Future of Animal Farming: Renewing the Ancient Contract*, eds. M. S. Dawkins, R. Bonney (Oxford: Blackwell Publishing).

UK Climate Change Committee (2019a), 'Net Zero: The UK's contribution to stopping global warming'.

UK Climate Change Committee (2019b), 'Reducing UK Emissions – 2019 progress report to Parliament', CCC.

UK Climate Change Committee (2020a), 'Land Use: Policies for a net zero UK', CCC.

UK Climate Change Committee (2020b), 'Sixth Carbon Budget', CCC.

Ulijaszek, S., Mann, N., Elton, S. (2012), *Evolving Human Nutrition: Implications for Public Health*, Cambridge Studies in Biological and Evolutionary Anthropology (Cambridge: Cambridge University Press).

United Nations Environment Programme (UNEP) (2020), 'Emissions Gap Report 2020', Nairobi.

van Hal, O., de Boer, I. J. M., Muller, A., de Vries, S., Erb, K-H., Schader, C., Gerrits, W. J. J., van Zanten, H. H. E. (2019), 'Upcycling food leftovers and grass resources through livestock: Impact of livestock system and productivity', *Journal of Cleaner Production*, 219: 485–96.

Van Kernebeek, H. R. J., Oosting, S. J., Van Ittersum, M. K., Bikker, P., de Boer, I. J. M. (2016), 'Saving land to feed a growing population: consequences for consumption of crop and livestock products', *The International Journal of Life Cycle Assessment*, 21: 677–87.

van Klink, R., van Laar-Wiersma, J., Vorst, O., Smit, C.

(2020), 'Rewilding with large herbivores: Positive direct and delayed effects of carrion on plant and arthropod communities', *PLoS ONE*, 15(1): e0226946.

van Vliet, S., Kronberg, S. L., Provenza, F. D. (2020), 'Plant-Based Meats, Human Health, and Climate Change', *Frontiers in Sustainable Food Systems*, 4: 128.

Van Zanten, H. H. E. (2016), 'Feed sources for livestock: recycling towards a green planet', Wageningen University.

Van Zanten, H. H. E., Herrero, M., Hal, O. V., Röös, E., Muller, A., Garnett, T., Gerber, P. J., Schader, C., De Boer, I. J. M. (2018), 'Defining a land boundary for sustainable livestock consumption', *Global Change Biology*, 24: 4185–94.

Vandermoere, F., Geerts, R., De Backer, C., Erreygers, S., Van Doorslaer, E. (2019), 'Meat Consumption and Vegaphobia: An Exploration of the Characteristics of Meat Eaters, Vegaphobes, and Their Social Environment', *Sustainability*, 11(14): 1–15.

Velasquez, M. T., Ramezani, A., Manal, A., Raj, D. S. (2016), 'Trimethylamine N-Oxide: The Good, the Bad and the Unknown', *Toxins* (Basel), 8(11): 326.

Veronese, N., Stubbs, B., Solmi, M., Ajnakina, O., Carvalho, A. F., Maggi, S. (2018), 'Acetyl-L-Carnitine Supplementation and the Treatment of Depressive Symptoms: A Systematic Review and Meta-Analysis', *Psychosomatic Medicine*, 80(2): 154–9.

Victor, K., Barnard, A. (2016), 'Slaughtering for a living: A hermeneutic phenomenological perspective on the well-being of slaughterhouse employees', *International Journal of Qualitative Studies on Health and Well-being*, 11: 30266.

Vilaça, A. (2005), 'Chronically Unstable Bodies: Reflections on Amazonian Corporalities', *The Journal of the Royal Anthropological Institute*, 11(3): 445–64.

Vince, G. (2020), 'The heat is on over the climate crisis:

Only radical measures will work', *The Observer*: https://
www.theguardian.com/environment/2019/may/18/
climate-crisis-heat-is-on-global-heating-four-degrees-2100-
change-way-we-live [accessed January 2021].

Viveiros de Castro, E. (1998), 'Cosmological Deixis and
Amerindian Perspectivism', *The Journal of the Royal
Anthropological Institute*, 4(3): 469–88.

Waller, S. J. (1993), 'Sound and rock art', *Nature*, 363: 501.

Walsh, P. K. W. (2019), 'Why foods derived from animals are
not necessary for human health', in *Ethical Vegetarianism
and Veganism*, eds. A. Linzey, C. Linzey (London:
Routledge).

Wang, C., Harris, W. S., Chung, M., Lichtenstein, A. H.,
Balk, E. M., Kupelnick, B., Jordan, H. S., Lau, J. (2006),
'n-3 Fatty acids from fish or fish-oil supplements, but not
α-linolenic acid, benefit cardiovascular disease outcomes
in primary- and secondary-prevention studies: a systematic
review', *The American Journal of Clinical Nutrition*,
84(1): 5–17.

Wang, F., Basso, F. (2019), '"Animals are friends, not food":
Anthropomorphism leads to less favorable attitudes toward
meat consumption by inducing feelings of anticipatory
guilt', *Appetite*, 138: 153–73.

Wang, Y., Lehane, C., Ghebremeskel, K., Crawford, M.
(2010), 'Modern organic and broiler chickens sold for
human consumption provide more energy from fat than
protein', *Public Health Nutrition*, 13(3): 400–8.

Wang, Z., Bergeron, N., Levison, B. S., Li, X. S., Chiu, S., Jia,
X., Koeth, R. A., Li, L., Wu, Y., Tang, W. H. W., Krauss,
R. M., Hazen, S. L. (2019), 'Impact of chronic dietary red
meat, white meat, or non-meat protein on trimethylamine
N-oxide metabolism and renal excretion in healthy men
and women', *European Heart Journal*, 40(7): 583–94.

Wannamethee, S. G., Jefferis, B. J., Lennon, L., Papacosta,
O., Whincup, P. H., Hingorani, A. D. (2018), 'Serum

Conjugated Linoleic Acid and Risk of Incident Heart Failure in Older Men: The British Regional Heart Study', *Journal of the American Heart Association*, 7.

Watts, J., Wasley, A., Heal, A., Ross, A., Jordan, L., Howard, E., Holmes, H. (2020), 'Revealed: UK supermarket and fast food chicken linked to deforestation in Brazil', *Guardian*: https://www.theguardian.com/environment/2020/nov/25/revealed-uk-supermarket-and-fast-food-chicken-linked-to-brazil-deforestation-soy-soya [accessed January 2021].

Weikert, C., Trefflich, I., Menzel, J., Obeid, R., Longree, A., Dierkes, J., Meyer, K., Herter-Aeberli, I., Mai, K., Stangl, G. I., Müller, S. M., Schwerdtle, T., Lampen, A., Abraham, K. (2020), 'Vitamin and mineral status in a vegan diet', *Deutsches Ärzteblatt international*, 117: 575–82.

Werdelin, L., Lewis, M. E. (2013), 'Temporal Change in Functional Richness and Evenness in the Eastern African Plio-Pleistocene Carnivoran Guild', *PLoS ONE*, 8(3): e57944.

Westbury, H. R., Neumann, D. L. (2008), 'Empathy-related responses to moving film stimuli depicting human and non-human animal targets in negative circumstances', *Biological Psychology*, 78: 66–74.

Weyrich, L., Duchene, S., Soubrier, J., et al. (2017), 'Neanderthal behaviour, diet, and disease inferred from ancient DNA in dental calculus', *Nature*, 544: 357–61.

White, N. C., Reid, C., Welsh, T. N. (2014), 'Responses of the human motor system to observing actions across species: A transcranial magnetic stimulation study', *Brain and Cognition*, 92: 11–18.

Whitley, D. (2006), 'Is there a shamanism and rock art debate?', *Before Farming*, 4(7): 1–7.

Whitley, D. (2009), *Cave Paintings and the Human Spirit: The Origin of Creativity and Belief* (Amherst, NY: Prometheus Books).

Willems, E. P., van Schaik, C. P. (2017), 'The social organization of Homo ergaster: Inferences from anti-predator responses in extant primates', *Journal of Human Evolution*, 109: 11–21.

Willerslev, R. (2007), *Soul Hunters: Hunting, Animism, and Personhood among the Siberian Yukaghirs* (Berkeley: University of California Press).

Willerslev, R., Vitebsky, P., Alekseylv, A. (2015a), 'Sacrifice as the ideal hunt: a cosmological explanation for the origin of reindeer domestication', *Journal of the Royal Anthropological Institute*, 21(1): 1–23.

Willerslev, R., Vitebsky, P., Alekseylv, A. (2015b), 'Defending the thesis on the 'hunter's double bind', *Journal of the Royal Anthropological Institute*, 21(1): 28–31.

Willett, W., Rockström, J., Loken, B., Springmann, M., Lang, T., Vermeulen, S., Garnett, T., Tilman, D., DeClerck, F., Wood, A., Jonell, M., Clark, M., Gordon, L. J., Fanzo, J., Hawkes, C., Zurayk, R., Rivera, J. A., De Vries, W., Sibanda, L.M., Afshin, A., Chaudhary, A., Herrero, M., Agustina, R., Branca, F., Lartey, A., Fan, S., Crona, B., Fox, E., Bignet, V., Troell, M., Lindahl, T., Singh, S., Cornell, S. E., Reddy, K. S., Narain, S., Nishtar, S., Murray, C. J. L. (2019a), 'Food in the Anthropocene: the EAT–Lancet Commission on healthy diets from sustainable food systems', *The Lancet Commissions*, 393 (10170): 447–92.

Willett, W., Rockström, J., Loken, B. (2019b), 'Healthy diets and sustainable food systems – Authors' reply', *The Lancet*, 394(10194): 215–16.

Willett, W., Rockström, J., Loken, B. (2019c), 'The EAT–Lancet Commission: a flawed approach? – Authors' reply', *The Lancet*, 394(10204): 1141–2.

Willett, W., Skerrett, P. J. (2001), *Eat, Drink, and Be Healthy: The Harvard Medical School Guide to Healthy Eating* (New York: Free Press; reprint edition, 2011).

Williams, A. C., Hill, L. J. (2017), 'Meat and Nicotinamide:

A Causal Role in Human Evolution, History, and Demographics', *International Journal of Tryptophan Research*.

Williams, P., 'Nutritional composition of red meat', *Nutrition & Dietetics*, 64 (2007): S113-S119.

Winkelman, M. (2010), *Shamanism: A Biopsychosocial Paradigm of Consciousness and Healing* (Santa Barbara: ABC-CLIO).

Wißing, C., Rougier, H., Baumann, C., Comeyne, A., Crevecoeur, I., Drucker, D. G., Gaudzinski-Windheuser, S., Germonpre, M., Gomez-Olivencia, A., Krause, J., Matthies, T., Naito, Y. I., Posth, C., Semal, P., Street, M., Bocherens, H. (2019), 'Stable isotopes reveal patterns of diet and mobility in the last Neandertals and first modern humans in Europe', *Scientific Reports*, 9: 4433.

Wong, K. (2012), 'Why Humans Give Birth to Helpless Babies', *Scientific American*: https://blogs.scientificamerican.com/observations/why-humans-give-birth-to-helpless-babies/ [accessed January 2021].

Wong, M-W., Yi, C-H., Liu, T-T., Lei, W-Y., Hung, J-S., Lin, C-L., Lin, S-Z., Chen, C-L. (2018), 'Impact of vegan diets on gut microbiota: An update on the clinical implications', *Tzu Chi Medical Journal*, 30(4): 200–3.

Wood, B., Collard, M. (1999), 'The Human Genus', *Science*, 284(5411): 65–71.

World Bank, International Bank for Reconstruction and Development (2012), 'Turn Down the Heat: Why A 4°C Warmer World Must Be Avoided', The World Bank.

World Health Organization (WHO) (2014), 'WHA Global Nutrition Targets 2025: Stunting Policy Brief, World Health Organization.

Wrangham, R., Jones, J., Laden, G., Pilbeam, D., Conklin-Brittain, N. (1999), 'The Raw and the Stolen: Cooking and the Ecology of Human Origins', *Current Anthropology*, 40: 567–94.

Wu, G. (2020), 'Important roles of dietary taurine, creatine, carnosine, anserine and 4-hydroxyproline in human nutrition and health', *Amino Acids*, 52: 329–60.

WWF-UK (2011), 'Soya and the Cerrado: Brazil's forgotten jewel', WWF-UK.

WWF-UK and RSPB (2020), 'Riskier Business: The UK's Overseas Land Footprint, Summary Report', WWF-UK.

Wynn, T., Coolidge, F., Bright, M. (2009), 'Hohlenstein-Stadel and the Evolution of Human Conceptual Thought', *Cambridge Archaeological Journal*, 19(1): 73–84.

Yildiz, A., Emhan, A., Bez, Y., Kıngır, S. (2012), 'Psychological Symptom Profile of Butchers Working in Slaughterhouse and Retail Meat Packing Business: A Comparative Study', *Kafkas Universitesi Veteriner Fakultesi Dergisi*, 18.

Yilmaz, B., Li, H. (2018), 'Gut Microbiota and Iron: The Crucial Actors in Health and Disease', *Pharmaceuticals* (Basel, Switzerland), 11(4): 98.

Young, J. F., Therkildsen, M., Ekstrand, B., Che, B. N., Larsen, M. K., Oksbjerg, N., Stagsted, J. (2013), 'Novel aspects of health promoting compounds in meat', *Meat Science*, 95(4): 904–11.

Zagmutt, F. J., Pouzou, J. G., Costard, S. (2019), 'The EAT-Lancet Commission: a flawed approach?', *The Lancet*, 394(10204): 1140–1.

Zagmutt, F. J., Pouzou, J. G., Costard, S. (2020), 'The EAT-Lancet Commission's Dietary Composition May Not Prevent Noncommunicable Disease Mortality', *The Journal of Nutrition*, 150(5): 985–8.

Zane, D., Irwin, J. R., Reczek, R.W. (2015), 'Do Less Ethical Consumers Denigrate More Ethical Consumers? The Effect of Willful Ignorance on Judgments of Others', *SSRN*.

Zani, C. F., Gowing, J., Abbott, G. D., Taylor, J. A., Lopez-Capel, E., Cooper, J. (2020), 'Grazed temporary grass-clover leys in crop rotations can have a positive impact on soil quality under both conventional and organic agricultural systems', *European Journal of Soil Science*, 1: 17.

Zaraska, M. (2016), *Meathooked: The History and Science of Our 2.5-Million-Year Obsession with Meat* (New York: Basic Books).

Zink, K., Lieberman, D. (2016), 'Impact of meat and Lower Palaeolithic food processing techniques on chewing in humans', *Nature*, 531: 500–3.

Zlatev, J., Persson, T., Gärdenfors, P. (2005), 'Bodily mimesis as "the missing link" in human cognitive evolution', *Lund University Cognitive Science-LUCS*, 121.

Notes

INTRODUCTION

1. The statuette in the Natural History Museum is a replica; in researching this book, I also sought out the original. See Lewis-Williams (2002), Conard (2003), Kind et al. (2014) and Ebinger-Rist et al. (2018).
2. Jeffers (1963), 'Vulture'.
3. See Prakash et al. (2012, 2019), BirdLife International and Vulture Conservation Foundation (2014) and Green et al. (2016).
4. Hughes (1957), 'The Jaguar'.
5. See WWF-UK (2011), Timmers (2018) and Rausch et al. (2019) for cattle grazing and soy in the Cerrado. WWF-UK and RSPB (2020) report that the land required overseas to meet the UK's annual demand for soy is roughly 1.7 million hectares, with 65 per cent of this land located in Argentina, Brazil and Paraguay, all of which are high risk in terms of ecological impacts. For the jaguar as a threatened species, see: https://www.iucnredlist.org/species/15953/123791436 [accessed January 2021].
6. Huxley (1956).
7. For species yet to be described, see Mora et al. (2011). For farm animal populations, see the FAO's dataset: http://www.fao.org/faostat/en/?#data/ [accessed January 2021]. For wild animal populations, see WWF-UK (2020): https://livingplanet.panda.org/en-gb/ [accessed January 2021]. For meat as the leading driver of species extinctions, see Machovina et al. (2015). For

the contribution of agriculture including animal farming to land degradation and wildlife loss, see IPBES (2019). For comparative biomass, see Bar-On et al. (2018). For projected global demand for meat, see FAO (2011). For diet change in this context, see Henry et al. (2019), Erb et al. (2016), WWF-UK (2017) and Benton et al. (2021).

8. Gerber et al. (2013) calculate that animal farming accounts for 14.5 per cent of all greenhouse gas emissions, with feed production and processing (including land use change) and enteric fermentation from ruminants the two main sources. Kim et al. (2015) calculate that if global trends in meat and dairy consumption continue, global mean temperature rise is likely to exceed the 2 °C target in the Paris Agreement, even with dramatic emissions reductions across non-agricultural sectors. GRAIN and the Institute for Agriculture and Trade Policy (2018) and Clark et al. (2020) reach similar conclusions. Statements concerning meat and dairy companies are derived from Feedback (2020a) and GRAIN and the Institute for Agriculture and Trade Policy (2018). The comparative emissions generated by JBS, Tyson, Cargill, Dairy Farmers of America and Fonterra relative to fossil fuel companies was calculated and stated by GRAIN and the Institute for Agriculture and Trade Policy (2018). For UK retailer and restaurant exposure to unsustainable soy, see Mighty Earth (2020) and Watts et al. (2020). Accusations of potential or purported involvement with ecological, social and human rights issues have been levelled against Cargill by Mighty Earth; see: https://stories.mightyearth. org/cargill-worst-company-in-the-world/ [accessed January 2021]. Cargill has disputed these claims. For a discussion 'fake farm' labels, see Feedback (2020a) and Griffiths and Morgan (2018).

9. For discussion of the financing of industrial animal farming, see Feedback (2020b). The statement regarding high street banks Barclays and HSBC is derived from Feedback (2020b).

10. See: https://plantbasednews.org/lifestyle/health/brits-want-urgent-ban-factory-farming/; https://www.aspca.org/sites/default/files/

impact_on_public_attitudes_toward_industrial_animal_
agriculture-final-111120.pdf; https://www.foodethicscouncil.
org/resource/public-back-farmers-with-high-standards/ [accessed
January 2021].

ONE: Meat

1. The 'sabretooth hypothesis' was voiced by Marean (1989)
   and modified by Marean and Ehrhardt (1995), the latter
   arguing that sabretooth cats would have provided hominids
   with scavengeable remains but not in the massive amounts
   hypothesised previously.
2. For archaeological evidence of hominid omnivory, see
   Domínguez-Rodrigo et al. (2005), Ferraro et al. (2013),
   Plummer (2004) and Pobiner (2013). For meat in the diet of
   Australopithecus africanus, see Balter et al. (2012), Sponheimer
   and Lee-Thorpe (1999) and Maslin (2017). For Olduvai Gorge,
   see Bunn and Kroll (1986) and Pante et al. (2018). For Dikika,
   see McPherron et al. (2010). For a discussion of *Homo erectus* as
   (arguably) the first early human species, see Wood and Collard
   (1999).
3. The contribution of animal foods to human anatomical
   evolution is discussed in Chapter 5, and their contribution to
   the evolution of the human brain in Chapter 7. For the relative
   importance of protein-rich outside-bone nutrients (meat) vs. fat-
   rich inside-bone nutrients (marrow and brains), see Thompson et
   al. (2019). Mann (2007), Ben-Dor et al. (2011) and Domínguez-
   Rodrigo and Pickering (2017) discuss omnivory and behavioural
   feedbacks. The quote is from Ulijaszek et al. (2012).
4. For the respective roles of animal and plant foods in the hominid
   diet throughout evolution, see Milton (1999, 2000, 2003), Smil
   (2013), Ulijaszek et al. (2012) and Williams and Hill (2017).
5. We were not at Bwlchwernen Fawr, but at Home Farm in
   Gloucestershire, hosted by farm manager David Wilson. I
   attended to discuss the Harmony in Education project at
   the invitation of Patrick Holden and head teacher Richard

Dunne, joining a group of teachers and educators. The events and conversations narrated in this chapter occurred throughout the day, as we toured the farm and held discussions as a group. Patrick's 'Kool-Aid' comment is from: https://sustainablefoodtrust.org/articles/interview-patrick-holden/ [accessed January 2021].

6. For discussion of the importance of herbivores and grazing animals in ecosystem recovery and maintenance, see Rewilding Europe (2015), Tree (2018), van Klink et al. (2020) and Jepson and Blythe (2020).

7. The manures of ruminant animals can pollute waterways and leach greenhouse gases, while excessive grazing and trampling can deplete soils and denude landscapes. Over three billion hectares of land worldwide are grazed by ruminants, and much of this land is in a degraded state. Large areas of the UK have been over-grazed. The UK has lost 97 per cent of its wildflower meadows in recent decades, with much of our grassland a sterile ryegrass monocrop. Swathes of rainforest and savannah in the Americas have also been destroyed to make way for ruminants, positioning animal farming as a leading global driver of deforestation and wildlife loss. While regions such as the Great Plains of North America and subtropical grasslands in Africa have historically supported millions of herbivores, it is not always the case that existing grasslands evolved under significant grazing pressure, calling into question whether regenerative farming in these contexts is really mimicking natural ecosystems. See Carter et al. (2014) for a critical discussion.

8. See Bengtsson et al. (2005), Tuck et al. (2014) and Sanders and Hess (2019) for organic farming and wildlife.

9. See: https://www.nhs.uk/live-well/eat-well/eat-less-saturated-fat/ [accessed January 2021]. For the evidence underpinning UK dietary recommendations pertaining to saturated fat, see SACN (2019).

10. Barabási et al. (2020).

11. For the TMAO hypothesis, see Koeth et al. (2013) and Senthong et al. (2016). It's not known whether TMAO is a mediator of heart disease risk or a marker of other processes; fish is a rich

source of preformed TMAO and is not understood to be a risk factor for heart disease. For a critical discussion ('the TMAO story may be a red herring'), see Landfald et al. (2017). See also Velasquez (2016), Wang et al. (2019) and Papandreou et al. (2020). For the gut microbiome, see Spector (2015).

12. See Barabási et al. (2020) for the Mediterranean diet, van Vliet et al. (2020) for the divergent outcomes related to red meat consumption and health, and Leroy and Cofnas (2020) for a discussion of ambiguities in the evidence.

13. The long-chain omega-3 polyunsaturated fatty acids (LC n3 PUFAs) eicosapentaenoic acid (EPA) and docosahexaenoic acid (DHA) are essential for foetal development and cognitive functioning, adequate intake being associated with health benefits. EPA and DHA are only found in animal foods (and some microalgae), primarily oily fish and seafoods. Theoretically, the precursor n3 PUFA α-linolenic acid (ALA), which is found in plant foods such as dark leafy vegetables, walnuts and linseed (flax), can be elongated in the body to EPA and DHA, but the conversion rate is very low, especially for DHA; see Gerster (1998), Burdge and Calder (2005), Brenna et al. (2009) and Lane et al. (2014). It's uncertain whether ALA consumption delivers the same benefit as the consumption of EPA and DHA. See Wang et al. (2006), Harris et al. (2021), Shahidi and Ambigaipalan (2018), Chang et al. (2009) and Bentsen (2017) for discussion. For Scottish farmed salmon, see Sprague et al. (2016). For poultry, see Wang et al. (2010), Ponte et al. (2008) and Eating Better (2020). Środnicka-Tober et al. (2016a, 2016b) found significant differences in fatty acid composition between organic meat and dairy and conventional meat and dairy, with significantly higher concentrations of LC n3 PUFAs in organic meat. Given the health benefits associated with consumption of LC n3 PUFAs, this research suggests that organic meat and dairy can play a beneficial role in nutritional security, perhaps alongside increased microalgae consumption. The role of LC n3 PUFAs in human evolution is discussed in Chapter 7.

14. Vegans generally have good intakes of most nutrients, including

higher intakes of fibre, vitamin C and folate. Some studies have also found higher vegetable consumption among vegans compared to omnivores. Potential health benefits of vegetarian or vegan diets have been reported by Clarys et al. (2014), Le and Sabaté (2014), Dinu et al. (2017), Tong et al. (2019), and Kim et al. (2019), among others. These studies cohere with Ashfin et al. (2019) who found that low intakes of wholegrains, fruits, vegetables, nuts and seeds, and high intake of sodium are the highest global risk factors in non-communicable disease morbidity and mortality, suggesting a global shift towards more plant-based diets is a public health priority. For EPIC-Oxford, see Davey et al. (2003). For the Adventist study, see Orlich et al. (2013). For the BDA statement, see BDA and The Vegan Society (2017). For the AAND statement, see Melina et al. (2016).

15. Research suggests that vegetarian and vegan diets foster a more diverse gut microbiome associated with health benefits – see e.g. Tomova et al. (2019), Wong et al. (2018) and Sakkas et al. (2020) – but variability deriving from the interplay of the microbiome, genes and the individual metabolism might also complicate vegan dietary health in some contexts. Berry et al. (2020) found high variation in individual metabolic responses to the same plate of food, even among identical twins, suggesting individual responses to vegan eating are likely to vary. Such processes are known to shape LC n3 PUFA blood levels among vegans. Burdge and Calder (2005) and Burdge (2006) found that women are generally more adept than men at converting ALA to LC n3 PUFAs, especially DHA. Kothapalli et al. (2016) found that conversion of ALA to EPA and DHA is influenced by a genetic mutation that is more prevalent among traditionally plant-based populations. See also Innis (2008) and Brenna (2002). Tang (2010) observes, on a parallel tangent, wide individual variation in the conversion of carotenoids (provitamin A) to retinol (vitamin A), depending on the genetic variability between individuals, with some individuals known to be unable to obtain sufficient retinol when subsisting solely on plant foods. While we have a good idea at a population level of what constitutes a healthy dietary pattern, such variability means

there is no correct way of eating that will work for everyone. This passage quotes Spector (2015).

16. Walsh (2019). For the Faunalytics study, see: https://faunalytics.org/a-summary-of-faunalytics-study-of-current-and-former-vegetarians-and-vegans/ [accessed January 2021].

17. See Bakaloudi et al. (2020) for a literature review of nutritional deficiencies in vegan diets. For LC n3 PUFAs, see Rosell et al. (2005), Kornsteiner et al. (2008), Craig (2009), Sanders (2009), Chamorro et al. (2020). For vitamin D, see Elorinne et al. (2016) and Crowe et al. (2011). For B12, see Gilsing et al. (2010) and Allès et al. (2017). For calcium and fracture risk, see Appleby et al. (2007), Ho-Pham et al. (2009) and Tong et al. (2020). For iodine and selenium, see Kristensen et al. (2015). It's likely that the popularity of veganism in the past decade has translated into increased understanding of some nutritional challenges, such as B12. Weikert et al. (2020) found that vitamin B12 status was similarly good in vegans and non-vegans in Germany, though urine samples revealed lower calcium excretion and markedly lower iodine in vegans compared to non-vegans; in one-third of the vegans, iodine excretion was lower than the World Health Organization threshold value for severe iodine deficiency. See Hovinen et al. (2021) for further discussion of the challenges which can persist on a vegan diet, namely for children, even with nutritional guidance.

18. See Weikert et al. (2020) for the iodine status of German vegans. Leung et al. (2011) raise similar concerns about vegan women in the US. A robust body of evidence recommends regular DHA intakes during pregnancy and for at least the first six months of an infant's life, with higher levels at birth associated with better neurodevelopmental health and other beneficial health outcomes; see Innis (2008), Coletta et al. (2010), Guesnet and Alessandri (2011) and Brenna and Carlson (2014). Sanders (2009) is among those to observe notably lower levels of DHA in vegans. Mun et al. (2019) highlight that adequate choline and DHA intakes are not being met by most American adults, especially women of child-bearing age. The potential of algal-derived DHA supplementation in pregnant vegan women and

infants (as well as for vegans more broadly) requires further research, with Burdge et al. (2017) noting that the effect of low maternal DHA status in vegans on cognitive function in infants has been inadequately studied. Beyond DHA, Avnon et al. (2020) found a vegan diet to be associated with an increased risk for small-for-gestational-age newborns and lower birthweight. Koebnick et al. (2004) warn that pregnant women consuming a vegetarian or vegan diet have an increased risk of vitamin B12 deficiency, while Rashid et al. (2020) called for additional guidance on antenatal diagnosis and management of vitamin B12 deficiency among pregnant women who are vegan. See also Castro et al. (2020) and Baldassarre et al. (2020). For the German, Belgian, Spanish and Danish positions, see Richter et al. (2016), ARMB (2019), Ferreiro et al. (2019) and Lund (2019).

19. On some calculations we have already reached 'peak phosphate', with supplies set to decline in the next two decades. Other scholars say that we have longer, but our reliance is problematic either way, for phosphate is supplied through geopolitically unstable supply chains. The UK, like most countries, has no domestic source. Germany imports half a million tonnes each year. At current rates of use, those countries that do have a domestic supply, including the US, China and India, will exhaust it in the next generation. The world's remaining reserves are highly concentrated, with Morocco and the Moroccan-controlled Western Sahara holding 85 per cent of the store. See Soil Association (2010) for discussion.

20. By how much should ruminant populations be reduced? It depends on the context. While ruminants can perform a host of positive ecological functions, analysis by Garnett et al. (2017) found they typically contribute more emissions than are sequestered in soils in the long run, implying that a reduction in populations globally would be of climate benefit. The best modelling to date suggests that an organic system would require a decline in average meat consumption (in Europe) of at least 50 per cent, primarily as declines in pig and chicken meat but also in ruminant meat and dairy. See Poux and Aubert (2019),

the Food, Farming and Countryside Commission (2021), Van Zanten et al. (2018), Bajželj et al. (2014), Aubert et al. (2019), Tirado et al. (2018), Muller et al. (2017), Benton et al. (2021), the UK Climate Change Committee (2020b) and Heller et al. (2020) for further discussion of meat reduction as a response to the climate and nature crises. Some research suggests a vegan food system might be the most sustainable. The IPCC (2019) summarise evidence from studies showing that vegan diets have the greatest potential for demand-side mitigation of greenhouse gas emissions, while Poore and Nemacek (2018) conclude that vegan diets would have 'transformative potential' if adopted globally. The ecological rationale for a shift towards more plant-based diets is unambiguous, but the rationale for a fully vegan farming system is debatable. The vegan scenario implied in the oft-cited Poore and Nemacek (2018) remains reliant on fossil fuel fertilisers and chemical pesticides; their analysis excludes consideration of how to address malnutrition or meet the nutrient requirements of a growing population; and considerations such as co-products, on-farm biodiversity and food sovereignty were not addressed. While some farmers, such as Iain Tolhurst in the UK, have developed successful 'veganic' systems, and there is rich potential for research and development on this front, it's not clear whether these systems could feed the global population or be applied in every context. Poux and Aubert (2019) found that organic farming could only feed a growing population if animals were included in the system, with a 40 per cent nitrogen shortfall in the veganic scenario. Phosphorus could be an even greater challenge in a veganic system. Cooper et al. (2018) and Martin et al. (2007) note that stockless (animal free) organic farms are prone to phosphorus deficiencies. See Fairlie (2010), Soil Association (2010) and Schmutz and Foresi (2017) for further discussion. Beyond nitrogen and phosphorus, animals can contribute to soil health by helping to capture carbon, nurturing microbial abundance and activity, and can contribute to soil structure, making soils more resilient in the face of extreme weather. See e.g. Fließbach et al. (2007), Zani et al. (2020), Lori et al. (2017), Lotter et al. (2003), Neal et al. (2020), Skinner et al. (2019), Ghabbour et al. (2017) and Gattinger et al. (2012). Animals could be farmed but not eaten in organic systems, though this could pose land-use and nutritional challenges; such a scenario offers rich potential for future research. For recognition that organic or 'agroecological' farming represents our best hope of feeding the world a healthy, sustainable and equitable diet, see IAASTD (2009), De Schutter (2014), Food, Farming and Countryside Commission (2019) and European Commission (2020). For further benefits of organic farming, see Bengtsson et al. (2005), Tuck et al. (2014), Sanders and Hess (2019), IFOAM and FIBL (2016), Lampkin (2020), Hurtado et al. (2017) and Pieper et al. (2020). See Eisler et al. (2014) for manures relative to fossil fuel fertilisers.

21. Charles HRH The Prince of Wales et al. (2010). The association with hashish and hemp was not made by Prince Charles, but by Henri Michaux.

22. The frontiers of cellular agriculture are expanding rapidly, with 3D printed steaks, cell-based chicken and cultured seafood in development. There are regulatory, technical, social and political barriers to be overcome before these foods enter the mainstream, but it seems only a matter of time. Is cellular agriculture a good thing? I do not address the question in this book, though the short answer is 'hopefully'. If the products are safe, nutritious, and if production evades corporate capture, supporting social equity and food sovereignty, advancing a transition to nature-friendly farming while hastening the end of industrial animal agriculture, then cellular meat could have a hugely beneficial role to play. In an ethical context, considering the meat paradox, it seems obvious that it would be more ethical to consume cellular meat than meat that required the premature death of an animal. For a public health and food systems perspective on cellular agriculture, see Santo et al. (2020). For the ethical and ecological case, see e.g. Dutkiewicz and Rosenberg (2021), Dutkiewicz and Specht (2020), and Shapiro (2018).

TWO: Murder

1. The term 'speciesist' was introduced by Richard D. Ryder in 1970. See Singer (1975).
2. Bentham (1789).
3. Singer (1975).
4. See: http://fcmconference.org/img/ CambridgeDeclarationOnConsciousness.pdf [accessed January 2021]. For the richness, variety, and depth of animal subjectivity, see e.g. Safina (2016), King (2017) and Pribac (2021).
5. Regan (1983, 1985). For a discussion, see Donovan (1990).
6. Women have been at the forefront of animal advocacy and animal studies from the beginning. The anti-vivisection and animal defence movements of the nineteenth and early twentieth centuries were often led by women. The Vegan Society was founded in the 1940s by Dorothy Watson, with her husband and four friends. In the 1960s, writers Ruth Harrison and Brigid Brophy voiced influential critiques of factory farming, with Harrison's *Animal Machines* prompting the UK government to form the Brambell Committee which laid the foundations for animal welfare regulation in the UK. By the early 1970s, prior to Singer's *Animal Liberation*, the feminist movement had begun to establish connections with animal issues. Carol J. Adams and Constantine Salamone pioneered these connections, and Adams (1990) is a landmark publication in the field of animal ethics. In tandem, ecofeminist and 'care' strands of animal ethics were emerging, with women at the forefront of scholarship. Gilligan (1982) emphasised 'the activity of care ... responsibility and relationship' in animal ethics over more 'male' modes of ethics focused on rights and rules. Kheel (1985) advanced an ecological conception of ethics, 'a concept of holism that perceives nature (much like the new physics perceives subatomic particles) as comprising individual beings that are part of a *dynamic* web of interconnections in which feelings, emotions and inclinations (or energy) play an integral role'. Donovan (1996) emphasised the role of loving attention and sympathy, a passionate caring about animal wellbeing, as the basis of an ecologically informed animal

ethics. In as far as this book is concerned with empathy and the interplay of ecological and animal ethics, it is indebted to this tradition, including, more recently, Gruen (2015) on 'entangled empathy' and Aaltola (2018) on varieties of empathy. The meat paradox, as a focus of psychological research, was prefigured by scholarship authored by women, e.g. Adams (2001) which proposes that animal advocates should view non-vegans as 'blocked vegetarians', anticipating the dissonance dynamic of the meat paradox, and Joy (2010) who introduced the 3Ns (normal, natural, necessary) as rationalisations for meat consumption. The frontiers of the meat paradox continued to be expanded by women, with Aaltola (2019), for example, outlining her related concept of the 'omnivore's akrasia', exploring philosophical and psychological perspectives on moral agency. For a discussion of the feminist tradition in animal ethics, see Donovan and Adams (2007) and Adams and Gruen (2014).

7. See: https://www.thebureauinvestigates.com/stories/2018-07-29/ uk-meat-plant-injuries and https://www.thebureauinvestigates. com/stories/2018-07-05/us-meat-plant-injuries [accessed January 2021].

8. Victor and Barnard (2016).

9. For the psychological impacts of slaughterhouse work, see Kristensen (1991), Eisnitz (1997), Stull and Broadway (2004), Dillard (2007), Fitzgerald (2010), Purcell (2011), Pachirat (2011), Yildiz et al. (2012), Dorovskikh (2015), Victor and Barnard (2016), Baran et al. (2016). For PITS, see MacNair (2002).

10. See Eisnitz (1997), Victor and Barnard (2016), Dillard (2008) and the account recounted by Ashitha Nagesh: https://www.bbc. co.uk/news/stories-50986683 [accessed January 2021].

11. MacIntyre (2017) discusses the ethical demand as conceived by Knud Ejler Løgstrup, a Danish philosopher and contemporary of Levinas, who arrived at a strikingly similar conception of our ethical experience. See also Critchley (2007), who emphasises that for Levinas, 'the ethical demand is a traumatic demand'. See Levinas (1961, 1974) and Perpich (2008).

12. Neither Levinas nor Løgstrup wrote about animals in relation to the ethical demand. In 'The Paradox of Morality', Levinas

et al. (1988) recount an interview with students who ask whether animals demand recognition as ethical beings. 'One cannot completely refuse the face of the animal,' Levinas says, ambivalently. 'I don't know if a snake has a face. I can't answer that question.' Some scholars have nevertheless developed accounts of animal ethics based on Levinas's philosophy; see e.g. Crowe (2008), Atterton (2011), Edelglass et al. (2012), Coeckelbergh and Gunkel (2014) and Sözmen (2015).

13. Bob Comis ran a small pig farm in upstate New York, where his pigs were provided with a life that was 'as close to natural as possible'. Of his pigs, Comis says: 'they root, they lounge, they narf, they eat, they forage, they sleep, they wallow, they bask, they run, they play, and they die unconsciously, without pain and suffering.' Yet Comis could not escape the perception that he was 'a slaveholder and a murderer'. 'The simplest way to put it is that slaughter is a socially permissible ethical transgression; societal permission does not make it ethical, it makes it acceptable, non-punishable.' In 2014, Comis stopped farming pigs and became a veganic farmer. See McWilliams (2015) for further examples. Husserl is quoted in Donovan (1996).

14. There is a moral maxim, often attributed to Immanuel Kant, which says 'ought' implies 'can'; that we can only be morally obliged to do something if it's possible to do it. This is intuitively reasonable, and the maxim shapes the meat debate in scholarship and advocacy. See Linzey and Linzey (2019), for example. For *Sacred Cow*, see Rodgers and Wolf (2020) and: https://www.sacredcow.info/book. Earthling Ed's e-book can be downloaded from his website: https://earthlinged.org/. Watch Earthling Ed's film *Land of Hope and Glory* (go on, I dare you) at: https://www.landofhopeandglory.org/ [accessed January 2021].

THREE: Hunting

1. The words 'Eskimo' and 'Inuit' are not directly interchangeable. Both can refer to the indigenous peoples of the Northern circumpolar region living in Alaska in the US, Siberia in Russia,

and in Canada and Greenland. 'Eskimo' was commonly used in the ethnographic literature until the 1990s but it is considered by some northern peoples to be a derogatory term. 'Inuit' is used in most of Canada and has largely replaced 'Eskimo' in the literature as a generic term. My use of 'Inuit' to speak of indigenous peoples across the far north should not be read as implying cultural uniformity, but as the necessary shorthand for a nexus of lifeways, rituals and stories which bind diverse peoples in a cultural continuum.

2. Susqlak is quoted in Laugrand and Oosten (2015). The 'Eskimo people' quote is Nelson (1993). See Nelson (1980) for an account of breathing hole hunting.

3. Willerslev (2007).

4. There is a gender bias in the anthropological literature. Most of the authors are men, and they have often spent most of their time with the male members of the community. This is unfortunate, as women possess cultural identities every part as rich, and women also provide food by hunting and foraging. In keeping with the literature, I primarily refer to hunters as 'he', while acknowledging that this is a partial presentation.

5. Descola (2005) notes that such tales are common in hunting cultures; there are 'many myths and anecdotes that tell of a human being's stay among a people whose appearance and manners are altogether human ... [in such instances] it is always some unexpected detail in the customs of his hosts that suddenly alerts the visitor to the animal nature of those who have welcomed him; a dish of rotting meat politely served reveals vulture-people, an oviparous birth indicates snake-people, and a cannibalistic appetite points to jaguar people.' See also Vilaça (2005).

6. Speaking of the Inuit, Descola (2005) writes: 'If animals are indeed persons, eating them is a form of cannibalism ... This kind of dilemma is not faced solely by the inhabitants of the Far North. Many Amerindian cultures find themselves with the same problem.' Descola differentiates animism, naturalism, totemism and analogism among societies globally. Most of the discussion of 'hunting societies' in this book pertains to animist societies.

7. Liebenberg (2013). Liebenberg also contributed to the 1990 film *The Great Dance: A Hunter's Story*, which features Nqate Xqamxebe.
8. Brown (1983).
9. Kohn (2013).
10. Descola (2005) writes: 'Despite differences in language and ethnic affiliations, the same complex of beliefs and rites everywhere governs the hunter's relationship with his prey. As in Amazonia, most animals are regarded as persons with a soul, and this confers upon them attributes in every way identical to those of humans, such as reflexive consciousness, intentionality, an affective life, and a respect for ethical principles.' Willerslev (2007) explains that the personhood of animals in animist societies is not categorical: 'animals and other nonhumans are conceived as persons, not because personhood has been bestowed upon them by some kind of cognitive processing, but because they reveal themselves as such within relation contexts of real-life activity, such as during hunting.'
11. See Viveiros de Castro (1998), Vilaça (2005) and Descola (2005).
12. Viveiros de Castro (1998) warns of the risk 'of seeing the human who lurks within the body of the animal one eats'. See also Willerslev (2007).
13. For a discussion of bear rituals, see Hallowell (1926), Serpell (1986) and Descola (2005).
14. Reichel-Dolmatoff (1996, 1997).
15. The Tukano are a collective of tribes; they include the Desana, who are the focus of much of the literature. Reichel-Dolmatoff (1975, 1996, 1997) sometimes uses 'Desana' and 'Tukano' interchangeably, particularly when describing the Desana's vision of a cosmic energy circuit. I have adopted the same approach and refer to the Tukano, even when the literature speaks of the Desana. Where the literature speaks of tribes in the Tukano collective with distinctive beliefs or rituals, such as the Makuna or the Barasana, I refer to them directly.
16. Reichel-Dolmatoff (1997).
17. These manifestations of Vaí-mahsë are mostly derived from

Descola (2005). For the Tukano, see Reichel-Dolmatoff (1975, 1996, 1997). For the Cree, see Brightman (1993). Inuit and Innu accounts are from Laugrand and Oosten (2015). For the Yukaghirs, see Willerslev (2007). Viveiros de Castro (1998) writes: 'These spirit masters, clearly endowed with intentionality analogous to that of humans, function as hypostases [the underlying essence] of the animal species with which they are associated, thereby creating an intersubjective field for human-animal relations.' See also Serpell (1986) and Paulson and Auer (1964).

18. Descola (2005).

19. Reichel-Dolmatoff (1996, 1997).

20. The comparison might seem far-fetched, but Hugh-Jones (1996) has suggested it might be apt. See Victor and Barnard (2016) for the dreams and nightmares of slaughterhouse workers and Reichel-Dolmatoff (1997) for the dreams and nightmares of Tukano hunters.

21. Reichel-Dolmatoff (1996), Descola (2005).

22. Nelson (1993). The Inuit today are engaged in a longstanding dialogue with non-indigenous cultures in the lands in which they live. Colonial intrusion was often violent and exploitative and Inuit life has evolved over the past century, while the Inuit's cultural identity, in its varying guises, remains intact. See Laugrand and Oosten (2015) for a discussion.

23. Quoted in Laugrand and Oosten (2015).

24. Willerslev (2007).

25. Descola (2005).

26. The meat paradox, as defined by Loughnan et al. (2010), and as the term is typically employed in the literature, concerns the dissonance aroused by liking meat while not liking harming animals (or a similar formulation). I use the term in a distinct but complementary sense in this book, proposing that the crux of the paradox, at least in some contexts, resides in the tension between *necessity* and *murder* – the necessity of animal consumption asserted on nutritional, ecological or evolutionary grounds, and the perception that the animal consumed is an ethically demanding person whose death is forced upon them

in a manner akin to murder. The original formulation of the paradox is entirely apt, but there is, I believe, a deeper stratum to be explored. What sort of creatures are we, that we find killing for food so problematic? How did we evolve to become so conflicted? To suggest a stratum of necessity in our consumption of meat is to invite dispute or criticism. As Joy (2010) and Piazza et al. (2015) have observed, necessity is among the primary rationalisations that we offer to defend our choice of eating meat. The necessity for animal consumption in contemporary Western society, if it exists, is certainly highly restricted and very different to the way that we eat and farm today. Crucially, I do not assert this necessity as a moral justification. On the contrary, I suggest that meat might involve murder *even when it's necessary*. The meat paradox, in my use of the term, characterises our evolutionary predicament as an empathetic omnivore, a creature torn between the ethical demand and its biological and ecological entanglement. We are the paradox.

FOUR: Omnivore

1. Lewis-Stempel's 'compassionate carnivore's manifesto' can be read at: https://unherd.com/2020/06/let-them-eat-mutton-a-compassionate-carnivores-manifesto/ [accessed January 2021].
2. Rollin (2002).
3. Pollan (2006).
4. See: https://www.theguardian.com/books/2019/jul/27/the-disinformation-age-a-revolution-in-propaganda [accessed January 2021].
5. See: https://www.dailymail.co.uk/news/article-8372959/US-megafarm-locals-call-Cowschwitz-120-000-cattle-pumped-hormones-boost-growth.html [accessed January 2021].
6. Niman (2014).
7. Compassion in World Farming (2012).
8. Various 'consenting animal' adverts are documented on the Suicide Food blog, which was active from 2006 to 2011: http://suicidefood.blogspot.com/ [accessed January 2021].

9. Brightman (1993) notes the similarities between Cree conceptions of 'grateful prey' and imagery used by the advertisement industries. See also Willerslev (2007) and Laugrand and Oosten (2015).

10. Ingold (1994, 1998), Brightman (1993).

11. Festinger et al. (1956), Festinger (1957).

12. Rothgerber (2020a) writes: 'beliefs about farm animals and meat eating are not objective but instead are motivated, and hence susceptible to fluctuation. A general implication of the dissonance perspective is that the very act of consuming meat determines perceptions related to meat and to animal welfare.'

13. See Hestermann et al. (2019) and discussion in Rothgerber (2020a) and De Backer and Hudders (2015). With regards to how prevalent wilful ignorance is, Onwezen and van der Weele (2016) found that 27 to 28 per cent of individuals use strategic ignorance to manage the dissonance of meat-eating (others managing by being 'indifferent', 'struggling' or 'coping').

14. The dissociation of meat from its animal origins has been observed for decades; see Singer (1975), Serpell (1986), Adams (1990) and Joy (2010). Kunst and Hohle (2016) explore how language and meat processing interact with empathy. Subsequent research from Kunst and Haugestad (2018) showed that dissociation is moderated by cultural factors, including prior exposure to unprocessed meat. Tian et al. (2016) also found that prior exposure was important. Following exposure to visual stimuli making the animal origin of meat explicit, French but not Chinese participants rated cows as having diminished mental states, perhaps because food production is more hidden in France than China. For red versus white meat, see Kubberød et al. (2002). For a summary of the evidence, see Benningstad and Kunst (2020).

15. Descola (2005), Willerslev (2007, 2014a), Brightman (1993).

16. For a discussion of dissociation via processing and cooking, and red versus white meat in hunting societies, see Hugh-Jones (1996), Kohn (2013) and Reichel-Dolmatoff (1997). Descola (2005) writes: 'The resemblance between [human and animal]

interiorities is so powerful, affirmed so vividly in all the circumstances in which humans are involved with nonhumans, that it becomes really difficult to ignore it completely when cooking and eating ... one can do one's best to de-subjectivise this food, to make it just "a thing," by eliminating everything that recalls the being that provides it, all the shreds of interiority that still adhere to the tissues.' See Århem (1996) for 'food shamanism'.

17. See Loughnan et al. (2010), and further evidence in Bilewicz et al. (2011), Bastian et al. (2012), Rothgerber (2014) and Monteiro et al. (2017). Our denial is supported by categorical biases wherein we place some animals in a 'food' category and others in a 'not food' category, lowering our estimation of those in the former; see Bratanova et al. (2011), Rothgerber (2020a), Cole and Stewart (2014, 2020), Herzog (2010), Joy (2010) and Acari (2020).

18. Hallowell (1926), Laugrand and Oosten (2015).

19. Rothgerber (2020a), Serpell (1986), and Benningstad and Kunst (2020).

20. Willerslev et al. (2015b).

21. Ingold (1994) suggests the relationship between hunter and prey is characterised by 'trust', versus a relationship of 'domination' in pastoral and agricultural societies. Speaking of the Cree he says: 'the encounter between hunter and prey is ... basically non-violent' because 'animals intentionally present themselves to the hunter to be killed.' Willerslev et al. (2015a, 2015b) challenge Ingold's stance. 'Why is it that the selfsame ethnographies that describe animals as willing prey often also present drawings of an arsenal of devious spring traps, deadfalls, and self-triggering crossbows, designed to catch animals unaware?' Brightman (1993) and Laugrand and Oosten (2015) similarly observe the fragility and contradictions in the narrative of a 'willing' or 'grateful' prey among the Cree and Inuit.

22. Kohn (2007, 2013).

23. Lockwood (2016).

24. For the Save Movement, see Krajnc (2020). For a pioneering discussion of the psychology of meat and the significance of

bearing witness, see Joy (2010). See Bastian and Loughnan (2017) for 'imperfect cloak'.

25. Brightman (1993) observes that a 'sizable minority' of Cree refuse to eat bear meat: 'as the most hominid and most powerful animal, the bear synecdochically represents all animals that the Crees kill and utilize, symbolizing the ambiguity surrounding the hunting project more generally.' See also Willerslev (2007), Laugrand and Oosten (2015) and Serpell (1986).

26. RSPCA (2020).

27. King (2017), Bennett et al. (2018).

28. KFC UK & Ireland (2020).

29. Willerslev (2007) says the Yukaghirs perceive prey animals and certain species of birds, notably the raven, to be persons, while other kinds of animals such as insects, fish and plants are recognised as animate, but are hardly ever spoken of as such. See also Serpell (1986) and Reichel-Dolmatoff (1997).

30. For the Cree, see Ingold (1994) and Brightman (1993). For the Inuit, see Laugrand and Oosten (2015). For the Yukaghirs, see Willerslev (2007). For the Makuna, see Århem (1996). For the Tukano, see Reichel-Dolmatoff (1996, 1997). See also Descola (2005).

31. These prohibitions on unnecessary killing are associated with prohibitions on waste. Brightman (1993) says that the Cree insist that all parts of the animal's body are used or consumed; meat must not be thrown away; and the hunter should refrain from killing animals unless in genuine need. It must be stressed that these prohibitions do not mean that overhunting or waste do not occur. On the contrary, the hunters' worldview can sometimes lead directly to excess killing and profligate waste. When animals are understood to be a 'gift' from the Master of Animals, it can be disrespectful *not* to kill them when they present themselves. When hunting is viewed as regenerative, the hunter might feel an obligation to make the kill, even wantonly so. See Brightman (1993), Willerslev (2007) and Nelson (1993) for a discussion. See Joy (2010) and Piazza et al. (2015) for necessity as a rationalisation.

FIVE: Herbivore

1. The squirrel-eating can be viewed on YouTube: https://www. youtube.com/watch?v=v-cuT7q1dZ4&t=49s. For the CPS statement, see: https://www.cps.gov.uk/london-south/news/ men-who-ate-dead-squirrels-outside-vegan-stall-london-fined. For the pig's head, see: https://metro.co.uk/2019/04/13/ man-who-ate-raw-pigs-head-at-vegan-festival-stabbed-four-classmates-at-school-9184229/ [accessed January 2021].

2. See: https://www.vegansociety.com/go-vegan/definition-veganism [accessed January 2021].

3. Bruckner (2016).

4. Rozin and Fallon (1987).

5. Rozin and Fallon (1987), Rozin et al. (2008).

6. Rozin et al. (2008).

7. Horberg et al. (2009).

8. See: https://www.peta.org/about-peta/faq/is-it-ok-to-eat-roadkill/; https://www.peta.org/features/eat-chickens-period/ [accessed January 2021].

9. Rozin et al. (2008) hypothesised that vegetarians find meat more disgusting because they have adopted an anti-meat stance on ethical grounds, which leads them to (consciously or unconsciously) associate meat with emotions that provide additional motivational force. Other scholars have proposed an inverse process whereby meat avoidance is sometimes initially motivated by physical disgust, with the moral stance constituting a post hoc justification. It seems likely that the process can work in both directions, with moral and physical disgust serving to reinforce one another. See Fessler et al. (2003) for evidence that disgust reactions to meat are caused by, rather than causal of, moral beliefs.

10. Disgust also shapes the psychology of omnivory. Rothgerber (2020a) describes the 'moral outrage' characteristic of Western society wherein the consumption of animals in other cultures is 'disgusting' or reprehensible, while animal consumption in one's own culture remains unexamined. Hugh-Jones (1996), to give one example from a hunting culture, notes that the Kalapalo of

central Brazil preferentially consume fish and nothing else except a few small animals and birds, believing the meat of the large animals consumed by neighbouring tribes to be 'disgusting'.

11. See: https://faunalytics.org/a-summary-of-faunalytics-study-of-current-and-former-vegetarians-and-vegans/ [accessed January 2021] and Levy (2016). For a pragmatic approach to veganism and the purity question, see e.g. Gruen and Jones (2016), Shotwell (2016) and Leenaert (2017).

12. Philosopher David Hume said that 'ought' judgements should not be inferred from premises expressed only in terms of what 'is' and that systems of morality that employ such reasoning are flawed. Among philosophers, the principle is known as 'Hume's Law'. See Piazza et al. (2015) and Joy (2010) for naturalness as moral justification. See Ulijaszek et al. (2012) and Stiner (2002) for the role of omnivory within a flexible dietary strategy that facilitated migration into novel environments.

13. See: https://www.peta.org/living/food/really-natural-truth-humans-eating-meat/; and Mills' essay: http://www.vegsource.com/news/2009/11/the-comparative-anatomy-of-eating.html [accessed January 2021].

14. The WHO states that red meat consumption has 'known health benefits' and the classification for cancer risk 'is based on limited evidence'. The IARC's conclusions, summarised by Bouvard et al. (2015), have been contradicted by recent research; see e.g. Kruger and Zhou (2018), Anderson et al. (2018), Mejborn et al. (2021). See Spector (2020) and Leroy and Cofnas (2020) for a critical discussion of the evidence. Spector (2020) comments on the comparative risks of smoking and processed meat.

15. It's possible to obtain all necessary amino acids from plants, but this requires the consumption of a wider variety of foods in the right combinations, and affordability, knowledge and other constraints can make this more difficult in low-resource settings, meaning that animal foods are typically seen as important sources of complete proteins and amino acids in a development and food insecurity context. For global malnutrition and the importance of meat and animal foods to vulnerable populations, see Nordhagen et al. (2020), Adesogan et al. (2020) and FAO

(2018). Animals can also be socially and ecologically important in the context of global development, helping to cycle fertility, consume waste fodders, protect against food scarcity, provide traction, act as pest controllers, and provide materials as well as essential nutrition.

16. In *The Carnivore Code* (2020), Saladino claims that our ancestors in the Palaeolithic age and indigenous hunting and foraging people today preferentially consume a diet of meat and animal foods, eschewing plants, eating them 'only during times of scarcity or starvation.' This claim is contradicted by evidence concerning both our ancestral diet and subsistence patterns among indigenous peoples. See e.g. Melamed et al. (2016) and Smil (2013) for plants in our ancestral diet. The key reference text pertaining to contemporary hunting peoples has been the *Ethnographic Atlas* by Murdock (1967). The data in the *Atlas*, as calculated by Cordain et al. (2000), suggest that in tundra and circumpolar environments with limited plant foods, meat contributes approximately 85 per cent of the diet. This compares to hunters living in grassland ecosystems, where animal foods contribute 42 to 62 per cent of the diet, and to those living in forests, where animal foods contribute 52 to 80 per cent. In the past decade, scholars have argued that these plant-to-animal subsistence ratios are likely to overstate the contributions made by animal foods. The data in the *Atlas* was not collated in a robust manner, and may be skewed by observational biases arising from a focus on men's subsistence activities coupled with an excessive focus on peoples living in circumpolar and marginal environments. Other scholars suggest that plants make a much higher contribution to the diets of hunting peoples, approximately 65 per cent, with animal products (terrestrial and aquatic) making up the remaining 35 per cent. Ulijaszek et al. (2012) furthermore observe that there are many known cases where hunting peoples make use of an enormous range of plant foods: the Seri of northern California, the Bardi of north Australia, and the Wopkaimin of Papua New Guinea routinely eat foods from around thirty-five plant families, a far cry from Saladino's assertion that plant foods are only consumed during

times of scarcity. See Crittenden and Schnorr (2017) for current views on hunter and forager nutrition. Robert Ardrey and Raymond Dart are discussed in Hart and Sussman (2005).

17. Substantial alterations in cranial-dental and intestinal morphology apparent in *Homo erectus* from around 1.8 million years ago are taken by most scholars as evidence of omnivory. See e.g. Aiello and Wheeler (1995), Aiello (1997) and Milton (1999). Wrangham et al. (1999) argue that the controlled use of fire and cooking (more than omnivory) drove the advances seen in *Homo erectus*. Ulijaszek et al. (2012) are among those (with the majority of paleoanthropologists) who believe this is unlikely, partly because it's difficult to see how cooking could have left so few traces in the archaeological record if it was sufficiently widespread to cause digestive and social adaptation. Unambiguous evidence of cooking only appears within the past 800,000 years, and mostly within the past 200,000. Zink and Lieberman (2004) argue convincingly that the alterations in *Homo erectus* would have been initially made possible by stone tools used to process meat and animal foods, without the need to posit cooking as an explanation. For a discussion of haem iron, taurine, and *Taenia saginata* and *Taenia solium* as evidence of hominid and human meat eating, see Henneberg et al. (1998), Mann (2007) and Ulijaszek et al. (2012). For B12 deficiency and porotic hyperostosis, see Domínguez-Rodrigo et al. (2012). Long-term adaptation to animal consumption is also observable in the elevated signal of *Bacteroides* species in the human gut microbiome relative to other primates; see Berson (2019), Amato et al. (2015), Tomova et al. (2019). Ulijaszek et al. (2012) discuss the genetic basis of lipid metabolism in humans and chimpanzees. For a discussion of the stomach pH values of humans as akin to those of carrion feeders, see Beasley et al. (2015).

18. A review of the literature by Elizabeth et al. (2020) found a clear association between ultra-processed foods and poor health outcomes including overweight, obesity and chronic disease. See also Monteiro et al. (2018, 2019a, 2019b), Rauber et al. (2020), Baldridge et al. (2019) and Soil Association (2020b). For a

discussion of food processing in human evolution, see Zink and Lieberman (2004) and Ulijaszek et al. (2012).

19. It bears repeating (see the endnote in Chapter 3 above) that my use of the term 'meat paradox' is idiosyncratic. The crux of the meat paradox, as I describe it, resides in the tension between necessity and murder, our status as an empathetic omnivore, susceptible to the ethical demand yet sometimes compelled by biological or ecological necessity to consume animals. This formulation (necessity versus murder) is coherent with the original use of the term, but brings a different discussion to the fore, and it might also imply an inverse dynamic: while the omnivore might experience dissonance when they perceive that meat entails murder (or is morally wrong), the vegan might experience dissonance (so compelling is the ethical demand) when confronted with evidence that meat is nutritious, natural and sometimes necessary. This inverse dynamic might be understood either through classical dissonance theory as expressed by Festinger (1957), wherein dissonance arises when an individual realises that two of their cognitions are inconsistent, such as 'killing animals is always wrong' and 'killing animals is a good thing for human nutrition'; or through dissonance theory as it pertains to the self-concept (discussed in Chapter 10), such as 'I am someone who finds animal consumption abhorrent' and 'I evolved consuming animals and remain physiologically omnivorous'. While the meat paradox, in its original sense, has been thoroughly researched, my proposal of an inverse dynamic shaping (some) vegan thought is a hypothesis.

20. Testoni et al. (2017) discuss death as a contaminating principle. Rozin et al. (2008) similarly observe that 'anything that reminds us that we are animals elicits disgust,' with disgust serving to protect us from reminders of our mortality and animality. Bastian and Amiot (2020) discuss these reminders in relation to the meat paradox. For the prior study with omnivores, see Anderson and Barrett (2016). See also Becker and Lawrence (2021).

21. Evidence of hominid and early human hunting has been outlined

by Thompson et al. (2019), Faurby et al. (2020), Parkinson (2018), Pante et al. (2018), Domínguez-Rodrigo and Pickering (2017), Willems and van Schaik (2017), Plummer (2004) and Bunn et al. (2017). The case against hunting as a defining characteristic of early humans has been voiced by Binford (1985, 1987), Berson (2019) and Hart and Sussman (2005). The 500,000-year-old Boxgrove site in England is often seen as significant as it provides some of the earliest unambiguous evidence of our ancestors' position alongside the top predators in their environment; see Roberts and Parfitt (1999) and Stringer (2011). Within the past 100,000 years, we have robust evidence of large mammal hunting; see Agam and Barkai (2015, 2018) and Reshef and Barkai (2015). Within the past 50,000 years, there is evidence that diets in some contexts might have been mostly animal-based. See Bocherens et al. (2005), Richards and Trinkaus (2009), and Wißing et al. (2019) for evidence of carnivory among Neanderthals and contemporaneous modern humans, and Henry et al. (2014), El Zaatari et al. (2011), Weyrich et al. (2017) and Lippi et al. (2015) for contrasting evidence of plant consumption among related populations. Regarding the origins of agriculture, the transition from hunting and foraging to farming was long and diverse, with geographical and temporal variation. In so far as a pattern is evident, it is one of declining health associated with a lower quality diet, inclusive of less meat and animal foods. Angel (1984) and Eaton and Konner (1985) observe a decline in stature, associated with a lower quality diet. Larsen (1995, 2006) suggests that dependence upon plant foods over meat among agriculturalists reduced the intake of zinc, vitamin A and vitamin B12, with evidence of nutritional deficiencies in Neolithic skeletal samples as lesions in the form of porotic hyperostosis and cribra orbitalia, as well as a general trend of decreased stature. Cohen and Crane-Kramer (2007) similarly observe that following the onset of agriculture, humans became shorter and less robust and they suffered from more debilitating diseases than their hunter-gatherer counterparts. Latham (2013) attributes this poorer health to a decline in meat and animal foods in the diet. Smil (2013) and

Ulijaszek et al. (2012) concur. For Viva!'s claim that meat only became a regular part of our diets when we began farming, and other evolutionary claims, see: https://viva.org.uk [accessed January 2021].

22. Who experiences the more acute dissonance, the hunter standing over a slain elk or the farmer in the slaughterhouse? 'Putting quasi-similar beings to death and eating them is far more disturbing metaphysically than the passing prick of conscience that certain Westerners may feel when they eat meat,' Descola (2005) writes. In contrast, Serpell (1986) says: 'The moral dilemma confronted by farmers and livestock herders is far more serious than that faced by hunters of wild game.' Serpell argues that husbandry has traditionally required that farmers or shepherds have a close relationship with the animals in their care, knowing them as distinct personalities. 'The ethical problem is more serious for the farmer than the hunter because the relationship with the animal is different.' Knight (2012) voices a similar view, observing that while the hunter might develop a personal relationship with Vaí-mahsë (in whatever guise the figure appears), they do not form a personal relationship with the animals they hunt. Expressed differently, the hunter might be said to have a relationship with the species but not with the individual. Critics of Knight's stance have noted that in some cultures the animal's soul is understood to be reborn in a new body; the Inuit hunter believes that he hunts *the same animal* repeatedly, with respectful treatment ensuring the return of the animal's soul in new flesh, in which case the relationship *is* perceived to be personal. Descola offers the decisive insight, explaining that the hunter finds consuming animals more *metaphysically* challenging, whereas the farmer might face a distinct emotional challenge, rooted in the personal nature of their relationship. 'It is not so much a sense of culpability that grips the Amazonian or Siberian hunter when he takes an animal's life, but rather a muffled anxiety when faced yet again with the manifest porosity of ontological frontiers.' While the onset of farming altered the terms of our relationship with other animals, the common strategies of

dissonance reduction employed across societies suggest a similar set of psychological pressures. In virtue of our humanity, we all possess a faculty for empathy, and this faculty sometimes confronts us with the perception that the individual animal before us demands not to be harmed. See Peden et al. (2020) for a discussion of how farmers navigate the meat paradox.

SIX: Emergency

1. See Richardson (2018) and Willett et al. (2019a) for the contribution of agriculture and diets to planetary boundaries. For scientists declaring an emergency, see Gardner and Wordley (2019), Ripple et al. (2020), Bradshaw et al. (2021).

2. In a sustainable farming scenario (where 'food/feed competition' is eliminated and livestock are fed on 'leftovers', i.e. ruminants on grass and in organic/regenerative rotations, monogastrics on food waste and by-products from crop production), as calculated by Schader et al. (2015), Van Zanten et al. (2016), Röös et al. (2017) and Van Hal et al. (2019), there would be roughly 21g of animal protein produced per person per day. This can be visualised as 100g of raw bone-free meat but no milk, or 50g of meat and 300ml of milk, or some such combination. Fairlie (2010) similarly calculates that a farming system based around leftovers would produce 33g of meat and 68g of milk per person per day globally, an 80–90 per cent decline on the average UK or US diet today (and less than recommended in EAT-Lancet). Poux and Aubert (2019) and Aubert et al. (2019) have produced a model based on similar premises, where Europe has adopted organic farming while minimising food/feed competition (some crops are still fed to animals, but much less than today), finding that 87g of meat and 250g of milk could be produced per person per day, implying a 50–60 per cent decline in consumption relative to today. These leftovers scenarios broadly cohere with the change in consumption required to resolve the climate and nature crises as calculated by Van Zanten et al. (2018), Bajželj et al. (2014), Kim et al. (2015), Tirado et al. (2018), Muller et

al. (2017), Benton et al. (2021) and the UK Climate Change Committee (2020b).

3. Willett et al. (2019a). See also: https://eatforum.org/eat-lancet-commission/ [accessed January 2021].

4. Blythman was quoted in 'New Diet: Completely Nuts', *Big Issue North*, 1–7 April 2019. See also: https://wickedleeks.riverford. co.uk/opinion/veganism-meat/scrutinise-small-print-eat-lancet. Cornado's comments are quoted in Ingrid (2019). For the EAT-Lancet response, see: https://www.stockholmresilience.org/download/18.8620dc61698d96b1903f7/1553710278936/Letter_Co-Chairs_Lancet_Commission_26.03.2019.pdf [accessed January 2021].

5. See: https://veganuary.com/; https://www.fginsight.com/blogs/blogs/it-is-time-the-livestock-sector-reclaimed-january; https://plantbasednews.org/culture/meat-bosses-vow-reclaim-january/; https://www.fginsight.com/ahdb/ahdb-eat-balanced/eat-balanced-enjoy-the-food-you-eat-115487?s=09 [accessed January 2021].

6. See: https://www.farmdrop.com/blog/veganuary-2018s-latest-fad-diet-wider-cultural-shift/; https://veganuary.com/wp-content/uploads/2020/10/Veganuary-EndOfCampaignReport.pdf [accessed January 2021].

7. Hopwood et al. (2020) found that health motives are the most common reason that people would consider adopting a plant-based diet, while concern for animals was a stronger driver among those who were already vegan. Janssen et al. (2016) reported that people often have multiple motives for choosing vegan diets, with 89 per cent of respondents listing motives related to animals, 69 per cent motives related to personal wellbeing and health, and 47 per cent motives related to environmental protection; most respondents (82 per cent) cited more than one source of motivation. Jay-Z's post can be read at: https://lifeandtimes.com/22-days-challenge; de Boo wrote for the *Huffington Post*: https://www.huffingtonpost.co.uk/jasmijn-de-boo/beyonce-vegan_b_4414658.html [accessed January 2021].

8. See: https://www.vegansociety.com/news/media/statistics;

https://www.waitrose.com/content/dam/waitrose/Inspiration/ Waitrose%20&%20Partners%20Food%20and%20Drink%20 Report%202018.pdf. A Mintel study conducted at the end of 2020 found that 41 per cent of UK consumers say they are either not eating meat or actively reducing their meat consumption [accessed January 2021].

9. Garcia et al. (2019).

10. Much of the criticism of EAT-Lancet was voiced on Twitter and social media. Following Garcia et al. (2019), I have taken the social media response as legitimate grounds for discussion, including of the rumours and hyperbole that surrounded the report's publication. Throughout this chapter, I have only cited original tweets, not retweets, likes or quotes. Blythman's article, 'Why we should resist the vegan putsch', was published by *The Grocer* on 17 January 2019: https://www.thegrocer.co.uk/consumer-trends/ why-we-should-resist-the-vegan-putsch/575625.article. See also: https://twitter.com/bigfatsurprise/status/1085211032556052480; https://twitter.com/joannablythman/status/1085632265592418305 [accessed January 2021].

11. Teicholz posted the 'evidence' on her website: https:// ninateicholz.com/majority-of-eat-authors-vegan- vegetarian/. See also: https://twitter.com/bigfatsurprise/ status/1088862495668948992; https://twitter.com/ bigfatsurprise/status/1089248763959537665; https://twitter. com/JoannaBlythman/status/1088875854933999621; https:// twitter.com/JoannaBlythman/status/1107593357969276928 [accessed January 2021].

12. For EAT-Lancet funding, see: https://eatforum.org/eat-lancet- commission/eat-lancet-funding/. For the FReSH group, see: https://twitter.com/bigfatsurprise/status/1085937306740101120. Teicholz was not the first or only person to suggest the FReSH group funded or influenced the report, but with more than 90,000 followers she played a role in amplifying the claim. For GM nuts, see: https://twitter.com/JoannaBlythman/ status/1097951617385672704 [accessed January 2021].

13. See: https://www.nutritioncoalition.us/news/eatlancet-report- one-sided [accessed January 2021].

14. See: https://wickedleeks.riverford.co.uk/opinion/veganism-meat/ scrutinise-small-print-eat-lancet; https://www.bbc.co.uk/sounds/ play/m0009kxr [accessed January 2021].

15. See: https://twitter.com/bigfatsurprise/ status/1103404762764988416 [accessed January 2021].

16. For criticism of EAT-Lancet, see Leroy and Cofnas (2020), Adesogan et al. (2020), Zagmutt et al. (2019, 2020), Archer and Lavie (2019), Hadaad (2019), and Hirvonen et al. (2019), and responses from Willett et al. (2019b, 2019c).

17. If EAT-Lancet appears to endorse industrial animal farming, this is partly a consequence of the methodology adopted. EAT-Lancet set out, first and foremost, to define a healthy diet. They then calculated the share of the planetary boundaries the food system should legitimately occupy, and assessed whether the diet could be provided to a 2050 population within this share of the boundaries. This is a very different approach to one which asks: *How should we farm and use our land in region X to optimise health and environmental outcomes?* The healthy eating targets drove the model, with agricultural production only altered to the degree needed to deliver the diet within the established boundaries. An enhanced version of 'business as usual' was implicit in the methodology, and this leaves the EAT-Lancet model vulnerable to criticisms that pertain to considerations that lie outside the boundaries. Among these are the risks of zoonotic disease and antimicrobial resistance; animal welfare; the imperative to phase out chemical pesticides and synthetic fertilisers; the need to dismantle the fossil fuel industry; issues related to food processing and distribution; and how to achieve food sovereignty and social equity. See Willett et al. (2019a) for the methodology. The data on farm animal populations and fish weights are available on the University of Oxford website: https://ora.ox.ac.uk/objects/uuid:b5a8c0c6-293c-4420-90a7-. f9195d6631fa [accessed January 2021].

18. Rothgerber (2014).

19. The 'anti-vegetarian/vegan sentiment' paragraph is paraphrasing Hannan (2020) and Bastian and Loughnan (2017). For a

discussion of derogation as dissonance reduction, see Rothgerber (2014, 2020a). For anti-vegan discrimination, see MacInnes and Hodson (2015). For negative views of vegetarians, see Minson and Monin (2012). For further discussion, see Zane et al. (2015) and Vandermoere et al. (2019). For veganism in the newspapers, see Cole and Morgan (2011).

20. For Willett's longstanding promotion of an omnivorous diet (albeit one that limits red meat and saturated fat), see Willett and Skerrett (2001). See Garnett (2019) for an insightful discussion of contemporary attitudes towards veganism. Blythman's tweet is referenced in note 11 above.

21. For 'perceived behaviour change', see Rothgerber (2020a). For claimed and actual vegans in the UK, see: https://ahdb.org.uk/consumer-insight-plant-based-diets [accessed January 2021].

22. For the PETA documentary, see Rothgerber (2013). For gender as a predictor of attitudes towards animals and meat, see Miele et al. (1993), Eldridge and Gluck (1996), Gossard and York (2003), Knight et al. (2004) and Sobal (2005). See Rothgerber (2013, 2019, 2020a), Piazza et al. (2015) and Dowsett et al. (2018) for further discussion.

23. UK consumption figures are provided by the Agriculture and Horticulture Development Board (AHDB): https://ahdb.org.uk/Tags/Yearbook. These figures are based upon the calculated total supplies available for consumption, i.e. production plus imports minus exports divided by the mid-year population estimate, with data converted to carcass weight equivalent. An alternative dataset is provided by the United Nations Food and Agricultural Organization (FAO): http://www.fao.org/faostat/en/#data/FBS. The FAO figures show a decline in UK meat consumption, from 81.48kg in 2013 to 79.89kg in 2017. Such a modest decline is difficult to reconcile with one in three people in the UK claiming to reduce their meat consumption.

24. The 'one in four' figure is based on a Gallup telephone poll with US adults conducted in September 2019, see: https://news.gallup.com/file/poll/282776/200116MeatConsumption.pdf. US consumption figures are based on data from the United States Department of Agriculture (USDA): https://www.ers.

usda.gov/. For a discussion of 2018 as a 'record high', and of the difference between 'meat disappearance' and 'loss adjusted food availability' and the assumptions underpinning these datasets, see: https://www.ers.usda.gov/amber-waves/2018/june/per-capita-red-meat-and-poultry-disappearance-insights-into-its-steady-growth/. The FAO data for the US shows a steady rise in per capita meat consumption from 115.13kg in 2013 to 124.10kg in 2017 [accessed January 2021].

25. Consumption data for France, Spain, Italy, Germany, Australia, Brazil, Mexico, Argentina, Russia, Japan, Turkey and Iran, are provided by the FAO. For '40% of Germans cutting back on meat', see: https://www.theguardian.com/world/2020/sep/27/the-wurst-is-over-why-germany-land-of-schnitzels-now-loves-to-go-vegetarian [accessed January 2021].

26. Data on US and global 'factory farm' populations are provided by the Sentience Institute, based on data from the USDA Census of Agriculture and EPA definitions of Concentrated Animal Feeding Operations (CAFOs): https://www.sentienceinstitute.org/us-factory-farming-estimates and https://www.sentienceinstitute.org/global-animal-farming-estimates. For intensification in the UK, see Davies and Wasley (2017) and Colley and Wasley (2020). For the two surveys cited here, see: https://plantbasednews.org/lifestyle/health/brits-want-urgent-ban-factory-farming/ and https://plantbasednews.org/culture/ethics/brits-ditch-meat-2021/ [accessed January 2021]. For the effects of consolidation on farmers, see Hendrickson et al. (2020) and Kelloway and Miller (2020).

SEVEN: Evolution

1. Maslin (2017).
2. For a discussion of the archaeological evidence attesting to this transition from wooded areas to open savannah, see Mithen (2005) and Maslin (2017). The quote is from Marean (1989).
3. The first quote is from Guthrie (2006). For evidence of predation

on hominids and early humans, and the second quote, see Hart and Sussman (2005). For a discussion of predator threat and hominid adaptation, see Willems and van Schaik (2017), Mithen (2005) and Hodgson and Helvenston (2006).

4. Liebenberg (2013), Cordain et al. (2001).

5. Maslin (2017).

6. Mithen (2005). The 'bestiary ...' quote is from Guthrie (2006).

7. Krause (2015) writes: 'Bonded closely to the natural world, early humans would have first imitated the voices of these soundscapes ... the creature world of whirs, shrieks, scratches, hisses, bleats, clicks, barks, howls, moans, buzzes, and crunches.' Mithen (2005) concurs: 'As well as miming how animals moved, Early Humans could have imitated their calls, along with the other sounds of the natural world.' Donald (1991) writes: 'Even rudimentary imitations of animal and environmental sounds would have had very good uses, particularly in a hunting culture that lacked speech: simulated bird calls and animal cries are still used in hunting.'

8. Mithen (2005) writes: 'For hunting and gathering ... [communication] might have included utterances that meant "hunt deer with me" or "hunt horse with me", either as two completely separate utterances, or else as one phrase of "hunt animal with me" accompanied by mimesis of the particular animal concerned.' See also Englefield (1977).

9. The hand signals are described in Marshall (1976). The bird calls are from Lee (1979).

10. Hodgson and Helvenston (2006). The emphasis on storytelling recounting animal encounters coheres with the behaviour of contemporary hunters as described, for example, by Marshall (1976) and Lee (1979). For further discussion of mimesis in human evolution, see Donald (2001), Zlatev et al. (2005), Mithen (2005) and Hodgson and Helvenston (2006).

11. Falk (1983, 2014). For a discussion of endocasts, see Mithen (2005).

12. For the discovery of mirror neurons, see Rizzolatti et al. (1988). For the human mirror system and its role in communication, see Rizzolatti and Arbib (1998) and Gallese (2009).

13. Arbib (2000), Mithen (2005), and Hodgson and Helvenston (2006).
14. For 'the most hyped concept', see Jarrett (2012). For 'Gandhi neurons', see: https://www.gla.ac.uk/events/lectures/gifford/previouslectures/vsramachandran/ [accessed January 2021]. For mirror neurones and empathy, see Gallese (2005).
15. Niemyjska et al. (2018) found that decreased meat consumption was associated with increased recognition of human features of animals and increased empathy to animals, suggesting that animals' anthropomorphism predicts empathy. Bastian et al. (2012) and Amiot and Bastian (2017) similarly found that when encouraged to think of animals as 'human-like' volunteers expressed more moral inclusivity towards them. For phylogenetically similar animals in this context, see Amiot et al. (2015) and Westbury and Neumann (2008).
16. White et al. (2014) present evidence that the human action observation system can represent actions executed by non-human animals. See Spence (2017) and Spence et al. (2017) for a discussion. For chickens and the meat paradox, see Bottomley and Loughnan (2017), Loughnan and Davies (2020), Kunst and Hole (2016) and Bastian et al. (2012).
17. Broadhurst et al. (2002) and Cunnane et al. (2007) propose that humans are unlikely to have evolved large brains in an environment which did not provide abundant dietary EPA and DHA in the form of animal foods, primarily fish. Stewart (1994) notes that fish remains are associated with many hominid and early human sites, including five sites at Olduvai Gorge in Tanzania dating to around 2 million years ago; 80 to 90 per cent of the fish present in these assemblages were catfish, which could be captured with little or no technology. Further evidence is presented in Cunnane and Crawford (2003), Braun et al. (2010), Steele (2010) and Joordens et al. (2014). Not all scholars believe that fish or aquatic foods were critical. Chamberlain (1996) suggests that LC n3 PUFAs from both aquatic and terrestrial meat sources were necessary, whereas Cordain et al. (2001) argue that a combination of DHA-rich mammal brains and energy-rich bone marrow, scavenged from the carcasses

of herbivores, would have provided the necessary nutrition for encephalisation. See also Eaton et al. (1998), Milton (1999, 2003) and Ulijaszek et al. (2012). Carlson and Kingston (2007) voice the counterargument, proposing that ALA is sufficient for normal brain development and maintenance in modern humans and could have facilitated encephalisation among our ancestors. See Cunnane et al. (2007) and Cordain et al. (2001) for a riposte. For the importance of DHA for the brain and nervous system, see Horrocks and Yeo (1999), Chang et al. (2009), Bradbury (2011), Gupta (2016) and Guesnet and Alessandri (2011).

18. See Mithen (2005), Hawkes (2013), Wong (2012) and Maslin (2017).

19. See Mithen (2005).

20. For infant imitation, including in relation to the emergence of empathy, see Meltzoff (2004, 2005), Kinsbourne (2005), Goldman (2005), Thompson (2001), Garrels (2004) and Tomasello (2005).

21. See Goldman (2005) for role play in infant development. Laugrand and Oosten (2015) discuss role play among Inuit children. Marshall (1976) recalls extensive role play of animals among the !Kung: 'Mimicking animals is a pastime of men and boys. They mimic the walk and the way the animal carries and throws its head, catching the rhythm exactly ... Boys play little dramas of encounter and attack. One may imitate a lion, growling and springing at the other boys who run towards him ... They mimic peculiarities of posture and movement so cleverly that they leave no doubt as to who the model is.'

22. Gopnik (1998). For further discussion of infant/child relationships with animals and the meat paradox, see Bastian and Amiot (2020), Rothgerber (2020b) and Cole and Stewart (2014).

23. For a discussion of Aurignacian lifeways, see Fagan (2010), Guthrie (2006) and Lewis-Williams (2002).

24. For a discussion of cognitive fluidity, see Mithen (1996, 2005). In the latter, Mithen hypothesises that our modern linguistic abilities might be associated with mutations in the FOXP2 gene,

which appears to play a role in turning on and off other genes, some of which are vital for the development of neural circuits for language in the brain. Mithen (1998) suggests that animal mimesis and 'anthropomorphic thinking' might also have contributed to the evolution of cognitive fluidity.

25. Mithen (1996) writes: '"cognitively fluid" thought finds its first material manifestation in some of the earliest images of ice-age art, such as the lion-man carving from Hohlenstein Stadel.' Wynne et al. (2009) and Helvenston (2006) also say the Lion Man evidences an advance in cognitive capabilities.

EIGHT: Cave

1. There is a Eurocentric bias to cave art scholarship, partly resulting from the good preservation of the images and the study lauded upon them. Humans were making images elsewhere and at an earlier date. Paintings in Indonesia have been dated as 44,000 and 45,500 years old. In Western Australia, there are paintings and carvings believed to be up to 50,000 years old. In Africa, pieces of ochre adorned with delicate geometric patterns, recovered from Blombos Cave, are believed to be between 70,000 and 100,000 years old. There was probably nothing special about the humans who made images in Europe, though the imagery found in European caves is uniquely rich in its preservation. See Clottes (2010, 2016) for a discussion. The 'terra incognita ...' quote is from Lewis-Williams (2002).

2. For the discovery of Chauvet, see Lewis-Williams (2002), Fagan (2010), Hammer (2015) and Clottes (2010).

3. For felines in Aurignacian art, see Lewis-Williams (2002). Geneste is quoted in Hammer (2015).

4. See Lewis-Williams and Dowson (1988), Clottes and Lewis-Williams (1998), Lewis-Williams (2002). The 'shamanic' interpretation of cave art has its critics, most notably Bahn (2001). For a rebuttal, see Clottes (2010), Whitley (2006, 2009), Lewis-Williams (2004). For the biopsychosocial context

in which Palaeolithic shamanism and art developed, see Winkelman (2010).

5. Reichel-Dolmatoff (1996).

6. Reichel-Dolmatoff (1997).

7. Lewis-Williams (2002) suggests that entoptic phenomena are 'wired into' the human nervous system 'as an innate, biologically based capacity with adaptive significance'.

8. Eshleman (2003), 'The Death of Bill Evans'.

9. Murphy (2014).

10. Eshleman did not speak of the meat paradox, but he alluded to a 'crisis' rooted in the conflicted emotions associated with killing and consuming animals, these emotions expressing a 'catastrophic' separation from the animal world to which cave art was a response. The tale recounted here is derived from Eshleman (2003); I have elaborated on Eshleman's account with atmospheric details.

11. Le Barre (1970).

12. Horses account for roughly 30 per cent of all images in European caves; bison and aurochs (mostly bison) roughly 30 per cent; deer roughly 11 per cent; mammoths roughly 9 per cent; ibex roughly 8 per cent; reindeer roughly 4 per cent; bears a little less than 2 per cent; felines and rhinos around 1 per cent each; and there are a handful of birds and fish. The recurring focus on a few large herbivores has puzzled scholars, but Guthrie (2006) is less surprised. 'One is trying to find, stalk, spear, feel its surprise, fright and death, smell its mammal warmth, dismember, prepare, and take into one's body a species rather like one's own.' The description of seasonal change and hunting at La Vache is informed by Fagan (2011) and Pailhaugue (1998).

13. See Clottes (2016).

14. For a discussion of injured or dying animals, see Guthrie (2006), Lewis-Williams (2002), Clottes (2016).

15. Eshleman (2003), 'Permanent Shadow'.

16. For a discussion of psychotropic plants growing in Palaeolithic Europe, see Hancock (2005) and Clottes and Lewis-Williams (1998).

17. For a discussion of sensory deprivation and altered states in relation to Palaeolithic caves, see Lewis-Williams (2003), Clottes (2016) and Eshleman (2003).
18. MacLeod tells of her experiences in her 1980 essay 'Sensory Isolation and Vision Quest', recited in Eshleman (2003).
19. Clottes (2016) explains that these restitution rituals were very different to the 'hunting magic' proposed by cave art scholar Abbé Breuil, who saw image-making as 'explicitly aimed at subduing them [prey animals] through the power of images'. See also Clottes and Lewis-Williams (1998) and Lewis-Williams (2002).
20. Clottes and Lewis-Williams (1998) suggest the Lion Man represented either Vaí-mahsë or a shaman in trance, with Dowson and Poore (2001) embracing the latter interpretation. They note that the Lion Man exhibits 'an alert face indicated by the cocked ears and closed mouth' typical of a feline predator, but 'other features that, we argue, point to hallucinatory origins'.

NINE: Catharsis

1. Miller et al. (2019). For a discussion of yahé (or ayahuasca) in an ethnobotanical context, see Reichel-Dolmatoff (1975, 1996, 1997), Davis (1997), McKenna et al. (1998), Schultes et al. (1992) and Sheldrake (2020).
2. Benny Shanon, Professor of Psychology at the Hebrew University of Jerusalem, drank yahé more than 130 times across a ten-year period, including with a dozen Amazonian tribes. His experience coheres with the Tukano's vision of plant and animal communication. Speaking of one experience, Shanon (2010) wrote: 'The different visions that appeared all pertained to one common theme – the life of nocturnal animals. In each vision, a different species appeared: jaguars, jackals, several kinds of birds, insects, and organisms smaller than insects. In each case, I was shown how the animals in question behave. My eyes accommodated and I could see what the animals themselves

saw.' Jaguars appeared frequently – more so than any other animal – and Shanon came to feel a sense of affiliation. 'Overall, I would characterise the jungle cat as a manifestation of the energy of life in its full and pristine form.' See also Hodgson and Helvenston (2006) and Reichel-Dolmatoff (1996, 1997).

3. Gorman (2010).

4. Neruda (1989), 'Cóndor'.

5. See Tello (1942), Burger (1992) and Jay (2005, 2019).

6. Reichel-Dolmatoff (1997). For more on the Tukano's use of DMT snuffs, see Reichel-Dolmatoff (1975, 1996). For use throughout the Amazon, see Pochettino et al. (1999), Agurell et al. (1969) and Schultes et al. (1992). For evidence of use at Chavín, see Burger (1992) and Jay (2005, 2019).

7. Burger (1992).

8. For the identification of shaman with jaguar, see Reichel-Dolmatoff (1996), Descola (2005), Kohn (2013) and Shanon (2010).

9. See Reznikoff and Dauvois (1988), Waller (1993) and Fazenda et al. (2017).

10. Mithen (2003).

11. Lewis-Williams (2002).

12. For a discussion of music in Palaeolithic caves, see Lewis-Williams (2002). The first quote is Le Barre (1970) and the second is Lonsdale (1981).

13. Reichel-Dolmatoff (1996).

14. Burger (1992).

15. For a discussion of altered states, interpreted as the interplay of 'top-down' and 'bottom-up' processes, see Corlett et al. (2009). For Chavín's architecture 'as a visionary technology', see Jay (2005, 2019). For Palaeolithic caves as a kindred 'technology', see Lewis-Williams (2002). Leroi-Gourhan (1982) noted that felines are more commonly found in deeper and more remote chambers.

16. Clinical trials to date have affirmed the potential *feasibility* of psychedelic-assisted therapy, but not the *efficacy* of treatment. Most trials have taken place in single centres and cannot prove generalisability of any treatment effect they report. This

will require larger trials in many different centres around the world – only with this extended body of evidence can we begin to say that a treatment is efficacious. Yet the early evidence is promising. See Johnson et al. (2014), Bogenschutz et al. (2015), Gasser et al. (2014), Ross et al. (2016), Griffiths et al. (2016), Carhart-Harris et al. (2017), Rucker et al. (2016), Nutt et al. (2020). Yahé has not been thoroughly studied in a clinical context, but two small studies with participants who had clinical depression found that the brew effectively alleviated symptoms, with the effect sustained for at least three weeks. See Osório et al. (2015), Sanches et al. (2016), Barbosa et al. (2012) and dos Santos (2013). For the history of psychedelic research and a discussion of modern clinical trials, see Rucker et al. (2018).

17. Carhart-Harris and Nutt (2017), Nutt et al. (2020).
18. Reichel-Dolmatoff (1997). The metallurgy metaphor is from Carhart-Harris and Nutt (2017).

TEN: Futures

1. Schwalm et al. (2020) argue that RCP8.5 provides the best match for our emissions trajectory to mid-century under current and stated policies, and remains a 'highly plausible' scenario for 2100. This view is disputed by Hausfather and Peters (2020), who suggest that RCP4.5 or RCP6.0 are more plausible scenarios given current climate policies. The IPCC (2014) say that global heating in these scenarios would likely rise to 1.1 °C to 2.6 °C under RCP4.5; 1.4 °C to 3.1 °C under RCP6.0; or 2.6 °C to 4.8 °C under RCP8.5. The possibility of reaching 4 °C before the end of the century is implicit in the RCP8.5 scenario. Sherwood et al. (2020) describe a more finely honed 'climate sensitivity' range than used by the IPCC (2014), establishing that a doubling of atmospheric carbon dioxide compared to pre-industrial levels, from 280ppm to 560ppm, would result in a likely rise in global temperatures of 2.3 °C to 4.5 °C. Atmospheric carbon dioxide is currently roughly 417 ppm and is on track to exceed 560ppm by around 2080. UNEP (2020), in

the most up-to-date analysis at the time of writing, say the world remains on track for 3.2 °C heating by the end of this century, if the nationally determined contributions (NDCs) under the Paris Agreement are fully implemented. If countries go further and meet stated net-zero commitments, global temperatures could be reduced close to or in line with the targets set out in the Paris Agreement. The UK Climate Change Committee (2019b) recommend that adaptation strategies are developed for a 4 °C rise in global temperatures.

2. There is no scientific consensus as to what a planet heated by 4 °C looks like. A synthesis of the evidence is provided by Lynas (2020). This account also draws on Vince (2019).

3. The UK Climate Change Committee (2019a) warn of potential tipping points in the climate system at 4 °C.

4. See Gowdy (2020) on climate stability and agriculture in the Holocene. For a discussion of future climate projections related to the climate of the deep past, see De la Vega et al. (2020), Burke et al. (2018) and Bova et al. (2021). See also: https://www.theguardian.com/environment/2020/jul/09/co2-in-earths-atmosphere-nearing-levels-of-15m-years-ago [accessed November 2020].

5. This description of the Holocene climate and Vicdessos Valley is informed by Mithen (2003), Fagan (2010) and Don Hitchcock, https://www.donsmaps.com/ [accessed November 2020]. Guiot and Cramer (2016) and Vince (2019) describe the encroachment of the Sahara into Europe.

6. Aronson (1999).

7. Reichel-Dolmatoff (1997).

8. Huxley (1956).

9. Melanie Joy, Hal Herzog and Carol J. Adams should be recognised as among the pioneers and forerunners of the meat paradox. Nick Haslam was a fellow 'first zoologist', co-authoring the 2010 paper in which the term 'meat paradox' was coined.

Index